Labor Markets, Employment Policy, and Job Creation

Published in cooperation with
the Milken Institute
for Job & Capital Formation

The Milken Institute Series in Economics and Education

Series Editor
Lewis C. Solmon

Labor Markets, Employment Policy, and Job Creation
edited by Lewis C. Solmon and Alec R. Levenson

Economic Policy, Financial Markets, and Economic Growth
edited by Benjamin Zycher and Lewis C. Solmon

Labor Markets, Employment Policy, and Job Creation

EDITED BY

Lewis C. Solmon
and Alec R. Levenson

Westview Press
BOULDER • SAN FRANCISCO • OXFORD

The Milken Institute Series in Economics and Education

Copyright © 1994 by the Milken Institute for Job & Capital Formation

Published in 1994 in the United States of America by Westview Press, Inc., 5500 Central Avenue, Boulder, Colorado 80301-2877, and in the United Kingdom by Westview Press, 36 Lonsdale Road, Summertown, Oxford OX2 7EW

Library of Congress Cataloging-in-Publication Data
Solmon, Lewis C.
    Labor markets, employment policy, and job creation / edited by
Lewis C. Solmon and Alec R. Levenson.
        p.   cm. — (The Milken Institute series in economics and
education)
    Includes bibliographical references and index.
    ISBN 0-8133-8900-3
    1. Full employment policies—United States.   2. Employees—Effect
of technological innovations on—United States.   3. Skilled labor—
United States.   4. Occupational training—United States.
5. Industry and education—United States.   6. Labor market—United
States.   7. Job creation—United States.   I. Levenson, Alec Robert,
1966–   .   II. Title.   III. Series.
HD5724.S626   1994
339.5'0973—dc20   94-36049
                                                                          CIP

Printed and bound in the United States of America

(∞)   The paper used in this publication meets the requirements
      of the American National Standard for Permanence of Paper
      for Printed Library Materials Z39.48-1984.

10   9   8   7   6   5   4   3   2   1

Contents

Preface

The Milken Institute is a private non-profit foundation established to support research and discourse on the determinants of American economic growth, to provide a wide range of analyses to support effective policy decisions, and to help educate the American public in issues of economic growth and job creation.

In November 1993, the Institute convened its second economics conference in Washington, D.C. This book presents the research findings and analyses of eminent academic economists and discussion by several business leaders and policy analysts, all of whom participated in the conference. It is our intent that the discussions of these scholars and practitioners published herein will help to illuminate key issues in the areas of employment growth and job creation policy.

When the Institute set out to organize a conference on the general issue of jobs, it was clear to us from the outset that the number of relevant topics was large. The issues selected for discussion and presented here represent key but by no means the sole basis for dialogue.

It is our hope that this volume will make the best available thinking in this area of labor economics accessible to an audience that extends well beyond the scholarly economics profession to journalists, policy makers, and private sector participants in the fields that impact the creation of new jobs and prepare the American labor force to perform these jobs.

The goal of the Institute is to provide evidence, enhance thinking, and improve policy making in order to stimulate the American economy; this work is one of our chief means of doing so. In addition, through in-house and commissioned research studies, periodic seminars, and publications including our journal, *Jobs & Capital*, the Institute's resident, affiliated, and guest scholars and staff study the many issues related to jobs and capital and disseminate the results.

This book opens with an introduction from the Milken Institute's president and co-editor of this volume, Lewis C. Solmon, who offers an historical view on the topics covered in this work.

Lewis C. Solmon
Alec R. Levenson

Acknowledgments

This work represents the efforts of many people, and the editors gratefully acknowledge their assistance in the production of this book. Beverly Werber, Milken Institute editor, is responsible for many refinements to the manuscript and for supervising the publication of this volume. Sang Han, Karin Hsiao, and Cindy Zoghi provided extensive research support for the analysis of the data in the opening chapter. Jason Ing's word processing skill was an indispensable aid in guiding the volume through its draft forms. Lawrence Lesser, of the Milken Family Foundations, directed the technical expertise required to produce this book. Laura Janssen's desktop publishing skill—as well as her usual endless reservoir of patience—ensured a polished copy.

Thanks are due also to the staff members of the Milken Institute for Job & Capital Formation for arranging and producing, with skill as well as good humor, the conference at which these papers were first presented.

L.C.S.
A.R.L.

Introduction: The Historical Context of Current Labor Market Debates

Lewis C. Solmon

A strong society and a healthy private enterprise system are dependent upon each other. Thus, the Milken Institute for Job & Capital Formation was established to undertake and support research and public discourse on the determinants of economic growth and job creation. We focus upon access to financial capital by companies, the strength of our financial institutions, the effects of regulatory and tax policies, trade issues, and the role of entrepreneurship. Education as well is at the heart of the Institute's mission, for one of our central premises is that optimal economic growth can be achieved only if people are educated to their full potential and are offered opportunities to utilize their human capital in productive jobs. It is imperative to understand how we can keep the economy growing by providing access to capital and employing human potential to the maximum.

A main tenet of the Institute is that sound economic policy will be supported only if the public has an accurate understanding of economic and financial issues. And so, one of our chief aims is to convey our research findings not only to policy makers but also to the general public. Because the public receives so much of its financial and economic information from the media, we are committed to a continuing discourse with journalists to insure that our research findings are disseminated as broadly as possible.

Moreover, the Institute was established in the belief that not only must its research findings be made accessible to practitioners from the worlds of business and finance, but also that the experiences of these practitioners can inform our scholarship. Our view is that research is truly effective *only* if it is informed by and available to those who will be affected by its implications. Few issues today have more relevance to all in our nation than that of employment and job creation.

A major focus of the Clinton administration proposals on the budget and other matters has been the magnitude and nature of employment growth. It is safe to say that every administration keeps at least one eye firmly on the jobs picture and that the job security of public officials from presidents to senators to governors to city councilmen depends in no small part upon the job security enjoyed by the rest of us. It is no accident that both incumbents and challengers for public office use the jobs record as political ammunition, always and everywhere. And because even strong economic and employment growth inevitably vary on a geographic and sectoral basis, the jobs issue is never off the table for sizable parts of the electorate.

The last recession, both cyclical and structural in nature, illustrated clearly the many policy dimensions that influence job creation and economic well-being. The cyclical component underscored the importance of both the management and timing of monetary policy and of fiscal policy as it influences macroeconomic decision makers. The structural component of this past recession has reminded us of the importance of technological advances and of foreign competition as they yield immense long-run benefits often obscured by short-run dislocations. Regulatory policy as well carries both benefits and burdens not often compared clearly in public discourse, and such regulatory effects are felt, often unknowingly, in sectors and by people far removed from those of immediate regulatory interest.

What exactly is the jobs issue? It is far more than an ongoing focus upon changes in the unemployment rate or total employment. In an environment in which living standards are perceived or reported to be stagnant—in which many people reportedly believe that their children will not live as well as they have—"jobs" has come to mean far more. Whether articulated well or poorly, the jobs issue encompasses the rate at which employment is seen as growing. It comprises also the growth path of real wages; the *security* of employment, as shifts in the economic and political environment affect the structure of economic activity and thus the growth and contraction of employment in various sectors and geographic regions; the returns to various forms of human capital—which I believe are both monetary and non-monetary—and individual uncertainty about the education and training investment best suited for a world of rapid change in economic conditions. And, finally, the jobs discussion entails the distribution of the gains from economic growth across economic classes and population groups.

I think it is fair to say that since the founding of our country there have always been people who were unhappy with the conditions of employment in America. There has, in a sense, always been a jobs issue, and the sub-issues have remained strikingly constant. To illustrate by a few examples of these issues:

1. The debate over slavery—economic efficiency versus morality—can begin this discussion. Analysis of the issue has persisted even to recent times, as the 1993 Nobel Prize in economics, awarded to Robert Fogel and Douglas North, attests. We might ask whether despite the voluntary choices of migrant farm workers, their present day treatment is much improved from 15–20 years ago.

2. The attitudes revealed during the Luddite riots in England early in the nineteenth century reflected attitudes in America as well regarding the evil of replacing workers with machines. The debate over the role of technology persists to the present. For example, Paul Kennedy (1993) has observed a resistance in the United States, as compared to other countries, to the introduction of robots in manufacturing. This despite the fact that robots appear to increase productivity and quality, add flexibility, and reduce errors and waste. He attributes this resistance to (1) the absence of an overall shortage of labor in the United States; (2) the ability of manufacturers to relocate their plants to lower wage, primarily non-union areas; (3) robots requiring expensive redesign of plants; (4) job security being less certain in the United States than elsewhere; and (5) U.S. firms being reluctant to invest in retraining workers so that robots are seen as a greater threat to jobs here than is the case elsewhere. An alternative hypothesis is that various government regulations and tax policies have raised the cost of labor relative to that of capital in other countries, resulting in a shift toward robots elsewhere.

3. Occupational safety is an ongoing issue here. Formerly, factories and their dangerous machinery framed this discussion; and today exposure to dangerous chemicals and carpal tunnel syndrome are at the forefront.

4. Boredom on the assembly line became an issue when Taylorism led to an organization of work that subdivided tasks into a series of simple repetitive motions. This suggested for the first time the "good job/bad job" question.

5. We used to hear of problems of access or lack of access of various white ethnic groups to certain jobs. This is similar to current discussions regarding access of minorities and women to various occupations and professions.

6. The launch of Sputnik in 1957 caused a fear in the United States that this country lacked an adequate number of scientists and engineers. What followed was the never-ending discussion of whether we have enough scientists and engineers in needed specialties. Moreover, there have been periodic fears about oversupplies or

shortages of Ph.D.s in various fields. (If they cannot teach, what can they do instead?) I did research on "underemployed" Ph.D.s and found that many—even those in traditionally academic fields—did well in non-academic jobs (Solmon et al., 1981).

7. The GI Bill of Rights passed after World War II gave every returning American soldier the money to attend college and began the shift to a "knowledge society." Thus, the 1950s and 1960s saw the beginning of credentialism, the screening of job applicants by educational attainment.

8. The 1970s brought the fear of the "overeducated American" and "underemployment" due to an apparent decline in rate of return to college (Freeman, 1976). Now, we see the gap between high school and college earnings is widening. On the other hand, debate still continues about whether most new jobs that are created need people with high or low levels of schooling.

9. The process of matching skills people attain in school with job needs continues a discussion over vocationalism, career education, the education and work movement versus detracking, the self-esteem movement, school as clinic, away from and back to the 3Rs, to learning how to learn, learning how to think, and cultural awareness. Should schools prepare kids for jobs or prepare them for life?

This brings this introduction to the perpetual question, What are the goals of workers? Summarized, we can state that most workers want the following basic job benefits: a salary to live on or enough salary for upward mobility; provision of insurance by employers—worker's compensation, health, retirement; job satisfaction; jobs with the opportunity to use skills/abilities/talents to maximize potential productivity; the security not to lose one's job; and decision-making responsibility.

There are a range of problems to be confronted by job seekers in their attempts to secure employment. Without advanced schooling, workers may not be able to find much good work. (Are high school graduates prepared today to assume the demands of today's jobs?) Even with advanced schooling, virtually anyone who wants postsecondary education can get it. And so, people who stay in school after high school are not necessarily special any more.

We must ask why the workplace has changed. Why have workers started coming to work drunk? Is it that the work has become more boring, or that it is more difficult to fire people? What has changed in our world to make the assembly line now a bad job? Additional issues include the precipitous decline in the number of union members (except in the public sector). Productivity issues, and by association, issues of worker organization require study. (Is there any evidence—scientific evidence—that newer organizations in the workplace which have less hierarchy and fewer management prerogatives will yield higher productivity?) The ballooning high tech nature of work causes us to question how we can best organize for such advanced work. Zuboff (1988) describes the choice between (1) refining control of workers by "automating" versus (2) replacing hierarchical control and narrow division of labor by "informating" to tap the potential for reflective insight, for creative hypothesizing, and for collaborative troubleshooting in all workers. One has to wonder whether there is more to this than just buzz-words.

The Clinton administration's Secretary of Labor, Robert Reich (1991, pp. 81–86) has described the future by noting that the 1950s model of industrial mass production is moving toward dinosaur-type obsolescence. Reich says the reason is the shift from *high volume* production to *high-value* production. He says there are two basic forces behind this shift: The rush of product changes that accompany computer-assisted production and service, and the complex diversity of needs in the world market where business must now be done.

Reich says there are three different but related skills that drive this shift forward. First are the problem-solving skills required to put things together in unique ways, whether they be molecules, alloys, semiconductor chips, pension portfolios, or information. Second are skills required to help customers decide how their shifting needs can best be met by customized products. This requires an intimate knowledge of customers' whole operations and how they may achieve a competitive advantage. Third are skills needed to link the problem identifiers and problem solvers. These people must understand specific technologies and markets to see the potential for new products and how to assemble the problem identifiers and problem solvers to carry it out. Their special skill is in managing ideas and bringing the right people together for creative action.

Reich says that with these developments a new skill category is emerging beyond the routine production and service work skills. These are the skills of what he calls *symbolic analysis*. Symbolic analysts are people who "solve, identify, and broker problems by manipulating symbols" (p. 178). They operate with a distinctive work style. Often they work with associates or partners rather than under bosses. They may work alone or with small teams connected to the international networks. As neither problems nor solutions are known in advance, they communicate constantly, often informally, to see that insights are put to best use and ideas are evaluated quickly and critically. They produce plans, designs, drafts, layouts, scripts, or projections based on their skill in conceptualizing problems and solutions (Reich, pp. 177–180).

All of this seems to some observers like a massive revolution in industry. But so did the introduction of machinery during the Industrial Revolution and assembly lines after that. And, new products and new production methods have been introduced constantly over time.

In Peter Drucker's book, *Post-Capitalist Society* (1993), he argues that as our knowledge base has expanded over the centuries, knowledge has always been applied to work; first to developing new tools, processes, and products; then to organizing work to effect the "productivity revolution"; and more recently to the application of knowledge itself in the form of the "management revolution." He asserts that productivity increases have always resulted from application of the latest knowledge to work. But now that even manufacturing has evolved from "muscle work" to "knowledge work," some view the present as a time for the greatest revolution in production of goods and services that our nation has ever faced. We must ask, Is this really news?

At this time in our history, the question has been posed—even if only implicitly—as to whether our free market, profit seeking, capitalist system can handle the changes demanded by new technologies and globalization of the economy, or whether the time has come when further prosperity requires significantly greater government involvement in the affairs of American business and industry. This sounds like the arguments put forth in favor of the New Deal of the 1930s.

Every period of change in U.S. business history has been viewed as a crisis by some. However, the current changes are occurring at a time when every short-term dislocation can be dramatized on television on the evening news. Thus, the need for amelioration of pain is emphasized and the prospects for government involvement enhanced. Yet, just because we are more aware today of economic hardship, that does not mean that conditions now are worse than ever before, nor that there is a stronger justification for government intervention.

At the individual level, some very talented, highly educated young people are unable to get the jobs they expected when they began their education. We must, therefore, wonder: Is this lack of opportunity a failure of our labor markets? If, when 20% of our population attended college, all of them were upwardly mobile and got jobs viewed as "college level," is it to be expected that when 50% attend, there will be college level type jobs for all 50%? Can 100% of the population end up in the top quintile of anything? (Yes, if there is only 1 quintile, i.e., everyone is earning or doing the same.) Cannot better educated people "elevate" jobs that were formerly held by people with less education? My research in the 1970s (Solmon et al., 1977) on the relationships between education and jobs said this was the case. Do all Americans have the unalienable right to earn five times the minimum wage? Do they have the right not to be bored at work? or regimented? or supervised? or evaluated? or fired?

To answer these questions, it is useful to understand how the job situation has changed over the past several decades. Since 1972, total nonfarm employment has increased by almost 39 million despite a decline in manufacturing jobs of 1.4 million and a decline in the employment of Fortune 500 companies of over 3 million. Growth in service jobs has exceeded 38 million.

The service sector includes a broad range of professions and occupations, from attorneys and physicians to the proverbial hamburger flipper. Hence, growth of employment in the service sector per se tells us nothing about the availability of "good" versus "bad" jobs. By looking at relatively broad occupational categories within various service sectors, I have estimated that of the 38 million new jobs created over the past 22 years, roughly two lower-level or "bad" jobs might have been created for every one higher-level or "good" job. It is not obvious that this is any different from earlier times or that the result has been a "crisis" in job creation. It might be that with rising levels of educational achievement among most workers, expectations have risen and so more people are dissatisfied with jobs that formerly would have been perfectly acceptable.

The question remains: What is our obligation as a nation to high school graduates and dropouts, particularly given the extensive access to postsecondary education today? If the productivity of this group of workers is low, should not their earnings reflect that? If an uneducated, unskilled person is "poor," whose failure does that reflect: his own, his family's, the schools', the community's, employers', or the functioning of the labor market? Whose responsibility is it to raise the earning power of such people? Thus, discussions of labor market and employment issues today inevitably turn to debates about the appropriate roles of various government policies, our education system, and individual efforts. These are the themes that run through this volume.

The jobs issue figures prominently in discussions of tax and budget policy, environmental policy, trade policy, health care reform, education policies both federal and state, as well as much regulatory policy. This broad scope of the jobs issue naturally engenders a vast array of proposed "solutions," themselves often offered with great impatience in spite of the absence of a rigorous definition of the problem. Will government "investment" programs make matters better or worse? What about the jobs effects of the taxation, whether present or future, needed to finance such spending? Does government have a clearly beneficial role in defense conversion, or can market forces and the price mechanism yield an efficient reallocation of resources including labor? What is the tradeoff between the adverse employment effects of much regulatory effort and the beneficial effects of those regulations in other dimensions? Or *are* there substantial benefits emanating from regulation? That is part of the jobs issue as well.

When we set out to organize a conference on the general issue of jobs, it was clear from the beginning that the number of relevant topics even upon cursory thinking was enormous. We sought topics sufficiently broad so that modern empirical research at the academic level could be brought to bear. We sought topics sufficiently narrow so that policy relevance either is immediate or, at a minimum, is foreseeable over the medium term. We sought topics sufficiently complex so that the relevant issues can be delineated and direct debate can be joined, with conceptual and empirical issues addressed directly and—we hope—progress made in terms of issue clarification, resolution, and new-found agreement. At the same time, we sought topics that can be formulated and discussed at a level at which intelligent nonspecialists can participate, make significant contributions, and continue discussion among their respective groups of colleagues and associates.

It is hardly a secret that the U.S. economy is undergoing profound structural change. The Cold War is over. Economic powerhouses are emerging in the Far East, and new markets and competitors are developing in many parts of the world. The information age is more than merely upon us. In the jobs context, therefore, it is relevant to ask how the demand for labor is likely to evolve over the foreseeable future. The first part of this volume focuses upon the evolving U.S. economy of the twenty-first century. What skills and forms of human capital will receive the greatest rewards? Should we look primarily to manufacturing or service sectors for U.S. employment growth? Will employment increasingly be permanent or temporary, high wage or low, with or without familiar fringe benefits? Will the organization of work tasks change, and, if so, what are the resulting implications for workers, their needed skills, and their wages? And, are the needed adaptations ones that market processes can pursue efficiently, or is there a prominent role that government ought to fill?

It is important to know how we have arrived wherever we are, assuming of course that we can agree on just where it is that we stand, however temporarily. Hence, Part Two reviews past sources of employment growth. What sectors have accounted for much or little employment growth? Is it mainly small, medium, or large firms accounting for recent patterns, and what future implications are yielded, particularly in terms of the choices of public policy.

The growth of labor productivity carries important implications for trends in real wages and living standards, international competitiveness, and implicitly for the aggregate productivity of U.S. capital investment. The third session at our conference and Part Three in this volume focuses squarely upon the productivity issue. What have the trends been and are the data misleading? What explains this history? What are the ensuing implications for the future growth of U.S. employment and wages? What are the sources of any adverse trends, and how can they be reversed?

For better or for worse, government is everywhere. It is commonplace that a multitude of tax and regulatory policies have adverse employment effects, but the nature and magnitude of those effects are subject to considerable uncertainty. Part Four examines the issue of government mandates squarely in terms of direct effects upon labor costs and employment trends, a topic of enormous importance and timeliness, particularly as there are good reasons to believe that political constraints on increased federal borrowing and taxation may provide incentives for a renewed emphasis upon taxation by regulation.

Finally, the traditional debate over the returns to human capital and income inequalities seems to have become more prominent of late. Part Five examines this issue including the distribution of income: Has it become less equal? What is the source of the purportedly growing disparity? Is this trend, if it is a trend, a public policy problem? Given the shifting returns to various levels and kinds of human capital, how should individuals prepare for the world of work: How much schooling is necessary, of what kind, and for whom?

In short, a central goal of the Milken Institute's 1993 conference is the separation of the jobs issue into several components that are more manageable, that can be analyzed in terms of concepts and data, and that have important policy implications in their own right. The jobs issue is so broad, affected by and affecting so many other dimensions of economic and social policy, that no conference and no brief span of discussion, however intense, can hope to make progress on all important fronts. We hope that by having structured the issues into broad classes, the chapters in this volume offer important insights into what is known and not, and perhaps mold thinking on the precise nature of the important questions.

References

Drucker, P. F. (1993). *Post-Capitalist Society*. New York: HarperBusiness.

Freeman, R. B. (1976). *The Overeducated American*. New York: Academic.

Kennedy, P. M. (1993). *Preparing for the Twenty-First Century*. New York: Random House.

Reich, R. B. (1991). *The Work of Nations: Preparing Ourselves for 21st-Century Capitalism*. New York: Knopf.

Solmon, L. C., Bisconti, A. S., and Ochsner N. L. (1977). *College as a Training Ground for Jobs.* New York: Praeger.

Solmon, L. C., Kent, L., Ochsner, N. L., and Hurwicz, M. (1981). *Underemployed Ph.D.'s.* Lexington, MA: D.C. Heath.

Zuboff, S. (1988). *In the Age of the Smart Machine: The Future of Work and Power.* New York: Basic Books.

PART ONE

Job and Skill Demands in the "New" Economy

Introduction

Labor economists and policymakers are currently engaged in a fundamental debate about the changing characteristics of the American workplace and workplaces in both developing and developed countries around the world. The Commission on the Skills of the American Workforce defined the issues in a 1990 report entitled *America's Choice: High Skills or Low Wages*. This concept of a "new economy" took on added relevance when Robert Reich became Secretary of Labor in the Clinton administration, particularly in light of his then recently published book, *The Work of Nations: Preparing Ourselves for 21st Century Capitalism*.

To set the stage for subsequent sections of this book, Part One considers the implications of the new economy for job and skill demands in America. We begin with chapters by Ray Marshall, a Secretary of Labor in the Carter administration and co-chair of the Commission, and Gary Burtless, who with several colleagues has written an influential book, *Growth with Equity: Economic Policy Making for the Next Century*.

Professor Marshall defines the old economy—the one that evolved in the United States during the first two-thirds of the twentieth century—as having three distinguishing characteristics: a heavy orientation toward natural resource exploitation; supporting policies and institutions, especially a predominantly free enterprise system in which government and the private sector built infrastructures that facilitated rapid economic growth; and a mass production system. According to Marshall, mass production was made possible by large and growing internal markets for standardized products; its ability to achieve economies of scale; the need for few highly educated and skilled workers; a heavy reliance on front line workers who needed to have little more than basic numeracy and literacy; and almost complete control of the industrial process by a management system which modeled the "one best" method for performing a task.

Although the United States had huge advantages in the mass production economy—and still has the world's wealthiest economy—Marshall argues that this country has enormous disadvantages in the more competitive, global, knowledge-intensive, high-tech economy of the 1990s and beyond.

The policies that supported the old economy are becoming obsolete, and human capital must be the bedrock for economic success in the new economy. Computerized technology provides many of the advantages of economies of scale and scope through flexible systems that have significant advantages in a more dynamic and competitive global economy. The requirements of a more competitive, knowledge-intensive economy thus create new employment policy dilemmas. We can compete in only two ways: reduce wages and incomes or increase productivity and quality.

Marshall argues for national policies to create an environment that encourages companies to organize for high performance and discourages the low-wage alternative. High performance organizations are characterized by productivity, flexibility, and quality; worker participation and lean management systems; the need for higher-order thinking skills; group work requiring more communication, interpersonal skills, and teamwork; high performance workers who must manage their own work, solve problems without assistance, and deal with ambiguity; and, in general, workers who are more interactive in dynamic, consumer-oriented production systems where rapid response times convey significant advantages. Workers must come to their jobs with the ability to learn, to participate in more communal and cooperative activities than in the past, and with the willingness to share information. Thus, we need well-educated, well-trained, highly motivated workers who are much more flexible and productive, especially in supportive systems that stress equity and internal cohesion. They must be able to develop and use leading-edge technology and be rewarded for doing so. In this new economy, workers will be expected to participate in the design of work and its management.

In the new economy, Marshall argues, there is a significant role to be played by labor unions, as well as by education and training. Most of those who support changes in our organization of industry point to the successes of the labor markets of Germany and Japan as models for the prospective evolution of a new American system. In other, allegedly successful nations, but not in the United States, there is a national consensus-based policy to promote high performance work organizations that can maintain and improve incomes in a highly competitive global economy. There are high academic expectations for all young people, whether college-bound or not. Well-developed school-to-work transition systems are in place to provide young people with solid, recognized occupational skills. Public labor market organizations exist to provide training, counseling, information, and placement services for workers, all of whose skills are highly valued. One of the main problems that is a constant in discussions of the transition to the new economy is the claimed inadequacy of the American public school system and the inferior status of our school-to-work processes as compared with those of other industrial nations.

The United States must, according to Marshall, adopt macroeconomics policies that will better balance consumption and production by encouraging higher investments in physical and human capital to promote job growth. We must translate our world class accomplishments in science into leading-edge commercial technologies. He advocates an industrial extension service patterned after our agricultural extension system to help enterprises, especially small businesses, adapt technologies to meet small industry needs.

Marshall adopts the Commission on the Skills of the American Worker's major recommendations for the development of a highly skilled, high performance workforce. The commission advocates a new educational performance standard that all students must meet by age sixteen. Students passing a series of performance assessments that incorporate this standard will be awarded a certificate of initial mastery. States should take responsibility for confirming that virtually all students achieve the certificate. Through new local employment and training boards, states—with federal assistance—should create and fund alternative learning systems for those who cannot attain the certificate in regular schools. A comprehensive system of technical and professional certificates and associate's degrees should be created for the majority of our students and adult workers who do not pursue a baccalaureate degree. The standards for these certificates and degrees should be defined by business, labor, education, and public representatives. These programs should combine general academic education with the development of occupational skills and should include a significant work component. And, all students should have access to financing for these programs.

All employers should be given incentives and assistance to invest in the further education and training of their workers and to pursue high productivity forms of organization. He advocates a requirement that employers invest a certain percentage of their payroll for this purpose, and those who do not wish to participate will contribute to a general training fund. (Marshall proposes 1% of payroll; the Clinton administration proposes 1.5%.) A system of employment and training boards should be established by federal and state governments, together with local leadership, to organize and oversee school-to-work transition programs and training systems.

Marshall also recommends that labor laws be reformed to remove the barriers workers face in organizing and bargaining collectively as well as the legal barriers companies face in establishing labor-management committees and other forms of cooperation. Also, the federal government should establish technical assistance programs to help companies reorganize to meet high performance goals while mandating wage, full employment, income support, tax, trade, and other policies to discourage low-wage competitiveness policies. And finally, workers, employers, students, and others interested in jobs should have a ready source of information and counseling from highly automated local labor market offices staffed by exceptionally qualified professionals.

In his chapter, "Meeting the Skill Demands of the 'New' Economy," Gary Burtless agrees with Ray Marshall that the industrialized world has adopted the idea that improved workforce skills are critical if a nation's industries are to remain competitive and living standards raised. Evidence of the need for new investment in labor market skills is hard to overlook, particularly in the United States. Burtless discusses reasons for the widening gap between the wages of skilled and unskilled workers, in particular, the poor preparation of dropouts and high school graduates combined with the excellent education received by graduates of the nation's best colleges. If our secondary schools do not prepare graduates adequately for work, U.S. employers rarely remedy the deficiency.

Thus, Burtless focuses on proposals to improve workplace training. Although effective school reform could improve the work preparation of future workers, especially those who will not receive much postsecondary education, such reform cannot do much to solve the problems of today's working-age population. To improve the situation of active workers, policies are needed to boost workers' investment in their own skills or to provide incentives for employers to invest in employees' skills. He is also skeptical of the potential benefits of concentrating additional investments in a publicly managed training program or even in more generous subsidies to attend college.

To raise the level and quality of workplace training, Burtless favors a cooperative public-private effort with three main components: the establishment of nationally recognized credentials to certify workplace and occupational skills; the creation of a national apprenticeship system to help non-college-bound youngsters move from school to work through a carefully designed program of firm-based occupational training; and the imposition of a required employer contribution toward the workplace training of non-college-educated workers. Nationally recognized credentials will insure that skills acquired by workers are transferable and therefore will be an effective way of encouraging workers to participate enthusiastically in workplace training programs. A national apprenticeship program will raise dramatically the formal occupational training that young people receive in their first full-time job. To generate a source of funds, a simple assessment on company payrolls is recommended. To create an incentive for employers to provide training to their non-college-educated workers, the government can excuse employers from paying for all of this training assessment if they invest a minimum amount in their own workplace training programs. Burtless has argued for an investment target equal to 2 percent of a company's payroll, which is slightly higher than the figure recommended by Marshall or the current administration.

We originally invited three comments on the Marshall and Burtless papers. Laura Bassi, of the U.S. Department of Labor, was in general agreement with their approaches; however, in her own work she has found much greater levels of revamped organization at the workplace than did the Commission (referred to by Professor Marshall). She points out that we are a long way from understanding which (if any) aspects of work reorganization are critical to the ultimate success of firms and to the economic viability of those individuals who work within them. She points out that neither of the authors makes much of a connection between the interaction of the forces of global competition, the rising inequality of opportunity in the United States, and the soulful malaise this nation has experienced for well over 20 years. She is also more pessimistic about the ability of the U.S. economy to move from a low-cost to a high-quality environment.

Joel Stern, of Stern, Stewart and Co., presents the case for the reliance on voluntary innovations in human resource management to produce substantial impact on productivity gains, efficiency, and even rates of employment over the long term. His firm has developed a concept known as "Economic Value Added" which tries to measure rate of return on capital employed relative to a prescribed minimum required rate of return for risk taking. The important deviation from simple measurement of performance is the recognition of a need to align the interests of employees with those of shareholders. That is, Stern advocates an incentive compensation approach, with incentives reaching down into the lowest levels of unskilled workers in the corporation.

The third original discussant, Professor James Heckman of the University of Chicago, has taken the discussion of the "New Consensus" (a different designation for "new economy") in a number of different and expanded directions, so much so that he, along with colleagues Rebecca Roselius and Jeffrey Smith, have prepared a third chapter for this section of our book. Heckman et al.'s (hereinafter "Heckman") chapter addresses not only the points made in the Marshall and Burtless pieces but looks at a broader set of issues, particularly as they have been laid out in the recent book by Baily, Burtless, and Litan. The Heckman chapter elicited a reaction from Gary Burtless (see "Comment," p. 123–137) which in turn brought a response from Heckman (see "Comment," p. 139–141).

Heckman challenges the new consensus that the current American labor market and educational system are unable to equip workers with sufficient skills thereby causing a disorderly transition from school to work characterized by excessive job turnover and inadequate on-the-job training. Although increased investments in education and training have been suggested as the key to transforming the American workplace, Heckman calculates that the required investment in human capital would be excessive, if the goal were to restore the 1979 earnings ratios of less-skilled workers to workers with some college education, while holding the latter group at their 1989 level of earnings. The debate persists, however, as to whether Heckman's cost estimates are really "large" when compared to the nation's current stock of human capital and if spread over a number of years. Heckman also stresses the value of job shopping, or turnover, as a way of promoting efficient matches between firms and workers who do not suffer long-term harmful consequences from frequent spells of early joblessness.

Heckman's challenges to the effectiveness of the widely acclaimed German apprenticeship system are particularly interesting given that it often is held up as an ideal the United States should strive to emulate. Most people who have observed the German system up close realize that apprentices are simply a source of cheap labor and have heard the well-known exclamation that "the largest employer of former apprentice bakers is the Opel automobile factory." As Heckman put it, "Any positive effect that the German program has on youth employment is mainly due to the fact that apprentices are exempt from minimum wage laws and rigid employment protection laws that make it difficult to fire regular workers." This leads to advocacy of flexible wages and work rules rather than a literal adoption of the German system.

Heckman also questions conclusions about lower youth unemployment in Germany (due to a compulsory education or training age of 18), the link between training and jobs (apprentices leave the firms that train them at very high rates), and the productivity of German labor (data are contrary).

A fundamental paradox of the new consensus is why, if new methods of training and production offer such great promise, have they been so slowly adopted in America. Is this due to inadequate complementary institutions here, or because of deficiencies in the proposed new approaches? Alternatively, is our ability to change constrained by the fact that our educational system is asked to do other things than train and educate (e.g., encourage cultural diversity in a multiethnic society that does not exist to the same extent in Japan or Germany, or perform functions previously provided by families)? Do American values inhibit change? Here I refer to our national distaste for early tracking of students and a tax system in which income redistribution goals often take precedence over providing appropriate incentives.

Heckman points out that U.S. tax policy does favor on-the-job training over formal education even though it is unclear what the appropriate mix is for the most useful development of human capital. Certainly, there is no clear evidence that training provided by the government is more effective than that provided by the private sector. And, there appears to be a myriad of problems with national skills certification tests.

Gary Burtless agrees with many of the propositions explicated by Heckman—indeed, he feels that some of the characterizations of his own views are inaccurate—but disagrees with some of Heckman's conclusions. Burtless is more positive than Heckman about certain types of government training programs. He feels Heckman has been too negative in regard to the success of the German labor market. He also claims that, despite tax incentives, tax subsidies for firm-based training as well as direct public spending for formal education are heavily tilted toward college graduates, and this is unfortunate on both equity grounds and probably efficiency grounds as well. Burtless observes that the argument that there is underinvestment in firm-based training is still quite convincing for a number of reasons.

Burtless is not convinced by Heckman's arguments against skill certification and against incentives for greater training incentives for firms. He chides Heckman for being tilted towards the status quo.

Heckman's final reply restates his assertion that the standards of evidence generally used to evaluate policy proposals need to be elevated. Points remain unsettled even at the conclusion of this interchange; however, this section carries the debate well beyond previous discussions.

1

Job and Skill Demands
in the New Economy

Ray Marshall

The Old Economy

An analysis of the job and skill demands in the old and new economies must start with a definition of these economies. I will define the old economy as the one that evolved in the United States during the first two-thirds of the twentieth century. This economy had three distinguishing characteristics. The first was a heavy *natural resource* orientation. The second was *supporting policies and institutions*, especially a mainly free enterprise system in which government and the private sector formed pragmatic partnerships to build the education, transportation, and other infrastructures that facilitated rapid economic growth. These pragmatic policies renewed and sustained the system during the 1930s when private demand faltered. The third distinguishing characteristic of the old economy was the *mass-production system*. Mass production was made possible by a large and growing internal market for standardized products. The system's main economic advantage in basic industries was its ability to achieve economies of scale with a combination of relatively high fixed capital costs, a few highly educated and skilled workers, and a heavy reliance on frontline workers who needed little more than basic literacy and numeracy. This system's productivity was demonstrated by Henry Ford's assembly line, which reduced the cost of a touring car from $850 to $360 in about six years just before the First World War. Actually, the mass-production system's advantages had already been demonstrated in nineteenth-century America long before Henry Ford

---

Author's Note: As requested by the editors of this volume, I have written this chapter in what may be called a journalistic style, without all the language and documentation commonly used for academic audiences.

popularized it with his highly successful Model T. Andrew Carnegie, for example, used mass-production techniques to reduce the cost of steel from $36.52 to $12 a ton between 1878 and 1898 (Marshall and Tucker, 1992, p. 4). But the mass-production of automobiles, tractors, and trucks had a major impact on the U.S. economy by significantly increasing agricultural productivity, increasing the flexibility of the nation's transportation system, and contributing greatly to rapid urbanization. The advantages of the mass-production system caused its management practices to be widely emulated in governments and schools as well as in industry.

The mass-production organization of work was rationalized by Frederick Taylor's scientific management system, which sought primarily to give management almost complete control by modeling the "one best" method for performing a task and transferring ideas, skills, and knowledge to management and machines. Only managerial, professional, and technical workers needed higher-order thinking skills. Most workers could perform the "one best" method with routine skills and basic literacy and numeracy. Management's control of the work was facilitated by detailed rules and regulations enforced by supervisors and inspectors.

Despite its productivity, the mass-production system had a number of problems that were addressed in various ways by the end of the 1940s. Because of large capital requirements and high fixed costs, mass-production companies were vulnerable to competition that could depress prices to below-average costs for long periods of time. Mass-production companies consequently developed oligopolistic policies that "stabilized" prices and adjusted to changes in demand by varying capacity utilization and employment. With fixed prices for oligopolies and competitive prices for workers and farmers, who often were squeezed by falling prices and high costs, production periodically outran consumption, leading to recessions.

During the Great Depression of the 1930s, the United States and other industrialized countries addressed the business cycle problem through "Keynesian" demand management policies designed to reduce unemployment by stimulating aggregate demand. Many analysts thought that U.S. performance during World War II demonstrated the efficacy of these demand management policies. The Keynesian system also justified unions and collective bargaining and income support systems such as unemployment compensation, pensions, and agricultural price supports as ways to stabilize aggregate demand.

In the 25 years after World War II, a number of developments strengthened support for Keynesian policies, particularly their success in achieving high rates of growth in productivity and total output and relatively low levels of unemployment. Ironically, the apparent success of tax cuts in stimulating the U.S. economy during the 1960s strengthened political support for these policies at the very time that changes in technology and international markets were making them less effective and ushering in the "new economy."

The New Economy: Global Competition and High-Performance Work Organizations

As noted in the previous section, the United States developed economic policies and work organizations during the first half of this century that produced the world's strongest economy and highest standard of living. Indeed, between the late 1930s and the early 1970s the United States experienced the longest period of relatively equitably shared prosperity in its history. Schools and other learning systems reflected the economy's bifurcated skill requirements. Elite private schools and college tracks within public schools taught higher-order thinking skills, whereas public schools employed Tayloristic methods to mass-produce students with the basic skills needed for most routine jobs. This section traces the emergence of a very different economy requiring very different skills. Although the United States had huge advantages in the mass-production economy, and still has the world's wealthiest economy, it has enormous disadvantages in the more competitive, global, knowledge-intensive economy of the 1990s and beyond.

Toward the end of the 1960s, there were growing signs that America's traditional economic system was in trouble. The main forces for change were technology and increased international competition, which combined to weaken the traditional mass-production system and its supporting institutions. These changes also dramatically altered the conditions for economic viability. In this more competitive world dominated by knowledge-intensive technology, the keys to economic success have become human resources and more effective production systems, not natural resources and traditional economies of scale. Economies of scale are still very important, but now must be considered in a global context and are needed to recoup much more extensive research-and-development costs. Although no consensus has formed for a new economic policy paradigm, two things are reasonably clear: The policies that supported the old economy are obsolete, and human capital must be the centerpiece for economic success in the new economy.

Technology not only contributed to the globalization of markets, but also rendered the mass-production system and traditional economies of scale less viable in high-wage countries. Although the assembly line can be automated, that does not seem to be the most efficient use of the new technology (Piore and Sabel, 1984; Zuboff, 1988). Computerized technology provides many of the advantages of economies of scale and scope through flexible systems that have significant advantages in a more dynamic and competitive global economy.

Technology makes new organizations of production possible, but competition makes them essential for those who wish to maintain and improve incomes. This is so because a more competitive internationalized information economy has very different requirements for national, enterprise, organizational, and personal success than was true of largely national mass-production systems. Significant changes for public policy purposes include the following: (a) National governments have less control of their economies; (b) national companies have less control of markets; and (c) unions have less control of working conditions. A country can no longer maintain high wages and full employment through traditional combinations of monetary-fiscal and international trade policies, administered wages and prices, and fixed exchange rates. Keynesian policies were particularly inadequate for dealing with inflationary pressures induced by external supply shocks during the 1970s, and had almost nothing to say about productivity, the main determinant of economic success in a more competitive global economy. In the 1970s and 1980s, moreover, internationalization weakened the linkages among domestic consumption, investment, and output that formed the basic structure of the traditional "Keynesian" demand management system. In a global economy, a firm's success depends on global, not domestic, demand. The weakening of these Keynesian linkages became very clear when U.S. tax cuts in the early 1980s increased consumption, but—in marked contrast to the 1960s' tax cut that seemed to justify Keynesian policies—also greatly stimulated imports and therefore produced much smaller increases in domestic investment than had resulted from earlier tax cuts in less globalized markets. Indeed, imports accounted for a large share of the consumer goods and almost all of the increased demand for capital goods following the 1981 tax cuts (Lower, 1985).

The requirements of a more competitive, knowledge-intensive economy thus create new employment policy dilemmas. Competing at high wages requires sufficient growth to prevent rising productivity from increasing unemployment. At the same time, countries are less able to stimulate their economies through demand management policies. Indeed, Harold Wilensky presents evidence that demographic, structural, and social trends had more influence on employment growth during the 1970s and 1980s than national economic policies (cited in Barnet, 1993, p. 51). The United States faces particularly serious employment problems because most of the future workforce growth will take place among minorities who have not fared very well in U.S. labor markets and learning systems. The good news is that, if they are able to get it, education improves the incomes of minorities (Smith and Welch, 1986). Employment problems likewise could be exacerbated by the absence of a global "engine of growth," a role played by the United States during the three decades after World War II. The United States can no longer serve this function, and the absence of coordinated policies among major countries, especially the United States, Germany, and Japan, has hampered global growth and stability. Similarly, obsolete economic institutions and policies make it difficult for the United States to provide needed investments, development programs, and markets to permit growing demand in Third World countries to stimulate the global economy.

The global jobs problem is further complicated by rapid workforce growth in Mexico and other developing countries that are unlikely to generate enough jobs either to absorb millions of new entrants to the workforce or to reduce already high levels of joblessness. Third World labor surpluses will affect the United States through competitive pressures on wages, as well as through immigration. The entry of millions of illegal immigrants with limited educational achievements makes it much more difficult for the United States either to reduce urban poverty and unemployment or to develop the high-performance organizations needed for a high-wage economy (Marshall, 1991a). These employment problems are exacerbated by changing family structures, especially the high incidence of poverty among children and single-parent families (Marshall, 1991b), many of whom are becoming isolated in large metropolitan areas (Wilson, 1987).

The Basic Choice: High-Performance Organizations or Low Wages

With the internationalization of national economies, countries, companies, and people must yield to the imperatives of global competition. The most basic of these imperatives is that we can compete in only two ways: (a) reduce wages and income or (b) increase productivity and quality. We can rely no longer on natural resources and economies of scale by oligopolistic firms in domestic markets insulated from international competition.

Most high-income industrial countries have either implicitly or explicitly rejected the low-wage option because it implies lower and more unequal wages—which is exactly what most workers in the United States have experienced in the past 20 years. At current exchange rates, wages in many other industrialized economies are now higher than those in the United States. According to recent U.S. census data, as analyzed by the Economic Policy Institute, the median hourly wage of men was 14 percent less in 1989 than it was in 1979. The only workers whose incomes have increased since 1979 are the college educated. Young male high school graduates' earnings were 26.5 percent lower in 1991 than in

1979. Among all male college graduates, earnings increased only for those with advanced degrees; young male college graduates actually earned 5.1 percent less in 1991 than they did in 1979, with most of the drop coming after 1987 (Mishel and Bernstein, 1992).

The U.S. experience illustrates why most other industrialized countries have rejected the low-wage option—they see that lower and more unequal incomes threaten their political, social, and economic health. The only way for those following the low-wage option to improve total incomes is to work more, a reality that clearly limits economic progress.[1] The high-wage, high-productivity option, by contrast, could create very steep learning and earning curves, and therefore holds the promise of rapidly increasing personal, organizational, and national advancement.

What must we do if we want to pursue the high-productivity option? Worldwide experience suggests that we must first develop national consensus to follow that option and then support the policies and strategies to achieve it. National policies must create an environment that encourages companies to organize for high performance and discourages the low-wage alternative.

In a 1990 report based on more than 2,800 in-depth interviews of people at every level in 550 companies in a broad cross-section of industries, the Commission on the Skills of the American Workforce (CSAW) found that relative to six other countries studied (Japan, Singapore, Germany, Sweden, Denmark, and Ireland), very few American companies have moved to the high-performance option. The CSAW found that 95 percent of major American companies cling to the mass-production organization of work. Other studies (e.g., Osterman, 1993) have produced somewhat higher estimates of "high-performance" U.S. companies, but they use a looser definition than the CSAW's, or the one I use in this chapter. The CSAW also found that a much larger proportion of companies in the other countries studied are shifting to more competitive systems. Before I present a discussion of why most American companies have been so slow to abandon the traditional organizational forms, it would be useful to outline some of the characteristics that most effective high-performance organizations seem to be developing in the United States and other countries. Although there is as yet no agreement on the definition of *high performance*, a good guiding hypothesis is that these organizations will drive the policies of high-wage countries.

Characteristics of High-Performance Organizations

Productivity, flexibility, and quality. In a competitive global information economy, success requires emphasis on factors that were much less important in traditional mass-production systems. These new factors are quality, productivity, and flexibility.

Quality, best defined as meeting customers' needs, has become more important for two reasons.[2] First, as the mass-production system matured and personal incomes rose, consumers became dissatisfied with standardized products. Second, a more competitive environment is largely consumer driven; the mass-production system was more producer driven, especially after governments and oligopolies "stabilized" prices. The mass-production system depended heavily on a few companies controlling national markets; with internationalization, companies, like national governments, have much less market control.

Productivity and flexibility are closely related to quality. The difference is that now productivity improvements are achieved through the more efficient use of all factors of production, not, as in the mass-production system, mainly through economies of scale and compatible and reinforcing interindustry shifts (e.g., from low-productivity agriculture to high-productivity manufacturing). The mass-production system had enormous waste in the utilization of capital (especially inventory) and people, but these were more than offset by economies of scale. Once technology reduced traditional scale advantages, mass-production companies were left with labor and capital inefficiencies, but with much smaller-scale offsets.

Flexibility enhances productivity by facilitating the shift of resources from less to more productive outputs and improves quality by making possible quick responses to diverse and changing customer needs. Moreover, flexibility in the employment of workers and technology improves productivity by reducing the waste of labor and machine time.

Worker participation and lean management systems. The fundamental issue, of course, is how to achieve quality, productivity, and flexibility. The answer appears to be high-performance production systems that develop and use leading-edge technologies. Productivity is improved when work organizations reduce waste through better inventory control, more efficient use of labor, and effective quality controls to prevent defects rather than try to detect them, as was often the case in mass-production systems. High performance systems have extensive employee involvement in what were considered "management" functions in mass-production systems. Indeed, more productive and flexible systems blur the distinctions between frontline "managers" and "workers." In short, high-performance organizations are unlikely to be achieved through marginal changes in mass-production systems—they require fundamental restructuring of those systems or the creation of totally different organizations.

A number of features of high-performance production systems encourage worker participation and lean, decentralized management structures. First, workers must have more knowledge and skill, which in turn makes them less tolerant of monotonous, routine work and authoritarian managerial controls. Second, quality, productivity, and flexibility are all enhanced when production decisions are made as close to the point of production as possible. Mass-production bureaucracies were designed to achieve quantity, managerial control, and stability, not flexibility, quality, or productivity in the use of all factors of production. Mass-production systems were based on managerial information monopolies and worker controls; in high-performance systems, workers must be free to make decisions. To accomplish this, information must be shared, not monopolized, because machines handle more of the routine, direct work and frontline workers do more indirect work formerly done mainly by administrative staffs.

Several features of a high-performance system reduce the efficacy of hierarchical management systems. First, because machines perform more of the direct work and frontline workers assume more of the indirect work, there is less need for inspectors, schedulers, and other indirect workers. Second, because workers manage more of their own work, individually or in teams, fewer supervisors and inspectors are needed. Thus, the flow of information, a major function of Tayloristic managers, can be controlled more effectively by computers and other information technology, which can provide everybody a common database or "score," to use an orchestral analogy. The role of managers therefore shifts from "bossing" or supervising to teaching, building consensus, and enabling and supporting frontline workers, who assume more responsibility for quality, productivity, and flexibility.

One of the most important differences between high-performance and Tayloristic systems is found in the attitudes of managers and workers toward one another. Taylorism assumes that workers are naturally lazy and must be forced to work out of fear that they will lose their jobs or be reprimanded. Taylor's system posited, in addition, that most frontline workers should not have to think and, indeed, were incapable of the higher-order thinking done by supervisors educated in "scientific management." This attitude naturally created resentment and distrust of management by workers and their unions. Labor's distrust was exacerbated by the decline in upward mobility of skilled, non-college-educated workers who had fewer opportunities to move into managerial ranks. High-performance managements, by contrast, establish trust and respect between workers and managers by assuming that most workers want to do a good job that enhances their self-worth and gains them the respect of management and their fellow workers. High-performance managers believe, in addition, that workers and effective work organization are the keys to high performance; they believe that workers understand their jobs, are capable of higher-order thinking, and are motivated by positive reward systems.

Higher-order thinking skills. High-performance systems therefore require frontline workers to have different kinds of thinking skills than were expected in Tayloristic systems. One of the most important skills required for indirect work is the ability to analyze the flood of data produced by information technology. This means that workers must understand and be able to use models, metrics, and other quantitative tools. Workers who have the ability to impose order on chaotic data can use information to add value to products, improve productivity and quality, solve problems, and improve technology.

Indirect work also is apt be group work, requiring more communication, interpersonal skills, and teamwork. High-performance workers also must manage their own work, solve problems without assistance, and deal with ambiguity. These skills are necessary because productivity, quality, and flexibility require close coordination between what were formerly more discrete components of the production process (e.g., research and development, design, production, inspection, distribution, sales, and services). These functions were more linear in the mass-production system, but are more interactive in dynamic, consumer-oriented production systems where rapid response times convey significant advantages.

Another very important high-performance skill is the ability to *learn*. Learning is not only more important in high-performance than in mass-production systems, it is also very different. The simplification of tasks and the standardization of technology and production in Tayloristic systems limit the amount of learning needed or achieved. More learning is required in a dynamic, technology-intensive workplace, and more of that learning must be achieved through the manipulation of abstract symbols, simulations, and models. For line workers, mass-production systems stressed learning almost entirely by observation and doing.

Learning in productive workplaces also is more communal and cooperative than was true in mass-production systems. Taylor's system and cost competition encouraged adversarial relationships that impeded the sharing of information among workers, managers, and suppliers. A high-performance system, by contrast, encourages both the sharing of information and cooperative efforts to achieve common objectives. High-performance organizations must, in addition, find ways to measure learning and to make individual and group learning part of the organizations' collective memories. These quality-driven processes create communities of interest among all those involved in the system—managers, frontline workers and suppliers, and other components of high-performance networks. Tayloristic organizations emphasized short-run profit maximization, which tends to create conflicts; high-performance systems emphasize quality, which tends to unify workers and managers. There clearly is much more learning in a community-of-interest network than in an adversarial one. Communal learning becomes increasingly important in building the consensus needed to create more highly integrated production processes. High-performance workers not only are self-managers, but also perform a greater array of tasks and adapt more readily to change. This requires a reduction of the inflexibility of Taylor's detailed job classifications and work rules. Well-educated, well-trained, highly motivated workers are much more flexible and productive, especially in supportive systems that stress equity and internal cohesion. Indeed, humans are likely to be the most flexible components in a high-performance system.

Development and use of leading-edge technology. Other features of high-performance workplaces require greater employee involvement and higher-order thinking skills. One is the need for constant improvements in technology—or what the Japanese call "giving wisdom to the machine." *Technology* is best defined as how things are done. The most important fact about technology is not the physical capital itself, but, as noted above, the ideas, skills, and knowledge embodied in machines and structures. Technology becomes standardized when the rates at which ideas, skills, and knowledge can be transferred to machines or structures become very small. Standardized technology therefore requires workers to have fewer intellectual skills than they must have when they develop and use leading-edge technology. High-performance organizations emphasize leading-edge technologies because highly mobile standardized technologies gravitate to low-paid workers. Some American companies have responded to competitive pressures by combining high technology and low skills through automation (Keller, 1989). This combination has proved to be little, if any, more productive than standardized technology and low-skilled workers. General Motors, for example, spent $77 billion for a system based largely on this theory and was less competitive in 1986 than when the process started in the late 1970s. The most productive systems, therefore, have highly skilled workers who can adapt, develop, and use leading-edge technology in particular production systems. And the shorter life cycle of products and technologies in a more dynamic and competitive global economy provides important advantages to continuous innovation and creativity.

The need to pay more attention to quality and productivity is another reason for increased involvement in production decisions by frontline workers. In cases requiring direct customer contact, flexible, highly skilled employees can provide better service than is true of highly specialized mass-production workers who can offer only their narrow specialized service. In manufacturing systems, moreover, even the most sophisticated machines are idiosyncratic and therefore require the close attention of skilled workers to adapt them to particular situations. With the smaller production runs permitted by information technology and required by more competitive and dynamic markets, workers must control production and be able to override machines. The mass-production system's long production runs, by contrast, made it possible to amortize the cost of start-up defects over those long runs. Systems with short production runs cannot afford many start-up defects. They therefore must rely on workers to override machines that malfunction or produce defects. Quality-driven systems also require more self-inspection by workers on the basis of visible observation, so that defects are prevented rather than detected at the end of the production process. Quality improvement is facilitated by just-in-time inventory and other mechanisms that expose defects early in production processes. Productivity and quality are enhanced by early detection; otherwise, those faulty components become invisible when they enter the product, and are discovered only as the products malfunction when used by customers.

Positive reward systems. Because organizations ordinarily get the outcomes they reward, the explicit or implicit incentives in any system are basic determinants of its outcomes. High-performance organizations stress positive reward systems. Mass-production incentives, by contrast, tended to be negative—fear of discharge or punishment; they also were more individualistic and implicit. Mass-production incentives were sometimes even perverse in that they actually impeded productivity improvements. Process- and time-based mass-production compensation systems, for example, were often unrelated to productivity or quality and were sometimes even counterproductive, as when workers feared they would lose their jobs if productivity improved.

Positive rewards enhance flexibility as well as productivity and quality. Group incentives and job security encourage flexibility by simultaneously overcoming resistance to the development and use of broader skills and providing employers greater incentives to invest in education and training to develop those skills. Similarly, bonus compensation systems simultaneously provide greater incentives for workers to improve productivity and quality and create more flexible compensation systems. The ability to participate in production decisions is itself a positive reward. In essence, the high-performance system substitutes clearly defined goals and objectives and positive rewards for the mass-production system's rules, regulations, supervisors, and administrators.

It would be hard to overemphasize the importance of equity, internal unity, and positive rewards for high-performance, knowledge-intensive workplaces, because all parties must be willing to "go all out" to achieve common objectives. In traditional mass-production systems workers were justifiably afraid to go all out to improve productivity for fear they would lose their jobs. This is why employment security is one of the most important incentives a high-performance company can offer. Similarly, the fragmentation of work within mass-production systems gave workers little incentive to control quality—quality was somebody else's responsibility. A high-performance system, by contrast, makes quality control everybody's responsibility. Positive rewards are required, in addition, because the effective use of information technology gives workers greater discretion. It is difficult to compel workers to think or to go all out to improve quality and productivity.

One of the most important requirements of high-performance incentive systems is a high level of consensus and trust. Indeed, traditional American managers have so much trouble understanding this concept that they actually are surprised when workers refuse to accept unilaterally imposed "incentives" that will improve the workers' earnings and the firm's economic viability. It is, moreover, difficult to transform adversarial relations into cooperative ones. The most successful transformations in the United States have required demonstrable threats to jobs and company survival.

The role of labor organizations. One of the most controversial aspects of high-performance production systems is the role of labor organizations. My own view is that the rights of workers to organize readily and bargain collectively constitute an important element in a high-performance system. Independent power for workers also is required because of the fundamental nature of the employment relationship. It is difficult for parties of unequal power to establish cooperative relationships. Cooperation is weakened when the stronger party makes unilateral decisions, forcing the other party to seek countervailing power. Moreover, the relationships between workers and managers are inherently adversarial as well as cooperative. Indeed, adversarial relations are functional in that they provide processes for the resolution of differences. Workers therefore need an independent source of power to promote their interests in these adversarial relationships. The challenge, of course, is to maximize common interests and prevent conflicts from becoming "functionless" by making all parties worse off. Finally, workers are unlikely to go all out to improve productivity and quality unless they have an independent source of power to protect their interests in the process.

Workers and managers often clash over inherent conflicts in the components of a high-performance system. Management typically wants to restrain wages, for example, whereas workers want to increase them. Management stresses "flexibility," which threatens work rules and leads to "outsourcing" and the use of temporary contingent workers, whereas workers emphasize employment security. How such clashes are resolved determines the extent to which incentives remain positive. Because motivation is critical for a high-performance system, the nature of the relationship between unions and management is an important determinant of whether unionized firms can be high-performance organizations. A good orienting hypothesis, therefore, is as follows: With mutual acceptance and respect between unions and managers, unionized firms can achieve higher performance than can nonunion firms.

Evidence and Issues

As noted earlier, opinions about how to define high-performance organizations vary. The foregoing discussion represents my judgment based on considerable study and experience during the 1980s and 1990s.[3] In a recent study for the Economic Policy Institute, Eileen Appelbaum (1993) has identified "two distinct and coherent models of high performance work systems," a more hierarchical American version of "lean production" and "an American version of "team production" that combines the principles of Swedish sociotechnical systems with those of quality engineering [and] more thoroughly decentralizes the management of work and the flow of decision making" (p. 9). This latter version is close to my definition of a high-performance organization. Appelbaum concludes: "While the outcomes for firms in the two models appear to be quite similar, evidence suggests that the American version of team production provides employees with greater autonomy, more employment security, and a greater guarantee of a share of any performance gains" (p. 9; see also Appelbaum and Batt, 1993).

Therefore, another good guiding hypothesis is that a high-performance organization, as defined in this chapter, is more compatible with democratic values and a more equitable distribution of income than are mass-production systems, and will do more to improve productivity and quality, which could help strengthen the effectiveness of such workplace regulations as training, pensions, and occupational safety and health. At the same time, however, high-performance organizations create external employment problems, such as technological unemployment and the growth of temporary workers with limited benefits and job security, that must be addressed by public policies. In the remainder of this chapter I will explore the evidence for these conclusions.

Worker Participation

I have argued that greater worker participation will improve productivity, quality, and flexibility. Unfortunately, the evidence for this proposition is difficult to establish because many worker participation processes in the United States are relatively new, have different meanings, are qualitatively different from place to place, and never occur in isolation from

other factors. There is, however, growing evidence that worker participation and work reorganization are important factors in improving productivity and economic competitiveness (Dertouzes, Lester, and Solow,
1989). A 1990 Brookings Institution report edited by Alan Blinder acknowledges the positive contribution of worker participation, though Blinder
considers such productivity improvements to be "transitory" albeit potentially "impressive" (see also Blinder, 1989/90). Blinder (1989/90), like most
orthodox economists, believes that "the best way to raise productivity
growth, and perhaps the only way to do so permanently, is to speed up the
pace of technological innovation" (p. 33). The trouble with this view, of
course, is the implication that technological innovation is an external,
rather than integral, part of the production process. This view also fails to
recognize that high-performance production systems with positive incentives, skilled workers, continuous learning processes, and a high degree of
worker involvement are able to improve productivity and technology
continuously. The ideas, skills, and knowledge embedded in the latest
machine technology can indeed improve quality and productivity, but
this is done most effectively with high-performance organizations and
highly skilled workers. The Brookings studies nevertheless show that incentive compensation systems raise wages about 11 percent an hour more
than for other workers, and do so without reducing fringe benefits or
hourly wages (Blinder, 1989/90, p. 37). Blinder (1989/90) concludes that
"worker participation apparently does help make alternative compensation plans...work better—and also has beneficial effects of its own. This
theme was totally unexpected when I organized the conference [that led
to these studies]" (p. 38).

It should be noted, however, that the mere existence of a formal
worker participation system will not necessarily improve productivity
and quality—the degree of participation and whether or not workers
have independent sources of power seem to be key characteristics related to productivity. For example, David Lewin and others at Columbia
University studied the relationship between the financial performance of
500 publicly traded companies and the degree of employee involvement.
Their analysis of the data for 1987 concludes:

> The mere presence of an employee involvement process was not signifi-
> cantly related to positive improvements in any of the financial indicators.
> However, the further a firm moved up the employee involvement index
> [measuring degrees of employee involvement] and the more employees
> were involved in decision-making, the greater the magnitude of financial
> performance. What appears to be critical is the scope or comprehensive-
> ness of employee involvement and participation programs.

High employee involvement is associated with better financial performance, particularly on the return on investment and return on asset measures. (Economic Policy Council of the United Nations Association, 1990, p. 16)

There is, in addition, abundant case-study evidence of the relationship between worker participation and improved quality and productivity. Perhaps the most clear-cut and compelling evidence is from the New United Motor Manufacturing Co., Inc. (NUMMI), a joint venture between Toyota and General Motors in Fremont, California. GM closed this plant in 1982 because its managers could not make it competitive. Toyota re-opened it as NUMMI in 1984 with a new management system, but with mostly the same UAW members and essentially the same equipment, which was much less automated than in GM's most modern plants. One of the most important changes NUMMI made was to guarantee the workers a high level of job security. Other changes included a reduction in job classes from about 100 to 4; the elimination of such management perks as private dining rooms, separate parking lots, private offices, and separate dress codes; and the establishment of work teams of 5 to 10 people who set their own work standards, lay out the work area, determine the workload distribution, and assign workers to specific tasks.

From a production standpoint, there can be little doubt that NUMMI has been a success. In 1989, productivity at the plant was 50 percent higher than at the former GM plant, and NUMMI ranked first among all GM plants in the United States. A 1988 MIT study reported that productivity at NUMMI was about 40 percent higher than at traditional GM plants and was about equal that of Toyota's Japanese plants (Krafcik, 1988). *Consumer Reports* judged NUMMI's Chevrolet Nova to be the highest quality of any American-built car. As a result of these successes, there has been strong interest in NUMMI among American managers.

It also should be noted that although the NUMMI experience is an improvement over the Tayloristic GM model, worker participation at the plant actually is restricted to production processes. Further, the work is still highly standardized, though the work of each employee is less standardized. GM's experience with its Saturn project (an autonomous high-performance company in Tennessee) has gone beyond NUMMI, especially in the important worker-participation factor; at Saturn, as in most German or Swedish companies, workers have greater control of the production process at every level than is true at NUMMI or most Japanese companies. Worker autonomy and control are key ingredients in steep learning curves and high performance. To some degree, NUMMI involves a Tayloristic fragmentation of work and a much faster pace than is found in the traditional GM plant. This system is nevertheless popular with NUMMI employees; indeed, "even the critics are enthusiastic about the system.... The criticisms are, with few exceptions, directed at what workers see as flaws in the implementation of the standardized work system, not the system itself" (Adler, 1991, p. 72).

Levine and Tyson (1990) contend that formal worker-participation systems are most likely to increase productivity when they include the following elements:

1. Workers share the benefits.
2. Wage differentials between firms are relatively narrow.
3. There are long-term employment guarantees.
4. Workers are protected from unjust dismissal.

Unions and Competitiveness

The diversity of union experiences makes it difficult to generalize about unions' impact on productivity. There is, however, abundant case-study evidence that unionized firms generally are more productive than nonunion firms. In their thorough review of the econometric evidence on this subject Harvard University economists Richard Freeman and James Medoff (1984) conclude: "Modern quantitative analysis of productivity in organized and unorganized establishments and sectors offers striking new evidence on what unions do to productivity. The new work suggests that in general, productivity is higher in the presence of unionism than in its absence" (pp. 162–163).

Eaton and Voos (1992), among others, have shown that union firms are more likely than their nonunion counterparts to be involved in workplace innovation, especially those cooperative arrangements, such as teamwork and production gain sharing, that yield higher productivity. Nonunion firms are more apt to concentrate on profit-sharing plans that have little direct impact on productivity.

Maryellen Kelley and Bennett Harrison (1992), in a study of 1,015 U.S. metal and machinery companies, found that union shops were as much as 31 percent more productive than nonunion shops. In fact, even unionized branches of large companies were more productive than nonunion branches of those companies using the same technology, paying similar wages, and making the same products. Kelley and Harrison found, in addition, that sites with various employee-management problem-solving teams, which sprang up in many U.S. firms during the 1970s and 1980s as an alternative to unions, were less productive than those without them. Freeman and Rogers (1993) have reviewed many studies that show the critical role of effective labor relations on economic performance and the dependence of effective labor relations on worker representation.

A study of unions and competitiveness conducted by Mishel and Voos (1992) and sponsored by the Economic Policy Institute (EPI) concludes as follows:

1. At the general economywide level, collective bargaining and unionization have had "few if any" adverse effects on competitiveness.
2. It is commonly argued that unions reduce competitiveness by raising prices above competitive levels. There is, however, strong empirical evidence that although unions do increase wages and benefits, they do not necessarily reduce competitiveness, for two reasons:

   • Competition is over quality, not just price. Quality is more likely to be maintained and improved by highly participative systems in which workers are unionized.
   • Because most studies show unionized firms to be more productive than nonunion firms, higher union wages are offset in part by higher productivity and in part by the reduction of oligopolistic profits. Although both union and nonunion sectors were trying to become more competitive through the introduction of various workplace innovations, "by the end of the 1980s, the large union employers either equaled or surpassed the large nonunion employers with regard to virtually all flexibility and productivity-enhancing workplace innovations, with the sole exception of profit sharing" (Mishel and Voos, 1992, p. 9). Many studies have shown, moreover, that profit sharing has much less effect on productivity than do team production and gain sharing. Eaton and Voos (1992) show that gain sharing and team productivity not only have greater potential than profit sharing for increasing firm performance, but also are a continuation of a long tradition of productivity bargaining by U.S. unions, which permits them to maintain union employment despite higher union wages.

The foregoing is not to argue, however, that unionized industrial relations systems never have negative effects on productivity and economic performance. In Japan during the 1950s and in Germany and other countries during the 1960s, evidence suggests that poor labor-management relations contributed to weak economic performance (Marshall, 1987). There also is evidence that the industrial relations climate influences economic performance. Belman (1992), for example, notes, on the basis of an extensive review:

The structure of bargaining, the history of labor management relations, the environment in which firms and employees operate, and the consequent attitudes of labor and management affect firm performance. In plants and firms in which there is little trust between employers and employees, in which production workers are largely excluded from decisions affecting them, and in which there is ongoing conflict over the boundary between subjects of bargaining and those under unilateral managerial control, there will be little incentive for workers and managers to share information, workers will only produce under compulsion, and the rules of the work site—originating from conflict—will be used to assert or limit control rather than improve output. In contrast, in environments in which there is high trust, where employees and their unions are integrated into the decision process, and in which the parties accept the legitimacy of one another's goals, productivity gains and cost reductions can be realized through creative bargaining, cooperation in development of better production techniques, and a reduction in the use of restrictive work practices and monitoring. (pp. 45–46)

A final observation about unions and competitiveness is that the viability of labor organizations depends heavily on their ability to transform themselves into high-performance organizations that protect and promote their members' interests while improving productivity and quality. Industrial unions were natural responses to Taylorism and therefore have developed attitudes, policies, and procedures that strengthen adversarial relationships and minimize cooperation. As noted above, although adversarial relations are inevitable and can be functional, they can become functionless if the parties involved ignore their common interests. High-performance unions therefore will give greater weight to cooperation and will stress flexibility and not merely stability through contracts, rules, and regulations. Like the oligopolies and regulated monopolies with which they bargained, unions originated to "take labor out of competition" through rules and regulations. In a competitive global economy, it is difficult, if not impossible, to remove labor from competition by traditional means. As is the case for noncompetitive companies, their best option is to stress competition through productivity and quality, though minimum labor standards remain an important part of high-productivity national economic strategies.

Skill Requirements in the New Economy

The foregoing discussion raises a number of important issues concerning whether future jobs will require higher-order thinking skills, as I have argued; whether educational achievement improves productivity, as I claim; and what policies are required to create a prosperous, high-income country where opportunities for advancement are widely shared by all major groups. There is little question that education is highly correlated with positive social and economic outcomes. There are, however, doubts that most jobs in the United States will require significantly higher skills (Teixeira and Mishel, 1991, 1993). There seems to be little doubt that in a sense the critics are right: Unless we adopt a high-productivity competitiveness strategy, most jobs in the United States will not require much more than basic literacy. Of course, policies that accelerate the movement to high-performance organizations will increase the demand for workers with higher-order thinking skills.

Richard Rothstein (1993) is among those who argue that the skills shortage in the United States is exaggerated. He notes that many college graduates are underemployed, and that some categories of workers, such as paralegals, are predicted by the U.S. Bureau of Labor Statistics to increase 75 percent between 1988 and 2000, whereas maids and janitors will grow by only 19 percent. Even so, the absolute increase in paralegals will be only 62,000, whereas maids and janitors will increase by 556,000. He points to the ability of U.S. companies to introduce "high-performance work organizations" in developing countries using workers with limited levels of formal education. In Mexico, for example, the Ford Motor Company achieved high performance in its Chihuahua plant using workers with an average of only nine years of formal education. Rothstein also cites GM's high-performance Saturn plant in Tennessee, where "America's schooling was no impediment" (p. 23). Rothstein concedes, however, that Ford gave the Mexican workers in Chihuahua extensive on-the-job education and training. The argument that *schools* need not do any better if companies will do the training is not the same as arguing that higher skills are not needed in sophisticated production processes. Evidence from Germany, Japan, and Western Europe, cited below, shows that students who meet high standards before leaving school are able to learn more complicated tasks on the job. It should also be noted that Saturn screened extensively before selecting its Tennessee workforce—as did Ford in Mexico. Arguing that a few companies, through extensive screening, can find workers with adequate learning skills is not the same as arguing that a general movement toward high-performance workplaces, as I have defined them here, would not encounter skill shortages in the United States. And I would not classify the Ford Chihuahua plant as a "high-performance organization," although I would put Saturn in that category. It remains to be seen, moreover, whether *most* Mexican or American companies can compete with high-performance Japanese or German companies with well-trained, highly paid workers—not whether *some* companies can compete.

Education and Productivity

Another issue is whether or not education improves productivity. The empirical research of the past 30 years generally supports the human capital perspective, whatever the method used—growth accounting, rate-of-return, or productivity studies—though each approach has limitations. A limitation of growth accounting is its assumption that earnings differentials accurately measure productivity improvements. However, this criticism is overcome by productivity studies, which bypass markets altogether and relate physical productivity to specific educational skills (Fuller, 1976; Jamison and Lau, 1982; Lau and Yotopoulos, 1989; Min, 1987). A 1993 summary of numerous rate-of-return studies for many countries by the World Bank concludes that overall "the evidence...suggests that the economic payoff to education is high and remains sizable with economic growth, even as educational systems expand the supply of educated workers" (Middleton, Ziderman, and Adams, 1993, p. 42).

Some critics of the human capital approach concede the value of education but argue that empirical studies inflate rates of return because of the "screening" effects of schooling (Phelps, 1972; Stiglitz, 1975; Taubman & Wales, 1973). These analysts agree that employers pay higher salaries to educated workers, but, they argue, employers do so because of these employees' innate aptitudes and behavioral traits, not solely or evenly mainly because their education makes them more productive. Although the screening hypothesis has some validity when it refers to schooling, it is less important in physical productivity studies, or in studies that relate various outcomes to specific skills instead of years of schooling. I am, moreover, very skeptical that educational attainment is largely the result of "innate ability." The evidence suggests that educational achievement is related to supportive learning systems and hard work.

As noted above, work is a very important learning system for productivity purposes. Econometricians have consistently found that only 40 percent of competitive improvements come from direct investments, whereas 60 percent are the result of "advances in knowledge" or "innovation" (Baumol, Blackman, and Wolff, 1989). In other words, some technologies, representing the distilled ideas, skills, and knowledge of others, can be acquired externally, but most (60 percent) are developed through individual and organizational learning, most often in the production process (Hulten, 1993). There is additional econometric evidence of high returns to companies that invest in the education and training of their workers (Lillard and Tan, 1986). Similarly, Denison (1985) attributes 26 percent of the productivity growth between 1929 and 1982 to education (schooling) and 55 percent to on-the-job learning.

Econometric studies likewise tend to confirm the conceptual view of the changing structure of U.S. industry outlined in this chapter. There is clear evidence of a large increase in the relative wages of educated workers during the 1980s that cannot be explained by quantitative changes in the demand for and supply of labor. For example, John Bound and George Johnson (1992) tested the impact of various traditional demand and supply factors on wage differentials for the 1980s; they state: "Our analysis points strongly to the conclusion that the principal reason for the increases in wage differentials by educational attainment...is a combination of skill-based technical changes and changes in unmeasured labor quality" (p. 389).

There also is a growing body of case-study evidence that confirms the positive correlation between workforce skills and productivity. Studies of matched plants making similar products in Britain and the Netherlands conducted by the National Institute of Economic and Social Research in London found Dutch manufacturing companies to be 25–30 percent more productive than their British counterparts, despite rapid upgrading and productivity growth in Britain during the 1980s (Mason and van Ark, 1992). This study found that Dutch workers were more highly skilled and therefore capable of more self-management, experienced fewer equipment breakdowns, and performed continuous maintenance to prevent problems. The researchers conclude that companies in Britain and Europe are being forced by international competition to move away from the Tayloristic mass-production model, but that British plants are having more trouble than their Dutch rivals because of "slower investment in new capital equipment" and "lower average levels of workforce skills and knowledge" (p. 16). The Dutch skills advantage is a result not only of more extensive skills training and education, but of higher standards for students in Dutch junior and intermediate technical schools, which

> give Dutch employers a considerable "head start" over their British counterparts in terms of the trainability of their workforce, both as new entrants to the labour market and subsequently as adult workers who may need retraining and updating.
>
> In this context, Dutch employers are able to carry out training to given standards more quickly and cost effectively than is possible in Britain, and in many cases are able to set their training standards much higher than is possible for their British counterparts. (p. 17)

A comparison of productivity and foreman training in Britain and Germany reached similar conclusions. Because almost all German students who are not in full-time education at ages 16 through 18 receive apprentice training, "two-thirds of the German workforce attain examined specialised vocational qualifications (at 'craft level' or higher)—which is probably at least double the proportion attaining comparable levels in Britain" (Prais and Wagner, 1988, p. 34). Training also is facilitated by the fact that "the level of mathematical competence of the average school leaver (at age 15–16) in Germany is substantially higher than in Britain" and the German youths' mathematics skills are developed further as an integral component of the German apprenticeship system (Prais and Wagner, 1988, p. 34).

In large part, the skill training system contributed to an estimated production advantage for German manufacturing establishments of 52 percent in 1977 and 40 percent in 1987 (Prais and Wagner, 1988, p. 37). Germany had better-trained workers and foremen, contributing to German companies' superior ability to organize work for high performance. In industrial occupations, "the German training system produced about seven times as many formally qualified foremen as the British system" (p. 36). Studies in matched manufacturing plants showed that, relative to the British, German plants had higher levels of coordination, smaller ratios of supervisors to workers, smaller rates of machinery breakdown, a higher level of automation and machine technology, and more timely product deliveries. Moreover, because their workers were not as well trained, British companies were forced to rely much more heavily than their German counterparts on wage competition. There was, of course, much more to the British competitiveness problem than workers' skills. The British labor movement had less influence on national policies than the German; Britain therefore adopted a low-wage development strategy that included weakening the unions.

Schooling and Education

Some confusion in debates about the influence of education on productivity arises from analyses that equate education and schooling. The finding that educational achievement (i.e., ideas, skills, and knowledge) improves productivity does not necessarily mean that *schooling* is a measure of educational achievement. This is especially true for the United States, where the outcomes of schooling vary widely, reflecting the absence of performance standards for high school graduation. Similarly, only a small part of productivity-enhancing educational achievement results from schooling—most is acquired at work or within the family. We therefore have two related issues: First, is more education required for high performance? Second, are schools efficient purveyors of ideas, skills, and knowledge?

The prevailing answer to the first question is yes, though, as noted, some critics disagree. The consensus answer to the second question is that, despite much discussion of school reform and many increases in school expenditures, performance in U.S. schools has deteriorated in the past 20 years.

Have American Schools Deteriorated?

Critics of America's public schools commonly argue that the United States has doubled per pupil spending and greatly increased teachers' salaries since 1965, yet SAT scores have fallen and dropout rates remain very high. This evidence is used by critics who argue that more money will not improve school performance. Defenders of public schools counter by pointing out that there have been important improvements in school performance and that most of the increased spending has been for things other than regular educational improvements. Richard Rothstein (1993), for example, notes in a recent article that nearly 30 percent of additional school spending has been for "special education," almost 10 percent for school breakfast and lunch programs, nearly one-third for smaller classes, and 5 percent for transportation. In real terms, teachers' salaries account for only 8 percent of increased spending and have increased only 21 percent since 1965. Beginning salaries for teachers increased only 149 percent between 1975 and 1990, less than the rate of inflation. Comparable increases for other occupations requiring college degrees were as follows: engineers, 153 percent; marketing reps, 169 percent; business administrators, 171 percent; mathematicians and statisticians, 163 percent; economists and financiers, 161 percent; workers in liberal arts, 183 percent; chemists 144 percent; and accountants, 130 percent (Rothstein, 1993, p. 25). Indeed, teachers' pay has not increased enough relative to competing occupations to attract and retain the most qualified people (Task Force on Teaching as a Profession, 1986).

It also is not necessarily true that school performance has deteriorated. The proportion of 25–29-year-olds who had completed high school rose from 75 percent in 1970 to 86 percent in 1990; the rates for minorities increased from 12 percent in 1940 to 58 percent in 1970 and 83 percent in 1990.

Many critics interpret the decline in SAT scores from 937 in 1972 to 899 in 1992 as evidence that schools have deteriorated. But these measures tell very little about what is happening in schools, because many other factors affect SAT scores, especially what is happening in families and the number and characteristics of students taking the tests. There has, for example, been a significant increase in the proportion of test takers who are minorities—from 13 percent in 1972 to 29 percent in 1992. Moreover, the scores for black students, who are concentrated disproportionately in urban public schools, which are presumed to have deteriorated most, increased from 686 in 1976 to 737 in 1992; SAT scores for Mexican-origin students increased from 781 to 797; and Puerto Ricans' scores rose from 765 to 772; while those of whites declined, mainly because of an increase in test takers from lower-income families (Rothstein, 1993, p. 27).

There likewise has been an increase in the proportion of test takers who do well. The proportion who scored above 600 on the verbal portion of the SAT, well enough to get into top-ranked universities, rose from 1.9 percent in 1976 to 2.2 percent in 1992. Comparable proportions scoring 600 or above in math rose from 3.8 percent in 1976 to 5.4 percent in 1992 (Rothstein, 1993, p. 27).

In many ways, the National Assessment of Educational Progress (NAEP), a performance examination, is a better measure of student achievement than SAT scores, which do not necessarily reflect educational achievement. NAEP reading and math scores for white students have been stagnant for the past 20 years, but those for minorities have improved during that time. Minorities also have increased their NAEP science scores, but not as much as in reading and math.

Another schooling indicator, college enrollment of 18- to 24-year-olds, also increased between 1970 and 1991: from 27 percent to 34 percent of whites, from 16 to 24 percent of blacks, and from 13 to 18 percent of Hispanics.

The argument that schools have deteriorated is not only difficult to prove, it is not the most important point, which is that we have never had the kinds of schools we need for success in the new economy. Moreover, America's public schools perform reasonably well for what they were designed to do earlier in this century—namely, to mass-produce students with basic skills. They are less successful at mass-producing students with higher-order thinking skills. In 1992, for example, the average 13-year-old read adequately to "'search for specific information, interrelate ideas, and make generalizations,' but only 11 percent could 'find, understand, summarize and explain relatively complicated information'" (Rothstein, 1993, p. 27).

More important for competitiveness purposes is how American students perform relative to students in other countries. On this point, few analysts argue that American students perform as well as they should (Marshall and Tucker, 1992, p. 66). American students consistently score relatively low in international examinations, especially in math and science. In math, only 2–3 percent of Americans matched the median

Japanese score on the Second International Mathematics Study. In science, 25 percent of Canadians knew as much chemistry as the top 1 percent of Americans. In the First International Assessment of Educational Progress, released in 1989, the United States performed less well than some newly industrialized countries, such as Korea.[4]

Thus, whatever one's conclusion about the deterioration of schools, it seems clear that Tayloristic schools, driven more by time than by student achievement, are inefficient at producing students with thinking skills. We need to assess student achievement with performance measures to find out how to restructure schools to improve achievement, and we need to reward teachers and administrators for student performance, not average daily attendance. The good news is that many effective schools have significantly improved student performance. Some of my favorite examples come from the work done by James Comer and his colleagues, at first in New Haven, Connecticut, and now in schools all over the United States (see Comer, 1980, 1986, 1988). By changing attitudes and school governance, the Comer schools have achieved remarkable improvements in student achievement with low-income minority students. The attitudinal changes have involved demonstrating and convincing teachers, parents, and students that all students, however disadvantaged, can learn. This is particularly important for poor minorities, like those in Comer's original New Haven schools, where most students, teachers, and parents had been conditioned to expect students to fail. Comer's experiences, and those of other behavioral and cognitive scientists, have demonstrated the validity of the claim that "any student can learn."

The second major change introduced by Comer and his colleagues was to make student achievement the schools' main objective and to focus the efforts of parents, teachers, and child development specialists on achieving that objective. At each Comer school, a governing committee is chaired by the principal, who works with representatives of parents, teachers, and child development specialists. This governing mechanism, which includes a high degree of parental involvement at every level, is designed to overcome the cultural barriers between students and the school that often prevent students from understanding the school's requirements and make it difficult for teachers to help students learn. Comer's is one successful model; there are many others (see, e.g., Fiske, 1991; Marshall and Tucker, 1992).

Unfortunately, most American schools are still organized to mass-produce students with only basic literacy skills, lack uniform achievement standards, and therefore do not necessarily produce educated students who can think. The keys to restructuring are as follows: Make student achievement the main driving force; staff schools with highly professional teachers, administrators, and support workers; and reward student achievement. In other words, schools must become high-performance organizations. They must be restructured for much the same reason that traditional mass-production companies must be restructured. Indeed, the "scientific" management system developed in American companies during the early part of this century was applied at least as rigorously to American schools as it was to any industry (Callahan, 1962).

What Other Countries Do to Compete in the New Economy

As noted earlier, the CSAW found that enterprises in other countries are much more committed to high-performance work organizations than are most of their American competitors. Despite very different cultures and social systems, these other countries have adopted the same goals and strategies, though implementation varies widely. They all agree on the following fundamental principles:

1. There is a need for national consensus-based policies to promote high-performance work organizations that can maintain and improve incomes in a highly competitive global economy.
2. There should be high academic expectations for all young people, whether college bound or not.
3. Well-developed school-to-work transition systems need to be in place to provide young people with solid, recognized occupational skills.
4. Public labor market organizations should exist to provide training, counseling, information, and placement services for all workers. (The United States invests much less in employment and training policies than do other countries. In 1987, for example, we invested only 0.9 percent of GDP in these programs, compared with 5.9 percent in Denmark, 4.8 percent in Ireland, 3.7 percent in France, 4.2 percent in Sweden, and 3.2 percent in the United Kingdom; CSAW, 1990, p. 64. The United States also has no coherent labor market policies and institutions to provide information and services to workers or potential workers. Federal employment and training programs are stigmatized, fragmented, and inefficient.)
5. The skills of frontline workers should be very highly valued. Companies and governments must be strongly committed to providing lifelong training and employment opportunities to workers. (Whereas American companies spend only 1–2 percent of payroll on training, two-thirds of which goes for management, companies in leading foreign countries spend up to 6 percent of payroll on training, devoting a significant share to frontline workers.)

Germany and Japan

These points can be illustrated more clearly through a comparison of Germany and Japan, our strongest international competitors. Limited natural resources have forced both of these countries to rely heavily on human capital for economic development. Both derived some advantage from the destruction of obsolete institutions caused by World War II and from having to unify for postwar reconstruction. Their consensus-based economic policies contrast vividly with the more adversarial public-private United States relationships. Germany and Japan stress market forces, but government plays a significantly more active role than in the United States. Within companies, there are strong consensus processes between workers and managers in both countries, but the Japanese processes are less extensive and more voluntary. In Germany, by contrast, workers have stronger unions and the right to serve on company boards and participate in most management decisions. Economic policies and social customs in both countries nevertheless combine to limit companies' ability to pursue low-wage strategies. In Japan, unlike in the United States, social pressures, economic necessity, and high growth, full-employment economic strategies prevent companies from discharging workers at will. Japanese workers therefore have greater commitment to their companies, which are, in turn, motivated to invest more in educating and training their employees.

Germany and Japan provide comprehensive and effective education and training for students who do not intend to receive regular university degrees immediately after leaving secondary schools. Both countries have high standards for secondary-school graduates, and school performance and recommendations from teachers and administrators translate into better postsecondary employment and training opportunities. In Germany, more than three-fourths of non-college-bound students enter apprentice programs at age 15 or 16. Apprenticeship positions, typically lasting three years, are highly valued, and apprentices earn wages while they learn; training consists of supervised instruction four days per week and one day of classroom work. This system is voluntarily financed by employers, and, although a high degree of employer participation is in part a result of peer and social pressure, the strongest incentive is recognition by employers that educating and training frontline workers is essential to competitiveness.

Thanks largely to the apprentice system, Germany possesses perhaps the world's most highly skilled workforce. There is, moreover, considerable mobility among the apprentice system, universities, technical schools, and managerial positions, facilitated in part by the high standards required of secondary school and apprentice graduates. It is not at all uncommon, for example, for the top managers of German companies to have served only apprenticeships after leaving secondary schools. Workers who have served apprenticeships can, and often do, pursue regular university degrees, which are free to all qualified students. German and Japanese workers not only are able to master sophisticated technical subjects better than most American workers, they are also better able to manage their own work. There are, therefore, more workers per manager in Germany and Japan than in the United States.

In Japan, companies pursue high-productivity strategies because of public policy, business strategies, and social and peer pressure, not because of strong political and economic labor organizations. Major Japanese companies practice "lifetime employment" and invest heavily in frontline workers, and full employment ensures little resistance to job rotation, technological change, or shifting low-wage work to less-developed nations. The Japanese system is more paternalistic and informal and less legalistic than the German. Japanese workers identify more with their companies and the Germans more with their crafts or occupations, but both countries have what many regard as among the world's most highly skilled workers. Because of heavy emphasis on elementary and secondary education, reinforced by private schools and family learning systems, Japanese secondary schools probably have the highest math, science, and native language standards in the world. Their public vocational training programs and universities, by contrast, do not meet the highest U.S. and German standards, but company training for frontline workers in the largest companies is more rigorous and extensive than it is in the United States. High school graduates often undergo demanding company-based technical training before starting entry-level jobs, and are able to master much more difficult technical material than their American counterparts. Indeed, German and Japanese companies report that they often are unable to use their most sophisticated technology in their U.S. plants.

The German and Japanese economies are experiencing structural problems and change during the 1990s. However, the chances are good that their attention to education and training will provide the flexibility needed to adapt to these changes.

Labor Force Quality in the United States

Despite its importance for economic performance, we lack adequate measures to compare workforce quality between the United States and other countries. The evidence we do have suggests that the United States has some advantages, but also serious disadvantages. We possess some of the world's leading public and private research institutions, and the top 20–25 percent of our workforce is world-class. Our best institutions of higher education are considered excellent, owing mainly to the existence of some outstanding universities and graduate schools and to past successes and a high degree of academic freedom, which has attracted many of the world's leading scholars and scientists. American learning systems also provide second-chance opportunities for people who have failed at various stages in the education process, and some of our leading companies have high-performance learning systems. We also have done more than at least the Japanese to provide opportunities for women and minorities.

Our main disadvantages relate to the uneven quality of our colleges and universities, many of which have poor standards for entry or graduation; the absence of effective mechanisms to commercialize scientific knowledge, which becomes a free good to foreign competitors who have adopted high-performance organizations and strategies and therefore have stronger incentives than most of their American competitors to commercialize basic research; and the poor quality of most of our noncollege learning systems. Families are the most basic learning systems, but we have a much larger proportion of children in poverty than do most other developed countries. Further, we do less to support families than do most other major industrial countries. Similarly, our elite schools are very good, but, as noted, most of our public schools mass-produce literates, rather than ensure that all students have higher-order thinking skills. And there are no uniform standards that all students are expected to meet. Our schools therefore channel students into or out of elite tracks at very early ages. The United States probably has the weakest school-to-work transition system of any major country. We spend more than other countries for students who are going to college, even though we do not make college or university education free to all qualified students, as it is in Germany and some other countries. Our most apparent weakness is that we devote a much smaller percentage of our resources than do other countries to those who do not pursue baccalaureate degrees (Rasell and Mishel, n.d.). Finally, as noted previously, most American companies do not provide education and training opportunities to frontline workers.

A major problem for the United States is the quality of education for minorities. Even though the educational achievement gaps between disadvantaged minorities and whites have been closing, they remain very large (Quality Education for Minorities Project, 1989). The importance of minority education is heightened by the recent rapid increase in the minority proportion of the U.S. workforce. Indeed, during the 1990s minorities will constitute just over half (52 percent) of the net growth in the U.S. workforce (Marshall, 1991b), and sometime in the twenty-first century non-Hispanic whites probably will become a minority of the U.S.

population. Minorities will become the majority in public schools during the first half of the twenty-first century.

Why is the United States so different? The evidence presented in this chapter suggests that most American companies have not shifted as rapidly to the new economy as have their competitors in other countries. It is not at all clear why this is true, but several hypotheses can be advanced. One is that the United States had more success with the old economy than did these other countries. We therefore developed institutions, attitudes, and policies that were deeply rooted in the mass-production, natural-resource-oriented economy, making change difficult. The hierarchical organization of schools, governments, and companies is one example of this development, and the Keynesian paradigm's preoccupation with consumption and demand to the neglect of productivity and efficiency is another. Similarly, the apparent success of laissez-faire policies during the early part of this century created resistance to consensus building and incentives for companies to organize for high performance. Indeed, the U.S. economic environment contains many incentives for companies to pursue low-wage alternatives. In Europe and Japan, in contrast, consensus-based public policies (the empowerment of workers, social support systems, labor standards, or full-employment and education policies) discourage low-wage strategies and encourage companies to organize for high performance.

Recommendations

If we in the United States want to continue to live in a world-class, high-income country, we must build consensus for that outcome and develop the strategies to achieve it. It is naive to assume that these outcomes will result from "natural" forces or passive strategies. Unlike our major competitors, the United States has no process to facilitate consensus. Adversarial relations like ours focus attention on differences, however small; consensus processes focus on, and therefore encourage, cooperation to achieve common objectives.

In addition to developing consensus-building mechanisms, the United States should adopt macroeconomic policies that will better balance production and consumption by encouraging higher investments in physical and human capital. We must, in addition, translate our world-class science into leading-edge commercial technologies. The foundation required to encourage high-performance production systems includes market conditions that promote rivalry between producers, supportive networks of high-performance suppliers, ready access to leading-edge technology, ready availability of capital at competitive rates, and high-quality factors of production, especially human resources (Porter, 1990). An industrial extension service patterned after our fairly successful agricultural system could help enterprises, especially small businesses, adapt technologies to fit their needs.

The CSAW (1990) makes the following five major recommendations for the facilitation of the development of the highly skilled workforce needed for high-performance work organizations:

1. *A new educational performance standard should be set for all students, to be met by age 16.* This standard should be established nationally and benchmarked to the highest in the world. Students passing a series of performance assessments that incorporate this standard would be awarded a certificate of initial mastery (CIM). Such a standard would provide greater incentive to students, better information to employers, and a way to provide success indicators for restructured schools.

2. *The states should take responsibility for assuring that virtually all students achieve the CIM.* About 20 percent of our students drop out of high school. We cannot give up on these students, because they will constitute one-third of our workforce growth during this decade. Through new local employment and training boards, states—with federal assistance—should therefore create and fund alternative learning systems for those who cannot attain the CIM in regular schools. There are many examples of creative alternative learning systems at the local level, including the Job Corps and the Comprehensive Competencies Program developed by Remediation and Training, Inc., and U.S. Basics. Once alternative learning systems are in place, children should not be allowed to work before the age of 18 unless they have attained the CIM or are enrolled in a program to attain it.

3. *A comprehensive system of technical and professional certificates and associates' degrees should be created for the majority (70–75 percent) of our students and adult workers who do not pursue a baccalaureate degree.* The standards for these certificates and degrees should be defined by business, labor, education, and public representatives. These programs should combine general academic education with the development of occupational skills and should include a significant work component. All students should have financing for these programs. It would be a wise public investment to guarantee to everyone who has attained a CIM four years of education and training in an accredited institution. An alternative approach would be to provide postsecondary loans, to be repaid as a surtax on earnings or

through national service. This system could be patterned after the very successful GI Bill of Rights, which provided education and training to millions of veterans after World War II.

4. *All employers should be given incentives and assistance to invest in the further education and training of their workers and to pursue high productivity forms of work organization.* The CSAW proposes a system whereby all employers would be required to invest at least 1 percent of payroll for this purpose. Those who do not wish to participate would contribute to a general training fund. Public assistance should be provided to help employers restructure their businesses to become high-performance work organizations. The Clinton administration initially proposed raising this requirement to 1.5 percent of payroll, but has deemphasized this proposal because of fairly uniform business opposition. The administration should not give up on this important objective. Instead, it should work with the private sector to provide incentives for all companies to invest in education and training for all workers (Bishop, 1993).

5. *A system of employment and training boards should be established by federal and state governments, together with local leadership, to organize and oversee the proposed school-to-work transition programs and training systems.* These boards could consolidate many of the fragmented, incoherent, and largely ineffective councils and advisory committees that currently characterize many contemporary human resource development activities. Two of the most important improvements that could be made in the U.S. employment and training system are the simplification of the human resource development infrastructure and the establishment of a cadre of highly motivated human resource professionals, particularly at the local level.

To the CSAW's list, I would add three additional recommendations:

6. *Labor laws should be reformed to remove the barriers workers face in organizing and bargaining collectively, as well as the legal barriers companies face in establishing joint labor-management committees and other forms of cooperation.* Further, joint labor-management committees should have responsibility for occupational safety and health, training, pensions, and other employee benefits.

7. *The federal government should establish a technical assistance program to help companies reorganize for high performance while wage, full-employment, income support, tax, trade, and other policies discourage low-wage competitiveness policies.*

8. *A global strategy should be developed.*

The above recommendations would help the United States develop a decentralized, world-class human resource development and labor market system. Workers, employers, students, and others interested in jobs would have a ready source of information and counseling from highly automated local labor market offices staffed by highly qualified professionals. Such entities would greatly improve the effectiveness of other economic and social policies.

No one should assume, however, that even highly effective human resource and labor market policies could function, or even be developed, without an overall high-productivity, high-wage economic growth strategy. Education, training, and labor market systems will not guarantee enough growth to provide good jobs for everyone who needs them. Indeed, without growth, high-productivity strategies could displace workers and contribute to rising unemployment. There is thus a need for macroeconomic policies to promote job growth. Macroeconomic policies not only must reflect competitive realities of the new economy, but must be considered in international context. We need to be concerned about increasing job growth in an open and expanding global economy. It is particularly important for the United States and other developed countries to help stimulate growth in the developing countries, which offer great potential for increased demand. Indeed, it is fairly clear that transactions among the industrialized countries alone are unlikely to generate sufficient growth to prevent global stagnation (Sewell and Tucker, 1988).

However, just as national and enterprise policies must change to reflect the realities of a more competitive world economy, international economic policies and institutions should be reexamined and ultimately based on more appropriate economic theories. They currently are rooted in the realities of the 1940s and 1950s, and assume mainly national economies in which international transactions are "second-order" considerations and where rapid growth, at first in the United States and then in other countries, can provide an international "engine of growth." These institutions and policies are inappropriate for a dynamic, competitive, knowledge-intensive globalized world economy in which "international" transactions are "first-order" considerations and growth requires much greater international cooperation. Comparative advantage, the dominant international trade theory, no longer provides an adequate guide for international economic policy. Comparative advantage is a static, short-run concept that assumes voluntary transactions mainly in final goods and services, not the mobility of whole companies, industries, and technologies. Under modern conditions, *competitive* advantage is a more strategic concept. All countries and international institutions should be encouraged to adopt high-productivity, high-wage strategies to improve the conditions of people everywhere. A low-wage strategy, by contrast, will diminish the incomes of most people in high-wage countries such as the United States, and could suppress the conditions of workers in countries such as Mexico. It is in our interest for productivity and wages in Mexico and other developing countries to rise. The United States should therefore follow the example of most other major industrialized countries and adopt a high-productivity strategy. We should also take the lead in urging this strategy on the GATT, the IMF, the World Bank, regional trade agreements such as NAFTA, and other international institutions.

Notes

1. According to Juliet Schor (1991), the average American worker works about one month more now than in the 1960s for about the same real wage.

2. There actually are at least two basic quality concepts. Within a firm, *internal quality* refers to zero defects, but this is not as appropriate, for competitiveness purposes, as meeting customers' needs. Timely delivery or convenience might be more useful to customers than zero defects. Some firms have extended the "meeting customers' needs" concept to include "customers" within the firm.

3. My experience includes working with the Commission on the Skills of the American Workforce, which I cochaired; the Work in America Institute; the Economic Policy Institute; the Economic Policy Council of the United Nations Association; and my present work as a member of the Clinton administration's Commission on the Future of Worker/Management Relations and chair of that commission's international working group.

4. As with most subjects, there can be technical disagreement on the extent of, and reasons for, poor performance by American students relative to those in other countries. See the exchange between David Baker and Ian Westbury that appeared in the April 1993 issue of *Educational Researcher*.

References

Adler, P. (1991). "Capitalizing on New Manufacturing Technologies: Current Problems and Emergent Trends in U.S. Industry." In National Academy of Engineering and Commission on Behavioral and Social Sciences and Education, National Research Council (Ed.), *People and Technology in the Workplace*. Washington, DC: National Academy Press.

Appelbaum, E. (1993, August). "Empower Workers for High-Performance Firms, High Wages." *Economic Policy Institute Journal*, vol. 3, no. 2, pp. 1, 9–10.

Appelbaum, E., and Batt, R. (1993). *High Performance Work Systems*. Washington, DC: Economic Policy Institute.

Baker, D. (1993, April). "Compared to Japan, the U.S. Is a Low Achiever...Really: New Evidence and Comment on Westbury." *Educational Researcher*, vol. 22, no. 5, pp. 18–20.

Barnet, R. J. (1993, September). "The End of Jobs." *Harper's*, vol. 287, pp. 47–52.

Baumol, W. J., Blackman, S. A., and Wolff, E.N. (1989). *Productivity and American Leadership: The Long View*. Cambridge: MIT Press.

Belman, D. (1992). "Unions, the Quality of Labor Relations, and Firm Performance." In L. Mishel and P. Voos (Eds.), *Unions and Economic Competitiveness* (pp. 41–107). Armonk, NY: M. E. Sharpe.

Bishop, J. (1993). "Underinvestment in Employee Training: Is a Mandate the Answer?" Working Paper No. 93–102, Cornell University, Center for Advanced Human Resource Studies.

Blinder, A. S. (1989/90, Winter). "Pay Participation and Productivity." *Brookings Review*, pp. 33–38.

Blinder, A. S. (Ed.). (1990). *Paying for Productivity: A Look at the Evidence*. Washington DC: Brookings Institution.

Bound, J., and Johnson, G. (1992). "Changes in the Structure of Wages in the 1980s: An Evaluation of Alternative Explanations." *American Economic Review*, *82*, pp. 371-392.

Callahan, R. (1962). *Education and the Cult of Efficiency: A Study of the Social Forces That Have Shaped the Administration of the Public Schools*. Chicago: University of Chicago Press.

Comer, J. P. (1980). *School Power*. New York: Free Press.

Comer, J. P. (1986). "Parent Participation in the Schools." *Phi Delta Kappan*, vol. 67, pp. 442–446.

Comer, J. P. (1988, November). "Educating Poor and Minority Children." *Scientific American*, vol. 259, no. 5, pp. 42–48.

Commission on the Skills of the American Workforce (CSAW). (1990). *America's Choice: High Skills or Low Wages*. Rochester, NY: National Center on Education and the Economy.

Consumer Report 1987 Buying Guide, vol. 51, no. 12, p. 58.

Denison, E. (1985). *Trends in American Economic Growth: 1929–1982*. Washington, DC: Brookings Institution.

Dertouzes, M. L., Lester, R. K., and Solow, R. M. (1989). *Made in America: Regaining the Productive Edge*. Cambridge: MIT Press.

Eaton, A., and Voos P. (1992). "Unions and Contemporary Innovations in Work Organization, Compensation, and Employee Participation." In L. Mishel and P. Voos (Eds.), *Unions and Economic Competitiveness* (pp. 173–215). Armonk, NY: M. E. Sharpe.

Economic Policy Council of the United Nations Association. (1990). *The Common Interests of Employees and Employers in the 1990s*. New York: Economic Policy Council.

Fiske, E. B. (1991). *Smart Schools, Smart Kids*. New York: Simon & Schuster.

Freeman, R., and Medoff, J. (1984). *What Do Unions Do?* New York: Basic Books.

Freeman, R. B., and Rogers, J. (1993). "Who Speaks for Us? Employee Relations in a Non-Union Market." *Employee Representation: Alternatives and Future Directions*. Madison, WI: IRRA (Industrial Relations Research Assn.).

Fuller, W. P. (1976). "More Evidence Supporting the Demise of Preemployment Vocational Trade Training: A Case Study of a Factory in India." *Comparative Education Review, 20*, 30–41.

Hulten, C. R. (1993). "Growth Accounting When Technical Change Is Embodied in Capital." *American Economic Review, 83,* 964–980.

Jamison, D. T., and Lau, L. J. (1982). *Farmer Education and Farmer Efficiency.* Baltimore: Johns Hopkins University Press.

Jencks, C. (1972). *Inequality: A Reassessment of the Effect of Family and Schooling in America.* New York: Basic Books.

Keller, M. (1989). *The Rude Awakening.* New York: William Morrow.

Kelley, M., and Harrison, B. (1992). "Unions, Technology, and Labor-Management Cooperation." In L. Mishel and P. Voos (Eds.), *Unions and Economic Competitiveness* (pp. 247–286). Armonk, NY: M. E. Sharpe.

Krafcik, J. (1988, Fall). "Triumph of the Lean Production System." *Sloan Management Review,* pp. 41–52.

Lau, L. J., and Yotopoulos, P. A. (1989). "The Meta–Production Function Approach to Technological Change in World Agriculture." *Journal of Development Economics, 31,* 241–269.

Levine, D. I., and Tyson, L. D. (1990). "Participation, Productivity, and the Firm's Environment." In A. S. Blinder (Ed.), *Paying for Productivity: A Look at the Evidence* (pp. 183–243). Washington DC: Brookings Institution.

Lillard, L. A., and Tan, H. W. (1986). *Private Sector Training: Who Gets It and What Are Its Effects?* Santa Monica, CA: RAND Corporation.

Lower, M. (1985, December 29). "The Industrial Economy and International Price Shocks." Presidential Address delivered at the meeting of the Association for Evolutionary Economics, New York.

Marshall, R. (1987). *Unheard Voices: Labor and Economic Policy in a Competitive World.* New York: Basic Books.

Marshall, R. (1991a). "Immigrants." In D. W. Hornbeck and L. M. Salamon (Eds.), *Human Capital and America's Future.* Baltimore: Johns Hopkins University Press.

Marshall, R. (1991b). *Losing Direction: Families, Human Resource Development, and Economic Performance.* Milwaukee, WI: Family Service America.

Marshall, R., and Tucker, M. (1992). *Thinking for a Living: Education and the Wealth of Nations.* New York: Basic Books.

Mason, G., and van Ark, B. (1992, January 17). "Education, Training and Productivity: An Anglo-Dutch Comparison." Paper presented at the meeting of the ESRC Study Group on the Economics of Education, London Business School.

Middleton, J., Ziderman, A., and Adams, A. (1993). *Skills for Productivity.* New York: Oxford University Press.

Min, W. (1987). "The Impact of Vocational Education on Productivity in the Specific Institutional Context of China." Unpublished doctoral dissertation, Stanford University.

Mishel, L., and Bernstein, J. (1992, May 14). "Declining Wages for High School and College Graduates." Economic Policy Institute briefing paper.

Mishel, L., and Voos, P. (1992). "Unions and American Competitiveness." In L. Mishel, and P. Voos, (Eds.), *Unions and Economic Competitiveness* (pp. 1–12). Armonk, NY: M. E. Sharpe.

Osterman, P. (1993, January). "How Common Is Workforce Transformation and How Can We Explain Who Adopts It?" Paper presented at the meeting of the Allied Social Science Association, Anaheim, CA.

Phelps, E. S. (Ed.). (1972). *Altruism, Morality and Economic Theory.* New York: Russell Sage Foundation.

Piore, M., and Sabel, C. (1984). *The Second Industrial Divide: Possibilities for Prosperity.* New York: Basic Books.

Porter, M. (1990). *The Competitive Advantage of Nations.* New York: Free Press.

Prais, S. J., and Wagner, K. (1988, February). "Productivity and Management: The Training of Foremen in Britain and Germany." *National Institute Economic Review,* no. 123, pp. 34–47.

Quality Education for Minorities Project. (1989). *Education That Works.* (Report of the Action Council on Minority Education). Cambridge: MIT.

Rasell, M. E., and Mishel, L. (n.d). "Shortchanging Education: How U.S. Spending on Grades K–12 Lags behind Other Industrial Nations." Economic Policy Institute.

Rothstein, R. (1993, Spring). "The Myth of Public School Failure." *American Prospect,* pp. 20-34.

Schor, J. (1991). *The Overworked American: The Unexpected Decline of Leisure.* New York: Basic Books.

Sewell, J., and Tucker, S. (Eds.). (1988). *Growth, Exports and Jobs in a Changing World Economy: Agenda 1988.* Washington, DC: Overseas Development Council.

Smith, J. P., and Welch, F. (1986). *Closing the Gap: Forty Years of Economic Progress for Blacks.* Santa Monica, CA: RAND Corporation.

Stiglitz, J. (1975). "The Theory of Screening, Education, and the Distribution of Income." *American Economic Review, 65,* 283–300.

Task Force on Teaching as a Profession. (1986). *A Nation Prepared: Teachers for the 21st Century.* Washington, DC: Carnegie Forum on Education and the Economy.

Taubman, P., and Wales, T. (1973). "Higher Education, Mental Ability and Screening." *Journal of Political Economy, 81,* 28–55.

Teixeiria, R., and Mishel, L. (1991). *The Myth of the Coming Labor Shortage: Jobs, Skills and Incomes of America's Workforce 2000.* Washington, DC: Economic Policy Institute.

Teixeira, R., and Mishel, L. (1993, Summer). "Whose Skills Shortage—Workers or Management?" *Issues in Science and Technology,* vol. 9, no. 3, pp. 69-74.

Wilson, W. J. (1987). *The Truly Disadvantaged: The Inner City, the Underclass, and Public Policy.* Chicago: University of Chicago Press.

Zuboff, S. (1988). *In the Age of the Smart Machine.* New York: Basic Books.

2

Meeting the Skill Demands of the New Economy

Gary Burtless

Everywhere in the industrialized world, it has become an article of faith that workforce skills must be improved if a nation's industries are to remain competitive and its living standards raised. Even clichés are sometimes true, and this one is. However, it is an unhelpful cliché, for two reasons. The same observation could have been made with equal accuracy in the 1950s—or in the 1890s. In no way does it distinguish the current labor market situation from the situation at any other time in the past century. More important, it offers no guidance on the skills that will be needed in the new world economy or on a mechanism that could reliably produce them here in the United States.

The Surge in the Demand for Skill

Evidence of the need for new investment in labor market skills is hard to overlook, particularly in the United States. Pay premiums received by the best-educated and most-experienced workers have risen sharply since the late 1970s. The jump in the pay premium for skill has been largest among young Americans, especially men, but the trend is apparent among workers of both sexes and at every age. One consequence of the increase in the skill premium has been a rapid increase in overall wage inequality, which in turn has spurred a sharp rise in family income inequality.

Author's Note: This chapter was originally prepared to be presented at the "Labor Economics, Employment Policy, and Job Creation" conference sponsored by the Milken Institute for Job & Capital Formation, Washington, D.C., November 10–13, 1993. The views expressed are those of the author and should not be ascribed to the Brookings Institution or the Milken Institute.

The growth in wage inequality has taken place in the context of painfully slow growth in *average* real wages. If average wages are growing very slowly while inequality around the average is rising, workers at the bottom of the wage ladder may actually experience wage losses. For less-skilled American men, this consequence of rising inequality is more than just a theoretical possibility. It has been a depressing reality that has blighted men's labor market prospects for the past two decades.

Wage Movements

Figures 1.1 and 1.2 show what happened to American wages over the 20-year span from 1969 to 1989 (wages fell after 1989). The numbers are calculated from data gathered in census interviews conducted in 1970, 1980, and 1990; they cover earnings received in 1969, 1979, and 1989. Male and female workers between the ages of 25 and 64 are separately ranked by their annual earnings and then divided into five equal-sized groups. The figures show how fast inflation-adjusted wages grew within each of these groups between 1969 and 1979 and between 1979 and 1989.

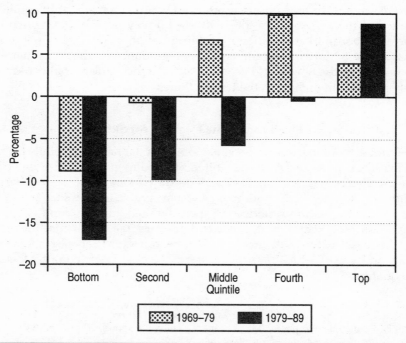

FIGURE 1.1 Changes in Male Earnings, by Quintile 1969–89. *Source*: Author tabulations of the U.S. Census Bureau's *Current Population Surveys*, 1970, 1980, and 1990.

The lighter bars show real wage growth in the first decade; the darker bars, real wage growth in the second.

The long-term trend in male wage growth can hardly be described as encouraging (Figure 1.1). Except in the highest quintile, wages grew more slowly (or fell more quickly) between 1979 and 1989 than between 1969 and 1979. In both decades, wage disparities widened. The fall in earnings at the bottom is remarkable. Wages dropped 9 percent in the first decade and 17 percent in the second. In contrast, average wages in the top fifth of the distribution rose 4 percent between 1969 and 1979 and 9 percent between 1979 to 1989.

The labor market climate has been much less hostile to women. Figure 1.2 shows what has happened to the real earnings of women who work at least 32 hours a week on a year-round basis. Earnings rose everywhere in the distribution between 1969 and 1989. But the trend in wage *inequality* was just the same for women as it was for men in the second half of the period. At the top of the wage distribution, women

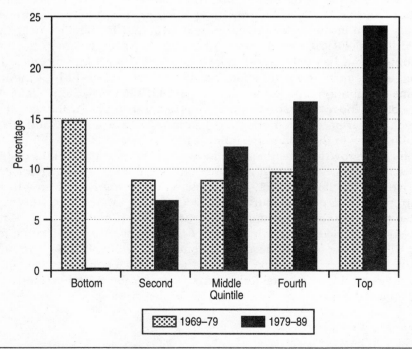

FIGURE 1.2 Changes in Females' Earnings, by Quintile (Full-Time, Full-Year Earners) 1969–89. *Source*: Author tabulations of the U.S. Census Bureau's *Current Population Surveys*, 1970, 1980, and 1990.

saw their earnings rise almost 25 percent in the decade after 1979. At the bottom, women's annual earnings edged up less than 1 percent.

The implications of these trends for long-term wage disparities are striking. From 1969 to 1989, earnings in the bottom quintile of 25- to 64-year-old male earners fell 24 percent. In the same period, real earnings in the top quintile of male earners rose 13 percent. The trend in inequality among women on full-time, year-round work schedules is broadly similar. Although working-age women enjoyed earnings gains everywhere in the distribution between 1969 and 1989, the percentage increase in earnings was almost three times larger in the top quintile than at the bottom.

Family Income

Slow growth in real earnings and a steep climb in wage inequality have produced large effects on family income. Income growth fell off dramatically starting the early 1970s. In the two decades before 1970, median family income in the United States grew 89 percent; in the two decades after 1970, it grew just 13 percent. The slowdown in income growth occurred at the same time as a rapid rise in overall inequality. Before the 1970s, income growth was strong for American families everywhere in the distribution, but was strongest for families near the middle. Since 1970, income growth has slumped everywhere in the distribution, but has fallen most among Americans with low incomes. In fact, after adjusting for inflation, families in the bottom fifth of the income distribution received less income in 1991 than they did in 1970. At the other end of the spectrum, income gains continued, though at a much slower pace than in the years before 1970. Between 1970 and 1991, real incomes in the top income quintile rose 28 percent.

Income growth for families and individuals in most parts of the distribution has slowed for one main reason: The pace of productivity improvement declined after 1973, sharply reducing the rate of growth in earnings. An important source of growing family income inequality has been the sharp rise in earnings disparities. David Cutler and Larry Katz (1991) have calculated the influence of this development on income inequality among families headed by nonelderly adults. In 1969, primary earners in the poorest income quintile received 5.3 percent of the labor earnings received by nonelderly primary earners. By 1979 this share had fallen to 4.3 percent, and by 1989 to just 3.7 percent.

Skill Premiums

The link between growing wage inequality and rising skill premiums is illustrated in Figure 1.3, which shows the premium that college-educated workers can expect to receive in comparison with workers with only high school education or less. The pay advantage is measured as a percentage of the average annual earnings of those who do not go beyond high school. The figure shows the size of the wage premium for different age groups at two points in time, 1978 and 1987. Among men 18 to 24 years old in 1978, those with a college education earned 20 percent more than those who had just a high school education or less. By 1987, the college earnings premium had tripled, reaching nearly 60 percent. For all men under age 44 there was a similar increase in the pay differential. The earnings premium for college graduates did not grow because better-educated men were receiving sharply higher real wages. As we have already seen, earnings rose only moderately, even among affluent males. Instead, the premium climbed because young, less-educated men received steadily *lower* real earnings. At older ages, the college premium increased, too, but by a smaller amount.

The increase in the premium workers receive from additional job experience also rose after the early 1970s. A worker's job experience, like his

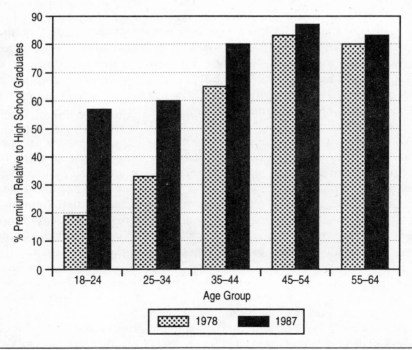

FIGURE 1.3 Pay Premium Received by Male College Graduates, by Age, 1978 and 1987. Note: Tabulations exclude men without wage earnings. *Source*: U.S. Bureau of the Census, 1979, Series P-60, no. 123 Series P-60, no. 162.

or her educational attainment, offers a rough measure of labor market skill. The rise in educational and experience pay premiums suggests that employers have been placing increasingly greater weight on the job skills of workers when making decisions on hiring and promotion.

Explanations

Journalists and other observers sometimes attribute the trends noted above to the shift in American employment from manufacturing to lower-paying industries. In fact, this factor plays a fairly small role in recent wage developments. Wage inequality has grown strongly *within* industries in both manufacturing and the service sector, accounting for the lion's share of the growth of inequality since 1979. To understand developments in earnings inequality, it is important to understand why wage inequality is growing across so many different kinds of industries.

Trade developments and industrial deregulation can explain part of this wage shift. As the rest of the world adopts U.S. production methods, the terms of trade have gradually turned against American producers. The worst side effects are felt by workers whose skills are similar to those of overseas workers, mainly less-skilled workers. The manufacturing industries that rely on mass-production methods and unskilled and semiskilled labor have been particularly hard hit because their methods are easiest for foreign producers to duplicate. To remain competitive, U.S. producers have turned to production methods emphasizing highly skilled labor, methods in which the United States continues to enjoy a substantial advantage. International competition thus produces a disproportionate effect on unskilled and semiskilled U.S. workers.

The effects of deregulation mirror those of more intensive international competition. Forced to compete freely with new low-cost entrants, deregulated firms such as St. Johnsbury trucking and Trans World Airlines have laid off less-skilled workers or cut the real wages of those who remain on their payrolls. Most new firms entering deregulated markets pay their workers wages only slightly above the market wage. Because these firms are not protected by regulation, they cannot afford to pay generous wage premiums to their less-skilled workers. As a result, the wages of airline baggage handlers and interstate truck drivers have fallen. Wages for highly skilled workers in deregulated industries have not fallen as far because job opportunities for them have always been reasonably good outside the regulated industries.

The adverse effects of international trade and industrial deregulation on less-skilled workers create spillover effects in other industries. Unskilled workers who cannot find decent jobs in industries affected by international competition or deregulation are forced to find jobs in other sectors. The presence of so many unskilled job seekers thus pushes down the wages of the unskilled in *all* industries.

Technical Change

Most labor economists think the best explanation for widening wage disparities is a shift in the structure of demand for workers tied to the introduction of new kinds of production techniques. This technological change has occurred in service-producing as well as goods-producing industries, as employers have modified their production techniques in ways that require a more skilled workforce. Companies have persisted in this strategy in the face of growing wage premiums for the better skilled, a development that makes it more costly to hire a skilled workforce—and cheaper to hire the unskilled—than it was in the 1960s and 1970s.

Direct evidence about the influence of technological progress on wage developments is surprisingly scarce. Almost no one asks employers whether and how much their skill requirements have changed. Economists must tease out the effects of technical change using evidence about changes in the relative price and relative supply of different kinds of labor. The shift in employment from high-wage sectors (such as manufacturing) to low-wage sectors (such as retailing) can explain only a minor share of the change in the structure of wages. In addition, changes in the composition of the workforce explain only a trivial percentage of the growth in low-wage employment. This leaves technological change as the major explanation for shrinking wages among the low skilled and the soaring wage premiums of managers and technically skilled workers.

It is a common misconception that technological change inevitably boosts employers' demand for advanced skills. But even if this were true, it would not necessarily lead to wider pay differentials between skilled and unskilled workers. Relative wage changes also depend on trends in the relative abundance of skill. If the supply of skilled workers is keeping pace with the increased demand, pay differentials might remain unchanged, as they did during the 1960s, when the number of college graduates entering the workforce surged.

Nor can we always count on technical progress to increase the demand for advanced skills. Advances in technology can sometimes lead to a dumbed-down production process. Many factory assembly lines require workers to repeat a set of very simple tasks. Before the introduction of the assembly line, production workers performed a wider variety of tasks, which often required considerable effort and ability to learn. Retail clerks once had to use arithmetic to calculate bills and make change. Technical advances have given us electronic cash registers illustrated with pictures of all the items offered for sale. Bills, taxes, and change are calculated by the register rather than the clerk, who may have only a hazy knowledge of math. If technological advances breed dumbed-down jobs, skill differentials should not widen. They may actually narrow. The labor market position of unskilled labor can only improve when employers create large numbers of jobs requiring limited skill.

A great deal of evidence suggests, however, that recent technological changes favor the more skilled over the less skilled. The pay premium offered to highly educated workers soared starting in the late 1970s, as we have seen. In addition, pay increases have been larger in high-skill than in low-skill occupations. The fast-growing occupations within most industries are those requiring high levels of education and skill. Well-publicized projections by the U.S. Bureau of Labor Statistics and the Hudson Institute (Johnston, 1987) show that the biggest employment gains have been and will continue to be in occupations requiring advanced skills. Another piece of evidence is also suggestive. Industries with faster technical change, as indicated by high R&D spending, offer larger pay differentials to their highly educated workers.

Alan Krueger (1993) recently found that workers who used computers on their jobs enjoyed faster wage increases in the 1980s than did workers who did not use or know how to use computers. Although the number of computer-literate workers is comparatively small, this fortunate group received a disproportionate share of all wage gains in the middle and late 1980s. Use of computers is particularly common among well-educated workers in skilled occupations; it is increasingly common among all types of workers. Krueger's research suggests that the introduction of microcomputers conferred a major advantage on workers who possess the skills and background necessary to learn how to use them. Unskilled workers, by definition, do not fit this description.

It is worth emphasizing that the soaring payoff to advanced skill is a comparatively recent phenomenon in the United States. Workers with advanced educational attainment and occupational skills have always commanded a wage premium. The premium has gone up and down over the postwar period. But workers with limited skill have always shared in general earnings growth, at least to some degree. In some decades their wage gains have outpaced those of better-skilled workers. Since the 1970s, less-skilled workers have not shared the wage gains received by the highly skilled; in fact, their real earnings have shrunk at an alarming rate.

It is also worth stressing that the dwindling fortunes of workers on the bottom of the U.S. wage distribution cannot be explained entirely by the declining market value of unskilled workers. Many workers near the bottom of the earnings ladder have accumulated average or above-average educational credentials and lengthy job experience. Their wages are low not because they lack skills, but because their skills have shrinking market value.

Shortcomings of American Training

Many recent trends in U.S. wages and employment can be explained by a growing demand for skilled workers and a declining demand for the less skilled. This has occurred not so much because there has been a shift in the level or distribution of demand across different kinds of industries, but because companies and industries have attempted to change their production methods in ways that require a more able and skilled workforce. Because skilled workers remain relatively scarce, their wages have been bid up, raising the gap between them and workers with less skill and lower educational attainment. This trend is evident in Canada and much of Western Europe as well as the United States, but the adverse wage trends among the less skilled have been most visible in the United States.

In considering remedies that could improve the fortunes of workers with average and less-than-average skills, it is worth bearing in mind some of the major weaknesses in our present system of labor market preparation. The advantages of American workers—which were once formidable—have shrunk in recent years. The productivity of workers in other industrialized countries is rising in comparison with productivity here. In some industries, foreign workers now outproduce American workers. American workers *do* work longer and perhaps harder than workers in most other industrialized countries (except Japan), but our long hours are partly explained by the trend in real wages. As workers at the bottom and in the middle of the earnings distribution have seen their wages fall, many have increased their hours in order to maintain their standard of living. This strategy has not been successful for all workers. Men at the bottom of the skill distribution have seen their incomes fall in spite of recent increases in their hours of work. Their problems originate at least partly from their uneven and faulty labor market preparation.

Preparation in the Schools

American high school graduates typically bring modest skills to the workplace. Notwithstanding recent improvements in primary school education, U.S. students continue to rank low in international comparisons of student knowledge and achievement. Tests of basic student achievement reveal that nearly half the nation's 17-year-olds cannot convert 9 parts out of 100 into a percentage (Carnegie Commission, 1981). The general math and science preparation of American secondary school students is abysmal. Figures 1.4 through 1.6 display results from identical tests of math and science competency administered to a cross section of students in eight countries around the world, including the United States. American performance is indicated by the dark bar in all the figures. It is easy to identify quickly; it is almost always the shortest bar.

Figure 1.4 shows results from a mathematics test administered to eighth graders. It contains some good news. U.S. eighth graders scored only slightly worse than children of the same age in England and Finland. They actually performed better on the test than did Swedish eighth graders. But American eighth graders are less proficient at mathematics than are students in Canada, and substantially less proficient than students in Hungary and Japan.

Figure 1.5 shows results from a test of science knowledge among 14-year-olds. American schoolchildren know less about basic science than do students of the same age in all the other countries. The American students' performance on an algebra test administered to 17-year-olds was even more dismal (see Figure 1.6). On average, U.S. schoolchildren achieve lower scores in algebra than do students in other countries; they achieve substantially lower scores than do students in Ontario, Canada, and in England, Sweden, and (especially) Japan.

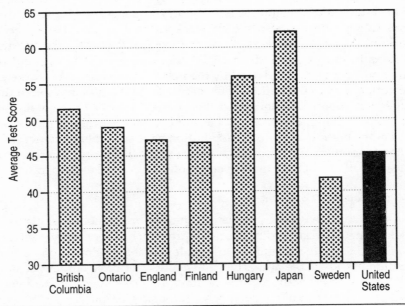

FIGURE 1.4 Average Mathematics Test Scores, Eighth-Grade Students. *Source:* Baily et al. (1993, p. 113).

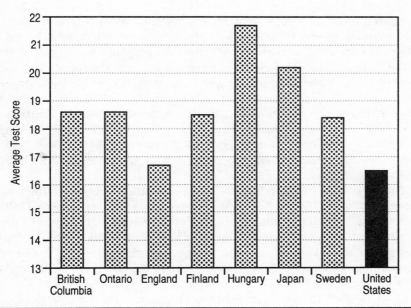

FIGURE 1.5 Average Test Score in Science, 14-Year-Old Test Takers. *Source*: Baily et al. (1993, p. 113).

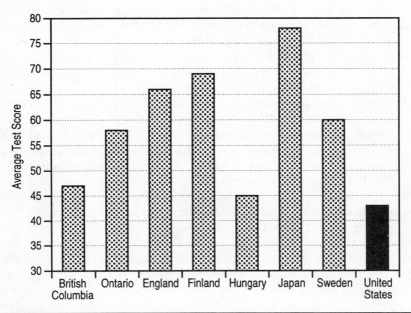

FIGURE 1.6 Average Algebra Test Scores, 17-Year-Old Test Takers. *Source*: Baily et al. (1993, p. 113).

International tests of student achievement are often criticized because they examine the performance of students who are selectively chosen in other countries but who are drawn from the general student population in the United States. This criticism does not apply to the results shown in Figures 1.4–1.6; however, these figures are all based on the performance of a representative cross section of each nation's students. American schoolchildren simply know less math and science than do children in other industrialized countries. The gaps in their knowledge grow larger as they grow older. Americans graduate from high school with much less knowledge than average secondary school graduates in other industrialized countries.

The ill effects of poor high school preparation are offset for many Americans by enrollment in good postsecondary schools. The United States sends a high percentage of its secondary school graduates to community and four-year colleges. About 55 percent of high school graduates go on to college or other postsecondary institutions (U.S. General Accounting Office, 1990). But many Americans learn in college what their Japanese and European counterparts learned in high school.

Graduates of the best American colleges and graduate schools certainly receive a good education. Their preparation is equal to that received by the best college graduates of other industrialized countries. Unfortunately, graduates of good four-year colleges constitute only a small minority of labor force entrants. Fewer than one in five 25-year-olds has graduated from any four-year college. Students whose postsecondary schooling ends after one or two years at a community college probably receive a less demanding education than that received by high school graduates in Western Europe and Japan.

Taxpayers also spend much less educating and training workers who receive no education beyond high school. Figure 1.7 displays estimates of the average amount of public funds spent on the schooling and training of four types of young Americans—high school dropouts, high school graduates who receive no schooling after high school completion, high school graduates who attend college but fail to graduate, and graduates of four-year colleges and universities. The dollar amounts reflect total public spending on formal schooling and subsidized training programs (such as Job Corps and the Job Training Partnership Act). Cost estimates are restricted to spending on students and young adults between the ages of 16 and 24. For a high school dropout, total public spending between these two ages is a bit more than $5,000. For a college graduate, the average taxpayer subsidy is just short of $25,000. Of course, the large college investment finances an education that often gives an excellent preparation for the labor market. But the poor preparation of dropouts

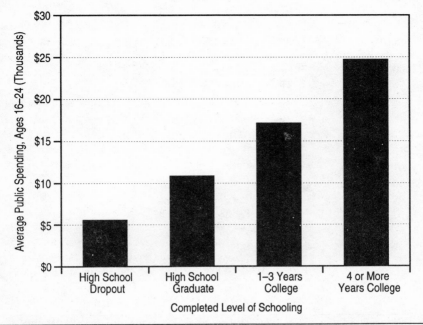

FIGURE 1.7 Average Public Spending per Person Ages 16–24 for Education and Training. *Source*: U.S. General Accounting Office (1990).

and high school graduates and the excellent education received by graduates of the nation's best colleges combine to create a significant factor pushing up earnings disparities in the United States.

Workforce Preparation by Employers

If our secondary schools do not prepare graduates adequately for work, U.S. employers rarely remedy the deficiency. Few American companies invest very much to improve the work skills of their young employees. Figure 1.8 shows the percentage of 16–30-year-olds who receive formal training on *any* job during their first eight years in the labor market. It shows the cumulative percentage of young workers who receive formal education or training by the end of their first year in the job market, by the end of their second year, and so on.

The upper line shows the percentage of young workers receiving training from *any* source, including a community college, a technical institute or proprietary school, or even a government training program. Much of this training—probably the great majority—is actually financed by workers themselves, not by their employers. This kind of training

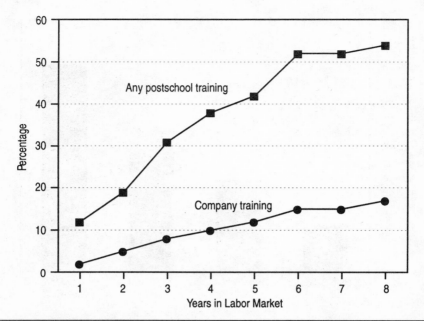

FIGURE 1.8 Probability of Receiving Training after Completion of Education, Young Men. *Source*: Tan et al. (1991).

rises fairly steadily until, by the end of the sixth year in the labor force, about half of young Americans have received some kind of formal training. Little of this training is obtained in a company training program, however. The lower line shows the percentage of workers who have participated in formal, company-financed programs. By the end of workers' sixth full year in the job market, only 10 percent have participated in formal, company-based training programs. A much higher percentage of young workers has participated in some kind of *informal* company training, but this kind of training seldom provides skills that are transferable to other employers.

The reluctance of employers to invest in their young workers is based on a hard-headed economic calculation. Few young workers remain on the payroll long enough for an investment in training to yield the company a big dividend. Turnover rates among young American workers are discouragingly high. High turnover may not be surprising among teenagers and workers in their early 20s, many of whom are trying to combine work with schooling, but high turnover persists even when Americans reach their late 20s. Among men who have graduated from high school and are between 29 and 31, one in three has held his current job for less than a year. Among dropouts of the same age, one-half have held their current jobs for less than a year. This makes company-financed training look like a high-risk investment. The investment often walks out the door when trained employees quit or are laid off.

Only about 40 percent of U.S. workers report they have taken training to improve their skills in their current jobs. Formal training is much less likely to occur in small companies than in large ones. Perhaps equally significant, the probability that a worker will receive company training is strongly related to the worker's educational attainment. Highly educated workers are much more likely to obtain training in company-financed programs. Many of the benefits of company training are thus conferred on workers who have already received extensive schooling before entering the job market. This pattern is exactly the opposite of that in Germany, where company investments in apprenticeship training are heavily concentrated on the majority of German workers who do *not* go on to college.

In contrast with American companies' typical practice, employers in Germany and Japan make large investments in training their young employees. Workplace training in Germany occurs in the context of an extensive and well-established public-private apprenticeship system. After completing compulsory full-time schooling, most young Germans enter apprenticeships that typically last two or three years. When they finish their apprenticeships, trainees take comprehensive exams to certify their mastery of occupational skills.

The Japanese system of postsecondary training does not involve as much government participation. Japanese employers take responsibility for developing the occupational skills of their employees. They take this responsibility seriously, and invest a great deal of time, money, and effort in it. Most Japanese firms enjoy an important advantage over their counterparts in the United States. Large Japanese companies take it for granted that nearly all their young male workers will remain with them throughout most of their careers. This greatly reduces the riskiness of investing in a worker's training.

Young Americans receive little formal training upon entering their first jobs, as just noted. The situation changes a little as Americans grow older, but the amount of company-financed training is fairly modest in comparison with levels observed in Germany and Japan.

Crucial Failing of the U.S. System

Because of high employee turnover, many employers, especially small businesses, fail to invest in developing the general occupational skills of their workers. For reasons of their own—including short time horizons, poor information, and inadequate access to credit—many American workers do not invest enough in improving their own general skills, either.

These workers are thus left stranded in low-productivity jobs with little prospect of internal promotion or upward mobility outside the firm. Their low level of general skills contributes significantly to America's main labor market challenges—anemic earnings growth and surging wage inequality.

Remedies

Youngsters who are not bound for college receive substandard formal schooling before they enter the job market. Many of them then obtain very poor or uneven general skill training after they become employed. These two problems require distinctive solutions, one focusing on the nation's public school system and the other on the private labor market institutions that provide postschool training.

In the remainder of this chapter, I will focus on proposals to improve workplace training. Effective school reform could greatly improve the work preparation of future workers, especially those who will not receive much postsecondary schooling. The statistics presented in Figures 1.4–1.6 show that secondary school reform is urgently needed. But such reform cannot do much to solve the problems of *today's* working-age population. To improve the situation of active workers, the nation must boost workers' investments in their own skills or employers' investments in their employees' skills.

I favor a policy that stresses incentives for employers to increase their investment in training. I am skeptical of the potential benefits of concentrating our extra investments in publicly managed training programs or even in more generous subsidies to encourage high school graduates to attend college. The government already offers a variety of inducements— such as student loans and low community college tuition—for individual workers to invest in their own general training. Raising the current generous public subsidies for general training would probably have little effect on the behavior of young workers who now refrain from investing in themselves—that is, the youngsters who now fail to attend college or postsecondary training courses.

To promote new training investments on the part of private employers, the nation needs to do more than simply exhort companies to invest more. Such exhortations have been made for more than a decade, by officials in business-sponsored organizations and in government. So far, there has been little detectable effect on the training strategy of most employers, especially small employers. Most small and medium-sized businesses ignore well-meaning exhortations for a natural reason: Few can improve their bottom-line results through a *unilateral* policy of added investment in their workers' basic and occupational skills.

U.S. employers and workers would nonetheless benefit if the average worker possessed better occupational and basic skills. Jobs could be made more challenging, work could be organized in more demanding ways, and greater responsibility could routinely be transferred from line managers to workers themselves. All of these changes in the organization of production can raise worker productivity. But an individual company cannot raise the quality of its job applicants by itself. Only a few can afford to take the risk of investing in workers whose tenure with the firm may be brief.

To raise the level and quality of workplace training, I favor a cooperative public-private effort with three main components: (a) establishment of nationally recognized credentials to certify workplace and occupational skills, (b) creation of a national apprenticeship system to help noncollege bound youngsters move from school to work through a carefully designed program of firm-based occupational training, and (c) imposition of a required employer contribution toward the workplace training of non-college-educated workers.

Nationally Recognized Credentials

The value of training is enhanced if occupational skills picked up on a job are certified with nationally recognized credentials. It is particularly important to workers to have their occupational skills certified by credentials that are recognized by large numbers of employers. Because job tenures are often brief, the skills picked up informally in one job are only rarely transferable to the worker's next job. This makes workers skeptical of the benefits of workplace training they now receive. Prospective employers also find it difficult to assess the occupational skills that job applicants bring to the job. Job applicants with good occupational preparation cannot be distinguished from applicants who have poor preparation or none at all. The main goal of skill certification is to add value to skill training by making it transferable.

Occupational skill credentials must be developed by a public institution that includes participants from affected employers, worker organizations, federal and state departments of labor, and, where appropriate, educational institutions. The purpose of the credentials would be to provide formal recognition of workers' proficiency in particular occupations and their mastery of necessary occupational knowledge. The public-private authority would define an occupation; specify the minimum competencies needed to practice it; describe a training plan to guide employers or training institutions in developing the timing, sequencing, and organization of occupational training; and develop appropriate tests that would prove a worker's mastery of the occupation. The German, Austrian, and Danish systems of skill certification show that this method of recognizing occupational skills is not only workable but can be an effective way of encouraging school leavers to participate enthusiastically in workplace training programs.

National Apprenticeship Program

To improve the job market preparation of young, non-college-educated workers, the most effective reform would be one that dramatically raises the formal occupational training that young people receive in their first full-time jobs. Formal apprenticeship is a proven method of accomplishing this goal. Apprenticeships now train only a small percentage of American job entrants. Less than 2 percent of high school graduates become apprentices. In comparison with the 13.5 million students enrolled in two- and four-year colleges in 1990, only slightly more than 280,000 workers were registered in 43,000 apprenticeship programs in that year, mainly in the construction trades.

To establish a functioning apprenticeship system, it is necessary to establish standards for training and occupational certification in a wide variety of white-collar and blue-collar occupations. It is also necessary to provide companies with strong incentives to participate in the system by offering apprenticeships to young school leavers. I have already suggested a cooperative public-private mechanism for defining and assessing workplace skills. The same mechanism could be used to establish and assess apprenticeships in a variety of occupations. Incentives for employer participation are described below.

Mandatory Contribution to Training

To pay for the development of occupational credentials, company-based training programs, and a nationwide apprenticeship system, it will be necessary to generate a source of funds. A simple assessment on company payrolls would be the most defensible and appropriate source of financing. To create an incentive for employers to provide general training to their non-college-educated workers, the government can excuse employers from paying some or all of this training assessment if they invest a minimum amount in their own workplace training programs, including qualified apprenticeship plans. In our recent book, my colleagues and I argue for an annual training investment target equal to 2 percent of company payrolls (see Baily, Burtless, and Litan, 1993).

If it were to adopt this financing scheme, the United States would join Australia and France, which imposed similar training obligations over the past two decades. The French government established its training mandate in 1971. French employers must invest 1.1 percent of their annual money wages in worker training and an additional 0.5 percent of their payroll in qualified apprenticeship programs. If they invest less than this much in a given year, the difference between their actual investment and the mandatory minimum must be forfeited to the state, which in theory uses the money to finance public training programs. The policy has little effect on large French employers, which, like big American firms, usually spend more than the required amount anyway. The mandate has had a large effect on smaller companies, however. In the first eight years after introduction of the tax, the share of workers in small French firms receiving training rose from less than 2 percent to 4 percent a year. Small firms doubled their spending on worker training.

The French system needs major refinement if it is to work well in the United States, however. Many U.S. companies pour funds into an activity they classify as "training" or "employee development," but little of this spending trickles down to their less-skilled workers, which is where America's training shortfall is most acute. The only training investments that should be counted in determining whether an employer meets the investment target are those devoted to raising the skills of *less-skilled* employees. An employer's obligation to train less-skilled workers could be met if the employer could demonstrate that it is devoting 2 percent of its payroll to expenses directly related to training or to the wages of workers who are being withheld from current production so that they can participate in training. *Less-skilled workers* could be defined in a number of ways. One option is to include all "nonexempt" workers covered by the overtime pay provisions in the Fair Labor Standards Act. Training investments in workers who are exempt from coverage under the overtime pay provisions would not be counted toward the 2 percent training assessment.

For the immediate future, it makes sense to phase in the training mandate gradually. If an expense is classified as training in an employer's budget, it would be accepted as a qualified investment so long as the investment is directed toward less-skilled workers. The definition of qualified training investments should gradually be tightened to reflect the standards established by public-private occupational certification boards. When the nation develops an operating credentialing system to certify the mastery of occupational skills, an employer should be required to show that its training investment actually yields employee certification in publicly recognized occupations.

Another modification of the French system is also needed. Employers should be offered a less expensive alternative if they do not believe they can usefully invest the specified percentage of their wage bill in qualified training of less-skilled workers. If the specified minimum percentage is 2 percent, employers devoting less than 2 percent of their wages to qualified training should be obligated to contribute *one-half* the difference between 2 percent of wages and their actual training expenses to a public training fund. The maximum payroll tax is therefore just 1 percent of payroll. Viewed from one perspective, this proposal reduces by 50 percent the cost to employers of investing in their less-skilled workers, at least for investments that total less than 2 percent of employers' payrolls. For each $1.00 that a firm spends on qualified training, it avoids paying $0.50 to the public training fund. If the firm can find no useful way to spend $1.00 on training, however, it would be better off contributing $0.50 to the public fund. This will eliminate much wasteful spending that the present French system encourages.

A 2-percent-of-payroll training assessment would be equal to approximately $50 billion a year if the mandate is confined to private employers. (For purposes of comparison, public spending on education amounts to over $360 billion a year.) It is unclear how much of this $50 billion would represent net new spending on training. The current amount invested in workplace training is unknown. We know that some employers already spend more than 2 percent of their payrolls training less-skilled workers. But many other companies would be forced to establish or enlarge workplace training programs or to contribute a small percentage of their payrolls to a public-private training authority.

Businesses fiercely resist the idea of a publicly imposed training mandate. They regard such a proposal as equivalent to a tax on money wages as well as an unwarranted intrusion on private decision making. For employers who choose to pay the 1 percent training tax rather than invest 2 percent of payroll in a training program, the mandate is certainly equivalent to a tax. Businesses are naive, however, if they believe the burden of this tax falls exclusively or even mainly on business profits. Most of the tax will be passed along to consumers in the form of higher prices or to workers as lower wages.

For most businesses, however, the mandate is not really equivalent to a tax. Businesses that already spend more than 2 percent of payroll on training the less skilled will not be directly affected by the mandate, except insofar as they must document their current level of spending. The proposal may actually *reduce* expenditures on training in these firms. Because other firms are induced to raise their training investments, firms that already make heavy investments will have less need to train job applicants who show up at their hiring offices.

Businesses that now spend *less* than 2 percent of their payrolls on qualified training will be induced to spend extra money and reorganize their current training efforts so they lead to certifiable occupational skills. The effects of the mandate would be equivalent to those of a tax only if the extra spending is entirely wasted from the firm's point of view. This may be true with respect to employer contributions to Social

Security and Medicare, which provide benefits to retired workers and their dependents but not to firms, but it can hardly be true with respect to company spending on worker skills, which should provide direct benefits to firms in the form of higher employee productivity and improved work organization. If businesses nonetheless conclude that the effects of a training mandate are equivalent to those of a tax, they must assume that additional resources devoted to training would be wasted by company managers.

A typical tax takes money from employers or workers and places it in a public budget. The government then exercises control over resources purchased with the money. A training mandate leaves control over allocation of training resources to private decision makers—specifically, to company managers. A persuasive argument in favor of a private training mandate is that company managers are in a much better position than government officials to decide on the best allocation of training investments. One alternative to a training mandate is expansion of the government's existing education and training programs. This alternative relies on public officials to decide how added spending on training will be divided up. In light of the political preferences of most business owners and managers, I find it surprising that they favor government over private business allocation of training resources.

Conclusion

Many informed observers in business, labor, and public life believe the American workforce is poorly prepared for the challenges of the new world economy. The huge advantages once enjoyed by U.S. workers are shrinking. In some areas, they have already disappeared. Real-money wages are stagnant for large classes of Americans, and in a variety of industries they now lag behind the wages earned by their overseas counterparts.

One shortcoming of the American labor market is the uneven preparation it provides to new and inexperienced workers. Many new entrants to the workforce who have earned college or advanced degrees unquestionably bring skills that are highly prized by employers. Their credentials are equal to those of the best-educated workers anywhere in the industrialized world. But the great majority of new entrants bring less impressive credentials to the labor market. Their schooling has given them poor job market preparation in comparison with the preparation provided by schools in other advanced countries.

The defects of schooling in the United States are not remedied by the strengths of its workplace training institutions. Current American training arrangements are based on an internally consistent but flawed logic.

Most firms do not expect workers to remain with the same employers throughout their careers. High employee turnover makes it uneconomical for many companies to invest heavily in training their unskilled and semiskilled workers. Yet most employers and workers would gain if managers could rely on good employee skills when they design jobs and the organization of work.

To improve the flagging performance of U.S. workers, it is necessary to improve their formal schooling and increase the workplace training offered by employers. The educational preparation of non-college-bound Americans is inadequate to the demands of the modern workplace. And training in the workplace does not offset their educational disadvantages. The difficulties faced by low-wage workers contribute decisively to the skill shortage lamented by so many observers.

A good diagnosis of labor market problems holds only academic interest if it does not also suggest remedies. The remedies suggested here are controversial and will be politically difficult to achieve. Because they represent a major departure from current practice, no one can be sure of their exact effects. The proposed reforms are aimed at improving workers' general occupational skills as well as their job-specific skills. They seek to improve the skills of the least-skilled Americans, thus addressing the issue of growing wage polarization. They are designed to ensure that extra training takes place in those institutions where it can be provided most efficiently. These proposals emphasize improvements of training in the workplace rather than sharply increased spending on training in public schools, colleges, or government training programs.

Even readers who reject an employer training mandate should consider carefully whether the nation can afford to do nothing about the serious skill problems documented in this chapter. For the least-skilled Americans, anemic productivity growth and growing inequality have not meant simply slow growth or stagnation in wages. Their wages have actually declined. Benign neglect is not an appropriate response to their predicament.

References

Baily, M. N., Burtless, G., and Litan, R. E. (1993). *Growth with Equity: Economic Policymaking for the Next Century.* Washington, DC: Brookings Institution.

Burtless, G. (Ed.). (1990). *A Future of Lousy Jobs? The Changing Structure of U.S. Wages.* Washington, DC: Brookings Institution.

Carnegie Commission on Science, Technology, and Government (1981). *In the National Interest: The Federal Government in the Reform of K–12 Math and Science Education.* New York: Carnegie Corporation.

Cutler, D. M., and Katz, L. F. (1991). "Macroeconomic Performance and the Disadvantaged." *Brookings Papers on Economic Activity, 2*, 1–61.

Danziger, S., and Gottschalk, P. (1993). *Uneven Tides: Rising Inequality in America.* New York: Russell Sage Foundation.

Johnston, W. B. (1987). *Workforce 2000: Work and Workers for the 21st Century.* Indianapolis, IN: Hudson Institute.

Juhn, C., Murphy, K. M., and Pierce, B. (1993). "Wage Inequality and the Rise in Returns to Skill." *Journal of Political Economy, 103*, 410–442.

Katz, L. F., and Murphy, K. M. (1992). "Changes in Relative Wages, 1963-87: Supply and Demand Factors." *Quarterly Journal of Economics, 107*, 35–78.

Krueger, A. B. (1993). "How Computers Have Changed the Wage Structure: Evidence from Microdata, 1984–1989." *Quarterly Journal of Economics, 108*, 33–60.

Levy, F., and Murnane, R. J. (1992). "U.S. Earnings Levels and Earnings Inequality: A Review of Recent Trends and Proposed Explanations." *Journal of Economic Literature, 30*, 1333–1381.

Tan, H. et al. (1991). *Youth Training in the U.S., Britain, and Australia.* Santa Monica, CA: RAND Corporation.

U.S. Bureau of the Census. (1988). *Money Income of Households, Families, and Persons in the United States.* Washington, DC: Government Printing Office.

U.S. General Accounting Office. (1990). *Training Strategies.* Washington, DC: Government Printing Office.

3

U.S. Education and Training Policy: A Re-evaluation of the Underlying Assumptions Behind the "New Consensus"

James J. Heckman, Rebecca L. Roselius, and Jeffrey A. Smith

The American labor market has undergone dramatic changes in the past 15 years, and has worsened particularly for low-skill workers. The wages of many groups of workers have declined. The ratios of the wages of college graduates to those of high school graduates and high school dropouts have increased, and participation in the market by low-skill workers has fallen.

Policy analysts have been quick to recognize these changes and to recommend policies designed to reverse them. Most of the proposed solutions entail increased investment in "human capital," that is, training and education, to upgrade the skill level of the workforce and to transform the American workplace. A new consensus has emerged in influential policy circles that the American labor market and educational system are unable to equip workers with sufficient skills. American youth are said to experience a disorderly transition from school-to-work characterized by too much job turnover and too little training on the job. In contrast, the German apprenticeship system has been held up as a model of order that produces smooth school-to-work transitions and provides workers with human capital directly related to their career interests in a format especially helpful

Author's Note: Support for this research was provided by grants from the Russell Sage Foundation and the Lynde and Harry Bradley Foundation of Milwaukee, Wisconsin. The Russell Sage Foundation and the Bradley Foundation do not necessarily endorse the views expressed in this chapter. Gary Burtless, Robert LaLonde, Derek Neal, William Niskanen, Robert Solow, Eugene Steurle, Ernst Stromsdorfer, and Rainer Winkelmann provided helpful comments.

for workers poorly served by formal schooling. Features of this system have been advocated as applicable to the U.S. labor market. Further proposals have been set forth to use taxes and subsidies to encourage firms to produce higher levels of training for their workers and to encourage them to shift to "high-wage" workplace environments.

In this chapter, we examine the analytic and empirical foundations of the new consensus. We summarize the facts that motivate recent concerns about the labor market. We put the developments in the labor market in perspective by noting that under optimistic assumptions about the effectiveness of training programs, it would take a human capital investment of $1.66 trillion (in 1989 dollars) to restore the 1979 earnings ratios of less-skilled workers to workers with some college education, while holding workers with some college education at their 1989 levels of earnings.

Despite its widespread acceptance, the intellectual foundations of the new consensus consist largely of speculation and questionable interpretations of existing evidence on the U.S and German labor markets. For example, a key presumption of the new consensus is that job turnover among youth in the labor market is a wasteful activity. This view fails to recognize the value of job shopping in promoting efficient matches between workers and firms and fails to take account of the fact that most youth do not suffer long-term harmful consequences from frequent spells of early joblessness.

Similarly, there is no evidence that the widely acclaimed German apprenticeship system is especially effective in promoting skill formation, despite many claims to the contrary (see, e.g., Commission on the Skills of the American Workforce, 1990; Hamilton, 1990). Lower youth unemployment in Germany compared with that in the United States results from regulations compelling young Germans to stay in school or participate in apprenticeship programs until age 18 if they seek any but the most menial jobs. Any positive effect that the German program has on youth employment is mainly the result of to the fact that apprentices are exempt from minimum wage laws and rigid employment protection laws that make it difficult to fire regular workers. The real lesson to be learned from this program is that flexible wages and work rules promote employment. Moreover, German apprentices leave the firms that train them at very high rates (Witte and Kalleberg, 1994). The current romance with German institutions is based on a myth that German labor is more productive than U.S. labor. In fact, it is less productive in many industries including beer production and automobile manufacturing, although this difference depends on a number of factors of which labor quality is only one (McKinsey & Company, 1993).

Some proponents of the new consensus also claim that a significant transition is taking place in the methods of production and the organization of work in the global economy. Firms in other highly developed countries are purported to be changing from the mass-production methods of the past to flexible-technology, high-skill methods. They hypothesize that these methods require apprenticeship-type institutions, credentialing, and cooperation between employers and unions to prepare the workforce for more complicated and challenging tasks. These proponents presume that the reason American firms have been slow in adopting "flex-tech" methods is that these complementary institutions are not in place in the U.S. market, rather than that there are deficiencies in the methods themselves. In fact, these advocates have failed to demonstrate that either flexible-technology workplaces or the additional educational training institutions they are said to require actually increase productivity.

Another strong presumption of advocates of the new consensus is that U.S. government policy is biased toward formal schooling and away from vocational and on-the-job training. Although some evidence suggests that current U.S. expenditure policies favor formal schooling over job training at the postsecondary level, the total body of evidence is far from clear on this matter. A deeper consideration of the issue reveals that tax policy favors on-the-job training over formal education. Furthermore, no theoretical or empirical evidence has been presented that equal expenditures on formal schooling and vocational or on-the-job training represent the optimal allocation of limited government funds for human capital investments.

Proposals to promote skill formation by establishing national skills certification tests fail to recognize the value of job-specific skills that cannot be certified by exams. They exaggerate the ability of exams to measure the skills valued by employers. Tests that certify some skills but not others would tend to distort worker skill-acquisition choices. General, easily measured skills would be emphasized at the expense of harder-to-measure firm-specific skills. In addition, tests that publicly reveal previously private information on worker skills may worsen the problem of financing worker investment in training. Firms will have less incentive to pay for the training of their workers if their skills can be easily identified by rival firms.

Finally, proposals to expand government training programs ignore the existing evidence on the ineffectiveness of these programs and on the comparatively greater effectiveness of private sector training programs. In the following sections, we explore each of these weaknesses in the theoretical and analytic foundations of the new consensus in greater depth. We find that these foundations lack the strength to support the edifice of taxes, subsidies, skill certification boards, and other policies constructed upon them by advocates of the new consensus. In our conclusion, we suggest a set of more limited policies directed at the same targets, but built upon a firmer understanding of the economics of the problem and a more realistic assessment of the functioning of the labor market both in the United States and abroad.

The New American Labor Market

Although many of the underlying assumptions of the new consensus are unfounded, there is much evidence to support the view that wage gaps have widened across skill levels. In purchasing-power-constant or deflated dollars, male high school graduates earned 4 percent less per week in 1989 than in 1979. Male high school dropouts earned 13 percent less per week than in 1979. In contrast, male college graduates earned 11 percent more per week (Blank, 1994). These comparisons widen further if we consider annual earnings. By any measure, labor incomes for men have become more unequally distributed. For women, the story is somewhat different. The real weekly earnings of female high school graduates have risen, but the rise has been even greater for female college graduates.

Thus, for both men and women, inequality of labor incomes has risen. The returns to schooling and skill have increased. The relative earnings of workers at the bottom of the skill distribution (less than high school graduate) have definitely declined for persons of either gender. Youth have been hit hardest in the shifting market for skills.

A corollary phenomenon is the decline in labor market activity, especially among the unskilled. A variety of labor force measures show increasing joblessness and longer unemployment spells for workers at all skill levels. Particularly problematic are less-skilled youth (those with high school education or less), who appear to flounder in the market for years before they find stable jobs. These youth are a source of major social problems. Teenage pregnancy, crime, and idleness are important phenomena that are on the increase in most areas.

The problem of a deteriorating market for unskilled or semiskilled workers is not solely a problem of youth. Displaced adults, primarily factory workers, are also a major concern. Middle-age workers displaced from high-wage jobs are at a major disadvantage in the new market for labor that has emerged since many of these workers first took their jobs. Displaced workers constitute 10–20 percent of the unemployed, or roughly 1–2 million workers. Recent evidence on the patterns of earnings losses experienced by workers displaced by mass layoffs suggests that the losses are significant and long-lasting, especially for those previously employed in unionized industries or occupations (Jacobson, LaLonde, and Sullivan, 1993).

Level of Investment Needed to Reduce
Current Levels of Wage Inequality

There have been many proposals for investments in human capital designed to increase the wage levels of the less skilled. An investment generally yields returns over many years after initial costs are incurred. For human capital, a round, and roughly correct, average rate of return is 10 percent. Thus, for each $10 invested in a person, the expected annual return is $1. Some claim that this number is lower and some claim that it is higher, but most economists would accept a 10 percent return as a good starting point for estimating the aggregate investment needed to upgrade the skills of the low-skilled segment of the workforce.

At this rate of return, to add $1,000 in earnings per year to the average person it is necessary to make a one-time investment of $10,000 in that person. This is a large sum relative to the cost of most public and private training programs, but many college students make even greater investments each year. Using a 10 percent rate, the investment needed to reduce any wage gap is 10 times the amount of the gap.

To put the magnitude of recent developments in the labor market in perspective, consider the following two questions:

1. How much would we have to invest in our workforce in 1989 dollars to restore real earnings of male high school dropouts and graduates to their real 1979 levels?

This question is meaningful only for men, because real weekly earnings for women have risen or remained roughly constant over the period 1979–89. A second question is as follows:

2. How much would we have to invest in our workforce in 1989 dollars to restore 1979 earnings ratios between lower-education groups and college graduates, without reducing the 1989 earnings of college graduates?

Using the 10 percent rate of return, it would require an investment of $25,000 in each high school dropout, or a staggering $214 billion in 1989 dollars, to restore male high school dropouts participating in the workforce to their 1979 real earnings level. To restore all high school graduates to their real 1979 *levels* would take an investment of $10,000 per high school graduate, or more than $212 billion 1989 dollars, for a total of $426 billion in 1989 dollars. To gauge the enormity of the required investment it is useful to compare these costs with those required to finance the Manhattan Project, which built the first atomic bomb, and cost only $15 billion dollars.

The answer to Question 2 is even larger. Table 3.1 shows the amount needed to restore the 1979 earnings ratio between high school graduates or high school dropouts and college-educated full-time workers over age 25. To restore real earnings for both male and female workers over age 25 who are high school educated or less to their 1979 *relative* positions with respect to college graduates (holding the latter at 1989 real wage levels) would require an investment of more than $1.66 trillion. These numbers are conservative because they do not consider persons below age 25 or persons who do not participate in the workforce at the current wage levels. They are conservative for another reason: few—if any—government training programs have returns anywhere near 10 perecnt. Zero percent is a much closer approximation to the true return.

One might wish to qualify these calculations in many ways. One might want to adjust down the rate of return as more difficult-to-train persons receive training. Or one might wish to account for the fact that as persons have their skills upgraded, the real wages of the lower-skill workers are likely to increase as they become more scarce and the real wages of those with higher skills likely to decrease as their supply increases. Still, under most plausible scenarios, the costs of restoring skill parities to their 1979 levels are huge.

Investment in human capital may still not reduce income inequality. Raising the skills of a few need not reduce overall inequality. By moving some workers from low-skill to high-skill status, some standard measures of earnings inequality might actually increase. Many programs train only the high end among the low-skill workers. Such training efforts could polarize the labor market. In addition, it takes skilled labor to produce skilled labor. A large-scale increase in training activity might therefore *increase* earnings inequality in the short run because it would further expand the demand for skilled labor to train the unskilled labor. It takes educated labor to produce educated labor.

Finally, the most efficient training policy may not be to train the unskilled. As first noted by Mincer (1962), there is strong evidence of universal complementarity between postschool investment and formal schooling. It may be economically efficient to invest in higher-skilled workers and to alleviate concerns about income and earnings inequality through income transfers. However, to the extent that working fosters socially desirable values among those who work, it may still be desirable to invest inefficiently in order to promote those values.

TABLE 3.1
Investment in Human Capital Required to Restore Earnings to
1979 Levels and to Restore 1979 Relative Wage Ratios Using a 10 Percent Rate of Return
(in billions of dollars)

To Restore Earnings to 1979 Levels	
Males	
To restore average male high school dropout earnings in 1989 to average real earnings of male high school dropouts in 1979	$214
To restore average male high school graduate earnings in 1989 to average real earnings levels of male high school graduates in 1979	<u>$212</u>
TOTAL	<u>$426</u>

To Restore 1979 Earnings Ratios	
Males	
To restore average male high school dropout earnings in 1989 to the level needed to achieve the 1979 high school dropout/college earnings ratio (holding 1989 college graduate wages fixed)	$382
To restore average male high school graduate earnings in 1989 to the level needed to achieve the 1979 high school graduate/college earnings ratio (holding 1989 college graduate wages fixed)	$770
Females	
To restore average female high school dropout earnings in 1989 to the level needed to achieve the 1979 high school dropout/college earnings ratio (holding 1989 college graduate wages fixed)	$136
To restore average female high school graduate earnings in 1989 to the level needed to achieve the 1979 high school graduate/college earnings ratio (holding 1989 college graduate wages fixed)	<u>$378</u>
TOTAL	<u>$1.66 Trillion</u>

Source: Wages are from Blank (1994). We assume workers work 50 weeks a year. The figures on the educational breakdown for the labor force are from U.S. Bureau of the Census (1992, Table 616). We have deleted all persons out of the labor force and those less than age 25. On these criteria, our estimated investment costs are downward biased.

The New Consensus about the U.S. Labor Market

A consensus has emerged in certain circles about the abilities of the current U.S. labor market, and the educational and training institutions that complement it, to produce the necessary skills for that labor market. It is negative in tone and looks abroad, especially to Germany and other Northern European countries, for advice on how to restructure the

American labor market. The new view is stated most forcefully in the report of the Commission on the Skills of the American Workforce (CSAW), *America's Choice: High Skill or Low Wages* (1990), and in numerous lectures and articles by Ray Marshall (see, e.g., Marshall's chapter in this volume). Marshall and Ira Magaziner, architect of President Clinton's health plan, were the principal authors of the CSAW report, along with former Secretary of Labor William Brock. This report has had an enormous impact on the views of the Clinton administration. Secretary of Labor Robert Reich elaborates the themes set forth in the CSAW agenda in his book, *The Work of Nations* (1991).

The following core ideas underlie the new consensus.

1. The growing inequality in wages and incomes is a serious social problem. Especially troublesome is the decline in real earnings among young and unskilled workers.
2. The quality of the labor force is not growing rapidly enough. Included in the notion of "quality" are such elements as work ethics and attitudes of employees. The United States is perceived to be facing a skills shortage exacerbated by the immigration of low-skill workers. Productivity growth has declined in part because of the slow growth in the quality of American labor. The recent growth in output during the 1980s had more to do with expansion of inputs (primarily the surge of workers produced by the baby boom) than with workforce quality improvements. American schools have failed to produce high-quality students. They fail to motivate their students and leave them inadequately trained for academic or nonacademic alternatives. Most American education is only poorly connected in content or practicality with the demands of jobs. The low academic performance of Americans is manifest in poor test scores of U.S. students compared with those of other countries. (This comparison of levels overlooks recent improvements in trends, but the gap in test score achievement between the United States and other countries remains sizable.)
3. The productivity of the workforce cannot be improved by investing in physical capital because, as the authors of *America's Choice* write, "Low wage countries can now use the same machines and still sell their products more cheaply than we can" (CSAW, 1990, p. 14). (This view is not held universally even within the group of scholars advocating the new consensus.)
4. The CSAW blueprint for the future of the workplace claims that the key to enhanced productivity lies in the "Third Industrial Revolution now taking place in the world" (p. 41). Henry Ford-style mass production and specialization is becoming obsolete, although it is

still widely utilized in the United States. Instead, today's market requires "flexible technology," which allows the production of quality goods and is sensitive to changing consumer tastes. This technology requires more highly trained—though not necessarily more highly specialized—workers. Participation in the global economy requires that we move toward high-productivity work organizations built around highly trained workers.

5. The authors of the influential CSAW report claim that the "school-to-work" transition in the United States is chaotic compared with the orderly, smooth-functioning transition experienced by German youth. In Germany, youth apprenticeships, especially designed for nonacademically oriented youth, are said to motivate learning by making it tangible. They make learning relevant to market needs and foster achievement among nonacademically oriented youth. By granting nationally recognized credentials to apprentices upon successful completion of occupational skills tests, we could do for vocational training what we currently do for academic training by granting nationally recognizable and accepted degrees. Such certification would enhance incentives for the acquisition of skills in the workplace by guaranteeing an economic return to quality in a national market. In this way, the skill base needed for Americans to participate in the "Third Industrial Revolution" would be created.

The new consensus is a happy marriage of two recent lines of thought. One is the view that the craft economy, now called the "flexible-technology" economy, is coming back after a century and a half of the triumph of mass production. This view is expounded by Michael Piore and Charles Sabel in their 1984 book, *The Second Industrial Divide*, and has fired the imaginations of many planners and policy makers. Though it has proved hard to document as a widespread phenomenon, flex-tech is widely trumpeted as the leading-edge technology. The other line of thought in the new consensus is the view that a return to the apprenticeship system that supported the old craft system will provide the incentives for workers to acquire the right skills. This view is most strongly espoused by Stephen Hamilton (1990). To these lines of thought a third argument has recently been added, namely, that flex-tech is best implemented in job environments in which firms and unions cooperate, and in which workers with general skills perform a multiplicity of tasks. It is claimed that by defying the law of comparative advantage and forgoing the benefits of specialization of tasks in the workplace, organizations can enhance worker and firm productivity. Unions are viewed as essential ingredients for fostering the cooperation needed to sustain the new workplace, even though it is well known that unions reduce firm profitability (see, e.g., Freeman, Marshall, 1992; Mishel and Voos, 1992; Chapter 2, this volume). Coupled with the remarkable and unsupported claim that investment in physical capital cannot restore or boost American productivity in regard to other countries, the new consensus virtually dictates a cooperative strategy of workplace-based investment in human capital.

Whereas earlier advocates of the new consensus saw adoption of the new technology as an inevitable consequence of progress, more recent advocates are less sanguine. Indeed, if this new technology had been adopted on a wide scale, this would serve to explain why wage differentials among skill groups were growing. A shift in the demand for skills toward more skilled workers would explain the recent trend in wage differentials found between and within sectors (see, e.g., Murphy and Welch, 1992). However, it has been documented that firms have been slow to adopt "Third Industrial Revolution" technology and its associated training schemes voluntarily. Very few firms have participated in the new industrial revolution (Osterman, 1993). Instead of calling into question the arguments made about the superiority of the new technology, the response of new view advocates has been to criticize myopic American firms for failing to adopt an obviously superior technology.

Martin Bailey, Gary Burtless, and Robert Litan (1992) of the Brookings Institution endorse some—but by no means all—of the ideas in the new consensus. Burtless's chapter in this volume restates many of the main ideas in that work. Similar to the proponents of the new view, they emphasize the problems of growing wage inequality and declining real wages for unskilled workers. They claim that there are inappropriately low levels of investment in the workforce—especially among the unskilled—and they further claim that public policy is biased against such investment. They endorse *features* of the German apprenticeship system—especially skill standards, occupational certification, and subsidized apprenticeship programs with firms for non-college-bound youth. They propose payroll tax policies to finance training and "encourage" firms to organize training programs for their workers.

A central premise of their work is that the increased income inequality resulting from increased skill differentials is inequitable, and that this inequity justifies an active governmental response. They argue that the best way to reduce income inequality, and thereby to increase equity, is to invest in the skills of low-wage workers. They further claim that there is too little investment in human capital among workers at the low end of the skill distribution. They attribute this lack of investment to market failure, including borrowing constraints, and to the short time horizons of low-skill workers. While it may be that low-skill workers have short time horizons, the resulting lack of investment is *not* inefficient as this term is normally used in economics. These arguments confuse normative and positive statements regarding the amount of training undertaken at the low end of the skill distribution. It is important to disentangle the Brookings' authors concerns with equity and with the decision-making processes of the poor from their positive claims about the labor market. Claims about whether investment in unskilled workers is or is not efficiently low and whether in-kind transfers in the form of human capital investments are or are not an efficient way to reduce income inequality can and should be evaluated separately from these authors' normative concerns.

In the discussion presented in this chapter, we evaluate arguments both from the Brookings authors and the new consensus group.

Weak Evidence Concerning Public Policy Bias Toward Formal Education and against Employer-Based Training

One of the main tenets of new consensus authors and of the Brookings group is that improvements in the quality of the U.S. workforce, especially the less-skilled portion of that workforce, have not kept pace with improvements in other nations. Critics question the effectiveness of the postsecondary training options currently in place for non-college-bound youth. More than 75 percent of youth still do not complete college, and many never attend. Baily et al. (1992), among others, claim that there is a dramatic imbalance between public expenditures on postsecondary schooling for youth who attend college and public expenditures on other forms of human capital acquisition for youth who do not attend college. This imbalance in public spending motivates their advocacy of expanded funding for apprenticeship programs and mandated training expenditures for firms to increase the amount of occupation-specific training acquired by non-college-bound youth. In this section, we consider the evidence concerning the argument that current public policies for postsecondary education and training are biased toward formal academic education and away from vocational skills training.

Baily et al. (1992) state that non-college-bound youth receive an inadequate amount of postsecondary school training. They cite as evidence a relatively higher level of public spending per college attendee compared with high school graduates and high school dropouts. They do not explain that a large part of public spending on college education goes to community colleges, which provide both academic and vocational training. More than 40 percent of college students currently attend such schools, which receive substantial support from local, state and federal sources. In 1991, 29 percent of the federal education budget was spent on community colleges (U.S. Bureau of the Census, 1992, Table 225). Local governments devote considerable expenditure to these schools as well.

Moreover, federal student aid programs also support students in public and private vocational schools. Indeed, among students enrolled in the fall of 1989, the percentage of students enrolled in private vocational schools receiving federal support (82 percent, full-time; 60 percent, part-time) exceeded that among students in public four-year colleges (35 percent full-time; 18 percent part-time) (U.S. Department of Education, 1993, Table 311). Of the $5.7 billion given in Pell grants, 24.3 percent went to students enrolled in community colleges and 20.7 percent went to students enrolled in proprietary schools (Hansen, 1994). State and local governments play an even larger role in supporting community colleges and vocational training.

A full accounting of the extent of government subsidies to different types of postsecondary education and training has not yet been done. It would require measuring subsidy contributions from all levels of government and determining the amount of expenditures on purely academic education versus vocational training. Moreover, the level of government expenditures on formal education is not the best measure of the true scale of training activity in the U.S. economy. Baily et al. (1992) state that only 12 percent of youth report formal training on their first jobs, and only 2 percent report receiving formal company training. These figures understate the true volume of training due to a basic bias in the way training is measured in the literature from which they draw. On-the-job training, especially learning by doing, is a major source of human capital investment. Much of this activity is not captured by surveys that record only formal training programs on which the Brookings authors rely so heavily. Mincer (1993) has presented evidence from a variety of sources that there is a substantial amount of informal, hard-to-measure investment activity on the job. Omission of informal investment in human capital biases comparisons of the amounts of training acquired by youth attending and not attending college. The failure to measure informal training activity adequately underlies claims that there is an inadequate amount of training provided to non-college-bound youth.

A more complete view of public policy toward training and education accounts for both tax and expenditure policy. Even if it were the case that current government educational spending favors formal education over other forms of training, current tax rules tend to operate in the other direction (see Quigley and Smolensky, 1990). Firms can immediately write off all of their training expenditures; they do not have to be amortized as do investments in physical capital. This favors investment in human capital over physical capital. In addition, training expenditures can include tuition paid by employers for each employee up to $5,250 per year, though tuition support is restricted to undergraduate-level education (U.S. House of Representatives, Joint Committee on Taxation, 1992). As many community colleges qualify as undergraduate institutions, there is an incentive for firms to sponsor vocational training. The bias in the tax code favors vocational training, not academic education.

Because tuition paid by employers is exempt from federal personal income tax through educational assistance programs, individuals have an incentive to seek training on the job. Additionally, portable vocational or employer-based training can be sold to employees by firms and paid for by lower wages. The foregone higher earnings are de facto written off on personal income taxes. To the extent that direct costs of books and educational materials are paid for by lower wages, current tax laws favor on-the-job training activities over off-the-job training activities. Thus, they act to shift human capital investment activity away from formal schools and toward workplace environments.

Conversely, individuals cannot write off direct tuition costs for formal schooling if it is not expressly job related. Write-offs are not allowed for training in skills useful in other jobs. Thus workers training to switch occupations cannot write off their educational expenses for this activity. Moreover, there is a floor level of training and education expenditures that must be met before persons can write off such self-investment activity. To be eligible for this tax break, it is necessary to itemize deductions and to incur training costs that exceed 2 percent of adjusted gross income. This tax policy likely biases human capital accumulation toward vocational over academic training, because vocational training is typically more narrowly defined and justifiable.

Since 1986, it has not been permissible to deduct interest on educational loans from taxable income. This removes an important incentive that promotes investment in human capital of all forms (Heckman, 1976). However, because mortgage interest is deductible, it is possible for persons with home equity to take out mortgages to finance their education or to rearrange their portfolios toward mortgage debt in order to finance educational loans.

The tax code for individuals favors human capital accumulation for higher-income persons (and their children) who itemize and have equity in their homes. Low-income persons who pay no taxes receive little encouragement to invest in human capital from the current personal tax code. However, firms that employ them may write off training expenditures devoted to them. The personal tax code thus encourages low-skill workers to make training investments on the job. It does not encourage investment in general or academic education except for company tuition programs. Unfortunately, these programs (defined under section 127 of the 1988 Tax Code) have not received consistent treatment by the tax authorities. In recent years, companies have operated under uncertainty with regard to the likelihood that section 127 would apply to them in a given tax year.

Our examination of the claim that current tax and expenditure policies are biased against employer-based training reveals that it is necessary to examine specific tax and expenditure policies more closely. Simple comparisons of government expenditures on different types of training and education are irrelevant. First, such comparisons ignore the vast amount of informal private sector training and skill formation that is hard to measure but which appears to generate substantial wage growth after schooling (Mincer, 1993). Second, such comparisons typically ignore the vocational training portion of community college education. It is inappropriate to count expenditures on community colleges solely as spending on academic education.

At a deeper level, even if the public expenditure figures cited by Baily et al. (1992) were correct, they would not still reveal whether government training expenditures are divided between formal schooling and other types of training in the way best designed to increase social welfare. There is no reason the expenditures required to produce the optimal levels should be equal absolutely or on a per capita basis in the two sectors. It might in fact be the case that the existing levels is the proper remedy, or that a reversal of the existing levels is appropriate. A complete discussion requires a full empirical and theoretical investigation of why the market and educational institutions fail to produce the correct levels of the two types of human capital investment and of the responsiveness of these training levels to government expenditures. In the absence of such a complete analysis, the evidence presented by Baily et al., even if correct, sheds little light on the questions they purport to address.

There is a widespread belief that markets for financing human capital are fragile and require help from governments to be sustained. The Brookings group claims that many young people have excessively high discount rates and that credit markets for financing training are imperfect. Evidence presented by Cameron and Heckman (1994) indicates that *family* income plays a powerful role in determining which young persons undertake on-the-job training, participate in schooling and work. This evidence is consistent with the importance of borrowing constraints but it is also consistent with a strong role for family environmental factors. There is surprisingly little decisive evidence on this important issue. There is even less evidence that the discount rates of young persons are "too high" even though the Brookings group maintains that this is so. This blatantly paternalistic argument has not been subject to rigorous empirical scrutiny. The same can be said of arguments that claim that firms are "excessively" myopic in their training strategies for their workers.

Missing in this litany of market failures is any discussion of why the market for the provision of schooling may be inefficient. Schooling at the primary and secondary levels is primarily a government monopoly with little opportunity for choice by most parents. It would balance their discussion if the Brookings group recognized the possibility that introducing choice and competition in schools might be a fruitful policy option for improving the skills of young persons. In the next section, we document that the German apprenticeship program operates to enforce competition and improve choice in markets for the production of human capital.

Until the source of a market failure is found, the appropriate policy to address it cannot be formulated. Both the new consensus and Brookings policy recommendations are based on surprisingly weak empirical foundations. The new consensus is based on common beliefs and not hard evidence.

Background on the German Apprenticeship System

Based in part on the belief that there is too little public spending on the postsecondary vocational training of American youth, the new consensus looks to the German education and training system as a model that more appropriately balances formal and vocational education. In this section, we examine the German system and provide some background on how it operates. In the next section, we consider what lessons should be learned from it. We stress at the outset that no one advocates wholesale adoption of the German system. However, features of it that stress learning on the job, skill certification, and early links between specific firms and students are widely advocated. Specific legislation has been passed to fund programs that incorporate these principles. We question whether the correct lesson has been learned from the German experience.

German youth move through three academic tracks. By grade 4 or 6 students are sorted into three schools: *Hauptschule*, where they continue until grade 9 or 10; *Realschule*, where they continue until grade 10; and *Gymnasium*, where they continue until grade 13. *Hauptschule* leads to apprenticeships, which are usually of three-year duration. Typically, one day a week of an apprenticeship is spent in academic schooling suitable to the occupation for which the person is being trained. The rest of the apprentice's time is spent learning and working on the job. *Realschule* qualifies students for further vocational schooling that eventually culminates in work and learning ("dual system") activities. *Gymnasium* leads to university preparation and is considered technically outside of the apprenticeship system, although in certain sectors, such as banking, students certified to go to the university instead take a form of professional apprenticeship. *Hauptschuler* become carpenters, auto mechanics, and office assistants. *Realschuler* become laboratory technicians, precision mechanics, and personnel managers. They are placed in higher-level apprenticeships. Not all graduates of these schools become apprentices. (Only 38 percent of *Realschuler* and about 50 percent of *Hauptschuler* become apprentices.) Many youth, especially those from *Realschuler*, progress into postsecondary vocational schools. The German government pays the full cost of this additional schooling, and apprentices pay part of the costs of their training by taking lower wages.

Apprenticeship wages range from 22–33 percent of full-time professional wages for experienced workers. The training wage varies by sector with larger firms paying more than smaller firms. In the handcrafts sector (retail trade and services) training wages are particularly low. Many apprentices live with their parents and are unable to support themselves with the apprenticeship wage. Only 10 percent of the firms in industry and commerce participate in these training programs, whereas 40 percent of the smaller crafts firms participate at the lower apprentice wage levels in that sector. (Rainer Winkelmann suggests that these figures may overstate the lack of participation of German firms in the apprenticeship programs because solo entrepreneurs, of whom there are many in Germany, are required to register as firms but are unlikely to use apprentices.) These training wages thus operate like youth subminimum wages. Because the German economy is virtually 100 percent unionized, the variance from high union wage levels granted apprentices greatly facilitates their employment, given that their marginal productivity equals or exceeds the wages they receive. The apprenticeship system thus provides an escape route for firms from high union wages, and may be a mechanism for evading union-mandated minimum wage laws. In addition, apprentices are exempt from the rigid German laws that impose costs on firms that seek to terminate the employment of workers. This imparts a bit more flexibility to the German labor market for the group of apprentice workers.

Apprentices are tested for minimal knowledge of the basic skills of their trade at the end of their apprenticeships. The pass rate on these certification exams is 90 percent. Candidates may take their exams twice again if they fail on the first attempt, so overall success rates tend to be quite high.

A German apprenticeship does not necessarily lead to lifetime employment at the firm training the worker (see, e.g., Witte and Kalleberg, 1994). Most apprentices move on to take full-time positions at other firms. This is especially true for trainees in the crafts sector where firms are rather small. Apprentices often take jobs in occupations different from those they are trained for. For example, the leading trainer of bakers in Munich is the Ford Motor Company. Recent evidence suggests that after five years, more than half of all apprentices are working in different companies from the ones that trained them (see, e.g., Harhoff and Kane, 1993). Participation in apprenticeship programs postpones but does not eliminate job shopping.

Completion of an apprenticeship, like graduation from a school, often conveys more information about the tenacity of the trainee and his or her ability to finish a task than it does about the quality of the skills obtained. This information about the stamina and degree of socialization of the apprentice may be valued in the market. A recent study of the economic returns to the German apprenticeship program conducted by Kenneth Couch (1993) suggests that they are low. Dieter Harhoff and Thomas Kane (1993) found the rate of growth of earnings with work experience is the *same* for German and American youths. (The wage levels are different, of course). The rate of growth of earnings with experience is often a reliable guide to the amount of human capital invested in workers. This evidence suggests that there is little difference in the amount of youth investment in human capital in the two societies, or that lower investment by American youth in formal training is compensated by better job matches resulting from higher levels of job shopping.

The very narrow technical training and rigid curriculum of the apprenticeship program may contribute to diminished options in later life. This observation goes partway toward explaining the current anomaly of low youth unemployment rates and higher adult unemployment rates found even in the former West German part of Germany (see Schmidt, 1993).

Furthermore, the apprenticeship and schooling system in Germany has come under attack as rigid and unresponsive to developments in markets and to personal growth on the part of individuals. Students are tracked at early ages. There are many fewer second- and third-chance features in this system than are characteristic of schooling and training choices in the United States, a feature unlikely to be attractive in an American setting. Although some *Realschuler* become students at the universities, this occurs infrequently. It is often charged that minorities (especially Turks) are excluded from participation in the apprenticeship system because the informal nature of the workplace places a premium on personal ties as a basis for participating in work groups. Turkish participation rates among eligibles are only a third of ethnic German rates. These features of the German system would be unwelcome additions to the American workplace.

Lessons to Be Learned from the German Apprenticeship Program

Stripped to its essentials, the German apprenticeship system imparts some flexibility to an otherwise rigid labor market. The lesson to be learned from the German apprenticeship program is that reduced regulation of the employment relationship promotes employment. The German apprenticeship system provides relief from union-mandated minimum wage laws and regulations that make it difficult to terminate ordinary workers. It is no accident that those firms permitted that pay the lowest wages to apprentices (in the crafts sector) are more likely to train apprentices than are firms in the industrial and commercial sector, where the permitted reduction from the standard wage is not as great. Given that minimum wage laws in the United States prevent employers from training low-skilled workers, an apprenticeship system would allow employers to circumvent the minimum wage laws and hire workers at low wages, train them, and then give them higher wages later on in their careers. Evidence presented by Cappelli (1993) indicates that when wage subsidies for youth were introduced in Britain, unemployment declined dramatically for youth in the subsidized age groups. During the period of the wage subsidy, the British youth unemployment rate was lower than the young adult rate, just as it is in Germany. Parenthetically, his evidence should give pause to economists who argue that minimum wages have no disemployment effects on youth. Wage subsidies certainly produce employment effects.

The German apprenticeship system is also a device for permitting choice in schools in the sense that by selecting an occupation, a trainee also selects a school. He or she is thus able to shop around for better schools and better training, thus breaking the monopoly of public schools in Germany at the secondary level. This aspect of the German system could be useful in the U.S. market, where there is currently little choice among secondary schools, especially for children from lower-income households.

The Youth Labor Market in the United States

Comparing the United States and German labor markets, there can be no doubt that the latter is more orderly in the sense that a much smaller proportion of youth is not at work or not at school at age 17 in Germany than in the United States. This, however, does not prove that the German system is the more efficient one. This is especially true in light of the fact that the compulsory schooling age is effectively 18 in Germany, whereas it is 16 in most U.S. states. In order to qualify for all but the most menial positions, German youth have to be in school or in an apprenticeship program two years later than most American youth are required to be in school. Most German youth are *required* to be "off the street" at the ages when many young Americans are making their transitions to full-time jobs.

Advocates of the CSAW report that has helped to produce the new consensus deny the value of the job shopping and job searching that characterize the U.S. labor market. Joblessness and turnover are viewed as wasteful activities that are usefully curtailed. Yet a recent study documents the important role of job shopping in the career mobility of young male workers (over age 18) in the American labor market. During the first 10 years of labor force attachment, a typical male worker holds seven jobs and achieves about one-third of his realized wage growth by changing jobs (career paths for young women have not been studied in similar detail). Matching of workers to firms, characterized by the new consensus view as a time-intensive process that involves wasteful search and excessive turnover, is in fact a major source of productivity enhancement, with important long-term economic and social consequences (Topel and Ward, 1992).

Such matching activity is productive because the worker skills utilized by firms are idiosyncratic. A bright person with an acerbic personality may not be suited for one firm but may be ideal for another. Diversity is an integral feature of the skills embodied in persons. Diversity of opportunities in firms is an essential feature of the American economy. Job shopping is a productive activity that reveals the suitability of worker-firm matches.

Finding a successful match is only the beginning of the investment process that characterizes most worker-firm relationships. There are match- or firm-specific investments that enhance productivity and are not portable elsewhere. The available evidence contradicts the technocratic view of youth job turnover as a wasteful activity. Job shopping promotes wage growth. Turnover is another form of investment not demonstrably less efficient than youth apprenticeships.

The concern about "inefficient" joblessness that is characteristic of recent proposals for youth apprenticeships also ignores some important features of the youth labor market summarized by Richard Freeman, David Wise, Martin Feldstein, David Ellwood, and Harry Holzer (see, e.g., Feldstein and Ellwood, 1982; Freeman, 1992; Freeman and Holzer,

1986; Freeman and Wise, 1982). First, 83 percent of U.S. teenagers (men and women age 16–19) are either in school, working, or both. Most unemployed teenagers are either in school or seeking only part-time work. Only 6 percent of all teenagers are unemployed, out of school and looking for full-time work. Most teenage unemployment spells are short. The bulk of teenage unemployment is experienced by a small group of teenagers with long spells of unemployment. These teenagers are concentrated in disadvantaged (minority, poor family background) groups with low levels of education. Unemployment and nonemployment problems are very acute for high school dropouts. They constitute, however, only a small portion of the total teenage population. Dead-end joblessness is not a modal phenomenon for teenagers. Rather, it is a phenomenon for only a small minority of them.

For youth as a whole, early employment experience has little effect on later employment chances, controlling for age-invariant person-specific characteristics. Loss of work experience reduces wage growth but such effects are transient in the life cycle. Even when teenagers hold dead end jobs, most transit out of them by their early 20s. There appear to be few "permanent scars" (in the language of David Ellwood, 1982) from early "floundering" or job shopping during the teenage years. In the longer view, there is considerable evidence of wage growth resulting from job shopping.

None of this denies that there are disadvantaged groups that are not readily assimilated in labor markets. Special remedies such as apprenticeships and intensive job training programs may be appropriate for these groups. But in devising national strategies for revising education and training, it is important to keep in mind the broader picture of the youth labor market. "Churning" is a form of learning and most youth who are in dead end jobs work and search their way out of them. As noted above, this is true in both the U.S. and German labor markets.

Assessing the Impact of Turnover on
Investment in Training by Firms

In the new consensus view, excessive job turnover characterizes the U.S. labor market, especially among younger workers. This excess turnover is said to lead firms to underinvest in both the general and firm-specific human capital of their workers by shortening the period over which they can realize the returns to such investment.

The standard economic theory of human capital investment predicts that workers will bear the full costs of investments in general human capital (Becker, 1975). Such capital is by definition portable to other firms, so that workers can obtain the entire return to general training simply by switching jobs. Firms know this, and so will not finance investments in general human capital. In contrast, the theory predicts that the cost of investments in firm-specific human capital will be borne jointly by the firm and the worker, thereby providing both with an incentive to prolong the employment relationship so as to realize additional returns on these investments.

Little empirical evidence exists on the rules for sharing human capital investment costs that actually prevail in the labor market. If the theory is correct, turnover rates provide no information about the adequacy of investments in general human capital. Because workers bear the full cost (and receive the full returns to such investments), the level of investment in general human capital is unaffected by the expected tenure at particular firms and therefore unrelated to the rate of job turnover.

The actions of firms and workers in a competitive labor market jointly determine the level of firm-specific capital investment and the rate of job turnover. Though they claim that investment is too low and turnover is too high, Baily et al. (1992) and advocates of the new consensus view provide no theoretical or empirical evidence as to why the levels resulting from market forces are not appropriate. A full evaluation of the suitability of the existing levels of investment and turnover would require estimates of the returns to job shopping, the returns to firm-specific human capital, and the responsiveness of investments in firm-specific human capital to changes in the rate of turnover. Such an analysis remains to be done.

The views advanced by the Brookings group combine and confuse efficiency arguments with equity arguments, although it would clarify the policy debate to separate these very distinct issues. Evidence that low-skill workers receive low and declining real incomes does not bear on the issue of the efficiency of the existing levels of human capital investment in such workers. Concern over widening income inequality does not automatically imply that human capital investment is an efficient income transfer policy. Beliefs that low-skill persons, their families and communities, and society at large are better served by having such individuals work—rather than receive welfare—do not necessarily justify human capital investment strategies for low-skill workers.

There is an accumulating body of evidence that suggests that investments in low-skill persons past a certain age—sometimes placed in the early 20s—have a very low return. Conditioning on measures of ability like the Armed Force Qualifying Test administered in the late teens, scholars like Bill Johnson and Derek Neal (1994) find little evidence that additional years of schooling raise earnings. This evidence is consistent with the evidence summarized below that formal training programs for disadvantaged workers have little effect on the earnings of participants.

In thinking about policies to reduce income inequality, it is important to distinguish the question of the volume of resources to be transferred from the form the transfer should take. The evidence just reviewed suggests that skill investments may represent a very inefficient method for transferring resources to persons with low measured ability. Two important alternative methods for transferring resources to such persons are cash transfers and job subsidies. Neither alternative is perfect. Straight cash transfers have well-known, and well-documented, work disincentive effects. Job subsidies result in the creation of inefficient worker-firm matches, and, if funneled through employers, may have perverse distributional consequences. Nonetheless, transfers to low-ability persons through work subsidies may be the most politically palatable, and in the long run the most desirable, of the alternatives given that they reward persons who demonstrate a willingness to conform to the work ethic of the larger society. Subsidized work may also promote the socialization of the poor, may lead to the accumulation of marketable skills, and may alter the preferences of subsidized workers so as to promote future work effort. (Heckman, 1981, presents some evidence supporting this position.) Whether or not low-ability workers should receive resources from the rest of society is a separate question from whether or not they should receive more training. The universal complementarity of schooling and training emphasized by Mincer (1993) suggests that economically efficient investment strategies may entail more investment in the skilled and investment earlier in the life cycle. It has not been demonstrated by the Brookings group that investment in low-skill workers is the efficient way to allay concerns over economic inequality.

The Economic Consequences of
Using a Payroll Tax to Finance Training

Baily et al. (1992) argue that "for reasons of their own, including shortsightedness, poor information, or inadequate access to credit, many workers do not invest enough in improving their own skills" (p. 127). They present no evidence on the empirical importance of these factors, but suggest that if workers are unwilling to invest in their own general human capital, firms should be induced to do so through a combination of tax policy and longer expected job tenure brought about by the introduction of an apprenticeship system. In particular, they advocate a payroll tax to finance training by firms. This idea is borrowed from France. Firms that spend less than a specified percentage of their payroll on training would be taxed, with the revenues devoted to a general training fund.

Except in certain extreme limiting cases, any tax has adverse consequences on employment and on the wages received by employees. If labor supply is perfectly inelastic (i.e., the number of workers is fixed), wages are simply reduced by the amount of the tax. If labor supply is perfectly elastic (i.e., the wages of workers are fixed), the tax reduces employment. The actual response of firms is an empirical matter and is not known with any precision (see, e.g., the evidence summarized in Hamermesh, 1993, p. 170). Either response worsens the labor market position of workers by reducing their wages or their employment prospects.

For firms that already achieve the targeted level of worker training there are no adverse consequences. Indeed, employment might expand in such firms in response to the lower wages of workers in the market induced by the tax. For firms below the target level, the disemployment effects may be more severe than are predicted from the analysis of an ordinary payroll tax, because these firms are asked to spend resources in a certain way—by setting up training programs—that or may not be an efficient use of their resources. Allowing firms the option to pay the tax instead of conducting training guarantees that the adverse disemployment and wage effects of the proposed training tax will be less than that of a general training tax because some firms will meet the target and be unaffected. Nonetheless, it is still expected that a training tax will have adverse employment and wage effects, although precise empirical magnitudes are not known.

Even if workers do underinvest in general training, blunt policy instruments such as the payroll tax recommended by Bailey et al. and others might better be replaced by policies aimed more directly at providing information to workers and at overcoming financing constraints that impair the formation of human capital. Good policy requires good empirical foundations for the source of the policy problem. The Brookings group offers speculation in place of careful empirical analysis.

The Likely Ineffectiveness of a Testing System for Non-College-Bound Youth

In addition to providing incentives for firms to invest in training their workers, the advocates of the new consensus recommend the implementation of a national credentialing scheme to provide incentives for workers to invest in their own training. A central tenet of the new consensus is that incentives within education can be restored by linking students' performance on tests to the quality of their job placements. The case for national testing and credentialing is based on the premise that tests measure job-relevant skills. The Brookings group strongly endorses this idea as well.

One test of general skill has recently been studied: the General Education Development test (GED). It is of interest in its own right because a major goal of many government job training programs is certification of participants as being equivalent to high school graduates through completion of the GED. The GED has become a major source of high school diplomas in this country. One out of every seven new high school certificate holders achieves that status by passing a GED. In New York State and Florida the proportion is one out of four. High school completion levels, measured by the proportion of persons ages 20–24 who have high school credentials or more, have not deteriorated in the past 20 years only because GED certification has been rising. Advocacy groups, in particular the American Council on Education, which markets the GED, claim that it is easy to test for the job-relevant skills embodied in achievement of a high school diploma. Evidence on the earnings of GED recipients relative to high school dropouts, however, indicates that a GED fails to provide information about the level of job-relevant skills of a worker. Except for a tiny perecntages, GED-certified high school graduate equivalents earn roughly the same as high school dropouts. Controlling for their years of schooling completed, male GED certificate holders in their late 20s and early 30s earn the *same* as high school dropouts. For other groups of workers over the age range 20–60 there is little evidence that GED-certified workers earn the same wages or work the same hours as ordinary high school graduates (Cameron and Heckman, 1993).

These findings challenge both the wisdom of our current emphasis on GED certification and the folly of relying on tests of general skill to measure market-relevant skills. National tests that certify "skill" cannot capture the imagination, drive, or motivation of the persons being tested, nor can they produce scores that will successfully rank certificate bearers in all firms in the economy, or even within a particular industry. Markets value, and humans possess, richer and more diverse skills and attributes than can be captured by standardized exams. Whereas tests of general skill may have little value, tests of specific occupational skills may convey more information about the suitability of persons for particular tasks. They cannot, however, convey information about the motivation, personality, or fit of a person in a particular work environment.

Much occupational testing and credentialing already exists in the U.S. labor market. Currently, testing centers on skills that can be measured directly, such as typing or cutting hair. Other information sources, such as recommendations of coworkers and the reputation of the school or teacher providing training to a worker, act formally or informally to certify skills not readily measured. Even if national skill certification were desirable, private firms could provide this information as least as well as could public sector boards. It seems likely that private firms would also be more sensitive to changes in market demand for particular types of skills. If public goods problems prevent the generation of information about worker skills in the market, then general revenues could be used to subsidize private sector accreditation.

One potential problem with a formal testing system for non-college-bound youth is that teaching in vocational programs would quickly become directed toward performing well on a general standardized test rather than toward specific job-related skills needed in the current local labor market. It is unlikely that vocational tests can be changed quickly enough to keep up with the changing mix of skills needed in a vocation. "Teaching to the test" limits creativity and flexibility in a vocational training curriculum and may reduce its effectiveness. Tests also bias students toward investing in general skills measured by the tests rather than in human capital that is relevant to their occupations.

Two untested implicit premises in the argument for credentialing are that individuals lack information about the skills needed to perform jobs and that credentials provide such information. Information is scarce, and more information is preferred to less. But it is not clear to us, nor has it been documented by advocates of skill standards, that failure of students to know about the skills required in a particular occupation is a major cause of underinvestment in training.

Although the lack of incentives for firms to provide training to their workers is a major reason given in support of government intervention in the labor market, nationally recognizable measures of skill and vocational ability could further reduce existing incentives. In the presence of such certification, if a firm invests in training a worker in a specific skill, the worker can take a vocational test to certify the skill obtained and thereby become immediately marketable to other firms. As a result, the probability that the firm will lose its investment in the worker increases in the presence of such a credential; thus, firms will become less willing to finance certifiable skills. A "successful" skill certification program could exacerbate the financing problem for skill acquisition.

Evidence for Ineffectiveness of Public Training Programs

In addition to the policies already mentioned, a variety of public training programs have been proposed by advocates of the new consensus. Most are reworked versions of existing strategies already shown to be ineffective. In this section, we examine the evidence concerning the rate of return to government training. The evidence suggests that the 10 percent rate of return assumed in the calculations performed above is wildly optimistic.

Summer Youth Employment and Training Program

It has been proposed that the Summer Youth Employment and Training program under the Job Training Partnership Act be doubled in size. The stated purpose of this program is to preserve and upgrade the skills of low-income youth during the summers between school terms. The new twist on this program is that an "investment" argument has been given to support it. Barbara Heyns (1987) and her associates have argued that knowledge acquired in schools deteriorates through disuse during the summer. The new proposals recognize this possibility and suggest that summer youth programs should be enhanced through the addition of learning enrichment activities. "Make-work" has become an "investment" in the new vocabulary of Washington. Though the stated purpose of this program has been updated to reflect current fashions in educational theory, its activities and principles are similar to those of previous programs that have already been evaluated and can therefore provide evidence on its likely rate of return. Predecessor programs such as the Kennedy-Johnson Neighborhood Youth Corps were well known to be palliatives designed to keep inner-city youth off the streets. No firm evidence of any lasting effects of these programs on the employment, wages, or criminal or sexual behavior of their participants has ever been demonstrated.

What are the prospects for success of this program? A recent evaluation of a similar effort, the Summer Training and Education Program (STEP), has been presented by Public/Private Ventures, a Philadelphia-based nonprofit corporation that evaluates and manages social policy initiatives aimed at helping disadvantaged youth (Walker and Viella-Velez, 1992). STEP offered two summers of employment, academic remediation, and a life skills program to low-achieving youth ages 14 and 15 from poor families. The objective of the program was to reach youth at the crucial ages at which they are deciding whether or not to drop out of school or become pregnant. Part-time summer work at the minimum wage was supplemented with remedial reading and math classes and courses on the long-term consequences of drug use, unprotected sex, and dropping out of school.

Using randomized trials, 4,800 youths in five cities were enrolled into or randomized out of the program. Individuals in both treatment and control groups were followed for eight years, and then a high-quality evaluation was conducted using state-of-the-art demonstration methods for three cohorts of participants. The findings of this evaluation are disappointing. STEP participants experienced measured short-run gains, including increases of half a grade level in their math and reading competency test scores. These gains held up even after 15 months, though gains in the second summer were less than those in the first. Especially large was short-run growth in knowledge of contraceptive methods. This short-term promise did not translate into longer-term gains, however. Three and a half years after their STEP experience, at the ages of 17 and 18, the youths in both treatment and control groups had work rates and school completion rates that were identical and low. Some 22 percent of young women had children, and 64 percent of these were receiving public assistance in some form (Walker and Viella-Velez, 1992).

Given that STEP is, if anything, more intensive than the proposed summer youth programs, this evidence suggests that summer youths programs are *not* investments. There is no evidence that they have lasting effects on participants. They may protect the peace, prevent riots, and lower summer crime rates, but there is no evidence of such effects.

Conventional Workforce Training and Work-Welfare Programs

How effective are current programs in moving people from welfare to work and in increasing their employment and earnings? Our colleague Robert LaLonde (1992) recently addressed this question. His evidence is summarized below along with our own evidence on the Job Training Partnership Act (JTPA).

Adult Women. Employment and training programs increase the earnings of adult female AFDC recipients. Earnings gains (a) are modest, (b) are persistent over several years, (c) arise from several different treatments, and (d) are sometimes quite cost-effective. Table 3.2 displays evaluation results for a variety of programs. For example, participation in an Arkansas job search program was required for AFDC recipients with children older than 3 years. Participants attended a group job search club for two weeks and then were asked to search as individuals for an additional two months. A program in San Diego required all AFDC participants to take job search assistance and mandated work experience. The gains were high for participants in both programs. The National Supported Work program provided intensive training and job search assistance at a cost of about $16,550 per recipient. The estimated rate of return to this program was only 3.5 percent.

The results of the recent experiment evaluating programs initiated under the Job Training Partnership Act (shown in Table 3.3) corroborate these findings. The largest impacts are for adult women, many of whom were collecting AFDC during their participation in JTPA programs. The impacts are not sufficiently large to move more than a tiny fraction of women out of poverty. As a general rule, conventional employment and training programs are often cost-effective for adult women (especially if the opportunity cost of trainee time is ignored or is sufficiently low), but do not produce dramatic changes in participant earnings.

TABLE 3.2
Experimental Estimates of the Impact of Employment and Training Programs
on the Earnings of Female Welfare Applicants and Recipients

		Annual Earnings Gain (Loss)	
Services Tested/ *Demonstration*	*Net Cost per* *Participant*	*After* *1 Year*	*After* *3 Years*
Job Search Assistance			
Arkansas	140	220**	410**
Louisville (WIN-1)	170	350**	530**
Cook County, IL	190	10	NA
Louisville (WIN-2)	280	560**	NA
Job Search Assistance **and Training Services**			
West Virginia	320	20	NA
Virginia Employment Services	520	90	330*
San Diego I (EPP/EWEP)	770	600**	NA
San Diego II (SWIM)	1,120	430**	NA
Baltimore	1,160	190	630**
New Jersey	960	720*	
Maine	2,450	140	1,140
Work Experience and Retraining			
AFDC Homemaker-Health Care	11,550	460**	NA
National Supported Work	16,550	460**	810**

**Statistically significant at the .5 level. N.A. = not applicable.

Note: All figures in the table are expressed in 1990 dollars. *Source:* Bell and Reesman (1987), Tables 3 and 4; Couch (1992), Table 1; Gueron and Pauly (1991), pp. 15–20.

Adult Men. The evidence for adult men is consistent across programs. Returns are low but usually positive. Job search assistance is an effective strategy but produces only modest increases in mean earnings levels.

Youth. Evidence from the JTPA experiment indicates that this program produces only low or negative impacts on earnings. For male youth, the estimated negative effect is unbelievably low. If taken seriously, these results would suggest that participation in JTPA programs has a more negative impact on the earnings of male youth than being in the army, loss of work experience, or incarceration as measured by many studies.

TABLE 3.3
Impacts on Total 18-Month Earnings and Employment:
JTPA Assignees and Enrollees, by Target Group

Impact on:	Adults		Out-of School Youths	
	Women	Men	Female	Male
Per assignee				
Earnings				
In dollars	539***	550	–182	–854**
As a percentage	7.2	4.5	–2.9	–7.9
Percentage employed	2.1**	2.8**	2.8	1.5
Sample size	6,474	4,419	2,300	1,748
(assignees and control group combined)				
Per enrollee				
Earnings				
In dollars	873[b]	935[b]	–295[b]	–1,355[b]
As a percentage	12.2	6.8	–4.6	–11.6
Percentage employed[a]	3.5[b]	4.8[b]	4.5[b]	2.4[b]

[a] At any time during the follow-up period.
[b] Tests of statistical significance were not performed for impacts per enrollee.
* Statistically significant at the .10 level;
** statistically significant at the .05 level;
*** statistically significant at the .01 level (two-tailed test).

Source: Bloom, Orr, Cane, Bell, and Doolittle (1993). Enrollee estimates obtained using the procedure in Bloom (1984).

Only the Job Corps has a demonstrated positive impact on earnings. It is an expensive program, costing approximately $20,000 per participant, with an estimated return of roughly 8–9 percent. There is some basis for supporting the expansion of this program, but even here the evidence is weak. The primary existing evaluation of Job Corps is not experimental. A substantial portion of the high estimated return comes from the combination of a slightly lower rate of arrest for murder among Job Corp participants and a very large value imputed to human life (see Donohue and Siegelman, 1994).

Workfare and Learnfare. An evaluation of two programs conducted in Wisconsin tells us something about the effectiveness of recent learnfare and workfare programs (see Pawasarat and Quinn, 1993). One, the Community Work Experience Program (CWEP), required mandatory participation in unpaid community service jobs for nonexempt AFDC participants. A second program, Work Experience and Job Training, provided AFDC clients with assessment, job search activities, subsidized employment, job training, and community work experience. Participants who failed to find employment after completing their education and training were also required to participate in CWEP jobs.

Using randomized trials for one county and nonexperimental methods for the rest, researchers found *no effect* of these programs compared with existing program alternatives. The reduction in AFDC participation that is widely cited as a consequence of these programs is essentially the result of improvement in the Wisconsin economy during the time the programs were in place. These results are disappointing but consistent with previous studies of the efficacy of such programs by the Manpower Demonstration Research Corporation (Gueron and Pauly, 1991). Mandatory work experience programs produce little long-term gain. No cheap training solution has yet been found that can end the welfare problem. Lifting a welfare woman out of poverty by increasing her earnings by $5,000 per year ($100 per week) will cost at *least* $50,000. This is the scale of required investment. No "quick-fix," low-cost solution is in sight.

Training Programs for Displaced Workers

As noted above, displacement of older workers with substantial experience in the labor market has become an increasingly important phenomenon in recent years. In response to this trend, Congress passed Title III of the Job Training Partnership Act in 1982 and the Economic Dislocation and Worker Adjustment Assistance Act in 1988. Although studies directly evaluating programs related to these acts are not available as yet, evaluations of state-funded programs providing a similar mix of services have been conducted. Leigh (1990) summarizes the evidence gathered from a variety of these programs. Results of some of these evaluations suggest small to moderate wages gains (8 percent for men and 34 percent for women) lasting about a year. A more recent evaluation by Mathematica of training provided under the Trade Adjustment Assistance Program to workers displaced as a result of foreign trade found no evidence of any effect of this long-term training program on the earnings and employment of recipients (Corson et al., 1993). Consistent with the other studies of government employment and training programs already discussed, the overall pattern for programs aimed at displaced workers is one of weak impacts for most groups.

Private Sector Training

Because of a lack of data and a bias in favor of funding studies of government training, the returns to private sector training are less well understood. Studies by Lynch (1992), Lillard and Tan (1986), Bishop (1994), and Bartel (1992) have found sizable effects of private sector training. In comparison with studies of public sector training, most of these studies have not attempted to control for selection bias. The presence of selection bias would imply that if more able persons are more likely to take training, the estimated rates of return would overstate the true returns to training by combining them with the return to ability. Thus, part of the measured return may be the result of more motivated and able persons taking training. Estimated initial returns range from 10 percent to 20 percent (Mincer, 1993), but they tend to decline after a few years as technical progress renders the training essentially obsolete. To the extent that rapid technical progress in many fields causes the knowledge obtained through training to lose its value after only a few years, fears about the detrimental effects of turnover in the labor market on the volume of human capital investment may be exaggerated.

An important feature of private sector training is that the more skilled do more investing even after they attain high skill levels. Different types of training and learning have strong complementarities with respect to each other. This universal complementarity of formal schooling and postschool investment is a key conclusion of Mincer's (1962) seminal study of postschool investment.

Even though the evidence is weak, the direction of the evidence is clear. To the extent that effective training can be produced on the job, it is produced in the private sector and not in the public sector. At the current state of knowledge, the only hope of getting reasonable returns from job training is to encourage private sector initiatives.

It is important to note, however, that private sector training typically excludes low-skilled persons. Firms can be exclusive in a way that government training programs for disadvantaged workers are designed not to be. The lack of interest of private firms in training disadvantaged workers indicates the difficulty of the task and the likely low return to this activity. As previously noted, training is likely to be both an inefficient transfer policy and an inefficient investment policy for low-skill workers.

The Conflict between Economic Efficiency and the Work Ethic

To the extent that there are strong complementarities between different types of skill investments, there is a conflict between policies that seek to alleviate poverty by investing in low-skill workers and policies that maximize the output of society. Taking the available evidence at face value, the best economically-justified strategy for improving the incomes of the poor would be to invest more in the highly skilled, tax them, and then redistribute the tax revenues to the poor. However, many people view the work ethic as a basic value and would argue that cultivating a large class of transfer recipients would breed a culture of poverty and helplessness.

If value is placed on work as an act of individual dignity, and because of general benefits to families, communities, and society as a whole, then all individuals in society may be prepared to subsidize inefficient jobs. Job subsidies are not, however, the same as investment subsidies. The evidence points strongly to the inefficiency of subsidizing the human capital investments of low-skill disadvantaged workers. Such investment may have some additional nonpecuniary returns. In this case, a purely economic evaluation of investment policies may be inappropriate. If, however, economically inefficient investments are to be made, the cost of reducing the skill gap grows beyond the already enormous sums presented in Table 3.1.

Alternative Policy Recommendations

The policies advocated by proponents of the new consensus target low skill levels as a fundamental problem in the current U.S. labor market. In this section we review these policy proposals in light of the evidence considered above, and suggest alternative policies with firmer theoretical and empirical foundations.

In the long run, significant improvement in the skill levels of American workers, especially workers not attending college, is unlikely without substantial change and improvement in primary and secondary education. Mincer's (1962) evidence on universal complementarity demonstrates the value of early training in making subsequent training effective. Much of the current discussion about improving postsecondary education is misplaced when the value of early schooling is put in context.

Methods for improving primary and secondary education have received much attention in the general literature but very little attention by new consensus authors or the Brookings scholars. Increasing the extent of consumer choice in the educational system would help to realign incentives in the right way to produce more effective schools. Choice among secondary training venues is an important aspect of the German apprenticeship system. It is odd that neither advocates of the new consensus nor the Brookings group consider the failure of government to provide adequate skills to students at the primary or secondary schooling levels as a major cause of the slowdown in labor force productivity growth.

The evidence in support of introducing a nationwide system of skill credentials based on formal tests is weak at best. New consensus advocates fail to address the problematic relationship between what tests can measure and the skills actually valued by employers. They ignore behavioral responses to the introduction of such tests in the form of incentives for vocational programs to "teach to the test" and incentives for workers to overinvest in the types of human capital captured on exams and to underinvest in other forms of job-relevant human capital. They fail to note that psychometrically based credentials may not arise in the market either because they are not needed or because alternative mechanisms for certifying workers are more effective.

Credentials developed or enforced by the government have a poor track record. As demonstrated by Cameron and Heckman (1993), the GED test of general skills fails miserably at its stated goal of certifying skills equivalent to those possessed by high school graduates. Other government credentials in the form of occupational certificates function in part as barriers to entry that reduce the supply of workers in the certified occupations, and limit opportunities to new entrants.

Before taxing or threatening to tax firms into providing additional general training on the grounds that workers are unwilling or unable to purchase it for themselves, advocates of new training policies must be more specific about the sources of market failure the policies are designed to correct. In particular, they should demonstrate in a more rigorous way that credit market constraints or information costs prevent workers from undertaking valuable investments in general human capital. Policies aimed directly at empirically documented problems should result in fewer adverse consequences (and offer less scope for manipulation by interested parties) than imposition of another layer of taxation on every firm in the labor market.

In regard to the incentives facing firms to provide training to their workers, we have noted that new consensus concerns about excess job turnover are likely to be overstated. This fact weakens the case for implementing an apprenticeship system designed to remove such turnover.

To the extent that the German apprenticeship system does raise productivity, three aspects of that system have relevance to U.S. labor market policy. The first, which we previously noted, is that more choice among public schools may contribute to more productive investments. The second is that low apprentice wages stimulate employment and encourage firms to provide training. Similar results could be achieved in the United States through the repeal of the minimum wage laws or the reduction of the minimum wage level, thereby allowing firms to hire workers whose initial marginal product is worth less than the minimum wage but for whom training would be a worthwhile investment. Third, allowing greater flexibility to firms in discharging employees may make some persons more employable.

We have noted that existing tax policy appears to favor human capital acquisition, but that this effect is strongest for high-income workers who already have substantial skills. Changes in the tax laws for firms and individuals designed to bring these incentives to bear at the low end of the skill distribution are worth much more consideration. Finally, support of cooperative activity among employers could allow firms within an industry to overcome free-rider problems by contracting to provide similar levels of industry-specific training or general training to their employees.

The evidence on government training programs suggests that they can make at best only a modest contribution to aggregate human capital formation. Evidence from existing evaluations suggests that such programs should be targeted primarily at adults, particularly adult women. The evidence further suggests a focus on job search assistance and wage subsidies as the strategies most likely to yield small favorable returns. Further research on more intensive training programs, such as the Job Corps (currently the subject of a major experimental evaluation), is required before we can reach a clear answer on whether or not they are worth the additional spending they require.

Finally, given the strong evidence of complementarity between schooling and training, it may be more efficient to focus training on high-skill workers, and then use the tax system to transfer resources to the less skilled. If the goal is to raise their incomes, the extra surplus generated through more efficient investment can more than compensate low-skilled workers for the training they forego. Investment may be more efficiently placed in the very young. Teaching children how to learn is likely to be a much more valuable activity than attempting to train unmotivated adults to learn new skills.

However, as noted earlier, work itself may have inherent social value that must be weighed against efficiency considerations. The appropriate form for the transfer is a separate issue. Job subsidies may be socially more desirable than welfare payments.

Summary and Conclusions

In this commentary we have reviewed the new consensus about the problems of the U.S. labor market and the appropriate solutions to these problems. The American labor market has changed in recent decades, with adverse consequences for low-skill workers. Our calculations reveal the enormous magnitude of the human capital investments required to restore 1979 wage differentials by skill groups in the 1989 labor market. In the current era of tight budgets, investments of this scale are unlikely at best.

Once we move beyond basic facts about the labor market, we find that the evidence used to justify the proposed policies is weak. Policy advocates misread the lessons to be learned from the German apprenticeship program. A close look at how this program operates reveals that it builds flexibility in wages and employment into an otherwise inflexible German labor market. German apprentices turn over at a rapid rate and experience wage growth rates comparable to those experienced by American youth.

Informal training, job shopping, and worker turnover among firms are viewed in the new consensus as pathologies, not as sources of productivity. Both new consensus advocates and the Brookings group place an emphasis on certifying certain easily measured general skills rather than on developing productive skills that contain an important hard-to-measure, firm-specific component. Certification exams are endorsed to foster and measure general skills at the expense of firm-specific skills.

Evidence on bias in government tax and expenditure policy toward education and training cited by the Brookings group is ambiguous at best. What is clear is that current tax policies encourage on-the-job training by higher-income workers and by firms. New schemes designed to tax firms to pay for training will likely reduce employment and wages.

The evidence on the effectiveness of training programs reveals that publicly provided training is ineffective. Returns from private training programs are much greater. However, private training programs typically exclude disadvantaged workers because the private returns to their training is low. There is evidence that the highest payoff to training comes for highly educated workers. Economically efficient training strategies are likely to *widen* skill gaps, not reduce them. There is a basic conflict between efficiency and the socially accepted value of the work ethic.

Rather than investing in high-skill workers and then taxing them to pay for the consumption of low-skill workers, many persons would favor redistribution through human capital investments because of the socializing value of work. This view—most strongly espoused by the Brookings group—confuses job subsidies with training subsidies. It may be inefficient to invest in low-skill workers, but it may be socially useful to subsidize their employment. Given the universal complementarity among components of education and training, economically efficient programs would focus on early training and education at the primary and secondary schooling level rather than on postsecondary education and training as most of the recent discussion has done. In the short run, job subsidies may be the most palatable way to employ low-skill workers.

In the long run, investments in families and early childhood programs that boost skills for persons from disadvantaged families are likely to be much more economically efficient.

Our discussion suggests that a broader portfolio of policies should be considered. Reducing the minimum wage and instituting choice in schools, tax subsidies for employing and/or training low-skill workers, and modifications of the antitrust laws are alternative approaches to encouraging human capital formation that have received insufficient attention in current policy discussions.

Current discussions of human capital investment strategies ignore what cannot easily be measured and interpret productive turnover and job shopping as wasteful activities. This technocratic view favors a "planned" order in place of the "chaos" of market activities. It favors easily measured general skills over hard-to-measure, but productive, specific skills. It ignores the perverse incentive effects of payroll taxes and national skill-certification exams. A richer, more factually informed view of how labor markets actually operate and how incentives affect choices is required before further intervention in labor markets is justified.

References

Baily, M. N., Burtless, G., and Litan, R. (1992). *Growth with Equity: Economic Policymaking for the Next Century*. Washington DC: Brookings Institution.

Bartel, A. (1992). "Productivity Gains from the Implementation of Employee Training Programs." NBER Working Paper 3893, Cambridge, MA.

Becker, G. (1975). *Human Capital: A Theoretical and Empirical Analysis*. New York: National Bureau of Economic Research.

Bell, S., and Reesman, C. (1987). *AFDC Homemaker-Home Health Aide Demonstrations: Trainee Potential and Performance*. Washington, DC: Abt Associates.

Bishop, J. (1994). "Formal Training and Its Impact on Productivity, Wages and Innovation." In L. Lynch (Ed.), *Training and the Private Sector: International Comparisons*. Chicago: University of Chicago Press.

Blank, R. (1994). "Employment Strategies: Public Policy to Increase the Work Force and Earnings." In S. Danziger, G. Sandfur, and D. Weinberg (Eds.), *Combating Poverty: Prescriptions for Change*. Cambridge, MA: Harvard University Press.

Bloom, H. (1984). "Accounting for No Shows in Experimental Evaluation Designs." *Evaluation Review, 8,* 225–246.

Bloom, H., Orr, L., Cave, G., Bell, S., and Doolittle, F. (1993). *The National JTPA Study: Title II-A Impacts on Earnings and Employment at 18 Months*. Bethesda, MD: Abt Associates.

Burtless, G. (1993). *Meeting the Skill Demands of the New Economy*. Washington, DC: Brookings Institution.

Cameron, S., and Heckman, J. (1993). "The Nonequivalence of High School Equivalents." *Journal of Labor Economics, 11,* 1–47.

Cameron, S., and Heckman, J. (1994). "Determinants of Young Male's Schooling and Training Choices," In L. Lynch (Ed.), *Training and the Chicago: Private Sector*. Chicago: University of Chicago Press.

Cappelli, P. (1993). "British Lessons for School to Work Transition Policy in the U.S." Pennsylvania: National Center on the Educational Quality of the Workforce, Catalog Number WP19.

Chubb, J. and Moe, T. (1991). *Politics, Markets, and America's Schools*. Washington, DC: Brookings Institution.

Commission on the Skills of the American Workforce (CSAW). (1990). *America's Choice: High Skills or Low Wages*. Rochester, NY: National Center on Education and the Economy.

Corson, W., Becker, P., Gleason, P., Nicholson, W., Beaumont, L., and Stapulonis, R. (1993). *International Trade and Worker Dislocation: Evaluation of the Trade Adjustment Assistance Program*. Princeton, NJ: Mathematica.

Couch, K. (1992). "New Evidence on the Effects of Employment Training Programs." *Journal of Labor Economics, 10*, 380–388.

Couch, K. (1993). "High School Vocational Education, Apprenticeship, and Earnings: A Comparison of Germany and the United States." *Bierteljahrsheste zur Wirtschaftssorsh.*

Donohue, J., and Siegelman, P. (1994). "Is the United States at the Optimal Rate of Crime?" Chicago: American Bar Foundation.

Ellwood, T. (1982). "Teenage Employment: Permanent Scars or Temporary Blemishes?" In R. Freeman and D. A. Wise (Eds.), *The Youth Labor Market Problem*. Chicago: University of Chicago Press.

Feldstein, M., and Ellwood, D. (1982). "Teeenage Unemployment: What Is the Problem?" In R. Freeman and D. Wise (Eds.), *The Youth Labor Market Problem*. Chicago: University of Chicago Press.

Freeman, R. (1992). "Is Declining Unionization in the U.S. Good, Bad or Irrelevant?" In L. Mishel and P. Zoos (Eds.), *Unions and Economic Competitiveness*. Armonk, NY: M. E. Sharpe.

Freeman, R., and Holzer, H. (1986). *The Black Youth Employment Crisis*. Chicago: University of Chicago Press.

Freeman, R., and Wise, D. (Eds.). (1982). *The Youth Labor Market Problem*. Chicago: University of Chicago Press.

Gueron, J., and Pauly, E. (1991). *From Welfare to Work*. New York: Russell Sage Foundation.

Hamermesh, D. (1993). *Labor Demand*. Princeton, NJ: Princeton University Press.

Hamilton, S. (1990). *Apprenticeship for Adulthood*. New York: Free Press.

Hansen, J. (Ed.). (1994). *Preparing for the Workforce: Charting a Course for Federal Training Policy*. Washington, DC: National Academy Press.

Harhoff, D., and Kane, T. (1993, November). "Financing Apprenticeship Training: Evidence from Germany." Working paper.

Heckman, J. (1976). "A Life Cycle Model of Earnings, Learning and Consumption." *Journal of Political Economy, 84*, S11–44.

Heckman, J. (1981). "Heterogeneity and State Dependence," in S. Rosen (Ed.), *Studies in Labor Markets*. Chicago: University of Chicago Press.

Heyns, B. (1987). "Schooling and Cognitive Development: Is There a Season for Learning?" *Child Development, 58* p. 1151–1160.

Jacobson, L., LaLonde, R., and Sullivan, D. (1993). "Earnings Losses of Displaced Workers." *American Economic Review, 83*(4), 685–709.

Johnson, W., and Neal, D. (1994). "The Role of Pre-Market Factors in Black-White Wage Differentials." Unpublished paper, University of Chicago.

LaLonde, R. (1992). "The Earnings Impact of U.S. Employment and Training Programs." Unpublished manuscript, University of Chicago.

Leigh, D. (1990). *Does Training Work for Displaced Workers?* Kalamazoo, MI: W. E. Upjohn Institute for Employment Research.

Lillard, L. A., and Tan, H. W. (1986). *Private Sector Training: Who Gets It and What Are Its Effects?* Santa Monica, CA: RAND Corporation.

Lynch, L. (1992). "Private-Sector Training and the Earnings of Young Workers." *American Economic Review, 82*(1).

McKinsey & Company, Inc. (1993). *Manufacturing Productivity.* Washington DC: McKinsey Global Institute.

Mincer, J. (1962). "On the Job Training: Costs, Returns, and Some Implications." *Journal of Political Economy, 70* (suppl.), 50–79.

Mincer, J. (1993, November). "Investment in U.S. Education and Training." Discussion Paper 671, Columbia University, New York.

Mishel, L., and Voos, P. (Eds.). (1992). *Unions and Economic Competitiveness.* Armonk, NY: M. E. Sharpe.

Murphy, K., and Welch, F. (1992). "Industrial Change and the Rising Importance of Skill." In S. Danziger and P. Gottschalk (Eds.), *Uneven Tides: Rising Inequality in America* (pp. 101–132). New York: Russell Sage Foundation.

Osterman, P. (1993, January). "How Common Is Workplace Transformation and How Can We Explain Who Adopts It?" Paper presented at the meeting of the Allied Social Science Association, Anaheim, CA.

Pawasarat, J., and Quinn, L. (1993). *Evaluation of the Wisconsin WEJT/CWEP Welfare Employment Programs.* Milwaukee: University of Wisconsin, Employment and Training Institute.

Piore, M., and Sabel, C. (1984). *The Second Industrial Divide.* New York: Basic Books.

Quigley, J., and Smolensky, E. (1990). "Improving Efficiency in the Tax Treatment of Training and Educational Expenditures." *Research in Labor Economics, 11,* 77–95.

Reich, R. (1991). *The Work of Nations: Preparing Ourselves for 21st-Century Capitalism.* New York: A. A. Knopf.

Schmidt, C. (1993). "Ageing and Unemployment," in P. Johnson and K. F. Zimmerman (Eds.), *Labour Markets in Ageing Europe.* England Cambridge University Press.

Topel, R., and Ward, M. (1992). "Job Mobility and the Careers of Young Men." *Quarterly Journal of Economics, 107,* 439–480.

U.S. Bureau of the Census. (1992). *Statistical Abstract of the United States: 1992.* Washington, DC: Government Printing Office.

U.S. Department of Education. (1993). *Digest of Educational Statistics, 1993.* Washington, DC: Government Printing Office.

U.S. House of Representatives, Joint Committee on Taxation. (1992). *Description and Analysis of Tax Provisions Expiring in 1992*. Washington, DC: Government Printing Office.

Walker, G., and Viella-Velez, F. (1992). *Anatomy of a Demonstration*. Philadelphia: Public / Private Ventures.

Witte, J., and Kalleberg, A. (1994, January 5). "Matching Training and Jobs: The Fit Between Vocational Education and Employment in the German Labor Market." Working paper, Carolina Population Center.

Comment

Gary Burtless

Heckman, Roselius, and Smith have presented a clearly written, often very persuasive, chapter. I agree with a number of their arguments, but I see problems with some of their conclusions. There are areas where I do not agree with the authors on either the facts or their implications for public policy.

Core Ideas

I do not subscribe to all or even most of the propositions Heckman et al. imputed to the "new consensus" on labor market policy. For example, I have never argued—or even hinted—that the quality of the U.S. labor force is declining (core idea 2 of the new consensus). The quality of the workforce continues to improve, though more slowly than it did during the first 35 years after World War II. The rate of *increase* in average educational attainment (including some measure of the quality of educational attainment) has almost certainly slowed since 1980. My interpretation, along with that of most other well-informed labor economists, is that the trend increase in *demand for skills* by U.S. employers has accelerated since the late 1970s. The slowdown in the rate of improvement in the average supply of skills has probably contributed to the slowdown in productivity improvement and to the trend in inequality (see Bishop, 1989; Blackburn, Bloom, and Freeman, 1990). But I am very skeptical that the quality of the workforce has actually declined.

Second, I disagree with the view that investments in physical capital cannot improve worker productivity (core idea 3). A big part of my book with Martin Baily and Robert Litan, *Growth with Equity* (1992) (hereinafter referred to as *GWE*), is devoted to arguments for increasing U.S. investment in private physical capital, either through better fiscal policy (lower government dissaving) or explicit tax incentives (a revived investment tax credit). Having been attacked by several good economists for *favoring* the investment tax credit, I find it odd to see my views lumped with those of people who do not believe additional physical capital investment can be helpful.

I have no particular views on the "Third Industrial Revolution" or on the possible productivity effects of "flex-tech" production methods (core idea 4). In GWE we mention that new compensation schemes, combined with different methods of dividing responsibilities between line workers and managers, have proved helpful in raising productivity in many companies. On this point I find the evidence quite convincing, but so do a large number of other economists who have contributed to or read the relevant literature, including Martin Weitzman and Alan Blinder (see the essays in Blinder, 1991). At any rate, I have never proposed any activist government policy to encourage firms to adopt these compensation or management schemes.

I agree with the idea that job switching and high employee turnover can have advantages for both workers and firms, as well as for the broader labor market. In GWE we specifically mention one of the biggest economywide advantages of high turnover, namely, the enormous flexibility of labor in the U.S. market. Job shopping can certainly improve the match between worker qualifications and employer requirements, raising worker productivity. Some policy analysts have undoubtedly called for policies to reduce employee turnover (core idea 5), but I have never endorsed that suggestion. The point of Chapter 5 in GWE is to highlight the main disadvantage of high employee turnover, which is the reduction in the firm's (and possibly the worker's) incentive to invest in worthwhile training where the payoff may not materialize for years to come. Good economists may disagree with this conclusion (see below), but it is hard to interpret our book as suggesting that job shopping and high employee turnover are socially wasteful activities, even though they do have some undesirable consequences. Our book is silent on the issue. The policy recommendations offered in GWE are intended to raise employer investments in worker training while *preserving* firms' and workers' prerogatives to sever the employment relationship at will.

Nor do I disagree with Heckman et al.'s assessment of government-sponsored manpower training programs. I have published surveys of these programs myself, and my conclusions are similar to theirs. The payoff from the programs is almost certainly positive but modest for disadvantaged adults, is questionable and possibly negative for disadvantaged teenagers, and is unknown for older adults who have suffered economic displacement. The modest success of government manpower training programs is one reason that our book emphasizes further small-scale experimentation in government-sponsored training but major reform and investment in secondary schooling and firm-based training.

I would add, however, that two types of government-sponsored training *do* seem to offer exceptionally good returns. The first is job search training, where very small investments seem to yield consistent though modest earnings gains. Even though the earnings improvements might be just $150–$300 per participant, the costs of the programs are often less than $100 per person served. A second unusually successful approach to training is public subsidy for firm-based on-the-job training, which consistently turns out to raise significantly the earnings of participants. The recent Job Training Partnership Act experiment suggests that at least part of the apparent success of the approach is the result of a genuine effect.

I share Heckman et al.'s skepticism about a number of the core ideas in the new consensus, assuming they have accurately described the ideas of other writers. We do not disagree much about the facts or in our interpretation of the facts in these areas. In other areas, our disagreements are more significant.

German Apprenticeship

I find it astonishing that sensible people interpret favorable remarks about the *training effects* of the German apprenticeship system to constitute a defense of German economic performance in general or labor market policy in particular. On page 41 of *GWE*, we show that German manufacturing productivity continues to lag behind that in the United States. We are quite familiar with the McKinsey study cited by Heckman et al. (McKinsey & Company, 1993). Martin Baily was one of the study's principal authors. Several aspects of German law and institutional arrangements increase the rigidity of the labor market and reduce the well-being of German consumers. One reason that German productivity may lag behind that of the United States, however, is that its productivity was a small fraction of U.S. productivity 40 years ago, and it takes time to catch up. According to the best available statistics, living standards and economywide productivity in western Germany continue to close in on levels in the United States.

An important reason for lower German productivity levels—one stressed in the McKinsey report—is that Germans are less enthusiastic than Americans about embracing vigorous market competition. I do not share Germans' distaste for competition. On the whole, *GWE* advocates measures that would open up U.S. markets to even greater competition or would protect the competition we already have. By contrast, German laws sometimes provide a measure of protection to current domestic producers at the expense of potential new entrants, foreign and domestic, a bias that Martin Baily, Robert Litan, and I strongly oppose.

Even granting the disadvantage Germans suffer in *average* worker productivity, Heckman et al. grossly overstate the problems of the German labor market. At the beginning of 1994, the unemployment rate in western Germany was about the same as that of the United States. It has not been consistently higher, as Heckman et al. apparently assume. The U.S. Bureau of Labor Statistics compiles monthly statistics comparing unemployment rates calculated under the U.S. definition for the major OECD countries. In January 1994, the unemployment rate in western Germany was 0.1 percent below the U.S. rate. During most of the postwar era, including all but three years of the 1980s, German unemployment was below the U.S. rate. It has often been far below the U.S. rate. The labor market rigidities rightly criticized by Heckman et al. have apparently not caused higher rates of joblessness in Germany than in the United States.

Contrary to Heckman et al.'s apparent inference, unemployment rates in western Germany are fairly evenly distributed across age groups, certainly more evenly distributed than they are in the United States. Germany is unusual among OECD economies in having a low rate of unemployment, especially among workers under the age of 30 (and not just among young people who are apprentices, as Heckman et al. suggest). Moreover, German incomes—including before-tax incomes—are significantly more evenly distributed than are U.S. incomes. The disadvantage that Germany suffers in average productivity is not reflected in the incomes received by its less-skilled workers. Richard Freeman (1993) recently calculated the comparative well-being of workers in Europe and the United States at identical points in the earnings distribution. His calculations show that a worker in the bottom decile of the U.S. distribution receives a wage that is just 45 percent of the real wage received by a worker in western Germany in the same part of the distribution. (His calculations are based on purchasing-power-parity exchange rates.) The real wage advantage of German workers extends well up the earnings distribution, and it is very sizable.

So, unemployment rates in western Germany tend to be lower than rates in the United States. German earned incomes are more equally distributed, giving poorly paid German workers a higher standard of living than their counterparts in the United States. And German real wages continue to climb. The name of our book is *Growth with Equity*, not *Growth, Regardless of Its Consequences for Equity*. I see no reason for Germans to be apologetic about their performance relative to that of the United States. On the score of equity, I see excellent reasons for Americans to feel embarrassment.

Even if rigidities in the German labor market were as serious as Heckman et al. claim, it would not follow that the German training system offers no lessons for the United States. German labor market arrangements might cause adult wages to remain fixed at uncompetitive levels, but German workers could still derive important benefits from their training system. Incidentally, I agree with Heckman et al.'s proposed explanation for the attractiveness of apprentices to German employers. Apprentices may be appealing to hire because their hourly wages are well below the comparable rates paid to older workers. But our book does not argue for wholesale adoption of German labor market institutions. Rather, it argues for establishing standards for a variety of occupations that do not require a college education and for creating incentives for firms and non-college-bound youngsters to participate in formal apprenticeship programs.

Heckman et al. do not believe that Germany's dual system has been especially effective in providing training to the German youngsters who fail to attend college. German and American employers who actually hire these apprentices do not agree. Managers with whom I have spoken believe the German graduates are better prepared for work than their American counterparts. This is evidence that I take into account but that Heckman et al. do not mention. Perhaps they do not believe it. However, their chapter offers little evidence that would cause me to change my opinion.

The evidence Heckman et al. actually offer in their chapter is not very convincing. The burden of the authors' argument is that the rate of wage growth is the same for U.S. labor market entrants and German apprentices. This seems extremely unlikely on the face of it if the authors are right that apprentice wages are only 22–33 percent of full-time regular wages. By implication, apprentices' earnings climb by a factor of 3 or 4 within a few years of their entry into the labor market. I am not aware that American entrants' wages rise this fast. Data from the National Longitudinal Survey of Youth, which I have analyzed, certainly do not show wage increases this large for U.S. dropouts or high school graduates.

If the calculation does not include the wages workers earn during their apprenticeships, then it must reflect the rate of wage increase from some year after young workers enter their first regular jobs. Under that assumption, I do not think the rate of wage growth is the correct benchmark for assessing whether apprenticeships have offered a good return. Young German workers enjoy an *immediate* earnings advantage over their American counterparts as soon as they enter regular employment. Some of that advantage stems from their better qualifications, which are attributable primarily, I would think, to their superior training under the dual system.

If German workers begin their regular careers by earning higher wages than their U.S. counterparts, it seems odd to suggest that their moderate earnings growth after entering employment provides evidence that their apprenticeship training has given them no advantage. Do competent analysts find that German and U.S. entrants' wages are (a) nearly identical and (b) growing at exactly the same rate? The original version of Heckman et al.'s chapter mentioned evidence about b. To make a convincing case, I think the authors should tell us something about a *and* b. Young German workers who have completed apprenticeships typically earn higher wages than American youngsters drawn from the equivalent part of the ability distribution. That is, apprenticeship graduates earn better wages than young American workers drawn from the same part of the distribution. If they earn higher wages, isn't it reasonable to conclude they are more productive? If so, isn't it logical to infer that the dual system has contributed to their greater productivity? Why wouldn't American youngsters benefit under a similar system?

American Bias against Firm-Based Training

I agree with Heckman et al.'s analysis of the tax incentives for investment in formal education and firm-based training. In *GWE* we show that the actual distribution of public and private investments in these two kinds of training is heavily tilted in favor of people who end up with a college education. Figure 1.7 in my chapter in this volume shows the actual distribution of public subsidies on formal schooling and public training programs received by young people between the ages of 16 and 24. These tabulations reflect spending at *all* government levels, not just at the federal level. Most public spending in this area is derived from state and local sources, so I am baffled by the emphasis in the original version of Heckman et al.'s chapter on the issue of *federal* spending on education and training. Federal spending is one part of the overall system, but it surely does not play the dominant role.

In *GWE* we also mention a fact that is well known in this literature and that Heckman et al. repeat, namely, that firm investment in training is positively correlated with a worker's educational attainment. Combining this fact with Heckman et al.'s analysis of current tax incentives for firm-based training, a strong implication emerges: *Tax subsidies for firm-based training as well as direct public spending for formal education are heavily tilted toward college graduates.*

We can argue about whether or not this is economically efficient, but there can be little question about its equity. People with the lowest educational attainment, who also happen to earn the lowest lifetime incomes, receive the smallest direct and indirect public subsidies for training. On equity grounds, a powerful case can be made for offering non-college-bound youngsters and non-college-educated adults more generous help in obtaining training. Heckman et al. may be correct that these subsidies will have smaller payoffs than subsidies for educating and training people who receive college educations. (Of course, they may be wrong about that, too.) But this does not change our analysis of the equity of the current distribution of subsidies. In fact, Heckman et al.'s analysis of the tax subsidies available to education and training strongly suggests that our book *understates* the equity case for providing more generous help to less-skilled youngsters and adults.

In *GWE*, we offer suggestions for structuring new training incentives in a way that we think offers the best prospects for high payoffs from incremental investments. A careful reading of Heckman et al.'s chapter suggests that, in some measure, the authors agree with our basic strategy. Because they are skeptical of the effectiveness of government-sponsored training, they believe training that takes place within firms offers a better prospect for good returns. We agree. That is why our proposals emphasize firm-based training.

Underinvestment in Firm-Based Training of the Less Skilled

Aside from the equity case for increased investment in the workplace skills of less-skilled workers, I see a good argument on efficiency grounds for such investments as well. The economywide gains from firm-based investments look promising—not spectacular, perhaps, but promising.

One reason for my optimism is the actual experience of Japanese firms, where both the costs and benefits of training are internal to the firm. Most observers believe that Japanese companies offering lifetime employment provide more training to their workers, especially their young workers, than do typical firms in the United States. Detailed evidence on the differences between U.S. and Japanese behavior is hard to come by. We mention some of the evidence in *GWE*. Japanese auto companies seem to devote more money to worker training than do their American counterparts. Observers in an MIT manufacturing productivity study had the same impression about training investments across a variety of industries (Dertouzos et al., 1989). I think one reason for the difference is that Japanese companies and adult workers believe their employment relationship will last for most of the worker's career. U.S. companies and workers believe their employment relationship could easily end long before the worker retires. Under these circumstances, it would be surprising if U.S. employers were willing to invest as are much in their workers, especially their young workers, as are Japanese firms.

I am not making any judgment about the overall advantages and dis-advantages of the employment systems in the two countries. The U.S. system certainly has some important advantages. I am attempting to draw inferences about the implications of current employment relation-ships for firm investments in workplace training. The payoff to such training will look more favorable to firms where the payoff period is longer. It is longer in Japan than in the United States, especially for young workers. Japanese firms invest more in training, apparently under the impression that the investment offers a good return, even when the target of the investment is an unskilled or semiskilled worker. American firms invest less in training their young, non-college-educated workers, apparently concluding that the payoff from larger investments will be small. Part of the payoff from a larger investment flows to the workers themselves or to future employers. This portion of the gain rep-resents a potential social gain from the investment that is not taken into account by U.S. employers when they are devising their training strate-gies. In support of this conjecture, we point out in *GWE* that large U.S. firms such as IBM and Ford invest more in training than do small em-ployers, presumably because the large firms can plausibly offer their new employees a better chance of lifetime employment. However, even IBM and Ford offer worse prospects for career employment than do their counterpart firms in Japan.

Heckman et al. offer the standard complaint against this kind of rea-soning. If there are benefits from training that will last beyond a worker's employment with a single employer, the worker should be willing to in-vest in such training him- or herself. This would be true if the worker could be sure of capturing all of those benefits in the form of future higher wages. It is less clear if the worker's additional skills are not rec-ognized by future employers when he or she is trying to find a job. When the extra skills are not recognized by prospective employers, part of the potential social benefit of the investment will be lost. Neither the initial employer nor the worker can capture the full potential benefit from the training investment, so less investment will be made than would occur at the social optimum. For this reason, in *GWE* we stress a strategy that forces employers to certify some of the transferable occupational skills they provide to their workers. To the degree that the certificate recog-nizes a set of skills that would be valuable to other employers, the worker can capture some or all of these benefits in the form of shorter joblessness or higher initial wages on subsequent jobs.

In addition, of course, the training available to workers on typical jobs will represent a joint decision by workers and employers; it is not a deci-sion made by workers alone. U.S. firms will devise their training strate-gies on the basis of private calculations that exclude the benefits future employers would derive from a strategy that leads to higher investment in worker skills. The only way firms could be persuaded to participate voluntarily in a strategy requiring heavy training investment is if new workers would accept initial wages below their initial productivity. (This, I suspect, is what typically occurs in Germany.) Heckman et al. are correct to point out that the minimum wage may prevent initial wages from falling low enough. It seems more likely, however, that a combination of borrowing constraints and a high rate of time preference among less-skilled workers causes many of them to prefer jobs with higher initial wages and lower training investments to jobs with low wages and heavy training investment. These are factors mentioned in *GWE*.

Of the arguments I have advanced, only one would strike most economists as outside the usual framework for evaluating public policy toward human capital investment—my view that less-skilled workers have a high rate of time preference (or, equivalently for our purposes, a short time horizon). It strikes me, however, that there is better empirical support for this proposition than there is for almost any conjecture in economics. From a libertarian perspective, an economic agent's rate of time preference should not matter. Each agent will make the best of his or her situation in light of his or her rate of time preference. For a person who cares about disparities in lifetime earnings capacity—as I do—workers' time preferences matter a great deal. The social benefits from firm-based training might easily yield a return that exceeds 10 percent. But if less-skilled workers require that early wage sacrifices yield a 20 percent or 30 percent private return, very few of them will be persuaded to accept the wage sacrifices that firm-based training would require under the current U.S. system.

In sum, I find the case that there is underinvestment in firm-based training quite convincing. Contrary to the Heckman et al.'s claim that we provide "no theoretical or empirical evidence" for underinvestment in training, *GWE* offers both theory and evidence in support of our reasoning. Our theory and evidence seem to me more persuasive than the counterclaims offered in their chapter.

Standardized Tests and Measures of Transferable Skill

I agree with Heckman et al. that the case for standardized tests of occupational skills is not so clear-cut. My reasoning is based on three arguments. First, there is an informational externality from training credentials that cannot be captured when many individual firms offer competing certificates of occupational preparation. An analogy may be helpful. Every medical school offers its own certificate of preparation. Few patients, however, can be bothered to investigate the claims of each school. A standardized national or state test helps reassure patients that, whatever the variation in preparation at different schools, each newly qualified physician has at least minimal knowledge about a range of medical conditions and their treatment. Even if the certification test is used to restrict the entry of new competitors into the market, as Heckman et al. suggest, it is beneficial to consumers that the restrictions are based on test takers' knowledge about effective medical practice, not on some criterion that is unconnected to performance (e.g., friendship with people who control entry into the occupation).

Heckman et al. suggest that employer or coworker recommendations already provide good certification of workers' skills. This strikes me as naive beyond the ordinary range of academic theorizing. Many, perhaps most, U.S. employers now routinely refuse to provide their former employees with usable letters of reference. This policy should not surprise an economist. Providing honest information to another employer carries some risk of lawsuit and brings no obvious benefits. Moreover, prospective employers who receive letters of reference for job applicants have good reasons to be skeptical of their contents. Would a sensible employer prepare a glowing letter of reference for an employee he or she hopes to retain? Would an employer provide an honest assessment of an employee he or she would be happy to be rid of?

Second, unlike Heckman et al., I am confident that governments, worker organizations, and employer groups can cooperatively define useful sets of occupational skills. This is not based on wild conjecture, as some people might assume, but on the actual success of such efforts in German-speaking countries. Heckman et al. offer an excellent description of the problems in the GED program, but this discussion does not seem particularly relevant. The GED was intended as a certificate showing mastery of some academic subjects taught in high schools; it does not test occupational skills learned in particular jobs. People who prepare applicants to take this test assure me that for many students actual test preparation involves only a couple of weeks of carefully directed study. As Heckman's pioneering research on the subject has shown, the labor market return from this level of effort is about what one would expect: very small. The occupational credentials we propose in *GWE* would require much greater investment in on-the-job and classroom training.

To be sure, many of the graduates of apprenticeship programs will find work in occupations outside of the areas in which they have been trained. As Heckman et al. point out, this occurs on a large scale in the German system. In Berlin, I am told, many people who served as baking apprentices go on to work in the pharmaceutical industry. However, contrary to the inference many readers may draw from reading Heckman et al.'s chapter, the certificate still serves a useful purpose in conveying information about the occupational qualifications of different job applicants. The apprentice bakers in Berlin, for example, apparently receive an excellent preparation for jobs in the drug industry, even though the specific focus of their preparation is in baking.

Heckman et al. argue that successful graduation from an apprenticeship simply shows employers something about workers' tenacity rather than their occupational skills. There is something in this view, certainly. But it overlooks the fact that many youngsters actually learn more in the context of work-based training than they would in the classroom settings provided by U.S. high schools and community colleges. Furthermore, the pharmaceutical industry would have no reason to favor successful *baking* apprentices over graduates of other equally demanding apprenticeship courses if it were not for the fact that the training provided to apprentice bakers is particularly transferable to drug manufacturing. The baking apprenticeship must help prepare youngsters for some kinds of work outside the baking industry, otherwise it would be very difficult to explain why bakers' apprentices are so successful finding jobs in the drug industry. I infer from this fact that the German certification system has been successful in providing and recognizing training that offers tangible benefits to employers (and, by implication, to workers).

The last reason I favor some system of certifying occupational skills is that it provides a way to measure whether employers make required investments in training. This argument cannot seem very persuasive to people who believe the optimal amount of training is already offered in the U.S. workplace. For reasons mentioned earlier, however, I think there is a good case for believing that employers and less-skilled workers invest too little in firm-based training. Baily, Litan, and I have suggested a method for boosting investment in training while trying to minimize the adverse effects of our proposed incentives. One way to determine whether firms actually make claimed investments is to measure the output of their investments. I do not see any way to measure reliably the ultimate benefit from training (higher worker productivity), but occupational certificates provide a standard for measuring an *intermediate* output of such training, namely, the number of a firm's training graduates who actually meet minimum skill requirements.

Heckman et al. are certainly correct that occupational certification involves costs. Some training may not be used later on. The tests may not measure the most appropriate mix of needed skills. The case for occupational certification rests on the belief that the informational externality from the certificate, the extra training that occurs as a result of the certificate, and the beneficial effects of certificates in monitoring firms' training activity outweigh the negative consequences mentioned. The authors are justified in claiming that this is a hard case to make in light of the spotty evidence. I think they are flatly wrong in suggesting the available evidence is stacked against the proposition that nationally recognized occupational certificates can be effective. The high wages of German apprentices upon their entry into regular jobs, especially in comparison with the meager wages received by less-skilled young Americans, provides some evidence that nationally recognized certificates of skill can be beneficial, both for workers and for employers.

Payroll Tax for Training

On training taxes, I have little to add to the discussion found in *GWE* and in my chapter in the present volume. The training tax I recommend would increase the incentive for firms to invest in training their less-skilled workers. Several features of the tax are designed to reduce the adverse effects of this proposal in comparison with a similar French tax and in comparison with the training mandate that some other observers have suggested. The tax my colleagues and I endorse does not eliminate these distortions entirely.

The only taxes I know that completely eliminate distortions are optimal taxes imposed on negative externalites. No taxes of this kind spring readily to mind. Even the taxes that support local schools and state colleges and universities generate capital and labor market distortions of some kind. Most of us believe that the benefits of the schooling outweigh the losses arising out of these distortions. National income is higher with public education than it would be without it. That is the only claim I make for the training tax my colleagues and I propose. Because we think firms and workers invest too little in firm-based training, we suggest a method for inducing them to invest more. The social benefits arising from the greater private investments are expected to raise national income, notwithstanding the adverse side effects of the imperfect incentives. Equally important, the distribution of benefits across different kinds of workers should reduce earnings inequality.

Heckman et al.'s arguments about the adverse consequences of our proposed tax apply with equal force to the taxes that finance other public activities, though I notice they do not think these distortions are worth mentioning when they describe their own preferred public policies. This omission is particularly striking when they reveal their preference for directly redistributing incomes from the best to the poorest earners. As it happens, I favor this policy, too. But if empirical research has demonstrated adverse consequences of any public policy over the past two decades, it is hard to think of a policy for which the evidence is more persuasive than it is here. High tax rates and generous income support levels cause poor breadwinners to reduce their work effort below the level it would be without any transfer payment; higher rates and more generous basic support levels cause the distortion to rise. Taxpayers, who are aware of these responses (and who probably exaggerate them), oppose making transfer payments to able-bodied adults any more generous. Because the indirect effect of a more generous income distribution policy will partly offset the intended effect of raising poor families' incomes, many ordinary voters prefer policies that help poor breadwinners to earn more on their own. I think our suggested policy will accomplish that goal.

Heckman et al. suggest that our proposed incentives for higher training investment may perversely increase earnings inequality. I hope this suggestion is meant to be facetious. It would take a very large increase in *within*-group inequality to offset the reduction in *between*-group inequality that our policies would bring about. By requiring that added training investment be concentrated on workers with less than college-level education, our proposal reduces the average difference in training between college and high school graduates. The last time I checked, college graduates earn more than high school graduates. Every orthodox theory of labor economics known to me suggests that the change in investment patterns should reduce the pay premium received by college-educated workers. Of course, some people with large incomes have not received any education beyond high school, and some college graduates are poor. If all of the extra training investments were concentrated on poorly educated workers who would have been well off without the reform, inequality *could* rise. But Heckman et al. will have to be more creative than they have been in their chapter in this volume if they want to persuade me (and most economists) that this is a realistic possibility.

Final Comments

Let me close with two comments. I am not sure what inference readers are expected to draw from the estimates of "required" training investments that Heckman et al. present near the beginning of their chapter. The calculations seem interesting and useful. Assuming a 10 percent rate of return, an investment of $426 billion is needed to restore male dropouts and high school graduates to the same relative earnings positions they enjoyed in 1979. This seems like a plausible estimate. But this figure is then compared with the $15 billion spent on the Manhattan Project. I am not sure I see the relevance of the comparison. People who believe the bomb should not have been dropped on Japan probably believe $15 billion is infinitely more than the Manhattan Project was worth.

Those who think atomic weapons form an indispensable part of our arsenal no doubt believe the Manhattan Project was a tremendous bargain. But how does information about a World War II weapons program help us decide how much money we should spend on training programs today?

The proper benchmark for thinking about a $426 billion investment is the return it will generate in higher incomes and/or reduced inequality. Of course, it is difficult to predict these benefits with any confidence. Another standard we might use is the amount of money already spent on the same or similar activities. According to the Department of Education, states and the federal government spent $337 billion on formal schooling in 1989. I presume that employers spent tens of billions (no one knows exactly how much) on training their workers. Students and workers invested some resources of their own, either in tuition payments or in foregone earnings. One way to interpret the $426 billion figure is as follows: A 10 percent increase in annual education and training investment, if maintained for 10 years and correctly targeted, could restore male dropouts and high school graduates to the relative earnings positions they enjoyed 15 years ago. Viewed from this perspective, I am not sure why the required investment seems absurdly large. If one believes the gain in earnings and improvement in income distribution are sufficiently important, one should favor the investment.

The point of the calculations might be to show that the state and federal governments are unlikely to make the "required" investments. If so, I think Heckman et al. are right. But this is hardly relevant for weighing the pros and cons of the specific proposals advanced in GWE. My coauthors and I acknowledge that our proposals will require real resources. We identify a source of revenue to pay for the additional investments. Our proposals may not have much merit, as Heckman et al. claim, but their merit should be evaluated through a comparison of expected costs with expected benefits. To imply that stylized cost estimates for a hypothetical program show colossal or gigantic spending levels without offering any sensible basis for comparison seems to me very puzzling. Every statistic about the U.S. economy is gigantic, including statistics that show how much money we spend each year on education and training.

In spite of my disagreements with much of their analysis, I am grateful to Heckman et al. for considering our proposals with so much care and seriousness. Their chapter contains a great deal of interesting information and shrewd analysis. But lurking behind some of its reasoning is a standard of evidence that would have doomed many worthwhile policies in their infancy, including compulsory public schooling and state-supported colleges. No one could prove with the rigor that Heckman et al. demand that a new training system can offer advantages over the existing one. Their criteria would not permit Abraham Lincoln to recommend land-grant colleges or allow nineteenth-century legislators to compel attendance in primary schools. I detect a kind of logic that is heavily tilted toward the status quo: Existing private arrangements *must* be efficient, because otherwise the world would look different. This approach to thinking about policy is clearly convenient for people who prosper as a result of heavy public investments in their own education and training. It might seem less appealing to people who do not share the bounty.

References

Baily, M. N., Burtless, G., and Litan, R. E. (1992). *Growth with Equity: Economic Policymaking for the Next Century*. Washington, DC: Brookings Institution.

Bishop, J. H. (1989). "Is the Test Score Decline Responsible for the Productivity Growth Decline?" *American Economic Review, 79*, 178–197.

Blackburn, M. L., Bloom, D. E., and Freeman, R. B. (1990). "The Declining Economic Position of Less Skilled American Men." In G. Burtless (Ed.), *A Future of Lousy Jobs? The Changing Structure of U.S. Wages* (pp. 31–76). Washington, DC: Brookings Institution.

Blinder, A. S. (1991). *Paying for Productivity*. Washington, DC: Brookings Institution.

Dertouzos, M. L., Lester, R. K., Solow, R. M., and MIT Commission on Industrial Productivity. (1989). *Made in America: Regaining the Productive Edge*. Cambridge, MA: MIT Press.

Freeman, R. B. (1993, November 17). "Is Globalization Impoverishing Low Skill American Workers?" Paper presented at the Urban Institute conference, Policy Responses to an International Labor Market, Washington, DC.

McKinsey & Company, Inc. (1993). *Manufacturing Productivity*. Washington, DC: McKinsey Global Institute.

Comment

James J. Heckman, Rebecca L. Roselius, and Jeffrey A. Smith

We are delighted to be charged with elevating the standards of evidence used to evaluate policy proposals. In an era of tight budgets, the loose standards common in Washington policy circles should no longer suffice to justify large-scale spending programs. The poor track record of policies supported by idle speculation should be sufficient to demonstrate that the standards of evidence need to be elevated. Henry Aaron's dictum that the worst thing one can do to a policy is to evaluate it is surely right. Few policy proposals can withstand rigorous scrutiny, and few should be adopted.

Our chapter demonstrates the flimsy evidence that undergirds the human capital policies advocated by the Brookings Institution economists and the new consensus advocates. The comment by Gary Burtless does little to bolster this evidentiary base.

We fully agree that the Brookings group does not adopt all the extreme views advocated by proponents of the new consensus. Nonetheless, the case made by the Brookings economists is not well documented. Nowhere do they prove—in any common usage of that term—that there is market failure in the provision of human capital. Nowhere do they justify the claim that investment in low-skilled adult workers is efficient either in terms of raising total output or in terms of being the best way to transfer resources to low-skill workers. Both the Brookings group and the new consensus advocates presume what should be shown—that investment in low-skill adult workers is a wise social policy. Both groups advocate specific interventions to correct undocumented market failures.

Our chapter has raised the following points: (1) The problem addressed by both groups is a large one. It is not an impossible one. Nonetheless, the scale of investment required to arrest recent developments in the labor market is staggering even assuming optimistic rates of return.

(2) No government program produces returns as high as ten percent. Zero percent is a much better estimate. Some small activities like job search assistance are worth the cost, but these programs are limited in

scale and none can be shown to be able to move substantial numbers of persons out of poverty at low cost. The sums of money proposed by the Clinton Administration to end welfare or to retrain displaced workers are trivial compared to the magnitudes required to seriously address these problems.

(3) Government training has a much lower return than private training. In part, this is due to the lower quality of trainees in government programs. While private firms may do a better job than government bureaucracies in producing training for low skill workers, there is no evidence that either private or public groups can achieve reasonable rates of return when training such workers.

Our chapter has stated the unstatable: that investment in entire groups of low-skill persons may not be worth the money. What the Brookings group and new consensus advocates take as a premise, we take as a point of contention. Nowhere has it been proved that investments in low-skill workers are efficient transfers or efficient investments. It may be better to invest in high-skill high-ability workers and tax them to subsidize the living standards of the unskilled even if the goal is equity as well as efficiency. The form of the transfer to the unskilled could be a welfare payment but in the current environment it is probably better given as a wage subsidy. Work has virtues that we discuss in our chapter.

(4) Proposals to subsidize apprenticeship programs or work-motivated learning programs have appealed to the "success" of the German apprenticeship program. No one favors wholesale adoption of that program in the U.S. labor market.

Our chapter debunks many of the myths surrounding the German system. We note that German labor productivity is lower than American labor productivity. Because many factors determine productivity, this does not prove the inferiority of the German system, but it does raise doubts about proposals to emulate it.

We present four reasons for low German youth unemployment rates that are not considered either by the new consensus group or the Brookings analysts: (1) the German apprenticeship system is like a compulsory schooling law—keeping German youth in school and out of unemployment until a later age; (2) the German apprenticeship system acts like a youth subminimum wage in a high-wage union-dominated economy; (3) German apprentices are not covered by rigid labor laws governing the dismissal of workers; and (4) competition among institutions for apprentices produces more competition in schooling than that currently found in U.S. secondary education. This could be a force for efficiency in the provision of education in the German economy.

These features of the German system are systematically ignored by the Brookings analysts and the advocates of the new consensus. It strikes us as odd that the policy lessons they claim that should be learned from the success of the German system—if indeed that is the right term—do not include suggestions for reducing minimum wages, reducing restrictions on the ability of firms to hire and fire workers and instituting choice in schools.

(5) The lessons extracted from the German system by both groups of analysts focus on the value of national skills standards and occupational testing and the value of work-based formal instruction. We do not quarrel with the proposition that additional information about workers may be useful. But a major premise of their program—that scarcity of information is a major cause of under-investment in skills, and that skills testing and certification will remedy it—remains to be demonstrated. We show that certifying skills and creating national markets for them will make firms less likely to finance worker training. Work-based learning, if instituted in the Germany style, will tend to undermine the monopoly of public school provision of vocational training and will promote competition among schools. It is an idea worth trying out on a small scale.

(6) We also argue that the case made by new consensus analysts and the Brookings economists understates the importance of unmeasured on-the-job training and unmeasured productivity gains from job shopping. This leads to a systematic bias in discussions of the imbalance between human capital investment in college-educated workers and non-college-educated workers. Many sources of skill acquisition for the latter group of workers are discounted in assessing the appropriate level of investment.

These points remain unsettled after reading Burtless' comments on our chapter. Clever statements do not substitute for solid evidence.

Comment

Laurie J. Bassi

Although there can be little disagreement with the major points made by Gary Burtless and Ray Marshall in their chapters, I would be remiss in my duties as a discussant if I didn't have some differences of opinion with the authors. Ray Marshall and I see the world somewhat differently in terms of the amount of work reorganization that is taking place within U.S. firms. Dr. Marshall does point out that a recent survey by Paul Osterman (1993) at MIT found evidence that there is a greater degree of work reorganization under way than was found by the Commission on the Skills of the American Workforce (CSAW, 1990). I, too, have surveyed firms on the extent of work reorganization—although my surveys focused almost exclusively on small and medium-size firms—and found much greater levels of work reorganization than did the CSAW (Bassi, 1993).

There are at least two possible explanations for the differences between the CSAW's findings and those of the more recent surveys conducted by Professor Osterman and myself. The first explanation is that the latter two surveys are simply more recent. If, in fact, the phenomenon being studied—the reorganization of work—is undergoing rapid change, then the findings of the CSAW, which are based on interviews done in 1989, could be very different from the findings of Osterman's survey and my own (both of which were conducted in 1992).

The second explanation is that, as Dr. Marshall points out, Osterman (as did I) used a somewhat more liberal definition of *work reorganization*. Both Osterman and I found that according to a strict definition, only a small percentage of firms are engaged in a full-blown reorganization of work. This finding is quite similar to the conclusion of the CSAW. If, however, work reorganization is characterized along a continuum, rather than as an either/or phenomenon, the estimates indicate that a much higher percentage of firms have embarked on this path.

There are at least two reasons for arguing that work reorganization should be thought of and measured along a continuum, rather than characterized as a dichotomous event. The first is that we are a long way from understanding which (if any) aspects of work reorganization are critical to the ultimate success of an organization and the economic viability of those individuals who work within it. As a result, eliminating from consideration those firms that are not engaged in each and every aspect of what analysts have come to think of as work reorganization may be a mistake. The second reason for measuring work reorganization along a continuum is that it takes time to achieve. Although it is probably true—as Dr. Marshall concludes—that nothing short of true transformation is required if firms and their employees are to thrive in the new economic area that the United States has entered, it is undoubtedly also true that transformation is not achieved overnight. Rather, it is achieved through trial and error. Firms experiment with alternative strategies—abandoning some innovations along the way, expanding others, and implementing new ones. It may well be that many of those firms that have not yet achieved what might be thought of as "transformation" are, in fact, well on their way to doing so. Excluding these firms from consideration could lead to excessively pessimistic conclusions about many of the positive reformations that are under way. This leads me to a somewhat more optimistic view about the degree of reinvention of U.S. organizations than that held by Dr. Marshall.

On the other hand, however, I am somewhat more pessimistic than both Dr. Marshall and Dr. Burtless. Neither of these authors makes any real connections among the interaction of the forces of global competition, the rising inequality of opportunity in the United States, and the social malaise that this nation has experienced for well over 20 years. I realize that such connections are difficult to make using rigorous, quantitative research methods, but it is difficult to deny their existence. The rise in the percentage of children living in female-headed households and, therefore, subject to a disproportionately high risk of spending a large percentage of their formative years in poverty coincided with the growing inequality of opportunity for young men in the labor market. It is difficult to ignore that the frightening increase in violence within the United States, the decay of our cities, the failure of our youth to thrive, and a plethora of other indicators of social trauma all seem to coincide with the deterioration of labor market conditions—especially for men and the young. There is much more at stake than the assurance of more equal opportunity in the labor market. The very fabric of a civil society rests upon the events that are taking place at work.

Although economists have much to contribute to our understanding of the events that are under way in the labor market and in the fundamental nature of work itself, the discipline of economics is also going to have to undergo a transformation if it is to be able to contribute more fully to an enhancement of our understanding of the transition we are currently experiencing. The greater our understanding of this transition, the greater will be our ability—both as individuals and as a nation—to see and seize the opportunities that are inherent in this transition, while simultaneously avoiding the potential calamities that are the other side of lost opportunity.

In the language of economics, the fundamental dilemma involved in understanding this transition is that it is being driven by three economic forces—price, quantity, and quality. Both economics and economists have focused primarily on price and quantity, which, when put together, constitute per unit costs. Our models of economic production, taught to countless economics and business students, indicate that the way to maximize profits is to minimize costs. As labor is a major cost to most firms, the costs associated with labor must, of necessity, be minimized. This is a mass-production model, in which labor is disposable.

What we have learned the hard way over the course of the past two decades is that the United States is increasingly unable to compete on this basis. Continuing on this path will take us further and further down the road to a low-wage equilibrium and a society in which despair, and the violence that accompanies it, is increasingly evident.

The alternative is to pursue a high-wage equilibrium. This requires that we begin to develop and teach models in which firms explicitly compete not only on the basis of costs, but of the basis of quality as well. Because quality is a multidimensional concept, it is evident that firms will not be able to achieve all of the dimensions of quality that their increasingly fickle customers demand of them without full engagement of their workforces. But workers, who have been treated as costs to be minimized by managers schooled—either formally or informally—in economists' models of mass production, are unlikely to be fully engaged in the exercise of satisfying each and every aspect of customers' demand for quality. The only workers who will be willing to do so will be those who perceive it to be in their self-interest; these are certainly not the workers who have been treated as disposable by their employers.

Thinking along these lines—incorporating quality into our modeling and our understanding—leads to a very different view of the role of labor. It also leads to the necessity for a different set of labor-management relations than has characterized the mass-production era of our nation's history. This "new era," in which firms are increasingly forced to compete not only on the basis of per unit costs but also on the basis of rapidly evolving, multidimensional, amorphous concepts of quality, holds great promise. It could not only lead us to a high-wage equilibrium, it could begin to heal much of the social trauma that this nation has experienced for more than two decades.

References

Bassi, L. J. (1993, Winter). "Workplace Education and the Reorganization of Work," *International Productivity Journal* pp. 21–28.

Commission on the Skills of the American Workforce (CSAW). (1990). *America's Choice: High Skills or Low Wages.* Rochester, NY: National Center on Education and the Economy.

Osterman, P. (1993, January). "How Common Is Workforce Transformation and How Can We Explain Who Adopts It?" Paper presented at the meeting of the Allied Social Science Association, Anaheim, CA.

Comment

Joel Stern

Economic Value Added: A Case for Capital Accounting

In lieu of critiquing the previous chapters, I would like to spend time discussing some substantive issues related to my business practice. At Stern Stewart & Company, we believe that the reliance on voluntary innovations in human resource management will have a substantial impact on productivity gains, efficiency, and even rates of unemployment over the long term. More specifically, management incentives linked to a business's "economic profit" is what drives enhancement of shareholder value.

At Stern Stewart we accidentally came upon this new practice area. We were originally involved in strategic planning and corporate finance, providing advice to clients in the United States and Europe. Several years ago, a company that was engaging in a management buyout approached us and asked us to devise an incentive compensation approach for senior management. My response was straightforward: I said to the CEO, "We have no idea what you are talking about. What do you want us to do?" Stern Stewart is in the shareholder value-enhancement business and we involve ourselves in financial strategy, capital structure, and similar issues. I recommended he speak to firms such as Towers Perrin, Wyatt, and Hewitt Associates about management incentive programs. The company had already sought such counsel and was not satisfied. We discussed the concept further. What they were really interested in was linking incentive compensation to value enhancement by creating discretionary "value-sharing" incentive programs. The CEO said he wanted his people to behave as if they owned shares in the company, and he wanted this feeling not just among senior management, but pervading the entire organization.

I am very happy to report to you that in the 10 years since that initial conversation we have worked with scores of companies. In fact, I have recently returned from a trip to Australia and New Zealand, where one

---

Author's Note: EVA™ is a trademark of Stern Stewart & Co., New York, New York.

company has announced it is putting our program in place. The company's share price rose to $295, up some 83 points in one day, when it announced its intention to implement a value-sharing program.

The concept behind value-sharing is not new. Virtually all well-trained microeconomists are familiar with the theory of "residual value" or "economic profit." The concept simply states that shareholder value, or true economic profit, is only created in a business when the rate of return on capital employed exceeds a prescribed minimum, which is the rate of return required by shareholders in exchange for bearing the financial and business risks.

What Stern Stewart has done is operationalize the basic theory of economic profit by developing a fully integrated framework for financial management and incentive compensation. Called "Economic Value Added" or "EVA™," Stern Stewart's EVA™ framework forces a concern for creating value to pervade the entire organization. EVA™ measures an operation's economic profitability by taking into account the one critical factor that no conventional accounting measure includes: the cost of the total capital employed in a business to produce that profit. Capital consists of fixed assets (e.g., heavy equipment, real estate, computers), so-called working capital, inventories, and receivables. The cost of that capital is the shareholder's minimum required return. EVA™ is simply net operating profit after tax (NOPAT) minus a capital charge, or the total annual cost (c^*) of capital (C) [EVA™ = NOPAT − ($c^* \times C$)]. Thus, the true economic profit of an organization is the profit after all costs have been covered, including the cost of capital.

The important difference between traditional accounting-based performance measures and EVA™ is in the recognition of the need to align the interests of employees with those of the shareholders. We used to call this "making managers into owners." However, now I simply describe it as all employees throughout the organization operating in exactly the same fashion—focusing on value. Revco Drug Stores is a brief example of how this works.

Ohio-based Revco has implemented EVA™ at its 1,200 or so stores. We typically measure success by what happens to the value of the company's shares traded in the markets (if publicly traded). Revco's shares were trading in July 1993, at approximately 11⅝ on the New York Stock Exchange. In October 1993, I received a telephone call from the Chairman. He said his company's shares were trading at 15¾. When I asked him to tell me what had happened, he said the company had carried the EVA™ program to all employees at the store manager level and above, about 1,650 or more people. Now, for the very first time, the people who run the individual stores were taking competitive bids on furniture and fixtures. They had never done that before. I asked why that was, and he said that these people had done a calculation and realized that for every dollar they saved in the process, six cents would wind up in their own pockets. I asked him why Revco had not tried such a strategy before. He explained that the company had been in bankruptcy before this new management had been brought in. And, before that, Revco had been operating in a way that confirmed exactly what Stern Stewart believes is the major problem—how companies pay their people.

If you take a look at the distribution between fixed pay and variable pay in companies, you will find that some 85 percent of the total compensation of individual managers is based on what we would call fixed pay (debt-like claims such as wages, retirement income and medical benefits), while only about 15 percent is variable pay (equity-like claims such as profit-sharing and stock options), and not even truly variable pay the way Stern Stewart defines it. This imbalance is the first problem. The second problem is that in most companies, a manager's fixed pay is tied, in a sense, to his "Hay point" count. Hay Associates (compensation consultants) recommends that wages be tied to the size of the business managed. Thus, the way for a manager to get more pay is to grow the business, regardless of the impact on shareholder value.

We believe that if a company implements an EVA™ incentive program, both of these problems will be resolved. What Stern Stewart has tried to do is to encourage companies to change the distribution between fixed pay and variable pay. To truly align the interests of management and shareholders, the debt-equity balance must be closer to 50-50. However, in order to get managers to take on more equity-like risk, they must be offered greater potential reward. By offering a value-sharing program such as EVA™ where they receive a portion of the increment they generate, greater rewards can be achieved at no extra cost to the shareholders. As shareholders must receive their required return before incremental EVA™ is generated, management does not win unless shareholders win.

The size issue is also resolved, because with an EVA-based incentive plan there are only three basic ways to achieve increases in incentive pay—all, by definition, aligned with shareholder value. One simply needs to look at the definition of EVA™ in a different way. The "operating" definition of operating profit less a capital charge [$EVA™ = NOPAT - (c^* \times C)$] can be rearranged into a "hurdle rate" definition, or the rate of return on capital (NOPAT/Capital) less the minimum required return (c^*) times the amount of capital employed [$EVA™ = (r - c^*) \times C$].

With this definition, you find that it no longer pays to increase the size of the organization (e.g., invest more Capital) simply for the sake of size alone. Under EVA™, the only investments that will be made are for those projects where returns will exceed the minimum required return, thereby enhancing value for shareholders. The second thing to recognize is that a manager does not have to grow a business in order to achieve incentive goals. If he holds net assets constant, he can still increase EVA™ by improving the productivity of the existing asset base (e.g., increase return). And finally, where the rates of return are inadequate, relative to the prescribed minimum, a manager will be incentivized to quickly get rid of businesses with insufficient returns (with no chance of improvement) by selling them to users who can achieve higher returns on those very same assets. So all three techniques are available to earn additional incentive pay. Yet, this can only be achieved by increasing the productivity and efficiency of the entire organization.

EVA™'s strong link to stock prices is one of its most powerful properties. The two numbers move up and down together. In fact, empirical research has shown that changes in EVA™ account for nearly 50 percent of changes in share prices, a more direct link than any conventional accounting measure—earnings, EPS, ROE, even cash flow.

There are hundreds of corporate units, representing scores of companies, across the American industrial system, Western Europe, South Africa, Australia, and New Zealand that use EVA™ or value-sharing incentive programs. What we have found is exactly the same everywhere. The major reason EVA™ works is that we structure incentive awards based on a combination of absolute EVA™ and improvements in EVA™. Even if the EVA™ starts out negative, a manager can still earn awards by making it less negative. One major feature of this approach is that the company pays out only one-third of any declared bonus in the current year. The other two-thirds are held back in a deferred account, or "bonus bank," that is subject to loss if the results that produced the declared bonus in the first place are not sustained. This way, managers are working with rolling three-year periods, fostering an environment focused on continuous improvement in value enhancement.

A second feature is that there are no caps on the bonuses. We do not want anybody holding back on this year's performance and saving it for next year just because they have reached their bonus maximum. We want people to try their best to achieve maximum results now. And, shareholders are protected against accidents of good luck (e.g., overall industry improvements), which may cause enormous awards declared to the bonus bank. The lion's share of the bonus declaration is subject to loss in future years if the gains are not sustainable over the long term.

The implementation of our system at The Quaker Oats Company offers an excellent illustration of EVA™ principles in action. The cereal industry is measured by price relatives such as price-to-earning ratios. The number-one company for decades has been Kellogg's at about 23 times earnings. Numbers two and three in the industry were General Mills and Ralston Purina, at some 19 and 17 times earnings, respectively. The stepchild of the industry was The Quaker Oats Company. In July 1991, Quaker implemented an EVA™ system throughout the organization for plant managers and above. The results are truly startling. The operating results are up 81 percent since EVA™ inception. The share value is up 75 percent, and the PE ratio is competing with the number two and number three companies in the industry. The price-earnings ratio is up almost 70 percent. What has this company done differently? It has stopped a common industry practice called "trade loading." What used to happen was that inventory was pushed out to trade customers during the fourth quarter, allowing a company to record sales, thereby inflating earnings for very strong fourth-quarter results. Halting such a practice has created much smoother production cycles, lessened the need for extensive inventory build-up, and consequently tied up much less capital. The EVA™ improvement from greater efficiency was a key driver of the stock price takeoff.

Another good example of the effectiveness of an EVA™ program can be found in the CSX Company in Richmond, Virginia. CSX is making do with a locomotive fleet of 100 instead of the previous 150, and a $70 million reduction in capital. How? En route from New Orleans to Jacksonville, Florida, four locomotives used to power trains at 28 miles/hour. But the trains arrived at midnight, long before their cargo was loaded onto trucks or freighters. Spurred by the EVA™ imperative, CSX decided to run the trains at 25 miles/hour with only three locomotives and arrive three hours later, still in plenty of time to be unloaded at 4:00 or 5:00 am. The three locomotives also use some 25 percent less fuel than four. The company's EVA™ was $10 million in 1992 and, as of this writing, on track to triple in 1993. Wall Street has noticed as well. CSX stock was $28 when the firm introduced EVA™; as I write this, it is $75.

I am not aware of a single publicly-traded company that has implemented the EVA™ framework that has not increased its share price by more than 100 percent within four years. And, in some cases, such as Coca-Cola, it has quadrupled in value, with two 2-for-1 stock splits during a five-year period. EVA™ shows there is absolutely no need for further intervention and regulation of incentive compensation on the part of government and well-meaning labor economists who want government to be larger. We are interested in a voluntary program in which we, as innovators, show our clients that it is in everyone's interest to enhance the value of the shareholder's investment. And, the only way to accomplish this is to empower workers throughout the entire organization.

We are currently working with a company that has operations in Europe and South Africa. During some recent meetings, the chairman invited us to have tea at the mid-morning break. A woman came in to serve the tea and then left. The chairman turned to me and said, "We want the tea woman to be on the program too. There are to be no exceptions to this throughout the organization." I quickly responded, "Do you realize there will be less tea in the tea bags if she goes on the program?" He admitted that it is entirely possible that no tea drinking would be going on. Having everyone from the "tea woman" to the CEO on the same incentive plan offers a powerful motivator to propel the organization to enhance value. My point is that the relative value of EVA™ programs have been confirmed by the capital markets as well.

A government agency has implemented EVA™ in Johannesburg, South Africa—the South African Institute for Medical Research. When a group of pathologists introduced me to their workers, I asked, "What am I doing here? All the hospitals are owned by the government. All the diagnostic testing is being done by your laboratories with your pathologists. Why do you need anything along the lines that we suggest?" They answered that this was true until about five years ago, when a group of private pathologists decided to go into competition with the government group. Recently, a representative of the Institute contacted me and reported that economic returns since July 1993 are up 27 percent. I asked him what he thought had caused the run up. He said, "It's empowerment, it's decentralization, it's paying people as if they were owners, even if they are messengers on a bicycle delivering samples to the physician." EVA™ works.

PART TWO

Sources of Employment Growth: Sectors, Size, and Reasons

Introduction

The session, "Sources of Employment Growth: Sectors, Size, and Reasons," was assembled to clarify the debate about what types of firms have been creating jobs over the past decade or so. There have been two views on this. David Birch was the leading proponent of the notion that most new jobs came from small firms. As he said in his 1987 book, *Job Creation in America*, "indeed, pulling it all together, we can see that very small firms [1–19 employees] have created about 88 percent of the net new jobs in the period considered [1981–1985]" (p. 16). His figures show that firms with fewer than 100 employees created more than 100 percent of all new jobs, because job creation was negative for firms with 100–4,999 employees. At the high end, firms with 5000+ employees created 4.7 percent of new jobs.

The Birch view is reinforced by readily available national employment statistics. For example, although total nonagricultural employment has grown in the United States by 20.8 million since 1979, employment in the Fortune 500 Industrials has fallen by 4.6 million over the same period. Because the Fortune 500 has been synonymous with "large firms," Birch's point seems to be confirmed even if in a sense we are comparing apples and oranges, as we shall see below.

On the other side of this debate are Charles Brown, James Hamilton, and James Medoff, whose 1990 book, *Employers Large and Small*, said, "Perhaps the most widespread misconception about small businesses in the United States is that they generate the vast majority of jobs and are therefore the key to economic growth.... Small employers do not create a particularly impressive share of jobs in the economy, especially when we focus on jobs that are not short-lived" (pp. 1–2).

How can this disagreement be resolved? There are a myriad of definitional problems, the first being what we mean by "small" and "large." Does "small" mean fewer than 20 employees, fewer than 100, fewer than 500 (the Small Business Administration cutoff) or any firm not in the Fortune 500? Moreover, when do we determine the size of a firm: at the beginning of the period during which we are looking at job creation or destruction, or at the end of the period? Or, should we average these two numbers, or even take an average over a number of periods? Additionally, the question arises as to whether size should be measured at the plant or firm level.

Confusion also arises over gross versus net job creation: What if a firm creates 100 new jobs in sales, but reduces administrative positions by the same amount? And, what if a small firm creates some jobs in one year but closes down the next year? Must a job have a certain amount of durability before it counts as being created?

The debate also relies heavily upon the data used. If the universe of firms is not included, how would the addition of missing ones affect the results? If we focus on only one sector, like manufacturing, can we expect that generalizations hold for other sectors? Here the answer is probably no, because it appears that small firms probably have a different role and importance in the service sector than in manufacturing. Large firms account for the bulk of the job base in manufacturing, but this is less the case in other sectors.

Finally, the evidence can be skewed depending upon the time period studied. If job creation in small firms is affected significantly by access to outside capital, for example, we would be more likely to observe higher net job creation in the mid-1980s when outside capital was available to these firms, than in the late 1980's and early 1990s when FIRREA and other regulations, along with the recession and possibly other factors, effectively reduced the flows of capital to noninvestment grade companies.

The issue of what types of firms create jobs is important for a number of reasons. As new firms and small firms are more likely to fail than are established, larger firms, jobs created by the former are less likely to endure and to provide job security. Moreover, different size firms offer different fringe benefits, and so the "quality" of new jobs might differ depending upon where they are created. It is generally assumed that job quality, particularly in regard to fringe benefits, is better in larger firms.

Much current and prospective public policy gives special consideration to small business in regard to exemptions from some taxes and regulations and by providing certain subsidies. Other regulatory policies harm small firms by initially creating artificial scale economies. Of course, the impact of these policies depends upon how "small" is defined. Thus, it is important to understand the special contributions small business make to our economy and society. If the special treatment is based upon the notion that most new jobs come from small businesses, we must be certain that is in fact the case.

Thus, MIJCF invited papers by the leading protagonists on each side of the "size" debate (that is, David Birch and James Medoff) along with a relative newcomer, Steven Davis. Birch and Medoff decided to collaborate in an effort to find common ground in the debate. Davis took a somewhat different approach and used new data to answer similar questions.

The agreement reached by Birch and Medoff is that (1) the relative role of smaller firms in generating jobs varies enormously from time to time and place to place; (2) most small firm job creation occurs within a relatively few firms—the "Gazelles;" and (3) there is a great and growing instability in our nation's stock of jobs due to the rapidly changing fates of United States firms. The real question their chapter raises is how to identify these Gazelles before the fact. Is there a way to help potential Gazelles thrive and prosper? Or, is any attempt to identify potential Gazelles merely industrial policy that is difficult to implement and therefore doomed to failure.

Steven Davis, along with his co-authors John Haltiwanger and Scott Schuh, report new evidence on the relationship between employer size and job growth that clashes sharply with the conventional wisdom–particularly that suggested by David Birch in work published prior to his chapter in this volume. Davis et al. find that large firms and plants in terms of volume dominate the creation and destruction of jobs in the U.S. manufacturing sector. While gross job creation rates are substantially higher for small plants and firms, so are gross job destruction rates. They find no strong or systematic relationship between net job growth rates and either firm or plant size. Although they hold open the possibility that data from the nonmanufacturing sector might reinstate the "small firm" idea, they attribute the "conventional wisdom" about their job creating powers to faulty analysis by previous observers. They also argue against preferential tax, subsidy, or regulatory treatment of small business.

The two chapters are followed by discussions by Robert Bednarzik of the U.S. Department of Labor and Barry Rogstad of the American Business Conference. These authors explore the policy implications of the chapters as well as add their own perspectives.

Bednarzik looks at the extent of job growth in the recovery from the recent economic downturn and finds, among other things, that the current recovery has been accompanied by weak growth in high quality jobs. Nevertheless, United States employment growth looks strong in comparison to Europe over the longer haul (1960–1994). Contrary to what occurs in other OECD countries, more job creation and destruction is accounted for by firms being born or dying in the United States, rather than by existing firms expanding or contracting. Most countries' jobless rates were higher than in the United States in 1992, with joblessness in most all countries being worse for low-skilled workers.

Bednarzik's recommendation is that the government keep out of the way rather than do anything to promote Gazelles, which are usually unstable anyway. Also, the government should establish rules to facilitate job transfers, making it easier to change jobs while remaining employed through such methods as education/training, portability of pensions and health care plans, and labor market information systems.

Barry Rogstad stresses that size of firm is not a meaningful descriptor in job creation. The companies with which he deals do not think the government is the chief determinant of their bottom line. He looks to globalization, finding the appropriate "niche business," and weeding out lines that are no longer competitive as the keys to firm growth and job creation. These factors are independent of firm size.

Rogstad points out that most policy discussions in Washington today have implications for job creation, and he argues that policy makers should be aware of how every proposal might affect job creation by different types of firms.

4

Gazelles

David Birch and James Medoff

Perhaps the most pressing need in the United States today is the creation of jobs (Medoff, 1992). Although the economy as a whole has been quite anemic as a job generator, there are some firms that are exceptions to this rule. These companies, which have been labeled Gazelles (Birch, Hagerty, and Parsons, 1993), can be thought of as vehicles for providing good jobs to our labor market. But what do we know about these Gazelles? What do they look like? How can we best discover them? What public policies should be adopted so they can generate still more greatly needed jobs?

In all honesty, we cannot at this time give in-depth responses to these queries. But we do know something about Gazelles. The purpose of this chapter is to share our knowledge; to state what we know and to admit what we do not. The chapter is divided into three sections. In the first, we document the very troubling "great American job shortage." In the second section, we describe the piece's protagonists: the Gazelles. In the final section we offer some conclusions and some suggestions for future investigations.

The Great American Job Shortage

A recent study conducted for then-Senator Lloyd Bentsen found evidence indicating that the amount of hiring activity per unemployed worker plummeted in the years after 1980 (Medoff, 1992). Table 4.1 vividly displays the severity of the need for jobs. The civilian unemployment rate (UR) figures in the table are from the U.S. Bureau of Labor Statistics (BLS); the normalized help-wanted index (NHWI) is based on the Conference Board of New York's help-wanted index divided by the payroll employment index provided by the BLS. The last column in Table 4.1 indicates how many jobs exist per unemployed worker. For example,

TABLE 4.1
The Post-1980 Shortage of Jobs for the Unemployed

Year:Quarter	Civilian Unemployment Rate (UR)	Normalized Help-Wanted Index (NHWI)	NHWI/UR
1980	7.1	100.0	14.1
1984	7.5	97.3	13.0
1991	6.7	60.7	9.1
1992	7.4	59.4	8.0
1993:2	7.0	62.5	9.0

Source: UR figures from U.S. Bureau of Labor Statistics (1993); NHWI figures are from Conference Board of New York (1993).

in 1980 there were 14 jobs for each person who was unemployed, whereas in 1992 the ratio dropped to 8 jobs per person.

The data shown in Table 4.1 also point out that although unemployment rates may be similar, alone this figure cannot serve as an accurate measure of the labor market's health. Rather, by using the UR and the NHWI together, we can get a more reliable indication of the state of the labor market.

The post-1980 sharp decline in the NHWI/UR ratio motivated James Tobin, a Nobel Prize-winning Yale economist, to look closely at job creation in a presentation he made to the Joint Economic Committee on February 1, 1993. He noted that whereas in the 20 months after the November 1982 trough the change in employment was about 6.5 million new jobs created, in the 20 months after the trough of March 1992 the change was only about 0.5 million. These findings are consistent with the data presented in Table 4.1.

It is also important to look at the categories of workers that have been hardest hit by the shortage of jobs. Katharine Bradbury (1993) of the Federal Reserve Bank of Boston was one of the first to note that many of these newly unemployed came from occupations (and industries) in which median pay was relatively "low." Among all occupations, the group that suffered the largest growth of unemployment was that comprising "managers and professionals" (from 795,000 to about 1 million). This group, of course, is on average "very well paid" and thus attracted a great deal of media attention. Much less discussed was the fact that the only other occupational group that suffered increased unemployment between 1983 and 1992 comprised those in the on-average "poorly paid" "technical, sales, and administrative" (T,S,A) category (in which unemployment grew from 2.1 million to 2.3 million).

TABLE 4.2.
Long Unemployment among Low-Pay White-Collar Workers

Year:Quarter	Civilian Unemployment Rate (percentages)	Percentage of Unemployed in Each Occupational Group Who Were Unemployed 15 weeks and More		
		C	S	T,S,A
1971	5.9	23.1	22.0	NA
1977	7.1	28.0	28.3	NA
1982[a]	9.7	31.4	29.2	30.3
1983	9.5	NA	NA	36.6
1984	7.5	NA	NA	29.4
1992	7.4	NA	NA	37.4
1993:2	7.0	NA	NA	36.2

[a] Separate figures for the C, S, and T,S,A groups were produced in 1982 for comparison.

Source: U.S. Bureau of Labor Statistics (dates as shown). Note: NA = not available.

In the past two decades, those in the economically very vulnerable T,S,A group, which prior to 1983 was divided roughly into the "clerical" (C) plus "sales" (S) groups, have had great difficulty in securing employment and earnings, as indicated in Table 4.2. These figures demonstrate forcefully that, since 1980, unemployed workers in the near-poverty and economically quite insecure T,S,A group have found it harder and harder to earn a living and, by so doing, avoid crossing the poverty line. For example, in 1971 about 22 percent of clerical and sales workers were unemployed for 15 weeks or more. By 1992, that figure was up to 37.4 percent.

Those in the T,S,A group, however, were not the only vulnerable workers who suffered long spells of joblessness. This is supported by the fact that unemployed workers whose predicted earnings (based on age, sex, race, state of residence, and SMSA status) placed them in the third and fourth deciles from the bottom of the entire predicted earnings distribution had greater difficulty in gaining employment in May of 1992 than they did in May of 1979. Using 1992 dollars, people in the third and fourth deciles from the bottom earn between $15,000 and $20,000 a year.

Current Population Survey microdata, summarized in Table 4.3, demonstrate that the percentage of the unemployed in the third-from-the-bottom predicted earnings decile who were unemployed for 15 weeks or more rose by 4.7 percentage points, from 25.6 to 30.3 percent between 1979 and 1992. The analogous percentages for the fourth-from-the-bottom decile are 33.7 and 37.5, indicating a 3.8 percentage point increase. The fact that the unemployed workers in the third- and fourth-lowest

TABLE 4.3
Long Unemployment among Low-Predicted-Earnings Unemployed

Year:Month	Third-Lowest Predicted Earnings Decile	Fourth-Lowest Predicted Earnings Decile
1979:May	25.6	33.7
1984:May	27.1	35.4
1992:May	30.3	37.5

Source: U.S. Bureau of Labor Statistics (1993).

predicted earnings deciles had predicted earnings that in 1992 dollars were only $15,000 to $20,000 lends credence to the contention that a long spell of unemployment could lead to poverty. These unemployed individuals could be expected to have real economic problems after 15 or more weeks of joblessness.

Labor market facts of this nature help us understand why the percentage of persons in poverty *rose* by 3.1 percentage points (from 11.4 percent to 14.5 percent) between 1978 and 1992. To put this number in some historical perspective, note that from 1967 to 1978 the percentage of persons in poverty *fell* by almost the same number of percentage points, from 14.2 percent in 1967 to 11.4 percent in 1978. Another indicator of the health of the labor market is the consumer confidence index; since 1973, this index has *dropped* 37 percent.

Common Ground

Over the past decade there has been much debate about what size firms generate the most new jobs for U.S. workers. Thanks primarily to third parties, we have frequently been drawn into this battle. Before we go any further, let us state the three key "facts" of this matter about which we agree fully.

First, the relative role of smaller firms in generating jobs varies enormously from time to time and place to place. If one had to pick an average number of new jobs generated by firms employing 100 or fewer employees, it would be about 67 percent (versus their 45 percent share of the existing job base). However, this percentage has varied quite widely—from about 40 to about 140—depending on cyclical conditions.

Second, most small-firm job creation occurs within a relatively small number of firms—the Gazelles. During the 1988–92 period, among ongoing firms, 4 percent of all firms (about 350,000) created 70 percent of the jobs. Ongoing firms, in turn, accounted for 83 percent of all new jobs.

The Gazelles thus accounted for about 60 percent of all new jobs in the economy, with the remaining 40 percent being divided more or less evenly between the other (96 percent) ongoing firms and the net of starts over closings.

Third, there is a great and growing instability in our nation's stock of jobs because of the rapidly changing fates of U.S. firms. An examination of the set of Fortune 500 firms over the past three decades shows this clearly. In the 1950s and 1960s, for example, it took 20 years for one-third of the Fortune 500 to be displaced from the list; in the 1970s it took 11 years; in the 1980s it took only 5 years. Will Dell and AST and Gateway ever become as large as IBM and Digital and Wang were at their peaks? Will they stay in the Fortune 500 (they are all there now) as long? Or must we count on a constant replacement of one set of firms by another? Will Gateway fall prey to Acer before anyone learns what Gateway is, much less Acer? To answer these questions we must know much more than we currently do about the success and failure of our nation's firms.

The Gazelles

The relative roles of large and small firms are of only modest importance, because most jobs are created by firms that are neither large nor small. These Gazelles move between small and large quickly—at various times in either direction—and to classify them by their size is to miss their unique characteristics: great innovation and rapid job growth. What else do we know about them?

First, most of them start from small bases. As Table 4.4 indicates, the 4 percent that dominated growth during the 1989–92 period began very small and grew. Although most gazelle firms started small, those few that started with more than 100 people accounted for more than one-fourth of the new jobs.

TABLE 4.4
The Distribution of Gazelles by Starting Employment Size

Starting Employment Size	Percentage of Gazelles	Percentage of Gazelle Job Growth
1–4	43	19
5–19	41	29
20–99	13	25
100+	3	27

Source: Birch, Hagerty, and Parsons (1993).

In 1993, the average size of a Gazelle firm was 61 employees. Overall, Gazelles employ roughly 20 million Americans. Clearly, they are a nontrivial force in the economy. In fact, they employ more workers than the manufacturing sector does, but not many Gazelles are in manufacturing. In fact, there is no particular sector of the economy that is producing Gazelles. Contrary to much popular mythology, "high tech" accounts for only 2.5 percent of this group of firms. The rest are predominantly appliers of technology, not creators of it. They are found in health care, fish wholesaling, textiles, shoe and boot manufacturing, lettuce growing, cookie making, "yuppie" clothing retailing, car lubricating, and oil exploration, to mention only a few. If there is any pattern, it is that every industry has roughly the same proportion of its firms innovating and growing at a rapid rate.

Another characteristic of Gazelle firms is that they are extremely volatile. Over any two- or three-year period the best predictor of Gazelle decline is present growth, the best predictor of growth is present decline, and the best predictor of death is stability. These firms are inherently unstable. They are constantly taking risks, making mistakes, being pressured by other Gazelles in their industries (and being pounced upon with every misstep), and succeeding brilliantly when everything goes right. If, by chance, they try to "bottle it" and strive for stability, their odds of failing double.

Gazelles are not indifferent regarding where they locate. Cognetics, an economics research firm, has found that Gazelles seek places where skilled workforces want to live and where managers have easy home-to-work commutes (Birch, Hagerty, Parsons, and Rossell, 1993). This set of needs now strongly favors a relatively few places in the South and the West. Hawaii, Nevada, Georgia, Utah, and North Carolina top the list of states; Charlotte, Atlanta, Indianapolis, Nashville, and Raleigh-Durham are the most entrepreneurial cities. Interestingly, all but one of the cities listed in Table 4.5 are hub sites for major airlines. Further, almost all of the smaller cities are home to major universities. The location of Gazelle firms reflects the fact that their employees travel extensively and that the firms are global traders that rely on the intellectual core of universities.

Within cities, Gazelles are, in most cases, moving as far away from the centers as they can get and still be near airports, highways, and universities—to the places Joel Garreau had labeled "edge cities." In the process, they are leaving behind the Americans most in need of employment.

If neither size nor industry has much to do with Gazelle success, what does? We observe, anecdotally, that Gazelles tend to be dominated by single strong individuals (or families). An Wang, Ken Olsen, Edwin Land, Bill Marriott, Sam Walton, Bill Norris, Bill Gates, Thomas Watson, Joseph Wilson, Steve Jobs, Debbie Fields, and Fred Smith all come immediately

TABLE 4.5
Top 10 Entrepreneurial Cities

Rank	Metro Area
1	Charlotte, NC
2	Atlanta, GA
3	Indianapolis, IN
4	Raleigh-Durham, NC
6	Milwaukee-Racine-Sheboygan, WI
7	Salt Lake City-Provo, UT
8	Orlando, FL
9	Washington, DC-MD-VA
10	Birmingham-Tuscaloosa, AL

Source: Cognetics.

to mind. These are only a few of the most obvious and extreme examples of a generic tendency for an individual to play a strong role in exploring new and different territory where no collective, professionally managed firm would dare to wander. What professionally managed firm in its collective right mind would propose to bring a parcel from Boston to Memphis in order to deliver it in Worcester the next morning? In many cases, the useful life of the individual is the useful life of the firm. Many of the individuals just mentioned no longer lead the firms they started and grew, and many of these same firms are no longer growing.

To understand Gazelles, we must understand their founders and leaders. What do we know about these people? Not much. We have little sense of where they come from, why they do what they do, how they do it (from a management style perspective), and why they ultimately give it up. These are all questions we badly need answers to if we are to encourage the processes seen in Gazelles.

There are more global questions about Gazelles:

1. What are Gazelles' taxpaying habits? As companies, are they major taxpayers, or do they plow surplus revenue back into the business and avoid paying taxes whenever possible? Are the owners of Gazelles motivated more by income or by wealth? What tax structure would encourage them most?

2. What kinds of employers are they? Do they attract and hold skilled workers through superior wages, benefits, and working conditions, or do they grow at the expense of people who work for them?

TABLE 4.6
Preliminary Data on Benefits in Gazelles

Firm Type	Percentages of Firms Providing	
	Health Plan	*Retirement Plan*
Large firms	100	79
Gazelles	67	37
Small firms	44	25

Source: Cognetics.

3. How stable are the jobs that Gazelles create? We already know that, in general, their aggregate trajectory looks like a roller coaster. How does this affect the individual employee and his or her need for security?

Table 4.6 displays some preliminary survey data that suggest that Gazelles lie midway between large and small firms when it comes to providing basic employee benefits. Gazelle firms are beginning to emulate large firms in terms of providing health plans to their employees; however, the percentage of Gazelles offering retirement plans more closely resembles small firms. Clearly, we still have many unanswered questions regarding the nature of these (and other) benefits and the extent of employer contribution in each case.

In sum, Gazelles are a likely source of the significant job growth necessary for a full U.S. economic recovery. What public policies will facilitate this growth? This question must be addressed rigorously by U.S. policy makers.

Conclusion

The "great American job shortage" is very deleterious to the economic health of our country. One group of very rapidly growing firms—the Gazelles—can do much for our economic well-being. Therefore, it is essential that we learn enough to establish early identification and support for these job generators. There are very compelling economic reasons for doing so. However, we must fully understand that the jobs created by any new firm (including Gazelles) are likely to be here today and gone five years from now.

References

Birch, D., Hagerty, A., and Parsons, W. (1993) *Who's Creating Jobs?* Cambridge, MA: Cognetics.

Birch, D., Hagerty, A., Parsons, W., & Rossell, G. (1993) *Entrepreneurial Hot Spots.* Cambridge, MA: Cognetics.

Bradbury, K. L. (1993, July 23). "Note on Shifting Patterns of Regional Employment and Unemployment." Mimeo, Federal Reserve Bank of Boston.

Conference Board. (1993). Data available upon request.

Garreau, J. (1988). *Edge City: Life on the New Frontier.* New York: Doubleday.

Medoff, J. L. (1992, April). "The New Unemployment." Mimeo.

Tobin, J. (1993, February, 1). Presentation made to the Joint Economic Committee.

U.S. Bureau of Labor Statistics. (Various dates). Data available upon request.

5

Small Business and Job Creation: Dissecting the Myth and Reassessing the Facts

Steven J. Davis, John Haltiwanger, and Scott Schuh

Few ideas about the U.S. economy reap greater homage in public discourse than the belief that small businesses are the fountainhead of job creation. Claims about the job-creating prowess of small business appear with remarkable regularity in a wide range of public pronouncements, including speeches by prominent politicians, newspaper columns by leading opinon makers, statements from the U.S. Small Business Administration, and assessments by well-known analysts such as David Birch. Exhibit 5.1 contains a sampling of these claims.[1] As these quotations illustrate, claims about small business's ability to generate jobs are frequently presented as justification for tax incentives, regulatory policies, and other government programs that favor the small business sector.

But it is not only the public discourse that motivates our interest in the relationship between employer size and job creation. Previous academic research has convincingly established strong connections between employer size and important economic outcomes such as the level and inequality of wages, the incidence of fringe benefits, workforce quality,

Author's Note: This chapter draws heavily on our forthcoming book, *Job Creation and Destruction in U.S. Manufacturing.* We gratefully acknowledge the generous support of the National Science Foundation and the U.S. Bureau of the Census. In preparing the data for this study, we have greatly benefited from the assistance of Bob Bechtold, Mark Doms, Tim Dunne, Cyr Linonis, Bob McGuckin, Jim Monahan, Al Nucci, Arnie Reznek, Ken Troske, and other Census Bureau employees at the Center for Economic Studies. Steve Strongin and Janice Weiss provided helpful comments on a previous draft. Laura Power and Lucia Foster provided excellent research assistance. The views expressed in this chapter are our own, and do not necessarily reflect official positions of the Census Bureau or the Federal Reserve System.

EXHIBIT 5.1 Small Business and Job Creation: Reciting the Conventional Wisdom

From 1970 to 1980 small businesses accounted for most of the 20 million new jobs generated in the United States.

Leonard Silk, *New York Times*, April 9, 1986

Little companies currently employ 53% of the total U.S. work force, and during the past decade created virtually all net new jobs.

Adam Zagorin, *Time*, July 12, 1993

Small firms created virtually all new jobs between 1988 and 1991.

David Birch, Cognetics Inc. press release, 1993

As always, the key [to job creation] is to spur hiring by new companies, the small businesses of fewer than 500 workers that accounted for fully two-thirds of job creation in the 1980s.

Stephen Roach, *New York Times*, March 14, 1993

Clearly, the smallest firms have become recognized as the most dynamic growers in the economy.

Bruce Phillips, *Business Economics*, 1993

Small businesses have created virtually all of the new jobs in our country in the last ten years. Their inability to create more jobs than larger employers have been shedding is the central cause of stagnant employment in America.

President Bill Clinton in a speech to U.S. mayors, March 1993
(quoted by Steven Greenhouse, *New York Times*, March 28, 1993)

Moreover, government regulation tends to be especially burdensome to small business, which created most of the jobs in the 1980s.

Henry F. Meyers, *Wall Street Journal*, March 8, 1993

Small businesses have become the superstars of job creation, producing up to 80 percent of new jobs in recent years.... Considering the success of small businesses in today's service sector and their willingness to take on and retain new employees, it would be innovative and economically sound for the Clinton Administration and Congress to give business a tax credit for hiring additional people.

Muriel Siebert, *New York Times*, January 6, 1992

The large increase in the effective tax rate on many small firms is likely to retard the economy's recovery momentum because small firms account for practically all the job creation in the U.S. economy.

David Hale, *Wall Street Journal*, July 30, 1993

Because small business has created such a high percentage of all the new jobs in our nation over the last 10 or 15 years, our plan includes the boldest targeted incentives for small business in history. We propose a permanent investment tax credit for the small firms in this country.

President Bill Clinton, 1993 State of the Union Address

(continues)

EXHIBIT 5.1 *(continued)*

> We agree with the President that we have to put more people to work, but remember this: 80 to 85 percent of the new jobs in this country are created by small business. So the climate for starting and expanding businesses must be enhanced with tax incentives and deregulation, rather than imposing higher taxes and more governmental mandates.
>
> Representative Robert Michel, House minority leader, in the
> Republican response to the 1993 State of the Union Address
>
> What do Bill Clinton, George Bush and Bob Dole have in common? All have uttered one of the most enduring homilies in American political discourse: That small businesses create most of the nation's jobs. This old chestnut got a heavy workout recently as Washington wrangled over the $500 billion budget package. Clinton invoked it to defend an equipment-purchase tax break aimed mostly at small businesses; Republicans cited it while denouncing the packages's tax hike on upper-income earners.
>
> Susan Dentzer, *U.S. News & World Report*, August 16, 1993

the pace of technological innovation, and the likelihood of unionization (see, e.g., Acs and Audretsch, 1988; Brown and Medoff, 1989; Brown et al., 1990; Davis and Haltiwanger, 1991, 1992; Hansen, 1992). These findings prompt us to ask how job creation and destruction behavior varies by employer size. In this chapter, we address that question for the U.S. manufacturing sector.

We also evaluate the empirical basis for conventional claims about the job-creating prowess of small businesses. In this regard, we develop two sets of conclusions:

1. *The conventional wisdom about the job-creating prowess of small businesses rests on misleading interpretations of the data.* One common error entails the use of changes in the size distribution of employment to draw inferences about the relationship between job creation and employer size. A second problem—the regression fallacy—leads to overly favorable assessments of small business job creation whenever measurement error or transitory employment movements are present in the data. Finally, a common confusion between net and gross job creation distorts the overall job creation picture and hides the enormous number of new jobs created by large employers.

2. *The most widely cited studies of job creation rely upon unsuitable data.* We review previous research that documents severe data problems in the database that underlies the most prominent studies of small business job creation. Our review leads us to question whether any useful information can be gleaned from these studies about the relationship between employer size and job creation.

Our analysis of job creation and destruction behavior in the manufacturing sector relies upon the Longitudinal Research Database (LRD) housed at the Center for Economic Studies in the U.S. Bureau of the Census. The LRD contains plant-level data at annual sampling intervals for the U.S. manufacturing sector from 1972 to 1988. Information in the LRD permits classification of employers by various characteristics, including plant and firm size. Among U.S. data sets that have been used to study job creation and destruction, the LRD contains the most detailed information on plant characteristics, the most careful treatment of the statistical sampling frame, and the best treatment of plant entry and exit. We exploit the LRD to deepen our understanding of job creation and destruction in the U.S. manufacturing sector and, by extension, the entire U.S. economy.[2]

The chief findings to emerge from our study of the U.S. manufacturing sector fall into three categories:

1. *Large plants and firms account for most newly created (and newly destroyed) manufacturing jobs.* Plants that averaged at least 100 employees accounted for two-thirds of job creation over the 1972 to 1988 period. Firms with at least 500 employees accounted for more than one-half of job creation. These findings reflect the simple fact that large plants and firms account for the bulk of the manufacturing jobs base.

2. *Survival rates for manufacturing jobs increase sharply with employer size.* The one-year job survival rate at the biggest firms is 92 percent, compared with only 81 percent for the smallest firms. The one-year survival rate for newly created jobs at the biggest firms is 76 percent, compared with only 65 percent at the smallest firms. Similar patterns hold for large plants compared with small plants, and for multiunit firms compared with single-unit firms. Hence, in terms of both new jobs and the typical existing job, larger employers offer greater job durability.

3. *Smaller manufacturing firms and plants exhibit sharply higher* gross *job creation rates but not higher* net *creation rates.* The gross job creation rate averages 12.2 percent per year for firms with fewer than 100 employees, nearly double the rate for firms with 25,000 or more employees. In this sense, small businesses create a disproportionately large share of new jobs. In the same sense, however, smaller plants and firms destroy a disproportionately large share of existing jobs. The *net* job creation rate in the U.S. manufacturing sector exhibits no strong or systematic relationship to employer size.

In the sections that follow we will explain how and why we arrived at these conclusions. The next two sections describe our measurement procedures; subsequent sections present our results and central line of argument.

Measuring Job Creation and Destruction

Although the concept of a job is easy to understand, measuring and interpreting job creation and destruction requires careful definitions. In this study, a *job* is defined as an employment position filled by a worker. Our data do not distinguish among part-time, full-time, and overtime employment positions; all count equally as single jobs. We do not measure the number of vacancies (i.e., unfilled positions) at a point in time or the change in vacancies over time. Rather, we measure plant-level changes in the number of filled employment positions.

The basic observational unit underlying our job creation and destruction measures is the *plant*—a physical location where production takes place. In contrast to a plant, a *company* or *firm* is an economic and legal entity that encompasses one or more plants and, possibly, administrative offices specializing in nonproduction activities. Although we provide tabulations broken down by plant and firm size, all job creation and destruction measures are cumulated from plant-level employment changes.

We calculate job creation and destruction from plant-level net employment changes over 12-month intervals. If, for example, a plant expands by 10 employees between March 1987 and March 1988, then, according to our calculations, the plant contributes 10 jobs to the 1988 creation count. If another plant contracts by 8 employees over the same time interval, it contributes 8 jobs to the 1988 destruction count.

Because plants represent the observational units in the LRD, our calculations capture the effects of firms that shift employment between plants. By the same token, however, our calculations do not capture the effects of job shifts within plants. For example, if a plant replaces several secretaries with an equal number of computer programmers, no net change in plant-level employment occurs; hence, our calculations record no job creation or destruction associated with this event. Because of the point-in-time nature of LRD employment data, our calculations also do not record plant-level employment changes that are reversed within the sampling interval. For example, if a plant lays off some workers in July 1987 and recalls an equal number in September 1987, there is no net effect on the plant's employment change between March 1987 and March 1988; hence, no contribution to job creation or destruction would be recorded for this episode of layoff and recall. For both reasons—the failure to capture within-plant job shifts and the point-in-time nature of the employment data—our job creation and destruction measures understate the true magnitudes.

With these remarks as background, we supply the following definitions:

Definition 1: Gross job creation at time t equals employment gains summed over all plants that expand or start up between $t - 1$ and t.

Definition 2: Gross job destruction at time t equals employment losses summed over all plants that contract or shut down between $t - 1$ and t.

In line with these definitions, plants with unchanged employment contribute to neither job creation nor job destruction. We shall typically express job creation and destruction figures as rates by dividing through by a measure of the employment level.

To convert time-t job creation and destruction measures to rates, we divide by the average of employment at t and $t - 1$.[3]

Definition 3: The net employment change at time t is the difference between employment at time t and employment at time $t - 1$.

A simple and important relationship links the concepts described by these three definitions: *The net employment growth rate equals the job creation rate minus the job destruction rate.* In other words, job creation and destruction figures decompose the net change in aggregate employment into a component associated with growing plants and a component associated with shrinking plants.

The job creation and destruction components of the net employment change provide insights into employment dynamics that are unavailable from traditional sources of information on employment trends. For example, suppose that aggregate employment grew 2 percent during the past year. That figure could be produced by a 4 percent rate of job creation and 2 percent rate of job destruction, or by a 22 percent rate of creation and a 20 percent rate of destruction.

Important aspects of economic behavior and performance are likely to vary with rates of job creation and destruction. Higher rates of job creation and destruction mean larger numbers of workers compelled to shuffle between jobs and, most likely, a greater incidence of unemployment. For a given net growth rate, higher rates of job creation make it easier for displaced workers and labor market entrants to find employment, and higher rates of job destruction imply less job security for employed persons. Higher rates of job creation and destruction also imply greater heterogeneity in the behavior of employment growth across plants. Thus, job creation and destruction figures offer a window into the diversity of plant-level outcomes masked by aggregate employment statistics.

Measuring Employer Size

There are many related but distinct concepts of employer size. Our analysis considers four concepts: current plant size, average plant size, firm size, and ownership type. *Current plant size* equals the simple average of the plant's current employment and its employment 12 months earlier. In contrast, *average plant size* equals the weighted mean number of employees, computed over all annual observations on the plant during the 1972 to 1988 period. *Firm size* equals the number of manufacturing workers employed by the plant's parent firm as of the preceding Cencus of Manufactures.[4] Finally, *ownership type* indicates whether the plant's parent firm operates one or multiple plants.

A few remarks will help to clarify the usefulness, strengths, and weaknesses of these alternative measures of employer size. Plant size is a natural metric for the scale of operations at a geographically distinct production unit. Because employment often fluctuates from year to year owing to demand variation and other factors, average plant size provides a better indication of the production unit's intended scale of operations. Hence, for most purposes, we prefer average size to current size.[5]

Firm size is superior to plant size as an indicator of the overall scale of operations carried out by the plant's parent firm. Firm size corresponds closely to the notion of business size that underlies most public discourse on job creation behavior. In addition, patterns of government regulation and business access to financial markets are tied more closely to firm size than to plant size. Smaller firms enjoy exemption from or weaker enforcement of many government regulations related to the environment, affirmative action, financial reporting, and occupational health and safety (see Brock and Evans, 1986, chap. 5; Brown et al., 1990, pp. 82–88). Larger firms enjoy greater access to certain forms of financial credit, such as equity and debt issues (on the relationship between firm size and financing patterns, see Gaston, 1989; Gertler and Gilchrist, 1992; Kashyap and Stein, 1992; Walker, 1989).

Ownership type is a crude indicator of firm size. Its chief virtue lies in its widespread availability and easy use in government data on individual business establishments. Consequently, many other studies and government statistical publications report breakdowns of economic activity by ownership type.

Job Creation and Destruction Rates by Employer Size

With these remarks as background, we now turn to the empirical evidence. Table 5.1 displays average net and gross job flow rates by employer size. The table reveals strong regularities in the relationship between employer size and gross job flow rates. Consider, first, the average rate of gross job creation. By all four measures, gross job creation rates decline monotonically with employer size. The job creation rate averages 16.5 percent of employment per year for firms with fewer than 20 employees, 9.3 percent for firms with 500–999 employees, and 6.3 percent for firms with 50,000 or more employees. Similar patterns prevail for the ownership-type indicator and both measures of plant size. Thus, small employers create new jobs at a much higher gross rate than do large employers.

But gross job creation measures clearly reveal only part of the story. Table 5.1 also shows that the gross job destruction rate declines sharply with firm and plant size. It averages 18.8 percent of employment per year for firms with fewer than 20 employees, 9.8 percent for firms with

TABLE 5.1
Rates of Job Creation and Destruction by Employer Size, 1973–1988

	Gross Job Creation	Gross Job Destruction	Net Job Creation	Employment Share
Average plant size [a]				
0 to 19 employees	15.9	17.2	−1.3	4.4
20 to 49	12.6	13.8	−1.1	8.2
50 to 99	11.7	12.6	−0.9	10.1
100 to 249	10.0	11.5	−1.4	18.5
250 to 499	8.5	9.8	−1.3	16.6
500 to 999	7.5	8.5	−1.0	13.8
1,000 to 2,499	6.6	8.2	−1.6	12.5
2,500 to 4,999	6.5	8.2	−1.7	7.2
5,000 or more	5.9	6.5	−0.6	8.8
Current plant size [b]				
0 to 19 employees	18.7	23.3	−4.5	5.2
20 to 49	13.2	15.3	−2.1	8.6
50 to 99	12.2	13.5	−1.3	10.5
100 to 249	9.6	10.7	−1.1	18.5
250 to 499	7.7	8.7	−1.0	16.0
500 to 999	7.0	7.6	−0.6	13.5
1,000 to 2,499	6.3	7.3	−1.0	12.3
2,500 to 4,999	6.1	7.5	−1.3	7.0
5,000 or more	5.4	5.6	−0.2	8.4

(continues)

TABLE 5.1 (*continued*)

	Gross Job Creation	Gross Job Destruction	Net Job Creation	Employment Share
Firm size c				
0 to 19 employees	16.5	18.8	−2.3	5.2
20 to 49	12.3	13.3	−1.0	7.0
50 to 99	11.5	11.9	−0.4	6.8
100 to 249	11.1	11.2	−0.1	9.1
250 to 499	9.8	9.9	−0.1	6.8
500 to 999	9.3	9.8	−0.4	6.2
1,000 to 2,499	8.8	9.5	−0.7	8.2
2,500 to 4,999	8.0	9.4	−1.4	7.1
5,000 to 9,999	7.8	9.1	−1.3	8.5
10,000 to 24,999	7.1	8.6	−1.5	13.6
25,000 to 49,999	6.5	8.1	−1.6	9.2
50,000 or more	6.3	8.0	−1.6	12.4
Ownership type of parent firm				
single unit	12.7	12.9	−0.2	22.3
multiunit	8.1	9.4	−1.3	77.7

  a Equal to the weighted mean number of employees, computed over all annual observations on the plant during the period 1972 to 1988.
  b Equal to the simple mean of the plant's current employment and its employment 12 months earlier.
  c Equal to the number of manufacturing workers employed by the plant's parent firm in the preceding Cencus of Manufactures. Census years are 1972, 1977, 1982, and 1987.

Note: Job creation and destruction rates are defined in the text. Table entries for the creation and destruction rates and the employment shares are means of annual values for the period 1973 to 1988. *Source:* Table constructed by the authors from the Longitudinal Research Datafile, housed at the U.S. Bureau of the Census.

500–999 employees, and 8.0 percent for firms with 50,000 or more employees. Again, similar patterns prevail for the ownership type indicator and plant size measures. Thus, small employers also destroy jobs at a much higher rate than do large employers.

How does net job creation vary by employer size? On this score, the empirical evidence produces no strong pattern. Net job creation rates by firm size exhibit a shape: Manufacturing firms with 100–499 employees show mild net contraction rates between 1972 and 1988, whereas smaller and larger firms show sharper contraction rates. Neither plant size measure evinces any strong relationship to net job creation rates, although the net contraction rate is substantially smaller for single-unit than for multiunit firms. In a nutshell, net job creation behavior in the U.S. manufacturing sector exhibits no strong or simple relationship to employer size.

How can we reconcile this empirical result with the widely held belief that small businesses account for a disproportionate fraction of new jobs? One might think that the answer lies in our focus on the manufacturing sector. Perhaps in the nonmanufacturing sectors of the economy, smaller firms exhibit higher net job creation rates than do larger firms. But even if this were true, it is not the basis for the widespread belief about the job creation role of small business. Rather, that belief rests on fallacious and misleading interpretations of the data, as we explain in the next three sections.

The Size Distribution Fallacy

Many claims about the job-creating prowess of small business appear to be based upon changes over time in the size distribution of employment. We review below the calculation typically performed on the size distribution data and explain why the usual interpretation of this calculation leads to fallacious inferences about job creation.

The U.S. Small Business Administration (SBA) typically defines small businesses as firms with fewer than 500 employees, although the precise cutoff is not important to the point at hand. Given a particular cutoff, let $TOTAL_t$ and $SMALL_t$ stand for total employment and small business employment, respectively, in year t. In terms of these symbols, one can calculate the small business "contribution" to 1990 job creation as the ratio

$$\frac{SMALL_{1990} - SMALL_{1989}}{TOTAL_{1990} - TOTAL_{1989}}$$

In words, the small business contribution to 1990 job creation is equated to the ratio of net employment change among small firms to total net employment change.[6]

The fallacy arises because firms can migrate between size categories from one year to the next. The example presented in Exhibit 5.2 illustrates this point.

This example considers three firms, one of which (Firm 1) satisfies the SBA definition of a small business in year 1. The largest firm (Firm 3) grows dramatically in year 2, whereas the two smaller ones shrink. As it shrinks, Firm 2 migrates from the large to the small business category. On net, total employment increases by 100.

If one executes the typical calculation on data in this example, small business appears to contributes 90 percent of net job growth. But, as the construction of the example makes clear, this interpretation is fallacious. In the example, firm-level net job growth actually increases with firm size, an observation that can be made only by following individual

	Firm 1	Firm 2	Firm 3	Small Firms	Big Firms	All Firms
Year 1 employment	300	550	650	300	1,200	1,500
Year 2 employment	50	340	1,210	390	1,210	1,600
Net change	−250	−210	560	90	10	100

Small Firm Share of Net Job Creation = (390 − 300)/(1600 − 1500) = .9

This illustration uses data on the size distribution of employment to calculate job creation shares. The calculation uses only the data that appear in the three rightmost columns. Changes in the distribution of employment by firm size are fallaciously used to draw an inference about the share of job creation accounted for by small firms.

EXHIBIT 5.2 Illustration of the Size Distribution Fallacy

employers over time, as in the calculations that underlie the net and gross job flow figures in Table 5.1.

How important is such migration across firm size categories in reality? The large magnitude of gross job flows—and the concentration of job flows in plants that undergo big employment changes—indicates that migration across categories is frequent and important.[7] Especially during periods of slow overall employment growth, firm migration from large to small is likely to occur quite often. This pattern creates the appearance of a booming small firm sector.

In summary, many claims about the job-creating prowess of small businesses derive from a fallacious interpretation of data on the size distribution of employment. Size distribution data cannot tell us whether small businesses systematically grew faster than large businesses.

Netting Out Reality

Sophisticated proponents of the view that small businesses create a disproportionate fraction of new jobs recognize the fallacy described above.[8] Circumventing the fallacy requires longitudinal data on individual establishments or firms—that is, data that track individual employers over time. The most widely cited studies of job creation behavior rely upon such data, but they often present results in a way that can mislead the statistically naive.[9]

To understand the potential for confusion, consider the example in Exhibit 5.3. This example depicts a situation with moderate net job growth in the midst of much larger gross job flows. We know from Table 5.1 that

	Firm 1	Firm 2	Firm 3	Small Firms	Big Firms	All Firms
Year 1 employment	300	600	600	300	1,200	1,500
Year 2 employment	350	400	800	350	1,200	1,550
Net change	50	-200	200	50	0	50

Small Firm Share of Net Job Creation = 50/50 = 1
Small Firm Share of Gross Job Creation = 50/(50 + 200) = .2

This illustration calculates job creation shares from longitudinal data on individual firms. The calculation makes use of longitudinal data to calculate net firm-level employment changes. The net firm-level employment changes are aggregated over firms within a size class and then expressed as a fraction of the aggregate net change. Following the common practice of prominent analysts and government agencies such as the U.S. Small Business Administration, we have assigned continuing firms to a size category using base-year employment. The last two lines show how the small firm share of net job creation misrepresents the actual distribution of newly created jobs by size of firm.

EXHIBIT 5.3 Illustration of a Confusion between Net and Gross Job Creation

this situation typifies the experience of the U.S. manufacturing sector. It also typifies the experience in other sectors of the U.S. economy and in other industrialized nations (see Davis et al., forthcoming, for a review of the evidence). In this example, 100 percent of the net job increase between years 1 and 2 is accounted for by Firm 1, which is classified as small based on its employment in year 1. Thus, one might conclude that "small firms created virtually all new jobs" between years 1 and 2. Closer analysis reveals, however, that such a conclusion grossly mischaracterizes the distribution of newly created jobs by size of firm. In fact, in this example large firms created 80 percent of the new jobs in year 2.

Public discourse about job creation rarely distinguishes between the small business share of gross job creation (20 percent in the example) and its "share" of net job creation. Consequently, claims about the job creation role of small business often conjure up the image of an economy in which large firms inexorably shrink and small firms struggle valiantly to replenish the stock of jobs. This image deviates sharply from the facts set out in Table 5.1 and in Table 5.3 which show that both large and small employers create large numbers of new jobs.

To appreciate fully the misleading character of statements about the small business "share" of net job creation, consider a particular historical episode. Between March 1973 and March 1974, manufacturing employment as reported in the LRD increased on net by about 16,000 jobs. Over this same period, manufacturing plants with fewer than 100 employees as of March 1973 experienced a net increase of about 160,000 jobs. Thus, the net increase for small plants was 10 times as large as the overall net increase. If we were to summarize these data in the usual phraseology of public discourse, we would say that "small employers created 1,000 percent of the new manufacturing jobs in 1974." Proponents of the small business job creation view would likely eschew the usual phraseology in this case, because it highlights the absurdity of the underlying calculation.

Continuing with the historical episode, manufacturing plants of more than 500 employees created about 1.3 million gross new jobs between 1973 and 1974. Since net job growth was only 16,000 during this period, we could easily identify a set of large manufacturing plants that accounted for 50 percent, 100 percent, 200 percent, or 1,000 percent of net job growth. We could do so by choosing a set of large plants situated in states with robust employment growth or rapidly expanding industries. We could even identify several distinct sets of large plants, each of which accounted for, say, 100 percent of net job growth. Would useful economic policy prescriptions then follow from these characterizations of the data? Certainly not! Yet it is precisely this type of data characterization and argument that underlie claims that small businesses create most jobs and—therefore—ought to receive favorable tax and regulatory treatment.

In summary, longitudinal studies that focus on the "share" of net job growth accounted for by small businesses grossly misrepresent the actual distribution of newly created jobs by size of employer. A more meaningful way to represent this distribution is to focus on the small employer share of gross job creation.[10]

The Regression Fallacy

Most longitudinal studies of the relationship between employer size and job creation suffer from another statistical pitfall known as the regression fallacy, or regression-to-the-mean bias.[11] The potential for bias arises whenever employers experience transitory fluctuations in size and whenever measurement error introduces transitory fluctuations in observed size. Both phenomena are important features of longitudinal data on employers.

The simple example in Exhibit 5.4 illustrates the regression fallacy. The example calculates growth rates for individual firms and by size of firm for years 2 and 3. Following widespread practice, firms are assigned to size classes using base-year employment.[12] The base is the initial year of the time interval over which a particular growth rate is calculated.

	Firm 1	Firm 2	Firm 3	Small Firms	Big Firms	All Firms
Year 1 employment	450	550	600	450	1,150	1,600
Year 2 employment	550	450	600	450	1,150	1,600
Year 3 employment	450	550	600	450	1,150	1,600
Year 2 growth rate	.22	−.18	0	**.22**	**−.09**	0
Year 3 growth rate	−.18	.22	0	**.22**	**−.09**	0

This illustration calculates net job creation rates for individual firms and by size class of firms. Following the common practice of prominent analysts and government agencies such as the U.S. Small Business Administration, we have assigned continuing firms to a size category using base-year employment. Year 1 (year 2) is the base year when calculating year 2 (year 3) growth rates. Although each firm employs the same number of workers in year 1 as in year 3, the net growth rate for small firms—as calculated—exceeds the net growth rate for big firms in both year 2 and year 3. This apparent puzzle reflects a bias in the estimated size-growth relationship induced by temporary changes in the level of employment at individual firms.

EXHIBIT 5.4 Illustration of the Regression Fallacy

Boldface entries in the illustration represent average employment growth rates by size class in years 2 and 3. These entries convey the impression that small firms outperform large ones in both years. Yet, closer inspection reveals that each firm is the same size in year 3 as in year 1. Evidently, the seemingly appropriate calculations underlying the boldface entries provide a misleading characterization of the size-growth rate relationship. This misleading characterization is an example of the regression fallacy.

The fallacy arises because, each year, we reclassify firms into size classes using base-year employment. The interaction between this reclassification and transitory firm-level employment movements lies at the heart of the regression fallacy. On average, firms classified as large in the base year are more likely to have experienced recent transitory increases in employment. Because transitory movements reverse themselves, firms that are large in the base year are relatively likely to contract. Likewise, firms classified as small in the base year are more likely to have experienced recent transitory decreases in employment. Hence, firms that are small in the base year are relatively likely to expand. As in Exhibit 5.4, this regression phenomenon (i.e., regression to the firm's own long-run size) creates the illusion that small firms systematically outperform large firms. The magnitude of the bias associated with the regression fallacy depends on several factors: the extent of measurement error in the data, the importance of transitory employment movements for individual employers, the size distribution of employment, and the precise size-class boundaries chosen by the analyst. As a consequence, we cannot precisely quantify the extent of regression-to-the-mean bias in previous studies without direct access to their longitudinal data. We can, however, replicate their procedure for measuring employer size in the LRD and determine the resulting relationship between size and net job growth. We can then compare this size-growth relationship to the ones that emerge under alternative size measures.

Table 5.2 carries out this comparison using LRD data for the period 1973 to 1988. Following the standard practice described above, the first panel classifies continuing plants and plant deaths by base-year size. New plants are classified according to size in the entry year. As we have explained, the entries in this panel are subject to the regression fallacy. To avoid the regression fallacy, we measure employer size using average plant size or current plant size. Recall that current size equals the simple average of the plant's employment in the current and previous years, and average size equals a mean computed over all sample observations on the plant.[13] Repeating portions of Table 5.1, the bottom two panels of Table 5.2 display the figures for average and current plant size measures.

The results of the comparison are striking. In the first panel, the net job creation rate declines steeply over the first five size class intervals and then flattens out over the remaining intervals. The second panel presents a sharp contrast. It indicates that the net job creation rate shows no systematic relationship to average plant size. The third panel actually shows a positive relationship between net job creation and current plant size. The gross job creation and destruction patterns also look much more favorable for small plants under the base-year size measure (the first panel) than under either alternative measure. Evidently, the regression fallacy illustrated in Exhibit 5.4 operates with powerful effect in the LRD data for the U.S. manufacturing sector.[14]

There is good reason to suspect that the regression fallacy operates with even greater effect in the longitudinal data sets used in the widely cited studies by Birch (1979, 1987) and the annual SBA reports. In particular, measurement error is almost certainly more serious in their data sets than in the LRD, a point we develop in the next section. Given their procedures for measuring firm size, the more serious measurement problems in their data suggest greater susceptibility to the regression fallacy.

In summary, the standard practice of measuring firm or establishment size according to base-year employment leads to a regression fallacy, which in turn paints an overly favorable picture of the relative job growth performance of small employers. Our replication analysis with LRD data finds a substantial bias in favor of small businesses under the standard practice for measuring business size using base-year employment.

TABLE 5.2
Job Destruction and Creation Rates
by Three Measures of Plant Size, 1973–1988

	Gross Job Creation	Gross Job Destruction	Net Job Creation	Employment Share
Base-year plant size [a]				
0 to 19 employees	25.7	15.4	10.3	5.2
20 to 49	13.6	13.1	0.6	8.5
50 to 99	11.4	12.0	–0.7	10.4
100 to 249	9.5	11.1	–1.7	18.6
250 to 499	7.4	9.9	–2.5	16.0
500 to 999	6.3	9.0	–2.7	13.5
1,000 to 2,499	5.7	8.4	–2.6	12.3
2,500 to 4,999	5.4	7.9	–2.5	7.0
5,000 to 9,999	4.7	7.1	–2.4	8.5
Average plant size [b]				
0 to 19 employees	15.9	17.2	–1.3	4.4
20 to 49	12.6	13.8	–1.1	8.2
50 to 99	11.7	12.6	–0.9	10.1
100 to 249	10.0	11.5	–1.4	18.5
250 to 499	8.5	9.8	–1.3	16.6
500 to 999	7.5	8.5	–1.0	13.8
1,000 to 2,499	6.6	8.2	–1.6	12.5
2,500 to 4,999	6.5	8.2	–1.7	7.2
5,000 or more	5.9	6.5	–0.6	8.8
Current plant size [c]				
0 to 19 employees	18.7	23.3	–4.5	5.2
20 to 49	13.2	15.3	–2.1	8.6
50 to 99	12.2	13.5	–1.3	10.5
100 to 249	9.6	10.7	–1.1	18.5
250 to 499	7.7	8.7	–1.0	16.0
500 to 999	7.0	7.6	–0.6	13.5
1,000 to 2,499	6.3	7.3	–1.0	12.3
2,500 to 4,999	6.1	7.5	–1.3	7.0
5,000 or more	5.4	5.6	–0.2	8.4

[a] Equal to the number of employees in the initial year of the interval over which the growth rate is calculated.

[b] Equal to the weighted mean number of employees, computed over all annual observations on the plant during the period 1972 to 1988.

[c] Equal to the simple mean of the plant's current employment and its employment 12 months earlier.

Note: Job creation and destruction rates are defined in the text. Table entries for the creation and destruction rates and the employment shares are means of annual values for the period 1973 to 1988. *Source:* Table constructed by the authors from the Longitudinal Research Datafile, housed at the U.S. Bureau of the Census.

An Unsuitable Database

Still another weakness of many leading studies of the job creation process is their reliance on an unsuitable database: the Dun and Bradstreet Market Identifier (DMI) files. David Birch and his associates have used these data for their studies and, until recently, so did the SBA.[15] Although the Dun and Bradstreet database has many impressive attributes and represents an unparalleled source of information for many commercial purposes, it is not designed or maintained as a tool for statistical analysis. Numerous studies have highlighted severe problems with the DMI files as a tool for measuring job creation and destruction or business births and deaths (see Aldrich, Kalleberg, Marsden, & Cassell, 1988; Armington & Odle, 1982b; Birch & MacCracken, 1983; Birley, 1984; Evans, 1987; Howland, 1988; U.S. SBA, 1983, 1987). For the purpose of investigating the job creation process, the DMI files suffer from two key problems. First, there is an enormous discrepancy between U.S. total employment as tabulated from the DMI files and the corresponding employment figures produced by the Bureau of Labor Statistics (BLS) or the Bureau of the Census. In 1986, for example, total employment tabulated from the DMI files exceeds the corresponding BLS and Census Bureau figures by 9 million persons (see U.S. Bureau of the Census, 1989, p. 514). In an economy with roughly 110 million employees, a discrepancy of this magnitude raises serious doubts about the accuracy of any statistical portrait generated from the DMI files. Furthermore, previous research (Aldrich et al., 1988) has found that the most serious data problems in the DMI files involve younger and smaller businesses. This finding suggests that DMI-based claims about small business job creation should be interpreted with special caution.

Second, the DMI files do not accurately track business births and deaths or other important employment events. The U.S. General Accounting Office (GAO) has analyzed the accuracy of the DMI files in accounting for mass layoffs, with particular emphasis on layoffs caused by plant closures. The SBA provided the GAO with a sample of mass layoffs and plant closures from the DMI files for the 1982–84 period.[16] The GAO study found that 81 percent of the mass layoff events in the DMI files were mistakenly identified. In reality, these 81 percent represented other events, such as changes in ownership structure, not mass layoffs or plant closures.

The DMI files also inaccurately identify plant births. Birley (1984) compares three alternative sources of data for identifying new firms: the DMI file, the ES-202 data generated from administrative records maintained by state unemployment insurance agencies, and the telephone directory. She found that the DMI files failed to identify 96 percent of the new firms found in the ES-202 data. Using a similar methodology, Aldrich, Kalleberg, Masden, and Cassell (1988) found that the DMI files missed 95 percent of apparently new businesses in the ES-202 data and 97 percent of those in the telephone directory.

In short, previous research indicates that the DMI files are unsuitable for use in generating job creation and destruction figures. DMI data identifying plant births and deaths and tracking businesses over time are most unreliable concerning small employers. Thus, the DMI files are especially ill suited for use in the investigation of the role of small business in job creation.

The LRD, in contrast, is explicitly designed and maintained to avoid the types of problems that plague the DMI files. It is based on business surveys specifically designed to provide a statistical portrait of U.S. manufacturing activity. In addition, the Census Bureau draws on payroll tax records and other government data sources to verify and enhance the quality of LRD report in employment data.[17] Drawing on the longitudinal data in the LRD, we report in the next two sections additional findings about the job creation process in the U.S. manufacturing sector.

What Fraction of New Manufacturing Jobs Did Small Employers Create?

Table 5.3 reports the percentage of manufacturing employment and job creation and destruction by employer size for the period 1973 to 1988. As the table reveals, large employers created most new manufacturing jobs over the period. They also destroyed most of the lost manufacturing

TABLE 5.3
Shares of Gross Manufacturing Job Creation and Destruction
by Employer Size, 1973–1988

	Job Creation	Job Destruction	Employment
Average plant size [a]			
0 to 19 employees	7.6	7.4	4.4
20 to 49	11.3	11.0	8.2
50 to 99	13.1	12.5	10.1
100 to 249	20.3	20.7	18.5
250 to 499	15.6	16.0	16.6
500 to 999	11.4	11.5	13.8
1,000 to 2,499	9.1	10.1	12.5
2,500 to 4,999	5.2	5.8	7.2
5,000 or more	5.7	5.6	8.8

(continues)

TABLE 5.3 *(continued)*

	Job Creation	Job Destruction	Employment
Current plant size [b]			
0 to 19 employees	10.7	11.8	5.2
20 to 49	12.5	13.0	8.6
50 to 99	14.0	13.8	10.5
100 to 249	19.5	19.5	18.5
250 to 499	13.6	13.6	16.0
500 to 999	10.4	10.1	13.5
1,000 to 24,99	8.5	8.8	12.3
2,500 to 4,999	4.7	5.1	7.0
5,000 or more	5.0	4.6	8.4
Firm size [c]			
0 to19 employees	9.5	9.6	5.2
20 to 49	9.4	9.1	7.0
50 to 99	8.6	7.9	6.8
100 to 249	11.1	9.9	9.1
250 to 499	7.4	6.6	6.8
500 to 999	6.4	6.0	6.2
1,000 to 2,499	7.9	7.6	8.2
2,500 to 4,999	6.2	6.5	7.1
5,000 to 9,999	7.2	7.6	8.5
10,000 to24,999	10.5	11.4	13.6
25,000 to 49,999	6.6	7.3	9.2
50,000 or more	8.6	9.7	12.4
Ownership type			
single unit	31.1	28.2	22.3
multiunit	69.0	71.6	77.7

[a] Equal to the weighted mean number of employees, computed over all annual observations on the plant during the period 1972 to 1988.

[b] Equal to the simple mean of the plant's current employment and its employment 12 months earlier.

[c] Equal to the number of manufacturing workers employed by the plant's parent firm in the preceding Cencus of Manufactures. Census years are 1972, 1977, 1982, and 1987.

Note: Table entries show the shares of gross job creation, gross job destruction, and employment for U.S. manufacturing. Entries are average annual values for the period 1973–88.
Source: Table constructed by the authors from the Longitudinal Research Datafile, housed at the U.S. Bureau of the Census.

jobs. The first panel of the table reveals that plants averaging at least 100 employees accounted for roughly 7 of every 10 newly created and newly destroyed manufacturing jobs. The second panel shows that firms with at least 500 employees accounted for 53 percent of job creation and 56 percent of job destruction. The last panel shows that multiunit firms accounted for roughly 7 of every 10 newly created and newly destroyed manufacturing jobs. The table also reveals why large employers play the dominant role in job creation and destruction, despite the higher creation and destruction rates among smaller employers. The reason is that large employers account for the bulk of the manufacturing jobs base. Over the 1972–88 period as a whole, firms with at least 500 employees accounted for 65 percent of manufacturing employment.

The SBA defines small businesses as all firms with fewer than 500 employees. According to this definition, the third panel of Table 5.3 reveals that small manufacturing firms account for 46 percent of job creation. This figure reflects an expansive and generous definition of the small business sector. Political orations about the virtues of small business often bring to mind family-run businesses and struggling entrepreneurs with shoestring operations, not firms with up to 500 employees. In addition, a host of government regulations that entail exemptions for small businesses specify cutoff levels far below 500 employees. For example, Brock and Evans (1986) note that the "Office of Federal Contract Enforcement exempts businesses with fewer than fifty employees from filing affirmative action plans" (p. 74). As another example, the Worker Adjustment and Retraining Notification Act of 1988 requires employers to give workers and government officials 60 days advance notice before a plant closure or large layoff, but exempts establishments with fewer than 50 employees. The Family and Medical Leave Act of 1993 exempts employers with fewer than 50 workers. Returning to Table 5.3, firms with fewer than 50 employees account for only 19 percent of gross job creation in the manufacturing sector; plants with fewer than 50 employees account for only 23 percent. Thus, according to these definitions, only about one-fifth of all new manufacturing jobs are created by small employers.

Would this characterization of the small business role in job creation differ if we looked outside the manufacturing sector? Although we are currently unable to calculate gross job creation and destruction rates for nonmanufacturing industries, we know that small businesses account for a considerably larger fraction of the jobs base in most nonmanufacturing industries. This point stands out clearly in Table 5.4. Drawing on several data sources, this table reports employment shares for various concepts of large and small businesses. According to SBA figures, firms with fewer than 500 workers account for 50 percent of private sector employment but only 36 percent of manufacturing employment. According to *County Business Patterns* data, establishments with fewer than 100 workers account for 64 percent of nonmanufacturing employment but only 28 percent of manufacturing employment (U.S. Bureau of the Census, 1988). Thus, small businesses provide a much larger share of the

TABLE 5.4
The Share of Employment by Employer Size

Year	Sector	Data Source	Number of Employees			
			<50	<100	≥500	≥1000
By current size of establishment [a]						
1988	private	CBP	.43	.56	.19	.13
1988	nonmanufacturing	CBP	.51	.64	.14	.09
1988	manufacturing	CBP	.17	.28	.37	.24
1988	manufacturing	LRD	.11	.22	.40	.26
By average size of establishment [b]						
1988	manufacturing	LRD	.11	.22	.41	.27

Year	Sector	Data Source	Number of Employees			
			<50	<100	<500	≥5000
By size of firm [c]						
1988	private	SBA			.50	
1988	manufacturing	SBA			.36	
1987	private	ES	.28	.36	.51	.29
1987	nonmanufacturing	ES	.36	.45	.59	.21
1987	manufacturing	ES	.12	.18	.32	.48
1987	manufacturing	LRD	.09	.16	.35	.42

Year	Sector	Data Source	Single Unit	Multiple Units
By parent firm ownership type				
1987	private	ES	.45	.55
1987	nonmanufacturing	ES	.54	.46
1987	manufacturing	ES	.24	.76
1988	manufacturing	LRD	.20	.80

[a] For the LRD, equal to the simple mean of the plant's current employment and its employment 12 months earlier. For the CBP, equal to the number of employees during March of the current year.

[b] Equal to the weighted mean number of employees, computed over all annual observations on the plant during the period 1972 to 1988.

[c] Equal to the number of workers employed by the plant's parent firm.

Note: CBP: authors' calculations from U.S. Bureau of the Census publication *County Business Patterns* (1988). The CBP covers the nonfarm private sector, excluding railroad and domestic household workers. LRD: authors' calculations from the Longitudinal Research Database. Unlike the other data sources, the LRD excludes administrative and auxilliary establishments not directly engaged in production activity. SBA: from U.S. Small Business Administration (1991, Table 17). ES: authors' calculations from U.S. Bureau of the Census publication *Enterprise Statistics* (1987). The ES data exclude finance, insurance, real estate, public utilities, communications, and some service industries.

jobs base outside the manufacturing sector. In addition, the available evidence indicates that the gross job creation rate declines with employer size in the nonmanufacturing sector, just as it does in the manufacturing sector.[18] These facts make us confident that small business accounts for a larger share of job creation and destruction in most nonmanufacturing industries than in the manufacturing sector. A more precise characterization awaits the development and analysis of high-quality longitudinal data for nonmanufacturing businesses. Given that the manufacturing sector accounts for a small and declining share of U.S. employment—only 19 percent in 1988—we think the development of such data merits a high priority by government statistical agencies.

The Durability of Jobs by Employer Size

Laudatory claims about the job creation role of small businesses often fail to consider how the permanence of jobs varies with employer size. This failure is serious, because job durability differs systematically by employer size. Table 5.5 documents this pattern for the manufacturing sector.

TABLE 5.5
Survival and Persistence Rates for All Jobs, New Jobs,
and Lost Jobs in Manufacturing, 1973–1988

	One-Year Survival Rate		*One-Year Persistence Rate of*
	All Jobs	*New Jobs*	*Newly Destroyed Jobs* [b]
Average plant size [a]			
0 to 19 employees	.83	.62	.84
20 to 49	.84	.65	.84
50 to 99	.87	.69	.82
100 to 249	.88	.71	.82
250 to 499	.90	.71	.80
500 to 999	.92	.71	.80
1,000 to 2,499	.92	.71	.82
2,500 to 4,999	.92	.75	.80
5,000 or more	.93	.75	.82
Current plant size [b]			
0 to 19 employees	.77	.70	.86
20 to 49	.85	.70	.84
50 to 99	.86	.71	.83
100 to 249	.89	.70	.81
250 to 499	.91	.68	.79
500 to 999	.92	.68	.80
1,000 to 2,499	.93	.68	.81
2,500 to 4,999	.92	.73	.79
5,000 or more	.94	.71	.83

(continues)

TABLE 5.5 (*continued*)

	One-Year Survival Rate		One-Year Persistence Rate of
	All Jobs	*New Jobs*	*Newly Destroyed Jobs* [b]
Firm size [c]			
0 to 19 employees	.81	.65	.86
20 to 49	.87	.66	.82
50 to 99	.88	.67	.81
100 to 249	.89	.70	.81
250 to 499	.90	.70	.82
500 to 999	.90	.69	.81
1,000 to 2,499	.90	.70	.81
2,500 to 4,999	.91	.70	.82
5,000 to 9,999	.91	.70	.81
10,000 to 24,999	.91	.71	.81
25,000 to 49,999	.92	.70	.82
50,000 or more	.92	.76	.82
By parent firm ownership type			
single unit	.87	.67	.82
multiunit	.91	.71	.82

[a] Equal to the weighted mean number of employees, computed over all annual observations on the plant during the period 1972 to 1988.

[b] Equal to the simple mean of the plant's current employment and its employment 12 months earlier.

[c] Equal to the number of manufacturing workers employed by the plant's parent firm in the preceding Cencus of Manufactures. Census years are 1972, 1977, 1982, and 1987.

Note: The one-year survival rate for all jobs equals one minus the job destruction rate, as reported in Table 5.1. The one-year survival rate for new jobs equals the fraction created between year $t-1$ and t that are still present at the same location in year $t+1$. The one-year persistence rate of newly destroyed jobs equals the fraction of jobs lost between year $t-1$ and t that have not reappeared at the same location by year t. All table entries are average annual values for the period 1973 to 1988. *Source:* Table constructed by the authors from the Longitudinal Research Datafile, housed at the U.S. Bureau of the Census.

The table shows one-year survival rates for all jobs and newly created jobs by size of employer. The one-year survival rates for all jobs rise systematically with all four measures of employer size. The one-year survival rate for the biggest firms is 92 percent, compared with only 81 percent for the smallest firms. Furthermore, the one-year survival rates for new jobs rise systematically with average plant size, firm size, and ownership type.[19] The one-year survival rate for new jobs at the biggest firms is 76 percent, compared with only 65 percent at the smallest firms. Simply put, bigger employers offer greater job durability. Regardless of employer size, however, new jobs are much less durable than are typical existing jobs.

Table 5.5 also reveals that the persistence of newly destroyed jobs is greater for smaller employers, although the relationship is weaker. In a nutshell, both existing and newly created jobs are less secure at small businesses than at large businesses, and once lost, small business jobs are less likely to reappear. Thus, in terms of job durability, larger employers outperform smaller ones.

Conclusions

Drawing on U.S. Census Bureau data for manufacturing plants from 1972 to 1988, we have reported new evidence on the relationship between employer size and job growth. We have shown that large firms and plants dominate the creation and destruction of jobs in the U.S. manufacturing sector. This finding has a simple two-part explanation. First, for employers large and small, gross job creation and destruction rates are quite high—on the order of 10 percent of employment per year. Second, large firms and plants account for the bulk of the manufacturing jobs base.

Although gross job creation rates are substantially higher for smaller plants and firms than for larger ones, so are gross destruction rates. We find no strong or systematic relationship between net job growth rates and either firm size or plant size. However, we find clear evidence that larger employers offer greater security. For both new jobs and typical existing jobs, job durability increases with employer size.

These empirical findings clash sharply with conventional wisdom about the job-creating prowess of small business. One might suspect that the source of disagreement lies in differences between the manufacturing and nonmanufacturing sectors of the economy. We hold open the possibility that careful analysis of job creation activity in the nonmanufacturing sector might produce evidence more congenial to the conventional view, but that view does not rest upon a careful and balanced analysis of the data. Rather, the widely espoused claims about small business and job creation rest upon two common fallacies—the size distribution fallacy and the regression fallacy—and a confusion between net and gross job creation.

As illustrated by the quotations in Exhibit 5.1, the job-creating prowess of small business is often touted as an argument in favor of preferential tax, subsidy, or regulatory treatment of small businesses. Aside from its questionable factual basis, this type of argument is, quite simply, a non sequitur. It has two fundamental problems.

First, the argument neglects the issue of job quality. The mere creation of jobs is not an appropriate economic policy objective. Economic policy is appropriately directed toward wealth creation and the expansion of consumption opportunities. Here we mean *consumption opportunities* in a broad sense that encompasses not just material goods, but the many factors that influence the quality of life. For economic policy to serve these objectives, it must promote job quality as well as job creation. Although there are many exceptions to the basic pattern, the weight of evidence indicates that, on average, larger employers offer better jobs in terms of wages, fringe benefits, working conditions, opportunities for skill enhancement, and job security.[20] Few studies that purportedly demonstrate small business's disproportionate contribution to job creation effectively address the issue of job quality. Except for the matter of job durability, we have not addressed the issue in this chapter.

Second, the argument for preferential treatment of small business fails to comprehend the central theorem of economic policy prescription. This theorem directs attention toward marginal responses to proposed economic policy changes. In contrast, claims about the job-creating prowess of small business are statements about the average behavior of a class of firms. Even if accurate, these statements do not predict how the number (or quality) of jobs would respond to a proposed economic policy change. Careful, well-founded predictions about how the number and quality of jobs respond to changes in the economic environment are the appropriate yardstick for policy evaluation.

In practice, determining how policy changes affect job numbers and quality poses considerable challenge. Even greater challenges in the political arena confront efforts to implement economically sound policies that target specific sectors or types of firms. Targeted policy proposals invite political conflicts over the precise structure of subsidies, tax breaks, and preferential regulatory treatment. These conflicts are costly for two reasons. First, they inevitably turn into resource-consuming struggles over the redistribution of society's wealth. Second, the outcome usually reflects the relative political strengths of the parties to the conflict, rather than the economic criteria that shaped the original policy proposal. In our view, these practical barriers to successful design and implementation of targeted policies create a strong presumption in favor of neutral, untargeted policies.

Appendix

In Table 5.5, the one-year survival rate for new jobs shows a clear relationship to average plant size but not to current size. How can we reconcile these apparently contradictory results? First, consider some hypothetical employment histories in a simplified setting with only two size classes.

Suppose a plant is small at the beginning of the sample, becomes large for one period, and then returns permanently to the small category. This plant is classified as small under the average size measure. Under the current size measure, it is classified as small in most periods but as large in the period that coincides with its one episode of job creation.[21] Consequently, this plant's employment history pulls down the survival rate for small plants under the average size measure, but it pulls down the survival rate for large plants under the current size measure.

As a second hypothetical example, consider a plant that starts out large, becomes small for one period, and then returns permanently to large status. The plant's return to large status involves an episode of persistent job creation. This episode pushes up the new job survival rate for large plants under the average size measure, but it pushes up the rate for small plants under the current size measure.

These two hypothetical employment histories illustrate a more general point: Under the current size measure, plant-level employment histories that involve occasional, temporary movements across size-class boundaries increase the new job survival rates for small plants relative to large plants. Just how prevalent are these occasional boundary-crossing episodes? We know from Davis et al. (forthcoming, chap. 2) that job creation is concentrated in plants that experience large percentage employment changes, suggesting that much job creation involves boundary crossing. We know from other research that temporary layoffs in the manufacturing sector are quite important, especially during cyclical downturns (see, e.g., Lilien, 1980). These observations suggest that the second hypothetical example, in particular, captures an important aspect of plant-level employment dynamics.

These remarks reconcile the apparent discrepancy between results based on the two alternative measures of plant size, but they do not indicate which size measure is more appropriate. As we suggested earlier, average plant size is probably a more accurate proxy for the plant's intended scale of operations. More important, the average size measure assigns each plant to a fixed category. In contrast, as our examples reveal, the current size measure can attribute job creation to the small plant category, even though the plant is large during most periods—and vice versa.[22] We find this aspect of accounting for job creation by current size class to be discomfiting. We believe that using average plant size is a more informative way to examine job creation data, although the current size measure may be preferable for some purposes.

In any case, this issue becomes less nettlesome when we examine the survival of new jobs by ownership type and firm size. A plant's ownership type seldom changes. Because firm size reflects the firm's employment level during the preceding Cencus of Manufactures, the measured size of a plant's parent firm is unaffected by the plant's subsequent employment history.

Notes

1. See also the U.S. Small Business Administration's annual reports to the president, *The State of Small Business*, and Birch (1979, 1987). The chorus of praise for the job creation performance of small business has been challenged by only a handful of critics (see Armington and Odle, 1982a; Brown, Hamilton, and Medoff, 1990, chap. 3). For journalistic pieces that question conventional wisdom about the small business role in creating jobs, see Wessel and Brown (1988), Marshall (1993), and Kinsley (1993).

2. Our forthcoming book describes the LRD in much greater detail (see Davis, Haltiwanger, and Schuh, forthcoming).

3. The resulting growth rate measure has several technical advantages over more conventional growth rate measures. See Davis et al. (forthcoming) for further discussion of this point.

4. Only in census years can we measure total employment for every manufacturing firm. The Census of Manufactures was carried out in 1972, 1977, 1982, and 1987.

5. Most other studies focus on yet a different measure of employer size that we describe in our analysis of the regression fallacy, later in this chapter.

6. Zayas (1978) used data on changes in the size distribution of employment to calculate growth rates by size of business. This calculation is also subject to the size distribution fallacy identified below.

7. Table 5.1 shows that gross job creation and destruction flows are large relative to net employment changes. Additional evidence on this point and on the concentration of gross job flows at plants that undergo big employment changes is available in Davis et al. (forthcoming, chap. 2).

8. The SBA's 1983 report *The State of Small Business* clearly explains the fallacy (see U.S. SBA, 1983, p. 62). See also Birch and MacCracken (1983).

9. The most widely cited studies of the small business role in creating jobs are the SBA's annual reports, *The State of Small Business*, and Birch (1979, 1987).

10. For the record, we should note that not every statistical tabulation performed on longitudinal data by the SBA examines the small employer share of net job creation. For example, Table 13 in U.S. SBA (1988) reports gross job creation by firm size. Nonetheless, the surrounding text reverts to the misleading "net" calculation when characterizing the small business role in job creation.

11. Friedman (1992, p. 2131) suggests that the regression fallacy "is the most common fallacy in the statistical analysis of economic data." Leonard (1986) explains how regression-to-the-mean bias can distort the estimated relationship between employer size and growth rates. Friedman (1992) and Quah (1993) focus on the regression fallacy in the recent literature that investigates whether per capita income levels are converging across countries.

12. This classification practice is used, for instance, in the annual SBA reports to the president and in Birch (1979, 1987).

13. To the extent that transitory employment fluctuations require more than one year to reverse themselves, our current size measure is subject to a milder and more subtle version of the regression fallacy. However, random errors in measuring employment levels do not produce a regression fallacy under any of our plant or firm size measures.

14. Brown et al. (1990) stress a different potential problem with the standard size measure. They argue that classifying new firms according to size in the entry year creates a bias, because new firms often start small even when their intended scale of operations is large. This point clearly applies to new plants as well. However, a symmetric point is that dying plants often contract and become small on their way toward exit. A careful reading of Table 5.2 suggests that this latter effect dominates for manufacturing plants. Observe that, among the smallest plants, the difference between the gross destruction rate based on current size and the gross destruction rate based on average size exceeds the corresponding difference for the gross creation rate. Observe also that the creation and destruction rates align more closely when one compares the current and average size measures than when one compares either of these measures to the Birch/SBA measure. This last observation indicates that the regression fallacy—not the birth problem stressed by Brown et al.—accounts for the striking contrast between the first panel and the other panels.

15. The SBA has recently contracted with the Bureau of the Census to link longitudinally the federal government's Standard Statistical Establishment List for the purpose of studying job creation and destruction behavior. See Census Contract Number 61-93-41, "The Longitudinal Data Study."

16. The GAO defined a mass layoff as the dismissal of at least 20 percent of a plant's permanent workforce.

17. Given the need of policy makers to understand the job creation process, government statistical agencies should set a high priority on developing longitudinal establishment-level databases for other sectors of the U.S. economy. The Center for Economic Studies at the Bureau of the Census is currently conducting a pilot study to determine whether the federal government's Standard Statistical Establishment List can be effectively used to construct longitudinal data on firms and establishments for the entire U.S. economy.

18. Unpublished tabulations prepared by Ken Troske for the finance, insurance, and real estate sector in Wisconsin, and by Al Nucci for the U.S. nonmanufacturing sector during the 1982–87 period, indicate that gross job creation rates decline sharply with employer size.

19. In the appendix to this chapter we explain why current plant size and average plant size exhibit different relationships to the one-year survival rate for new jobs. The explanation relates closely to our earlier discussion of the regression fallacy.

20. Brown et al. (1990) review much of the evidence on how job quality varies with employer size.

21. Recall that our measure of current plant size equals the simple average of current and previous period's employment. Remarks in the text presume that

the plant crosses the size-class boundary—once during its job creation episode and a second time after it returns to its initial size.

22. The same problem arises if we use base-year employment to measure employer size.

References

Acs, Z., and Audretsch, D. (1988). "Innovation in Large and Small Firms: An Empirical Analysis." *American Economic Review, 78*, 678–690.

Aldrich, H., Kalleberg, A., Marsden, P., and Cassell, J. (1988). "In Pursuit of Evidence: Five Sampling Procedures for Locating New Businesses." *Journal of Business Venturing, 4*, 367–386.

Armington, C., and Odle, M. (1982a). "Small Business—How Many Jobs?" *Brookings Review*, vol. 1, pp. 14-17.

Armington, C., and Odle, M. (1982b). "Sources of Employment Growth, 1978–80." Unpublished manuscript, Brookings Institution.

Birch, D. L. (1979). *The Job Generation Process.* Unpublished manuscript, MIT Program on Neighborhood and Regional Change.

Birch, D. L. (1987). *Job Creation in America: How Our Smallest Companies Put the Most People to Work.* New York: Free Press.

Birch, D., and MacCracken, S. (1983). "The Small Business Share of Job Creation: Lessons Learned from the Use of a Longitudinal File." Unpublished manuscript, MIT Program on Neighborhood and Regional Change.

Birley, S. (1984). "Find the New Firm." *Proceedings of the Academy of Management Meetings*, vol. 47, pp. 64-68.

Brock W. A., and Evans, D. S. (1986). *The Economics of Small Business: Their Role and Regulation in the U.S. Economy.* New York: Holmes & Meier.

Brown, C., Hamilton, J., and Medoff, J. (1990). *Employers Large and Small.* Cambridge, MA: Harvard University Press.

Brown, C., and Medoff, J. (1989). "The Employer Size Wage Effect." *Journal of Political Economy*, vol. 97, 1027–1059.

Davis, S. J., and Haltiwanger, J. (1991). "Wage Dispersion between and within U.S. Manufacturing Plants, 1963–86." *Brookings Papers on Economic Activity: Microeconomics*, 115–200.

Davis, S. J., and Haltiwanger, J. (1992). "Employer Size and the Wage Structure in U.S. Manufacturing." Mimeo, University of Chicago.

Davis, S., Haltiwanger, J., and Schuh, S. (1990) "Published versus Sample Statistics from the ASM: Implications for the LRD." *Proceedings of the American Statistical Association, Business and Economics Statistics Section*, pp. 52–61.

Davis, S., Haltiwanger, J., and Schuh S. (forthcoming). *Job Creation and Destruction in U.S. Manufacturing.* Washington, DC: U.S. Bureau of the Census.

Dentzer, S. (1993, August 16). "Doing the Small-Business Shuffle." *U.S. News & World Report*, p. 49.

Evans, D. (1987). "The Relationship between Firm Growth, Size and Age: Estimates for 100 Manufacturing Industries." *Journal of Industrial Economics, 15*, 567–581.

Friedman, M. (1992). "Do Old Fallacies Ever Die?" *Journal of Economic Literature,* 30, 2129–2132.

Gaston, R. J. (1989). "The Scale of Informal Capital Markets." *Small Business Economics,* 1, 223–230.

Gertler, M., and Gilchrist, S. (1992). "Monetary Policy, Business Cycles and the Behavior of Small Manufacturing Firms." Working paper, New York University.

Greenhouse, S. (1993). "Clinton Plan: Small Businesses Smile," *New York Times.* March 28.

Hale, D. (1993, July 30). "Small Business, Tax Plan's Victim." *Wall Street Journal,* p. A8.

Hansen, J. A. (1992). "Innovation, Firm Size, and Firm Age." *Small Business Economics,* 4, 37–44.

Howland, M. (1988). *Plant Closings and Worker Displacements: The Regional Issues,* Kalamazoo, MI: W. E. Upjohn Institute for Employment Research.

Kashyap, A., and Stein, J. (1992). "Monetary Policy and Bank Lending." Mimeo, University of Chicago.

Kinsley, M. (1993, September 13). "Small Isn't Beautiful." *New Republic,* p. 6.

Leonard, J. (1986). "On the Size Distribution of Employment and Establishments." National Bureau of Economic Research Working Paper 1951.

Lilien, D. (1980). "The Cyclical Pattern of Temporary Layoffs in United States Manufacturing." *Review of Economics and Statistics,* 112, 24–31.

Marshall, J. (1993, March 29). "Dispelling a Small-Business Myth." *San Francisco Chronicle,* p. D1.

Meyers, H. F. (1993, March 8). "The Outlook." *Wall Street Journal,* p. A1.

Phillips, B. (1993). "The Growth of Small Firm Jobs by State, 1984–88." *Business Economics,* 48–53.

Quah, D. (1993). "Galton's Fallacy and Tests of the Convergence Hypothesis." London School of Economics Discussion Paper EM/93/265.

Roach, S. (1993, March 14). "The New Majority: White-Collar Jobless." *New York Times,* sec. 4, p. 17.

Siebert, M. (1992, January 6). "Hire Workers. Get a Tax Credit." *New York Times,* p. A21.

Silk, L. (1986, April 9). "Quiet Shapers of History." *New York Times,* p. D2.

U.S. Bureau of the Census. (1987). *Enterprise Statistics.* Washington, DC: Government Printing Office.

U.S. Bureau of the Census. (1988). *County Business Patterns* (U.S. Summary Statistics, Vol. I). Washington, DC: Government Printing Office.

U.S. Bureau of the Census. (1989). *Statistical Abstract of the United States.* Washington, DC: Government Printing Office.

U.S. Small Business Administration (SBA). (Annual). *The State of Small Business: A Report of the President.* Washington, DC: Government Printing Office.

Walker, D. A. (1989). "Financing the Small Firm." *Small Business Economics,* 1, 285–296.

Wessel, D., and Brown, B. (1988, November 8). "The Hyping of Small-Firm Job Growth." *Wall Street Journal,* p. A1.

Zagorin, A. (1993, July 12). "How the Small Business Owner Gets Clobbered." *Time*, p. 32.

Zayas, E. R. (1978). Testimony at *Small Business and Job Creation*, hearings before the Subcommittee on Antitrust, Consumers and Employment of the Committee on Small Business, 95th Congress (second session). Washington, DC September 25 and 26.

Comment

Robert W. Bednarzik

The basis for my comments is what the preceding chapter authors have to say about policy, especially labor policy. For example, are their findings sufficiently strong to warrant a change in policy or the setting of new policy? Perhaps the findings point generally to a direction that policy should take. With the policy goal in mind, I hope in the following sections to accomplish the following: First, I will review the findings of the studies presented in Chapters 4 and 5, looking for areas of agreement as well as disagreement. I will then discuss my view of the credibility of these findings. Next, I will attempt to push the analysis a little further by focusing on the current U.S. economic recovery and comparing the employment picture in the United States with that of other countries of the Organization for Economic Cooperation and Development (OECD), which encompasses the world's 25 largest industrialized nations. Finally, I will conclude with a discussion of policy.

Findings

The major finding presented by Birch and Medoff is that a small group of firms accounts for the vast majority of new jobs; Davis, Haltiwanger, and Schuh, in contrast, argue that the dominance of job creation among small firms is a myth. Both sets of researchers note that large firms (those with more than 100 employees) are important for job creation but that job creation among small firms is not *un*important. Birch and Medoff show that more than one-fourth of new jobs over the 1989–92 period were created in large firms, but most Gazelles start from small bases, fewer than 20 workers. Examining a much longer time period, 1972–88, Davis et al. found that two-thirds of job creation occurs in large plants. They note that small firms have much higher *gross* job creation rates than large firms.

Author's Note: The views expressed here are solely those of the author and may not necessarily reflect the positions or opinions of the U.S. Department of Labor or the U.S. Government.

A key difference between the studies reported in Chapters 4 and 5 has to do with job "quality." Birch and Medoff note that Gazelles are inherently unstable (leading edge, risk takers, many successes as well as failures). This would result in low job tenure, a typical measure of job instability among workers. Davis et al. show that larger employers offer greater job stability and fringe benefits because their survival rates are higher than those of small firms. The creation of "quality" jobs is an important policy issue that I will come back to later.

Credibility of the Findings

I am not sure of the strength of Birch and Medoff's major finding. Is it robust enough to base policy on? I wonder if the finding is unique to the time period studied, which encompasses an economic downturn and an anemic recovery. For example, Birch and Medoff note that in determining whether job creation occurred more in small versus large firms, the time period analyzed was crucial. Moreover, they do not give enough information about the data to make possible any assessment of its quality. What are their sources? Are the data longitudinal? Are we talking about gross or net job creation? What are its limitations (e.g., there may be transitory fluctuations)? Also, how did job growth by firm size affect firm size classification? For example, if a very small firm (one to four workers) in 1988 recorded substantial job growth, would it be categorized as a larger firm in subsequent years?

Answers to these questions and a discussion of the database would be useful if we want to gauge better or to weigh in a qualitative sense the strength of the findings. Right now, we must take these findings on faith. They provide interesting food for thought, but they need to be more thoroughly researched before they can lead to any specific policy outcomes.

My primary concern with Davis et al.'s study is that their data are limited to the manufacturing sector and, as the authors note, a larger percentage of service sector than manufacturing firms are small. This is significant from a policy point of view because more than 80 percent of *all* jobs are now in the service-producing sector, whereas only about 17 percent are in manufacturing industries. Adding the service-producing sector to the analysis could radically change the findings. Although Davis et al. add another piece to the puzzle, their findings are not convincing enough on their own to get policy moved in the direction of *less* public support for small firms.

Pushing the Analysis Further

The Current Recovery

A key question is the extent of job growth in the recovery. To push the data presented by Birch and Medoff a little further, I examine below the recovery for various worker groups. Birch and Medoff note that an overlooked group suffering job losses in the recent economic downturn is made up of white-collar workers in technical, sales, and administrative support occupations. Table 1 provides a comparison of postwar recoveries 30 months after the recoveries began.

TABLE 1

Change in Employment Indicators 30 Months After NBER Troughs for the Seven Recoveries Between 1948 and 1993

	Percentage Change						
NBER Trough	Mar91	Nov82	Mar75	Nov70	Feb61	May54	Oct49
30th Month Later	Sep93	May85	Sep77	May73	Aug63	Nov56	Apr52
Total payroll	1.9	9.6	9.2	8.8	6.5	7.9	13.2
Goods	−4.4	8.4	9.5	9.3	5.9	7.5	19.8
Manufacturing	−4.3	6.6	9.0	8.7	5.9	6.3	18.2
Services	3.7	10.0	9.1	8.6	6.8	8.2	8.9
Total employment	2.3	7.9	8.8	7.6	—	—	—
White-collar	3.4	8.2	9.2	6.1	—	—	—
Managerial and professional $655[a]	5.5	10.3	—	—	—	—	—
Technical, sales, and administrative support $407[a]	1.6	6.7	—	—	—	—	—
Blue-collar	0.2	9.4	10.3	8.5			
Precision production, craft and repair $491[a]	1.7	11.5	—	—	—	—	—
Operators, fabricators and laborers $357[a]	−1.0	7.8	—	—	—	—	—
Unemployed	0.6	−30.5	−15.4	−11.6	−19.7	−24.1	−63.2
Layoffs	−19.9	−57.2	−53.4	−42.0	—	—	—
Permanent separations	12.7	−41.9	−12.1	−22.9	—	—	—
Involuntary part-time	8.2	−13.8	−13.1	−11.7	−7.3	−23.1	—
Discouraged workers	14.3	−8.1	−34.2	−3.7	13.5	—	—

[a] 1993 annual average, median weekly earnings of full-time wage salary workers.

Source: Author tabulations from U.S. Bureau of Labor Statistics data.

An examination of Table 1 reveals the following:

1. Payroll job growth is far behind the growth recorded at the same point in earlier postwar recoveries.
2. This is in large part the result of the fact that job losses are still occurring in manufacturing, and service sector growth has also been sluggish.
3. White-collar employment growth is slower than in previous recoveries, especially among technical, sales, and administrative support workers, but blue-collar growth is barely visible.
4. There is an inkling of employment gains in the recovery in higher-wage occupations.
5. Companies are still shedding labor.
6. Involuntary part-time and discouraged workers, two other measures of labor market slack, have not come down as in past recoveries.

Job creation by wage levels is an especially difficult issue to sort out. The wage levels in Table 1 are for full-time wage and salary workers. To the extent that the occupations listed in the table had significant growth of part-time workers, which typically earn relatively less than full-time workers, the likelihood of the finding concerning job growth among higher-wage occupations is diminished. The fact that many would-be full-time workers are accepting part-time jobs lends credence to the uneasiness surrounding the job quality issue in the current recovery.

The Situation in Europe

Policy makers want to know how the employment situation in the United States compares with that in other industrialized nations. What can we learn from their experiences? Moreover, what does our situation imply for future trading patterns? For example, a robust world economy will help our manufacturing industry recover.

Figures 1 and 2 present data from a recently completed two-year OECD study on employment and unemployment in member countries. Figure 1 shows employment trends, which are indexed to take account of differing country size, in OECD country groups over the 1960–92 period, with estimates to 1994 (1994 data were unavailable as of this writing). Clearly, from a relative standpoint, U.S. employment growth—which is the dominant component of the North American figures that include Canada—looks great in comparison with Europe. The United States, along with Australia and New Zealand (Oceania) has experienced almost a steady upward employment trend since 1960, whereas the trend in

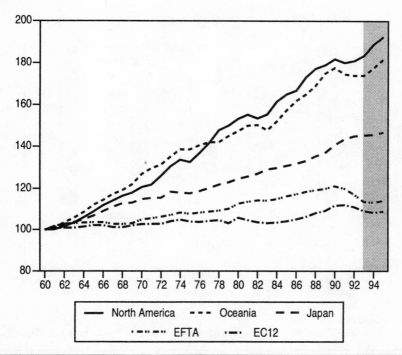

FIGURE 1 Employment Growth in OECD Regions, 1960–95 (OECD projections in shaded area) Note: Index 1960 = 100. *Source*: OECD.

Europe has been only negligibly upward. Two points often mentioned in the international literature to explain the higher employment growth in North America and Australia/New Zealand are (a) slower productivity growth here than elsewhere and (b) greater flexibility of wages.

Figure 2 shows (and this is broadly consistent with Davis et al.'s findings) that in the United States, more job creation and job destruction are accounted for by firms being born or dying than by existing firms' expanding or contracting. The opposite is the case in other OECD countries. Europeans feel that this entrepreneurialism also helps explain somewhat the differing employment trends shown in Figure 1.

An overview of the unemployment situation in the United States relative to other OECD countries is depicted in Table 2. Most countries' jobless rates were higher than those in the United States in 1993, particularly the share of unemployment that was long-term (one year or longer). The fifth column of Table 2 emphasizes the importance of education and

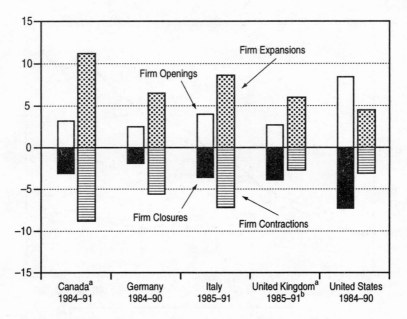

ᵃ Data refer to firms.
ᵇ Data in 1985–87 exclude firms with 1–4 individuals; data from 1987–91 include this size catagory.

FIGURE 2 Job Creation and Job Destruction: Percentage Contributions to Growth in Total Employment *Source*: OECD *Employment Outlook* (July 1994), Table 4.1.

training in combating unemployment. A ratio greater than 1 means that low-skilled workers have an unemployment rate higher than the national unemployment rate. In almost all countries, joblessness among low-skilled workers was well above the national average.

Policy

It seems clear that the U.S. economy is generating jobs, especially when viewed over the long term and relative to other countries. However, partly influenced by an anemic world economy, *net* job creation in the current recovery is quite slow. Many firms are still permanently shedding their workforces. Nevertheless, the smattering of job growth that is visible in the United States appears to be more high than low wage.

In any event, I do not think that creating jobs per se is a problem in the United States. Should the government be doing anything to promote Gazelles? I would suggest that it may be best simply to get out of their

TABLE 2
Profile of Unemployment

Country	Unemployment Rates[a] Total (1993)	Unemployment Rates[a] Youth (1992)	Unemployment Rates[a] Women (1992)	Ratio of Lower Secondary Education Unemployment Rate to Total Rate[b] (1989)	Long-term Unemployment as a Share of Total Unemployment[c] (1992)
North America	7.2	13.8	6.9	—	11.2
Canada	11.1	17.8	10.6	1.5	11.2
United States	6.7	13.3	6.5	2.3	11.2
Japan	2.5	5.1	2.6	2.7	15.4
Oceania	10.6	18.4	9.9	—	34.2
Australia	10.8	18.7	10.1	1.6	34.5
New Zealand	9.5	17.2	8.9	—	31.9
EC	10.6	20.6	12.2	—	42.2
Belgium	9.1	19.6	13.7	1.3	59.0
Denmark	10.4	11.4	11.3	1.7	27.0
France	11.6	24.6	13.7	1.3	36.1
Germany	5.8	4.9	6.1	2.0	33.5
Greece	9.8	24.6	15.4	—	49.7
Ireland	15.8	27.9	20.1	1.1	60.2[d]
Italy	10.2	30.6	14.6	0.9	58.2
Luxembourg	2.6	5.7	3.6	—	17.6
Netherlands	8.3	15.0	11.7	1.0	44.0
Portugal	5.5	12.0	6.5	1.7	30.9
Spain	22.4	43.2	28.9	1.2	47.4
United Kingdom	10.3	16.9	8.1	1.8	35.4
EFTA	7.4	12.6	7.0	—	13.1
Austria	4.2	4.7	4.9	—	16.9
Finland	17.7	30.8	15.6	1.4	8.2
Iceland	5.2	—	5.2	—	—
Norway	6.0	13.5	5.2	1.1	23.5
Sweden	8.1	18.4	6.6	1.4	8.0
Switzerland	3.7	6.8	4.7	—	20.6
OECD	7.8	15.1	8.2	—	28.6

[a] OECD standardized unemployment rates for total (national estimates for Austria, Denmark, Greece, and Luxembourg. For youth (aged under 25 years) and women, EC comparable unemployment rates and national estimates.

[b] For adults aged 25-64 years. Data refer to 1987 for Japan, to 1988 for Denmark, and to 1990 for the Netherlands.

[c] Long-term unemployed refers to all persons unemployed for 12 months or more.

[d] Data refer to 1991 for the EC countries.

Note: EC = European Community. EFTA = European Free Trade Association. Source: OECD data.

way, a *laissez-faire* approach, especially because it has been noted that jobs in Gazelles are unstable. What president wants to be remembered for creating unstable jobs?

Although Davis et al. found that survival rates for manufacturing jobs increase sharply with employer size, they also found that many, many firms, both large and small, go out of business each year. This finding, together with the unstable nature of Gazelles, points to a public policy focus on "employment stability," not "job stability."

Under such a policy focus, the government would act as a facilitator, not an initiator. It would establish rules to facilitate job transfers without losses—job-to-job flows instead of job-unemployment-job flows. This would include policies to make it easier for workers to change jobs while remaining employed, such as education/training to ensure that skills remain current, the portability of pensions and health care plans, flexible work schedules, and a nationwide labor market information system.

These policies would indeed help to promote the creation of "quality" jobs. The creation of quality jobs is a centerpiece of the Clinton administration's workforce strategy, which includes three broad components:

1. *Reform of primary and secondary education.* Highlights of the legislation now working its way through Congress—the Goals 2000: Education America Act—include development of national performance standards for students, improvement of teacher training and materials, and promotion of local school reform.
2. *Implementation of a school-to-work transition program.* In the last two years of high school and for at least one year beyond, students will be able to get on-the-job experience together with classroom training leading to *certified* skills. Voluntary national skill standards will be set.
3. *Establishment of a reemployment system* based on two broad components:

   a. Earlier identification, through screening of unemployment insurance claimants, of workers who clearly have permanently been displaced. Early identification followed by early readjustment and job search assistance cuts the time on unemployment. Long-term training will be reserved for those who really need it.
   b. Universal access to one-stop shops for employment and job information and assistance, available to the employed as well as the unemployed.

References

Boeri, T., and Cramer, U. (1992). "Employment Growth, Incumbents and Entrants: Evidence from Germany." *International Journal of Industrial Organization, 10,* 545–565.

Daly, M., Campell, M., Robson, G., and Gallagher, C. (1991, November). "Job Creation 1987-89: The Contributions of Small and Large Firms." *Employment Gazette,* 579–588.

Organization for Economic Cooperation and Development (OECD). (forthcoming). *Employment Outlook 1992.* Paris.

Comment

Barry Rogstad

What are the ramifications for small business growth and small business employees in the current policy setting? It is unfortunate, but it looks as if we will be in a wedge between 2 and 3 percent aggregate economic growth for a while. Some would argue that 2 percent is the "productivity frontier," and so businesses will focus on greater productivity. Yet, somewhere between 2.5 and 3 percent growth is needed before we have significant impact on aggregate net job creation in this country. As long as growth is at something less than that 2.5–3 percent level—where jobs are added in significant numbers—every public policy issue in Washington will focus on what the ramifications will be for job creation. The chapters in this volume on this topic caution policy makers: Watch targeting; be wary of drawing false conclusions from anecdotal information; be very clear that we can end up doing some real mischief in this area. I think Robert Reich is the second most important person in Washington for the foreseeable future because of discussion of these issues and discussion of how, in fact, the federal government will deal with job creation in this growth and policy environment.

Everyone has a bias; you ought to know mine. I am president of the American Business Conference (ABC), a group made up of 100 CEOs from midsize, high-growth companies. And, for purposes of my comments here, the emphasis is on *high-growth*, not midsize. To use some of David Birch's wording, I think the ABC can be described as a group of semipermanent Gazelles (my job is to try to keep them semipermanent). They are *not* permanent. There is turnover even in this group of excellent performers. The ABC has a numerical criterion: Membership is contingent on growth of either earnings or gross turnover of at least 10 percent a year. A firm must meet this level of growth for five years to gain membership. This level of growth is not automatic—I think the data from the preceding chapters have shown this to be true. Indeed, ABC has 5–10 percent membership turnover annually.

This is a perspective from an admittedly biased sample. It has been my professional hobby and good fortune to be able to look on a regular basis at some of the most successful companies (employers, if you will) to see why they do things as they do. Patterns do not immediately jump out at you; they are not so terribly obvious. But I have been at it for more than five years, and I think I have some useful observations to add to this discussion.

I agree with the policy ramifications discussed in the preceding chapters. These arguments illustrate the futility of chasing after idealized notions of business of any size—small, medium, or large. But on a broader plane, I think Chapters 4 and 5 highlight a debate that is ongoing in Washington. Policy makers desire to be very prescriptive, without looking at commercial evidence, without looking at the pattern of business behavior, the causes of the behavior, and the patterns created. Washington tends to emphasize clichés; indeed, the business community is partially responsible for that. Valid descriptors—research into what actually goes on in the economy—is very much needed in government.

The central issue to discuss is whether firm size is a meaningful descriptor in explaining job creation. The preceding chapters suggest that firm size is not the key determinant. I agree with that. The question then is, If not size, what other factors make a difference? I emphasize growth— although equating high growth with job creation does not make one a rocket scientist.

What, then, is the determining characteristic for job creation? I advance the notion of mind-set—the mind-set of the chief executive and, further, the business culture led by that CEO. I have found this to be true in my own experience. There is a positive, "glass is half full" attitude at the most successful companies. It is a decisive, action-oriented attitude. CEOs at such firms have a distinct view of public policy as well. They begin from the assumption that the government is not the chief determinant of the company's bottom line or top line. And they eschew the kind of targeting suggested as unproductive in the preceding chapters.

The authors of both chapters point out that there is no stability in this market system; perhaps there should not be. Instability is a source of the dynamism and growth that underlie American business. A second important issue is the notion that business can be maintained in a steady state; this is an illusion.

What are the key elements of success for a Gazelle company? There are three that stand out. The first is globalization; this is the key to business expansion. Business frames this issue in the following terms: If we are the dominant player in market share in our own industry, how do we expand that market? How do we increase the market share domestically? If we really are having difficulty increasing domestic markets, how can we gain markets worldwide? Access to international markets is absolutely essential.

The second element of success involves CEOs who have very clear definitions of the businesses they are in, and those are niche businesses. Their market niches may be valued in hundreds of billions of dollars on a worldwide basis, but they niches.

Finally, successful businesses are constantly engaged in a ruthless weeding out of product lines in which they are no longer at a competitive advantage. I suggest that the storm cloud for Gazelles is in dealing with firms with lines of business that are attempting to maintain their comparative advantage.

These three issues are largely independent of firm size in today's business world. Businesses that focus on these issues have a growth mind-set and view the role of public policy very distinctly. I want to keep that in the forefront of this discussion.

My view is that there is a great American job machine. It has a very fragile mechanism, and Americans should not take it for granted. The authors of Chapters 4 and 5 have discussed structural adjustments in the labor force, evidence of turnover, and the declining notion of lifetime employment. I suggest that the quality of jobs will become much more uniform throughout the size sector. What's the challenge? At the risk of getting back to rocket science here, jobs are coming from those companies that are engaged in growing markets. Job destruction is an increasing competitive reality. (I focus on that 7 to 8 percent year-in year-out job loss that Birch and Medoff talk about.)

The question I pose is, What actually starts an enterprise? This issue probably has very little to do with the public policy arena. But once a business is in fact started up, there are some issues I think are terribly important in how to encourage expansion and how to keep the Gazelle leaping in an upward direction as long as possible, thus lengthening its growth period. I think that is where public policy comes into play.

Davis, Haltiwanger, and Schuh point out that preferential treatment of small or any size business fails to comprehend the central theorem of economic policy prescription. This theorem, as they point out, directs attention toward business decision units that respond at the margin to proposed economic policy changes. I think that idea is the key. If we examine some key policy discussions that have major employment ramifications in this town today, what are the job creation ramifications?

1. *Tax reform*: If government is interested in fundamental tax reform, it ought to start off with a level playing field by removing the biases from existing code, to get the tax code to deal with all firms under all conditions as equally as possible. What do we do with the tax code now? We target like there is no tomorrow, and we have heard here that targeting does not make much sense.

2. *Health care*: Do I think that alternative health care proposals have different impacts on future hiring decisions? Yes, I think so. We are starting off with an assumption in the proposed health care reform that the system should be employer based. If job creation is our number-one policy outcome, then we should carefully reexamine that assumption and ask ourselves about the trade-offs implicit in making that kind of assumption for health care reform.

The American Business Conference is very much interested in accounting for options. We believe one of the means of promoting job creation is making stock options available for employees at all levels. Options will allow employees to identify with what the enterprise is all about. Option ownership promotes a sense of employee ownership. It lengthens the employee's time horizon and curtails job turnover.

The final point I would like to make follows on the last point made by Davis et al. in Chapter 5. Do we focus on Gazelles or try to pick out ABC-type companies and ask government to do something for them? That kind of activity is targeting. I think what we need to do is look at evidence of employer behavior and learn about what governs that behavior—what causes employers to employ which people under what circumstances. After observing, we must ask what kinds of policy situations and what kinds of economic environments caused them to behave one way or another. I believe a tremendous wealth of information is available. I think this kind of information will move the discussion of job creation forward.

PART THREE

U.S. Productivity Growth and Its Implications for Future Employment

Introduction

Economic growth by itself it not enough to guarantee that today's children will have better standards of living as adults than we do right now. As the population grows, the economy grows, too. But a growing number of jobs does not necessarily translate into better pay for those who are working. Rather, raising the productivity of individual workers is a key to raising the standard of living.

In the decades following the Second World War, labor productivity in the United States grew at an unprecedented rate. Not only was productivity growth faster than it had been historically, but it also exceeded that of other industrialized nations. However, in recent years the trend went in the opposite direction: even though our productivity has continued to grow, the rate of growth has been slower than that of our competitors. Does this signal the end of an era of American economic dominance? Persistent media reports about America's lack of competitiveness in recent years have led the public to believe that this is true.

The session, "U.S. Productivity Growth and Its Implications for Future Employment," was organized to address the issue of the apparent decline of American productivity. The chapter by William Baumol, "U.S. Productivity Revisited: It Remains Better Than You Think," details the performance of United States productivity growth relative to Canada, Japan, France, Germany, and the United Kingdom. While it is true that United States productivity growth has been slower in recent years, the level of United States productivity remains the highest of all nations. Baumol conjectures that other countries have been playing a game of economic "catch-up" with the United States in the post-war era because they started off with much weaker economies. An important implication of this diagnosis is that we should *not* expect that other countries will eventually overtake the U.S. level of productivity.

Despite his essay's optimistic conclusion about the prospects for United States productivity relative to that of other countries, Baumol does not dismiss the recent slowdown in productivity growth as unimportant. He shows, however, that the manufacturing sector is not the main source of the slowdown in overall productivity growth. This should help assuage the fears of those who worry that the recent growth in the service sector has been fueled by a lack of competitiveness in the manufacturing sector. Rather, he argues, productivity improvements in manufacturing have freed up workers to move into the rapidly expanding service sector.

If the manufacturing sector has not been the source of the overall productivity slowdown, then the service sector must be the culprit. In his paper, "On the Relation of Employment to Productivity," Walter Oi notes that service sector productivity, as reported in official government statistics, both is lower, and has grown more slowly, than manufacturing sector productivity. Yet he argues that the apparently low level of productivity in services is misleading because the definition of output is elusive. If, for example, the amount of time it takes a customer to get served goes down, then productivity goes up. But this would not show up in the official statistics, which only measure gross sales. If the improvements for consumer waiting times and the like have outstripped the gains in gross sales, then productivity in the service sector has increased faster than we had thought to be true.

Oi postulates that the increased presence in the labor force of women and part-time workers, who have less work experience than the older, full-time males they have replaced, could account for part of the slowdown in productivity growth in recent years. This has happened at the same time that there has been considerable growth in the number of jobs. Given the lack of a relationship between job and productivity growth, he emphasizes the need to focus public policy on the maximization of the total product of the economy, not the total number of jobs.

The overall impression left by the two authors is that (a) there is no cause for alarm over manufacturing sector productivity; and (b) we should be cautious about declaring a "crisis" in labor sector productivity. This may seem surprising, given the doomsday-like portrayals of these issues in the national media throughout the late 1980s and early 1990s. It is instructive that in the past year, as Japan has slipped into recession and the United States has shown emergent signs of economic growth, there has been a shift in the tone of reporting about the productivity of U.S. manufacturing. Now, it seems that the Japanese have the productivity problems and the United States can do no wrong. Because previous obituaries on the U.S. manufacturing sector were premature—as Baumol's paper shows—it is safe to assume that within a few years the media will find that the Japanese have made a "remarkable" comeback in manufacturing.

On a different note, some critics point out that even if there is a high rate of productivity growth in the economy, a large number of workers are permanently displaced from a job or an entire industry through labor-saving technological innovations. Oi's essay, and the comments by John

Haltiwanger and Patrick Savin, sound a warning against government intervention. All three acknowledge that there may be a role for the government to help out workers who are displaced by productivity improvements; but they argue that such assistance should be directed to individual workers, not entire firms or industries. If a firm or industry is destined to become extinct, their charge to government is to, at most, help the workers make a smooth transition to new employment, not to shield the firm or industry from the force of technological changes. For further insights into which workers have been adversely affected by economic growth in recent years, the reader is encouraged to turn to Chapter 6 for the session on "Labor Force Demographics, Income Inequalities, and Returns to Human Capital."

6

Productivity, Employment, and Wages

Walter Y. Oi

Productivity and Employment Prospects

Five of every eight American adults are gainfully employed. This is a historical high for the employment-to-population ratio and is higher than the employment-to-population ratio in any other industrialized country. Real wages have declined, but real per capita income is climbing at a modest rate. The American public is dissatisfied with the pace of the recovery from the most recent downturn in 1991. The administration wants to stimulate the rate of growth in labor productivity, which, it is hoped, will create more jobs and improve the competitive position of American workers in a global economy. The policy prescriptions are familiar—expand government spending to invest in the infrastructure, spend more for education and training, and provide incentives to encourage savings and R&D activities. These same policies were being pushed a decade ago, but at that time, there were concerns voiced about the dangers of technological unemployment, which acknowledges the possibility that there is no stable relation between the rate of productivity growth and employment.

The slower pace of productivity growth since 1973 has been attributed, in part, to the shift of labor toward the service sector, which has historically exhibited slower technical progress. Output is, however, not correctly measured in retailing and in the personal service industries. The statistics on output are even worse in the case of public and merit goods. I shall argue that the rapid growth in the allocation of resources to public and merit goods may be responsible for part of the productivity slowdown. The observed growth in labor and total factor productivity is a result of not only of technical progress and improvements in the quality of inputs, but of organizational innovations. Finally, the objective of public policy ought not be job creation, but the maximization of the total product of an economy.

Trends in Employment and Output

The U.S. economy has exhibited a remarkable capacity to generate employment opportunities. More than 117 million Americans were gainfully employed in 1992. Employment in nonagricultural industries has been growing at an annual rate of 1.6 percent.[1] The labor force has expanded even faster than employment resulting in a rise in the unemployment rate at the cyclical peaks from 3.8 percent in 1948 to 5.8 percent in 1979.[2] The composition of the workforce by age and sex is summarized in Table 6.1, which reveals that the employment-to-population ratio of women has climbed, and that of older men is declining. A higher fraction of women and part-time workers who have less work experience could account for part of the productivity slowdown of the past two decades.[3]

The gross domestic product in constant dollars grew at a rate of 3.75 percent a year over the 1957–73 period, but the growth rate slowed to 2.53 percent a year between the next two cyclical peaks, 1973–79.[4] The growth rate of labor productivity measured by GDP per employee (see the first panel of Table 6.2), which averaged 1.93 percent before 1973, slowed to 0.74 percent in the 1980s. The slowdown is evident in the time path of GDP per full-time-equivalent (FTE) employee shown in Figure 6.1 where two part-time workers are assumed to be equal to one FTE

TABLE 6.1
Employment by Age and Sex, 1948, 1973, 1992
(in thousands)

	1948	1973	1992
Employment	58,342	85,064	117,598
Percentage by age			
youth, 16–24	18.79	22.46	14.93
men, 25–64	56.10	46.78	44.77
women, 25–64	20.31	27.36	37.38
older, 65+	4.81	3.39	2.91
Employment-to-population ratio			
total 16 and older	0.5478	0.5616	0.5989
youth, 16–24	0.5284	0.5465	0.5212
men, 25–64	0.8963	0.8516	0.8195
women, 25–64	0.3142	0.4823	0.6627
older, 65+	0.2430	0.1340	1.1068

Source: Data is unpublished, obtained from Bureau of Labor Statistics.

TABLE 6.2
Annual Growth Rates of Output and Wages

Item	Annual Growth Rates (%)			
	1957–73	1973–79	1979–88	1957–88
Gross domestic product [a]				
total	3.75	2.53	2.44	3.13
per capita	2.41	1.50	1.48	1.96
per employee	1.93	0.00	0.74	1.21
per FTE employee	2.14	0.02	0.79	1.33
Business sector [b]				
output (X)	3.73	2.52	2.71	3.20
output per hour (X/H)	2.71	0.63	1.33	1.90
output per employee (X/E)	2.34	0.90	0.98	1.51
output per combined input (X/I)	2.75	0.67	0.29	1.62
hourly compensation (W)	2.65	0.45	0.30	1.53
Manufacturing [b]				
output X	3.98	1.78	2.86	3.23
output per hour (X/H)	2.96	1.43	3.46	2.81
output per employee (X/E)	2.97	1.03	3.80	2.83
output per comb. input (X/I)	2.21	0.52	2.76	2.04
hourly compensation (W)	1.87	0.89	0.02	1.14
Average hourly earnings [c]				
total nonagricultural industries	1.88	–0.04	–0.65	0.76
manufacturing	1.63	0.74	–0.55	0.82
retail trade	1.55	–0.14	–1.52	0.33

[a] Economic Report of the President 1993, Table B2.
[b] BLS Productivity and Related Measures. Index 1982=1.000
[c] Data is unpublished, obtained from Bureau of Labor Statistics.

Note: Growth rates are computed from peak periods to peak periods.

employee. Per capita GDP increased at a faster rate than GDP per employee (1.96 versus 1.21 percent a year), which is simply a result of the upward trend in the employment-to-population (E/P) ratio. U.S. Bureau of Labor Statistics data utilize a gross output measure for the business sector and exhibit a similar pattern for labor productivity, output per hour, X/H in the second panel of Table 6.2. Total factor productivity, X/I, also reveals the productivity slowdown; its growth rate averaged 2.75 percent a year over the first cycle, 1957–73, but slowed to 0.67 percent in the next interval. The BLS estimates for manufacturing, shown in the third panel of Table 6.2, reveal that both labor and total factor productivity have recovered in the 1980s even though both series are growing more slowly than they did in the pre-1973 period.

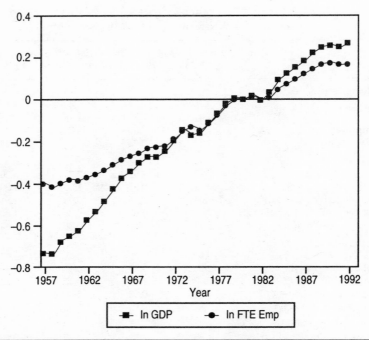

FIGURE 6.1 Gross Domestic Product and FTE Employment: 1957–92 (logs of indexes, 1982 = 1)

The onset of the productivity slowdown was accompanied by falling real wages measured by the BLS establishment survey, shown in the fourth panel of Table 6.2. Real average hourly earnings declined at an annual rate of –0.04 percent in the 1970s and fell even faster, –0.65 percent a year, between 1979 and 1988. There were some notable differences in the time path of real wages across industries, occupations, and demographic groups. Real wages of college graduates and women workers rose in the 1980s, whereas those of less-educated men and of retail employees fell sharply. Wages, however, are only part of total employee compensation. Employer costs for fringe benefits, which are included in the BLS data on real hourly compensation (shown in the second panel of Table 6.2), made up 10 percent of wages in 1970 and 16 percent in 1992. If the value of fringe benefits to workers is approximately equal to the employer costs, real hourly compensation is a superior measure of the real returns to labor. The growth rates of real hourly compensation in the business sector were always positive, but declined from an annual rate of 2.65 percent before 1973 to 0.43 percent over the 1973–79 period. The puzzle is that the growth of real hourly compensation in 1979–88 was even slower, +0.30 percent a year, than over the preceding cycle, even though labor productivity was growing faster in the latter period. The aggregate data do not reveal a stable long-run relation between the growth rate of labor productivity and the rate of job creation or the growth rate in real hourly compensation.

The Link between Productivity and Employment

The relation between productivity growth and employment can be traced to an aggregate production function in which output X depends on inputs of labor L and capital K given the state of technology τ.

$$X = f(L,K:\tau)$$

When the labor input is measured by person-hours, H, labor productivity grew at a rate of 1.9 percent a year over the 1957–88 period.[5] Savings and investment increase the stock of capital K, a cooperating input that raises labor productivity, employment, and wages. Investing in human capital via education and/or training improves the quality of each person-hour H and hence in measured labor productivity X/H. If, however, hours are measured in efficiency units, $H^* = \varepsilon H$ (where ε is an index of labor quality), output per efficiency adjusted hour, $X/\varepsilon H$, ought not to be affected by improvements in labor quality even though X/H will rise.

The historical growth of output can be explained only partially by larger supplies of inputs, even adjusted for quality. According to Solow (1957), the residuals from the fitted production function were the results of the uneven and unobservable pace of technical progress. Hicks neutral technical progress will lead to increases in employment, wages, and labor productivity. However, a labor-saving innovation could reduce the aggregate demand for labor. Innovations and technical advances are only two of the forces that can increase total factor productivity (TFP), the ratio of output to an index of all inputs combined, X/I. An increase in the demand for the final product can raise TFP if the production function exhibits economies of scale or if the more efficient firms in the industry capture a larger market share. In the opposing direction, a contraction in demand could be accompanied by an increase in X/I if the less efficient firms are pushed out of the market. A changing output mix also confounds the measurement of productivity. In 1990, the output of the airlines, measured by revenue passenger miles, rose by 4.5 percent, whereas labor productivity fell by 3.7 percent because employment was increased to meet demands for stricter inspections, tighter airport security, and pressures to improve on-time records.[6]

In addition to the long-run relation between output and employment, labor productivity is procyclical. Arthur Okun (1981) has observed that a 1 percentage point decrease in the unemployment rate (approximately equal to a 1 percent increase in employment) is associated with a 2 to 3 percentage point increase in GNP. This empirical regularity could be generated by (a) a model where production exhibits short-run increasing returns, (b) labor is a quasi-fixed input that is more intensively utilized in the upswing, or (c) labor is transferred from various internal activities, such as the maintenance and repair of equipment or training, in the downswing (which are not reported in the national income statistics) to producing goods in the upswing (I discuss these arguments in Oi, 1983a). A stimulus to aggregate demand in a slack period could lead to a short-run association between labor productivity growth and employment, but the causation is reversed. Employment in the short run is determined by exogenous changes in output. Robert J. Gordon (1993) has estimated a version of this sort of model. He relates trend-adjusted quarterly rates of change in employment (person hours) to lagged changes in output, an error correction term proxied by lagged labor productivity, and a vector of dummy variables to capture an "end of expansion" effect:

$$\Delta H_t = \mu + \Sigma \alpha_i \Delta H_{t-i} + \Sigma \beta_j \Delta Q_{t-j} + \Sigma \upsilon_k D_{t-k} + \phi \ln(Q_{t-1}/H_{t-1}) + e_t,$$

where $\Delta H_t = \ln(H_t/H_{t-1})$ is the first difference in the logarithms of person-hours, $\Delta Q_t = \ln(Q_t/Q_{t-1})$ is the first difference in the logarithms of output, and D_{t-k} is a dummy variable indicating a quarter preceding the end of an expansion. Gordon found that the end of the last expansion in late 1989 was characterized by an unusually high level of hours per worker. There were few layoffs in the downturn, enabling firms to expand total person-hours in this recovery with relatively few new hires, hence, the so-called jobless recovery. The Gordon model nicely describes the short-run, cyclical relation between output and employment changes. It still leaves us with the task of explaining the reason for the shift in the adjustment path in the most recent cycle, however.

Denison (1962, 1974), Jorgenson and Griliches (1967), and others have identified the factors responsible for the growth of the U.S. economy. Technical advances account for a third to half of the growth in output. However, the upward trend in productivity slowed and nearly stopped in 1973. The Council of Economic Advisers (1988) offered four reasons for the slowdown: (a) As more inexperienced women and teenagers entered the labor force, the average quality of the labor input deteriorated; (b) higher energy prices reduced the demand for a cooperating input; (c) more government regulations impeded the efficient allocation of resources across sectors; and (d) there was a decrease in R&D expenditures, slowing down the rate of induced technical progress.[7] The current policy proposals rest on a questionable assumption that there is a stable relationship between productivity growth rates and job creation rates.

Automation and the Relocation of Displaced Workers

Technological advances that reduce unit costs and push forward the production possibilities frontier are good for the economy as a whole. They are, however, frequently accompanied by unemployment, as displaced workers seek alternative employment. Stanback (1983) cites the example of a General Electric plant in Erie, Pennsylvania, where automation displaced 60 workers; they were replaced by 2 maintenance employees. Other examples of labor redundancies created by the adoption of new technologies are provided by Irving Bluestone (1983). In his opinion, the job losses caused by automation will force the government to institute a system of economic planning with a rational industrial policy. Shaiken (1983) claims that innovations in telecommunications and computers have facilitated the transfer of jobs around the world, a practice now called outsourcing. (He should have also included the cost saving innovations in transportation.) Cyert has projected that by the year 2000, only 3–5 percent of the U.S. workforce will be employed in manufacturing industries (cited by Bluestone, 1983). Disemployment caused by technical innovations, mergers, or foreign trade competition is costly to the displaced employee. A Nobel laureate wrote:

> The general theoretical proposition that the worker who loses his job in one industry will necessarily be able to find employment, possibly after appropriate retraining, in some other industry is as invalid as would be the assertion that horses that lost their job in transportation and agriculture can necessarily have been put to another economically productive use. (Leontief, 1983, p. 4)

The conventional wisdom calls for policies that will create jobs, establish retraining programs, and provide income replacement. Proposals that would reduce hours of work or introduce work-sharing plans have not been warmly received in the United States.[8] An industrial policy presumes that a government agency can achieve a more efficient allocation of resources than that attainable via the market. As a student, nearly 40 years ago, I recall hearing Milton Friedman say that in principle, the decisions to undertake certain projects will be no better or worse whether they are made by public agents or private entrepreneurs. However, the same cannot be said about decisions concerning when to cut one's losses. Public officials are far more reluctant to abandon projects. The returns to retraining are substantially greater for younger workers. Many older displaced workers elect to withdraw from the labor force, and those who do not experience longer unemployment spells before they find new jobs.[9] Lou Jacobson (1991) found that displaced workers who were put into a mandatory retraining program experienced a longer spell of unemployment between discharge and reemployment than did those who received no retraining. Further, the mandatory retraining had no effect on the average earnings on the subsequent job. Finally, higher income replacement rates are sure to extend the average duration of unemployment. William Niskanen (1983) argues that special programs for workers displaced by technical progress are contrary to the public interest. Needed adjustments can be more efficiently achieved through the normal functioning of the labor market.

Measuring the Output of the Service Sector

The productivity slowdown of the past two decades has been attributed, in part, to the relative expansion of the service industries, which have historically exhibited the slowest rates of productivity growth. Of the five industries identified in Table 6.3, personal services enjoyed the largest employment gain; their share of total employment climbed from 12.7 percent in 1957 to 26.7 percent in 1992. [10] BLS estimates reveal a considerably faster growth rate of labor productivity in manufacturing than in retail trade, 2.69 versus 1.67 percent a year over the 1948–87 period. [11]

The Bureau of Labor Statistics measures the output of the retail trade sector by sales volume, which is a crude and often misleading indicator. The output of a retail firm is a composite bundle of component activities that may include some or all of the following: (a) exchange, consummating transactions to transfer property rights to goods; (b) a product line, assembling and displaying goods and informing customers about them; (c) convenience, offering the product line at a time and place to reduce shopping costs; (d) ancillary services, supplying delivery, credit, implicit warranties, and return privileges; and (e) production, packaging and processing goods. A store that offers delivery and credit is engaged in downstream vertical integration into transportation and finance, whereas a grocer who bakes her own bread exemplifies upstream integration into manufacturing. Most vendors do not quote "prices" for supplying particular component services, but obtain their revenue by introducing a spread between wholesale and retail prices, the vendor's gross margin. These margins will vary across stores, being larger for firms providing a wider range and superior quality of services. Cafeterias realize a lower margin relative to restaurants because they supply fewer point-of-sale services.

TABLE 6.3
Employment, Person-Hours, and Earnings by Sector
(percentage distribution, 1957, 1979, and 1992)

	1957	*1979*	*1992*
Employment (thousands)	52,853	89,823	108,437
manufacturing	32.49	23.42	16.77
wholesale trade	5.75	5.81	5.52
retail trade	14.85	16.67	17.65
personal services	12.69	19.05	26.65
government	14.41	17.75	17.13
Person-hours (millions)	2,028.69	3,195.52	3,741.38
manufacturing	33.69	26.47	19.93
wholesale trade	6.03	6.34	6.11
retail trade	14.97	14.34	14.73
personal services	11.94	17.51	25.11
government	13.14	17.47	17.38
Earnings (millions of $)	4,050.06	20,248.12	43,054.62
manufacturing	34.60	27.99	19.83
wholesale trade	6.10	6.39	6.05
retail trade	11.02	10.25	9.14
personal services	9.39	14.81	23.00
government	15.86	19.76	23.97

Source: Data is unpublished, obtained from Bureau of Labor Statistics.

A production function for firms in distribution, transportation, education, and services differs from that in manufacturing in two important respects. First, the consumer/customer supplies an essential input. Without the consumer, there would be no output. Hence, the number of consumers/buyers B has to appear alongside hired labor and capital to produce a flow of services, $X = f(L,K,B)$. Second, demands are stochastic, and delays are costly. A person-trip is "produced" by combining the time of the trip taker with the resources (bus and driver) supplied by the vendor. Although some goods may be sold on consignment or "to order," a retailer ordinarily acquires title to the goods he or she sells. Stores maintain inventories and stay open even when there are no customers. On the other side, a customer may sometimes have to wait to be served. Someone is almost always idle. In the terminology of W. H. Hutt (1939/1977), resources and buyers are in a state of "pseudo-idleness." A retail production function, $X = f(L,K,B)$, exhibits increasing returns. A doubling of all inputs (clerks L, counters K, and customers B) leads to more than a doubling of output measured by completed transactions. These economies of massed reserves enable larger stores to offer lower prices and to pay higher wages.[12] These principles apply to most firms in the distribution, transport, and service industries. The largest airline on a given route will realize the lowest unit operating costs and the highest load factor. If the biggest hospital in a city has 60 percent of the available beds, it will supply more than 60 percent of all occupied beds. Larger cities and higher car ownership rates enabled firms in the trade and service sectors to exploit the economies of massed reserves.

The output of an establishment in the service sector is *not* proportional to sales volume. It is a composite bundle, the value of which can vary in response to changes in (a) the breadth and quality of services supplied by the vendor, (b) the inputs supplied by the customer, and (c) the interaction of vendors and customers, which determines the fraction of time that establishment resources (labor and inventories) and customer time are idle in the course of "producing" the output of this sector.

The Consumer and a Vertical Measure of Productivity

The idea for a self-service, cash-and-carry store was conceived in 1916 when Charles Saunders opened his Piggly Wiggly store in Memphis. The store had a large selling area located in a low-rent district outside of the city. It offered nationally branded goods at low prices, eliminated free delivery and credit, and used local advertising to attract customers. Appel (1972) claims that this was the institutional innovation that reduced retail prices. The prohibition of chain stores in some states, which has been analyzed by Tom Ross (1986), temporarily slowed the growth of productivity in food stores.[13]

Barry Bluestone (1981) has shown how this retail revolution was accompanied by a change in the composition of the workforce. Forty years ago, a customer could be served by a grocery clerk or butcher who might inform him or her about various products. National brands and trademarks have replaced trained clerks and reputable stores. Store-specific human capital is valuable when customers ask for particular clerks whose advice they seek and who can honor an implicit warranty in the event of a defective product. When impersonal transactions can be standardized, there is less to be gained from establishing durable, ongoing relations between customers and clerks who know one another. The increased use of part-timers reflects the move to less skilled and less specifically trained labor. In 1975, full-time employees outnumbered part-timers at the supermarkets responding to the Progressive Grocer survey, but by 1988, full-time workers made up only 41 percent of all employees at the independent supers. The ratio of part- to full-time clerks rose from 1.04 to 1.79 between 1981 and 1988.[14] These changes in the organization of work and pay are market responses to the reallocation of the various distributive functions performed by the retailer, manufacturer, and consumer.

Output depends on the components that are supplied by the vendor. A gasoline station can reduce its input of hired labor per dollar of sales by introducing self-service. The BLS index of productivity will rise because we do not count the labor provided by the customer.[15] Buying a cheesecake at a bakery instead of baking one at home is an example of the substitution of hired for home labor time, which is the mirror image of the self-service gas station or the automatic teller machine. Two additional examples illustrate the importance of an efficient allocation of distribution functions. According to Robert Steiner (1978), the national advertising of branded toys (a substitute for point-of-sales information) facilitated the mass merchandising of toys through discount outlets. This marketing innovation reduced the gross margin on toys from 40 percent to 20 percent. This development could not have taken place in the presence of resale price maintenance. Currently, dual distribution, wherein a refiner simultaneously markets through both independent and vertically integrated gas stations, is outlawed by divorcement laws in some states. Barron and Umbeck (1984) and Hogarty (1986) have found that retail prices are lower in states that permit dual distribution. If a state repeals a divorcement law, labor productivity in that state's gas stations will climb. This increase might be confused with technical progress.

It is surely reasonable to suppose that the component distribution activities will be allocated to the several parties to minimize the *full price* of the final good, the cheesecake on a plate or gas in a tank. Steiner (1978) proposes a vertical measure of productivity in which inputs at the manufacturing, wholesale, and retail levels are aggregated and related to the final output at retail to measure productivity. I would urge that the inputs provided by the consumer should also be counted. The problem is ubiquitous. A camera with a warranty is different from one that has none. If a carrying case is thrown in, the firm is producing more *output*. From its peak of 6.2 million employees in 1990, wholesale trade has lost more than 250,000 jobs. Nardonne, Herz, Mellor, and Hippel (1993) claim that some of the functions formerly performed by wholesalers have been assumed by the manufacturer.[16] The Steiner procedure would have consolidated the inputs at both wholesale and manufacturing levels and related the sum to output at the manufacturing plant to calculate a vertical measure of productivity. The logic of the Steiner procedure calls for us to include inputs at all levels, including the consumer. Vertical acquisitions and divestitures confound the task of measuring productivity changes when the prevailing methodology embraces a gross output measure.

Implications of a Rising Demand for Public and Merit Goods

A production function model tacitly assumes that (a) the economy is located on the production possibilities frontier, and (b) all goods are private goods, such as disposable diapers, eggs, and figs, whose values are determined by market forces. The first assumption has been challenged by Leibenstein (1966), who contends that for a variety of reasons (ignorance or lack of full information, inertia, custom, or rent-seeking behavior), firms sometimes locate inside of the frontier. The presence of a large public sector supplying some public goods contradicts the second assumption. Federal, state, and local governments are controlling an ever larger share of the nation's resources. One of every eight employees in 1957 worked for a government agency; by 1992, it was one of every six, as shown in Table 6.4. We like to think that the output of the government is largely composed of public goods (national defense, a justice system, parks and monuments, lighthouses), but this is not so. The government produces some private goods, such as electricity, books, and transit services, as well as *merit goods*. The latter are distinguished from private and public goods by a recognition that their value derives not from a norm of consumer sovereignty but from some alternative norm. The market values that would be determined by unimpeded individual choices would result in some goods being under- or overvalued in relation to some communal norm set by majority vote, fashion, or custom. The production of alcohol and tobacco is, for example, discouraged, because these are demerit goods. Education, health care, low-cost housing, energy for poor households, and school lunches exemplify some of the merit goods receiving government subsidies.[17] The impact of a rising demand for public and merit goods on the economy is different from that of increases in the demands for semiconductors or fructose.[18] The value of the output of the latter two industries is determined by consumer demands and the opportunity costs of producing them. This is not so for public and merit goods. The values of sports stadiums and baccalaureate degrees are not determined by market prices but by the budgetary outlays for the inputs needed to produce them. Additionally, there is no reason to suppose that least-cost techniques are adopted in producing tanks or school lunches.

Turn to the case of education, which was a major contributor to the growth of government from 1955 to 1970. The postwar baby boom increased enrollments at all schooling levels from 41.2 million in 1957 to 60.0 million in 1973. Although enrollments in grades K to 12 declined in the 1970s, college enrollments climbed. The data displayed in Table 6.4 reveal that per pupil expenditures for elementary and secondary schools (in constant dollars) increased by 52.3 percent. The average cost per college student rose by only 10.4 percent over the same 1973–92 period, which partially reflects the increasing proportion of college students enrolling in lower-cost two- and four-year state schools. Roughly 85 percent of all students in grades K to 12 are enrolled in public schools. Revenue per pupil in these schools (which is equal to expenditures) more than tripled over the 16 years from 1957 to 1973. The growth rate in revenue per pupil was 5.4 percent a year up to 1973, but this slowed to only 2.2 percent over the past 19 years. If *output* is measured by enrollments, there has been a clear decline in productivity, resulting in an increase in the unit cost of instruction.[19] Teachers made up 65.2 percent of all public school employees in 1957, but only 52.9 percent in 1992. A relatively larger support staff (administrators, counselors, nurses, bus drivers, and security guards) could arguably complement teachers, thereby improving the quality of instruction, meaning a larger quality-adjusted flow of educational output. Test scores indicate the contrary, however;

TABLE 6.4
Selected Data for Health Care and Education

	1957	1973	1979	1992
Employment (thousands)	58,800	80,260	93,170	111,644
goods producing (%)	35.7	31.0	28.4	21.0
services (%)	41.3	47.6	50.9	59.5
government (%)	13.0	17.1	17.1	16.6
health care (%)	4.4	6.2	6.8	8.8
education (%)	5.3	8.8	8.1	8.7
health/goverment/education (%)	16.44	23.19	23.66	25.76
Enrollment (thousands)	41,211	60,047	58,221	61,563
enrollment college	3,313	9,603	11,570	14,107
% college	8.04	15.99	19.87	22.92
Expenditures ($)	n.a.	251,888	274,911	378,700
per elementary/secondary pupil ($)	n.a.	3,159	3,696	4,809
per college pupil ($)	n.a.	9,638	8,859	10,640
School revenues (billions of $)	47.3	162.8	176.2	220.2
enrollment (millions)	30.7	45.7	42.6	41.2
revenue/pupil ($)	1,541	3,560	4,142	5,342
Students to employees				
per FTE staff	17.4	12.9	10.7	9.0
per FTE teacher	26.7	21.9	19.7	17.0
% teachers	65.2	58.9	57.7	52.9

Source: Data is unpublished, obtained from Bureau of Labor Statistics.

student performance is worse today than it was 35 years ago. In the official statistics, *educational output* is measured by outlays for hired inputs (superintendents and principals, teachers, media equipment, books, school operating expenses, and so on). I find it hard to believe that a student year of instruction in grades K to 12 is worth $5,342, judged either by a parent's willingness to pay or by the median voter's valuation.

Part of the increased demand for public and merit goods is directly produced by government agencies and public enterprises. Teachers are hired by community colleges, jails are built and staffed, and buses are operated by public transportation authorities. In addition, governments appropriate funds to retain private firms that supply prescribed goods and services. Hospital care, for example, is provided by both public and private units. The sharp increase of employment in the health care industries, shown in the top panel of Table 6.4, is largely the result of "in-kind" transfers awarded to the elderly and welfare clients on AFDC and SSI. To the extent that a recipient's valuation of a Medicare or Medicaid entitlement is below its cost, the *output* of the health care sector cannot be measured by expenditures in constant dollars, which have grown at an astronomic rate.[20] Education, health care, and government services (net of schooling and hospitals) make up a considerable proportion of all the public and merit goods produced each year. They collectively provided jobs for 25.8 percent of all employed persons. The outputs of these sectors are usually measured by deflated expenditures that almost surely exceed the utilities that consumers derive from these goods and services. An inflated measure of output for these three industries makes it hard to interpret the economywide estimates of labor productivity.

The ever-expanding demand for public and merit goods may have a darker side. The costs of meeting this demand necessarily raise taxes. A larger tax bite has to reduce the incentives to put forth more work effort and to undertake risky ventures. The disincentives generated by higher taxes to finance an ever-growing demand for public and merit goods may be responsible for part of the productivity slowdown exhibited by the private sector.

The Supply Side of the Labor Market

A production function model emphasizes the demand side of the market. Factors that affect labor supply, the organization of work, work effort and incentives, and the regulation of economic activity are pushed into the background. Variations in the employment-to-population ratio over time and across demographic groups have been driven mainly by supply-side factors. The doubling of the E/P ratio of adult women from

.314 in 1948 to .663 in 1992 can largely be explained by rising real wages and by a shift in preferences away from work at home to work in the market. Changes in the benefit and eligibility provisions of the social security retirement and disability insurance programs account for much of the decline in the E/P ratios of adult men and the elderly over 65 years of age. More important, the temporal movements in the E/P ratio are only weakly related, if at all, to changes in the growth rate of labor productivity or total factor productivity.

Maximization of the Total Product

The objective of public policy, according to Ronald Coase (1960), ought to be the design of an institutional structure that will promote the maximization of the *total product*. Productivity is the goal. Its relation to employment and job creation is only incidental. Leibenstein (1966) argues that a firm may, out of ignorance or inertia, operate in an inefficient fashion. Scientific management was introduced around 1913 by Frederick Taylor. Its signature was a stopwatch atop a clipboard, and its proponents tried to teach managers how to reach the efficient frontier.

> When pig iron is being handled (each pig weighing 92 pounds), a first-class workman can be under load only 43 percent of the day, and if the load becomes lighter (i.e., when only half pigs are handled), the percentage of the day in which the man can remain under load increases. Applying this law, Taylor got his Pennsylvania Dutchman Schmidt to load 47 and a half tons of pig iron per day instead of 12 and a half; i.e. he increased the output 276 percent. (Florence, 1924, p. 100)

Taylor and his disciples mainly dealt with the physical layout of a plant and the performance of employees. They believed that the acquisition of the requisite knowledge could increase output with only minor changes in the organization of work or minor investments in additional capital or labor. P. Sargant Florence (1924) embraced a broader concept of labor productivity. He found, for example, that a longer work schedule was associated with higher labor turnover rates, more absences and accidents, and higher rates of defective units. Conditions at the work site (length of the workday, temperature, humidity, and lighting) affected labor productivity. Output per hour was highest at temperatures between 60 and 72 degrees, and labor productivity was 8–10 percent lower when the temperature rose above 80 or fell below 55 degrees. By installing air conditioners, a firm could raise productivity and reduce the frequency of workplace accidents. The availability of low-cost air conditioning after 1965 was surely important in explaining the migration of the population and manufacturing activities to the South and South-west.[21] A firm that shortens the workweek and provides a work environment with a controlled temperature can set a faster work pace thereby raising productivity. Several economists, including Florence (1924) and Davidson, Florence, Gray, and Ross (1958), have urged that piece rates should be substituted for hourly rates of pay to give workers an incentive to put forth more effort. But such incentives often increase quantity at the expense of quality. Profit sharing and bonuses are now the preferred ways of providing incentives and are being incorporated into compensation packages.

Cash is usually the carrot of choice from the set of incentives that could elicit more work effort. But what is work? Amartya Sen (1975) asks if the beggar boy in *The Three Penny Opera* is or is not employed. Given that Jerimiah Peachum pays him a wage, the answer is yes, because (a) employment gives an income to the employed. But (b) employment yields an output, and here, Sen says the answer is no unless sympathy is an *output*. Finally, Sen is vague about the third criterion that distinguishes work, namely, (c) employment gives a person the recognition of being engaged in something worthwhile. The new industrial relations literature directs more attention to the nature and disutility of work. Leibenstein (1966) observes that (a) productivity is higher when work is organized in smaller groups, (b) generally supervised employees are more productive than closely monitored workers, and (c) individuals who are provided with more information about the importance of the job are more productive.[22] Team production and worker participation in quality circles are some of the human resource management (HRM) practices that can elevate the pride an individual takes in doing his or her job. A manager's acknowledging a job well done may elicit effort and can, at times, be substituted for cash or the fear of being dismissed.[23] Although incentives and job security are important, Ichniowski, Shaw, and Prennushi (1993) persuasively document the proposition that they must be embedded in a portfolio of complementary HRM practices to have significant effects on labor productivity.[24] The adoption of these HRM practices by a growing number of large firms suggests that organizational innovations may be as important as technical progress in raising productivity.

Downsizing and bifurcation are two recent developments that characterize a structural change in the corporate labor market. The Fortune 500 largest firms accounted for 26 percent of total employment in 1980, but only 21 percent in 1992. The Ford River Rouge plant once provided jobs for 50,000 employees. It was the world's largest manufacturing establishment, and we shall never see another one like it. The new steel and textile mill plants are much smaller than the ones they are replacing. A Commonwealth Fund survey of 438 large firms in 1992 revealed that 90 percent of them had downsized their workforces in the past five years (see Commonwealth Fund, 1993). This development is not surprising in light of falling transaction and monitoring costs. The costs of subcontracting (making the contractual arrangement and enforcing compliance) are lower because of reductions in communication and transportation costs. A firm no longer has to turn to vertical integration to ensure product quality and on-time delivery of parts. Downsizing allows a firm to form smaller teams, which are evidently more productive. The bodies for Boeing jets are now being produced in Japan. If the output-to-input ratio is higher in assembling planes than in fabricating bodies, divesting the latter activity can raise a firm's measured productivity. Downsizing and outsourcing can evidently achieve certain economies of organizational specialization. They are thus developments that should be encouraged.[25]

Bifurcation is the term I use to describe the growth in the relative size of the secondary labor force. It has been alleged that 23,000 job losses announced by manufacturing establishments are really only a shift across arbitrary industry lines. That is, they represent a substitution of regular manufacturing employees by temporary employees who are counted under a different SIC code.[26] Economic theory would have predicted that the secondary labor market for temporary and part-time workers would have expanded in relation to full-time employment. The ratio of social security taxes to earnings used to be higher for part-time workers, but advances in the maximum taxable earnings base have reduced the cost disadvantage of part-time workers. ERISA and other regulations are forcing employers to provide pension, health, and vacation time fringe benefits to part-timers on a prorated basis. Higher payroll taxes and more stringent regulations have thus reduced the relative costs of hiring these secondary workers, and firms have accordingly increased their demands for contingent and temporary employees. The incentives to invest in firm-specific training are substantially lessened when the workforce contains a large fraction of persons with weak attachments to the firm. The long-run consequences have to be decreases in labor productivity and earnings. The increasing bifurcation with more persons in the secondary labor force is a development that is contrary to economic efficiency. The maximization of the economy's total product depends not only on the acquisition of superior technology and high-quality inputs, but also on the organization of work.

Summing Up

Around 1973, the growth of the American economy and that of nearly every other developed country slowed. The current administration is dissatisfied with the speed of the recovery from the last recession. Administration officials argue that steps must be taken to raise labor productivity in order to create jobs and increase real wages. The policy proposals embrace a background model in which there is a stable relation between productivity and employment. The explanations for the productivity slowdown and the policy proposals embrace a simple production function model in which technology describes a relation between a well-defined output X and certain inputs. Because technical advances have been fewer in number in the service sector, part of the economywide slowdown has been attributed to the shift in consumer demands from goods to services. The problem here is that the consumer supplies an essential input to produce an *output* with several dimensions. The output of a retail firm cannot be equated to its sales volume. The official statistics are even worse in measuring the output of public and merit goods. Additionally, the taxes needed to finance a growing demand for these goods may result in a slower growth rate of output of the private sector. Finally, innovations in the ways in which work is organized and incentives are supplied to workers are surely as important as technological inventions in raising labor productivity. Regulations that impede the efficient allocation of resources or that prevent the adoption of efficient practices ought to be eliminated. The objective of public policy should be the maximization of the *total product* which is the net sum of the utilities derived from the goods consumed plus the utilities and disutilities of work.

Notes

1. If agricultural employees are added to the data in Table 6.1, total employment in the economy was 120.8 million in 1992 and 66.0 million in 1948. Technological advances have raised labor productivity in agriculture, resulting in a decrease in farm employment from 7.6 to 3.2 million over this period.

2. The unemployment rates of persons 16 and older at the peaks of the postwar cycles were as follows:

Year	Men	Women	Both
1948	3.6	4.1	3.8
1957	3.7	5.1	4.3
1973	4.2	6.0	4.9
1979	5.1	6.8	5.8
1988	5.5	5.6	5.5

Source: U.S. Bureau of Labor Statistics, *Handbook of Labor Statistics, 1989.* Bulletin 2340, Table 28, pp. 136–138.

The expanding coverage of unemployment insurance must surely have contributed to the increase in the equilibrium unemployment rate at full employment. The same pattern is also observed for married men, whose unemployment rate rose from 2.3 percent in 1948 to 3.3 percent in 1988. Notice that by 1988, the unemployment rate of women converged to that of men.

3. Women made up only 20.3 percent of all nonagricultural employees in 1948, but 34.4 percent in 1992. Part-time jobs made up 9.9 percent of all jobs in 1957, but this figure rose to 17.4 percent in 1992.

4. In Table 6.2, I report the level of each variable in 1992. The growth rate g is measured from peak to peak, indicated by the interval at the column heading. The growth rates between years T and $T+\tau$ is defined as,

$$x_{T+\tau} = (1+g)^\tau x_T.$$

5. The ratio of business sector output to employment, X/E, increased at a slower rate of 1.21 percent a year because hours per employee, H/E, fell at 0.38 percent a year. Labor productivity in manufacturing grew at a faster rate of 2.38 percent.

6. The output and employment data for the commercial airlines can be found in U.S. BLS (1992). If consumers demanded more safety inspections and closer conformity to schedules, they should have been willing to pay higher fares for a higher-quality final product. Most goods and services are bundles of several components, and changes in the composition of the bundles make it difficult to measure output changes over time and space.

7. Prior to the sharp rise in oil prices, energy was never an input in an aggregate production function. Capital (K), labor (L), energy (E), materials (M), and business services (S) are arguments in the KLEMS production functions fitted to data for manufacturing industries by Gullickson (1992). If τ is interpreted as knowledge, then R&D expenditures could serve as a proxy for increments to knowledge. The instability of the relation of technical progress to R&D spending may be caused by serendipitous discoveries that result in exogenous innovations.

8. Shorter hours and work sharing have been discussed at length in Europe, where unemployment rates are considerably higher than in the United States. Such policies raise the relative fixed costs of hiring and training a worker and thus discourage investments in firm-specific training. I suspect that workers oppose these proposals because they could reduce weekly earnings.

9. Robert Topel (1993) has found that the cost of job displacement is considerably greater for older workers.

10. Employment, a head count, overstates the magnitude of the sectoral shifts. Average weekly hours in retail trade fell from 38.7 to 28.8 owing to a sharp increase in the use of part-time workers. Retail trade provided more jobs in 1992 (its share of employment increased from 14.9 percent to 17.7 percent), but fewer hours of work (its share of total person hours fell from 15.0 percent to 14.7 percent). If the hourly wage on job A is twice that on job B, and if wages are proportional to efficiency units of labor services, then the decline in the relative importance of retail trade is magnified; its share of total earnings, shown in the third panel of Table 6.3, fell from 11.0 percent to 9.1 percent.

11. These data are from Oi (1992, Table 4.2). Data from the Council of Economic Advisers (1988) indicate that output of the manufacturing sector increased

at 4.5 percent a year, compared with only 0.6 percent for the nonmanufacturing sector over the 1982–86 period. I understand that the output of the nonmanufacturing industries is obtained by subtraction; there are no direct output estimates.

12. Robinson (1958) argues that these economies are the result of better coordination and synchronization. A formal analysis is provided by Mulligan (1983). The repairman's problem in queuing theory implies that repair workers and clerks in larger establishments will be idle a smaller fraction of the time. Because they get fewer idle moments, clerks at larger stores have to put forth more effort, are more productive, and hence are paid higher wages (see Oi, 1992).

13. Estimates of labor productivity in food stores that used a margins measure of output were developed by Ratchford and Brown (1985). In an earlier work, I have conjectured that the decline in productivity in the mid-1970s might have been in part a result of the expansion of the product line into more prepared foods, fish, and so on (Oi, 1992).

14. In addition to the trend over time, the ratio of part- to full-time clerks is positively related to store size. At the largest chain supermarkets, more than 70 percent of the workforce were on part-time work schedules. Further, the relative wages of part- to full-time clerks were higher at bigger stores, as shown in Oi (1992, Table 4.2).

15. Some might label this "unpaid labor," but this is wrong. It ought to be reflected in a lower pump price. The time needed to fill the tank and pay for it is evidently longer at a full-service station. I am indebted to Tom Hogarty for pointing out to me how the adoption of self-service has led to real efficiency gains.

16. This explanation seems to imply that the job losses in wholesale trade were offset by job gains in manufacturing. If so, the added workers should have increased the number of nonproduction workers in manufacturing, but the ratio of nonproduction to production workers did not rise. The wholesale functions may simply be more efficiently performed with new techniques involving more computers.

17. A donor, D, may prefer to give a gift "in kind" instead of in cash because the value that the recipient, R, attaches to the gift differs from D's valuation. Thus, D may prefer to donate a frozen turkey to R because R would have spent the money equivalent on beer. The several meanings that might be attached to the concept of a *merit good* are nicely discussed by Richard Musgrave (1987).

18. In the "semiconductor" industry, SIC 3674, output X expanded at an annual rate of 17.6 percent over the 1973–90 period, employment by 4.1 percent, and labor productivity by 12.8 percent a year. Fructose and glucose syrup are produced by the "wet corn milling" industry, SIC 2364, where the annual growth rates for the 1973–90 period were +6.6 percent for output X, -0.9 percent for person-hours H, and +7.6 percent for X/H. These were the two fastest-growing four-digit industries in the manufacturing sector.

19. In 1957, the public schools reported an average of 17.9 students per full-time employee, but this student-to-staff ratio fell to 9.0 by 1992. Classes also got smaller, from an average of 26.7 to only 17.2 students per teacher.

20. Health care outlays now account for more than 14 percent of GDP. We are healthier today than in 1973. Data from the Health Interview Survey reveal that

the average number of days of restricted activity or of bed disability have declined. Mortality and morbidity rates, which are other indicators of well-being, have improved, but at rates slower than in other developed countries. A consumer/recipient's valuation of an "in-kind" transfer will be less than the donor's when "too much" of the good or service is supplied to the recipient. Suppose that R would have purchased $2,400 worth of health insurance given the market "price" for such protection. If R is entitled to a policy costing $3,200, he is likely to utilize all of the benefits provided by the larger policy, but the "value" of the added protection will be worth something less than $800.

21. This explanation has been advanced by Raymond Arsenault (1984), who examined the impact of the air conditioner on culture, work, and lifestyles in the South.

22. Leibenstein appealed to the Hawthorne experiments at Western Electric to support this last proposition. An article by Parsons (1974) that appeared in *Science* challenged the validity of the Hawthorne results. Less-productive employees were replaced in the course of the experiments, and not all of the output data were reported.

23. Florence (1924, p. 157) cites Wagner, who identified five motives that would prompt an individual to work: a prompting of conscience out of a sense of responsibility or duty; desire for cash; desire for honor, fame, or approbation; pleasure in the activity for its own sake as in a hobby; and fear of punishment or hope of reward. I discuss in more depth the interactions among working conditions, work effort, and pay in Oi (1993).

24. Their measure of productivity in steel finishing mills was uptime, the fraction of time that the assembly line was operating and not on downtime. They show that the relation of productivity to each of the HRM practices in isolation was weak and sometimes of the wrong sign. Levine and Tyson (1990) reviewed six studies and found that in three, the adoption of an incentive plan significantly raised labor productivity.

25. In measuring the job losses resulting from downsizing, one has to count employment changes not only in the downsized firm, but also at any firms that acquire subcontracts. The net change in employment is the appropriate statistic to use in calculating the impact of downsizing on labor productivity.

26. This announcement on radio, which I heard on October 7, 1993, was attributed to Audry Friedman of the Conference Board. At a National Bureau conference some five or six years ago, a Japanese economist stated that across the four-digit manufacturing industries in Japan, 6–23 percent of all workers were contract or casual, irregular employees who, unlike firms' regular employees, do not receive bonuses and are not guaranteed lifetime contracts. Additionally, the costs of hiring these irregular employees are often reported in the published statistics under "purchased materials," making an accurate estimate of labor productivity impossible. The quality of Japanese cars may be superior to that of American cars, but the same cannot be claimed about Japanese statistics.

References

Appel, D. (1972). "The Supermarket: Early Development of an Institutional Innovation." *Journal of Retailing, 48,* 39–53.

Arsenault, R. (1984). "The End of the Long Hot Summer: The Air Conditioner and Southern Culture." *Journal of Southern History, 50,* 597–628.

Barron, J., and Umbeck, J. (1984). "The Effects of Different Contractual Arrangements: The Case of Retail Gasoline Markets." *Journal of Law and Economics, 27,* 313–328.

Becker, G. S. (1985, January). "Human Capital, Effort, and the Sexual Division of Labor." *Journal of Labor Economics,* vol. 3, pt. 2, S33–S58.

Bednarzik, R. W. (1993, February). "An Analysis of U.S. Industries Sensitive to Foreign Trade 1982–87." *Monthly Labor Review,* pp. 15–29.

Bluestone, B. (1981). *The Retail Revolution.* Boston: Auburn House.

Bluestone, I. (1983). "Technology and Employment: Effect on the Socio-Economic Structure." In *The Long-Term Impact of Technology on Employment and Unemployment* (National Academy of Engineering symposium) (pp. 21–23). Washington, DC: National Academy Press.

Commonwealth Fund. (1993). "Building the Competitive Workforce: Investing in Human Capital for Corporate Success." Mimeo, available from Commonwealth Fund, Harkness House, 1 E. 75th St., New York, NY.

Coase, R. (1960). "The Problem of Social Cost," *Journal of Law and Economics,* vol. 3, no. 1, pp. 1–44.

Council of Economic Advisers. (1988). *Economic Report of the President, 1988.* Washington, DC: Government Printing Office.

Davidson, J. P., Florence, P. S., Gray, B., and Ross, N. (1958). *Productivity and Economic Incentives.* London: Allen & Unwin.

Denison, E. F. (1962). *Sources of Economic Growth in the United States and the Alternatives before Us.* New York: Committee for Economic Development.

Denison, E. F. (1974). *Accounting for United States Economic Growth, 1929–1969.* Washington, DC: Brookings Institution.

Denison, E. F. (1984). "Accounting for Slower Economic Growth: An Update." In J. W. Kenderick (Ed.), *International Comparisons of Productivity and the Slow Down* (pp. 1–46). Cambridge, MA: Ballinger.

Florence, P. S. (1924). *Economics of Fatigue and Unrest and the Efficiency of Labour in English and American Industry.* New York: Henry Holt.

Gordon, R. J. (1993). "The Jobless Recovery: Does It Signal a New Era of Productivity Led Growth?" *Brookings Papers on Economic Activity,* vol. 24, no. 1, 271–306.

Gullickson, W. (1992, October). "Multifactor Productivity in Manufacturing Industries." *Monthly Labor Review,* pp. 20–32.

Hogarty, T. F. (1986). *Dual Distribution: Theory and Evidence.* Washington, DC: American Petroleum Institute.

Hutt, W. H. (1977). *The Theory of Idle Resources.* Indianapolis: Liberty. (Original work published 1939)

Ichniowski, C., Shaw, K., and Prennushi, G. (1993, August). "The Effects of Human Resource Practices on Productivity." Working paper, Carnegie Mellon University.

Jacobson, L. (1991, October). "The Trade Adjustment Assistance (TAA) Program in Pennsylvania, 1979–89: The Effect of Economic Conditions, UI, and TAA Program Changes on Benefit Receipt and the Ability of UI and TAA to Offset Earnings Losses." Unpublished paper, W. E. Upjohn Institute for Employment Research.

Jorgenson, D. W., and Griliches, Z. (1967). "The Explanation of Productivity Change." *Review of Economic Studies, 34,* 249–283.

Leibenstein, H. (1966). "Allocative Efficiency and X-Efficiency." *American Economic Review, 56,* 392–415.

Leontief, W. (1983). "National Perspective: The Definition of Problems and Opportunities." In *The Long-Term Impact of Technology on Employment and Unemployment,* (National Academy of Engineering symposium) (pp. 3–7). Washington, DC: National Academy Press.

Levine, D. I., and Tyson, L. D. (1990). "Participation, Productivity, and the Firm's Environment." In A. S. Blinder (Ed.), *Paying for Productivity* (pp. 183–236). Washington, DC: Brookings Institution.

Mulligan, J. G. (1983). "The Economies of Massed Reserves." *American Economic Review,* vol. 73, no. 4, 725–734.

Musgrave, R. A. (1987). "Merit Goods." In J. Eatwell, M. Milgate, and P. Newman (Eds.), *The New Palgrave* (pp. 452–453). London: Macmillan.

Nardonne, T., Herz, D., Mellor, E., and Hippel, S. (1993, February). "1992 Job Market in the Doldrums." *Monthly Labor Review,* pp. 2–14.

Niskanen, W. A. (1983). "Primary Policy Issues in Question." In *The Long-Term Impact of Technology on Employment and Unemployment* (National Academy of Engineering symposium) (pp. 52–54). Washington, DC: National Academy Press.

Oi, W. Y. (1983a). "The Fixed Employment Costs of Specialized Labor." In J. E. Triplett (Ed.), *The Measurement of Labor Cost* (pp. 63–116). Chicago: University of Chicago Press.

Oi, W. Y. (1983b). "Heterogeneous Firms and the Organization of Production." *Economic Inquiry, 21,* 147–171.

Oi, W. Y. (1992). "Productivity in the Distributive Trades." In Z. Griliches (Ed.), *Output Measurement in the Service Sector,* (pp. 161–191). Chicago: University of Chicago Press.

Oi, W. Y. (1993). "On Working." *Economic Inquiry, 31,* 1–28.

Okun, A. M., (1981). *Prices and Quantities.* Washington, DC: Brookings Institution.

Parsons, H. M. (1974). "What Happened at Hawthorne?" *Science, 183,* 922–932.

Ratchford, B. T., and Brown, J. R. (1985). "A Study of Productivity Changes in Food Retailing." *Marketing Science, 4,* 292–311.

Robinson, E. A. G. (1958). *The Structure of Competitive Industry.* Chicago: University of Chicago Press.

Ross, T. W. (1986). "Store Wars: The Chain Tax Movement." *Journal of Law and Economics, 29,* 125–137.

Sen, A. (1975). *Employment, Technology, and Development.* New York: Oxford University Press.

Shaiken, H. (1983). "Short Term Consequences of Technological Change." In *The Long-Term Impact of Technology on Employment and Unemployment* (National Academy of Engineering symposium) (pp. 28–31). Washington, DC: National Academy Press.

Solow, R. M. (1957). "Technical Change and the Aggregate Production Function." *Review of Economics and Statistics, 39,* 312–320.

Stanback, T. M., Jr. (1983). "Workforce Trends." In *The Long-Term Impact of Technology on Employment and Unemployment* (National Academy of Engineering symposium) (pp. 13–20). Washington, DC: National Academy Press.

Steiner, R. L. (1978). "Marketing Productivity in Consumer Goods Industries: A Vertical Perspective." *Journal of Marketing,* vol. 42, no. 1, pp. 60–70.

Topel, R. (1993). "What Have We Learned from Empirical Studies of Unemployment and Turnover." *American Economic Review, 83,* 110–115.

U.S. Bureau of Labor Statistics. (1992). *Productivity Measures for Selected Industries and Government Services* (Bulletin 2406). Washington, DC: Government Printing Office.

7

U.S. Productivity Revisited: It Remains Better Than You Think

William J. Baumol

There is no question that productivity matters. Its recent assignment, however, as perhaps the main source of widespread concern about the performance of the U.S. economy is unfounded. The central message of this chapter is that, although it would be foolish to believe that the United States is invulnerable to long-term decline and outpacing by rivals, its productivity performance is far better than is generally recognized and is, in itself, no reason for concern. As is true of any economy, there are some lurking threats, some of which we are in danger of ignoring. We also are vulnerable, like any industrialized economy, to cyclical economic downturns, the productivity consequences of which I will be illustrate strikingly below. However, our long-term performance is, in general, one of dramatic success, of a form that is, however, easily misinterpreted as the beginning of a process of secular decline.

Productivity Growth Does Matter in the Long Run

The importance of productivity growth in terms of its short-run influence on the economy may well have been exaggerated. Productivity gains amounting to half a percentage point per annum are exceedingly difficult to achieve, and a change of that magnitude can have little immediate power to bring down a disturbingly rapid rate of inflation or to reverse a deplorably resistant foreign trade imbalance. Yet, as we know, the magical powers of compounding do permit such a small yearly change in productivity growth rate to make an enormous difference over

Author's Note: I am very grateful to the Alfred P. Sloan Foundation and the C. V. Starr Center for Applied Economics, New York University, for support of the work reported here.

a period such as that since the Second World War. Figure 7.1, which is merely introductory to my main topic, shows what productivity growth has contributed to living standards of six of the leading industrial countries since early in the Industrial Revolution. In each country shown, except for the United Kingdom, real GDP per capita rose more than 1,000 percent between 1820 and 1989, with the United Kingdom growing only some 850 percent because by 1820 it had already grown far richer than any of the others. This growth is, of course, attributable to the productivity performance of those nations almost by definition, because unless there had been a sharp rise in the ratio of employed persons to total population, output per capita could have risen only through an increase in output per worker. Figure 7.2 shows how the productivity levels of the five leading industrial countries have been cumulating for more than a century.

The expansion in productivity is even greater than Figure 7.1 indicates, because during the period in question, work hours per year probably fell some 40 percent in each of these countries, with the exception of Japan. Yet the rise in standard of living is so enormous it is virtually

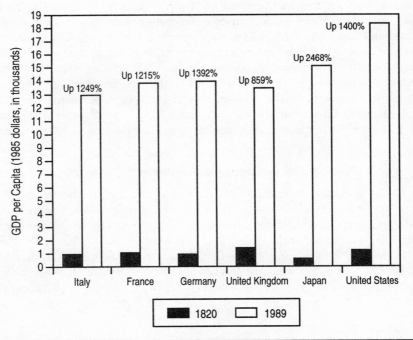

FIGURE 7.1 Improvement in Living Standards: Six Countries, 1820 versus 1989 *Source:* Maddison (1992).

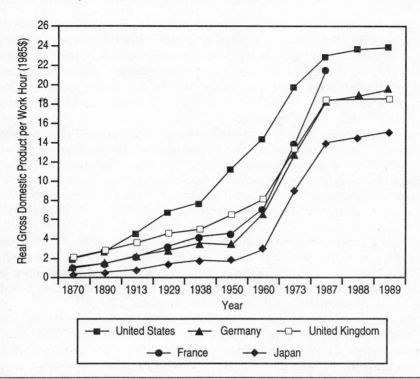

FIGURE 7.2 Labor Productivity, 1870–1989: Five Countries, Real GDP/Work Hour (1985 $)
Source: Maddison (1991).

incomprehensible. For example, the numbers indicate that in 1820 the real income of an average American was about one-fifteenth as large as it is today. Just try to imagine what this would mean in concrete terms for our daily lives, and you will see what I am suggesting when I say that the meaning of the rise is virtually incomprehensible.

The Apparent U.S. Productivity Failures: Deindustrialization

Three central concerns are expressed in discussions of U.S. productivity performance. First, it is noted that there has been a marked *slowdown* in U.S. productivity growth. Second, it is noted that the *rate of growth of productivity* in the United States is below that of most if not all the other industrial countries. Third, it is observed that the share of the labor force that is devoted to services has been expanding, leading to the conclusion that the United States is undergoing *deindustrialization* and is thus becoming a service economy.

The fact is that each of these statements is fundamentally true. It may, then, well be asked, How, in light of these observations, can one possibly conclude that American productivity performance is not in crisis? The answer is that these facts, legitimately interpreted, have implications very different from those they seem to offer. I will demonstrate this below, after a brief review of the evidence confirming unambiguously each of these three developments.

First, there can be no question that somewhere near 1973 there was a sharp decline in the rate of growth of this country's overall labor productivity, and that the growth rate of the period before that date has not yet been reattained. During the period since 1970, the average rate of productivity growth has fallen by about 65 percent below that in the earlier period, surely a marked decrease (U.S. Department of Labor, various years).

Second, according to the U.S. Bureau of Labor Statistics (1993a), the American growth rate of productivity for the period 1960 to 1991 (the years for which the BLS provides continuous data) was below that of the United Kingdom, Canada, France, Germany, Japan, and every other of the 14 industrialized market economies for which statistics are supplied. Surely, in itself, this is hardly an enviable record.

Finally, in the period 1967–92 the share of the U.S. labor force engaged in service sector employment rose by more than 20 percent (OECD, various years). At the same time, there was a fall in the share of manufacturing employment. Certainly, the rise in service employment's share is no minor matter and no statistical aberration.

Let us see, then, how one can nevertheless conclude that, from the long-run point of view, our economy is not in desperate trouble.

The Growth Slowdown—Everyone Is Doing It

Let me begin with the slowdown in productivity growth that occurred in the early 1970s. As just indicated, it did happen, and it was considerable. But it certainly was not a failure of the U.S. economy alone. A slowdown occurred at approximately the same time in *every* industrialized market economy for which I have compiled data. Figure 7.3 shows the situation in the United States, Canada, Japan, France, Germany, and the United Kingdom, comparing average growth rates since 1970 with those before that date. We see that, although the percentage decline (the numbers at the tops of the bars) was greatest in the United States (66 percent), the declines in Japan (58 percent) and Germany (60 percent) were nearly as great.

Obviously, something else was going on about that time that produced a universal slowdown, and if failure of performance it was, it was not a failure of this country alone. The conjecture offered most widely is

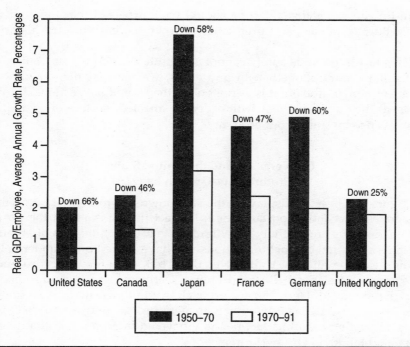

FIGURE 7.3 Productivity Growth Rates, 1950–70 versus 1970–91 *Source:* U.S. BLS (1993a).

that the source of the problem was a hybrid of the mid-decade recession and the oil crisis, which entailed startling rises in petroleum prices and led to dislocation of industry. These undoubtedly played a role, but one may well wonder, if these alone are the main causes of the slowdown, why productivity growth has not resumed its earlier course now that real oil prices have fallen drastically and the latter half of the 1980s was characterized by prosperity.

One additional conjecture that seems highly plausible is that a substantial portion of the slowdown may be attributed to the end of the "catch-up" period after World War II, when industrial activity was stimulated by the rebuilding of shattered economies; when a backlog of inventions, such as television, had not yet been brought to market; when accumulated savings and long unsatisfied consumer demands all added up to what has been described as the "golden age" of prosperity and productivity growth. These were stimuli that were, for obvious reasons, stronger in Europe and Japan than in the United States. Moreover, these were not inexhaustible stimuli, meaning that when the backlog of inventions had been brought to market, and production had caught up with pent-up consumer demand, one should have expected that the golden age would terminate, and productivity growth go back toward historic levels.

This last hypothesis surely cannot constitute the entire story, but it is difficult to reject altogether. In any event, we see that the slowdown problem, if real problem it is, is not one of the United States alone. It follows, at the very least, that with everyone affected, no loss of competitiveness need result for our economy.

Convergence and the United States as Productivity-Growth Laggard

Figure 7.3, besides displaying the slowdown in productivity growth, illustrates a second important point, the fact that throughout the postwar period our productivity growth rate has been behind that of all our leading industrial competitor nations. We have lagged only moderately behind Canada and the United Kingdom, but, as will surprise no one, our growth rate shortfall behind France, Germany, and Japan has been very large indeed. Here, our record is clearly unique—there is no other free-market industrial economy with a record as undistinguished as ours. How, then, can this fact possibly have an interpretation that does not entail failure in U.S. performance?

The answer is most easily understood if one thinks back to the era of the Marshall Plan. At that time, the U.S. economy stood alone, an island of prosperity in a sea of poverty. No nation in Europe or Asia had a real per capita income anywhere close to ours. The Marshall Plan rested on the premise that U.S. assistance to other countries, designed to help them on the way to prosperity, was an act of enlightened self-interest. It was based on compassion encouraged by the realization that poor neighbor countries are also necessarily poor customers, and that hope of international tranquility was slim in a world of widespread poverty. The combination of market forces, self-help, and pump-priming assistance clearly accomplished what was hoped for. The industrial market economies began to draw ever closer to U.S. levels of productivity and per capita income.

Figure 7.4 confirms this observation, one that has been supported by innumerable studies using more extensive data and more systematic analysis. This *convergence* literature shows that during the postwar period the leading industrial countries have moved closer and closer to the United States, *though none of them has yet overtaken it, and none seems about to do so.* Figure 7.4 reports labor productivity *levels* (rather than growth rates) for the six countries on which we have been focusing. The levels are reported not in absolute values, but as percentages of the U.S. level

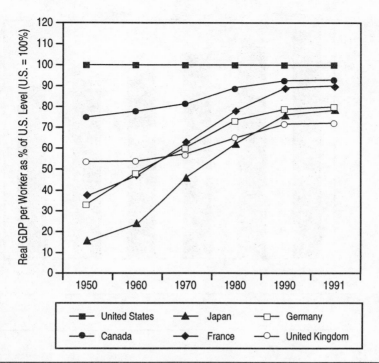

FIGURE 7.4 Productivity Levels as Percentages of U.S. Level, 1950–91 *Source:* U.S. BLS (1993a).

(so that the U.S. figure is always 100 percent). As we see in the graph, in 1950, Japan, France, Germany, and the United Kingdom had productivity levels averaging about one-third that of the United States. Today, that number is closer to 80 percent. In short, instead of the United States being surrounded by extremely poor neighbors, we now share the world with countries only a little less affluent than we. That, surely, is what we hoped for when the Marshall Plan was instituted.

What has that to do with the fact that U.S. productivity growth has been slower than that of every one of the other countries in the group? The answer is that the two observations, productivity convergence and comparatively slow U.S. productivity growth, are just two inseparable sides of the same phenomenon. If a country starts out with 30 percent of our productivity level, the only way it can reach 80 percent of our level is by growing faster than we. Clearly, a group of runners cannot draw more closely abreast of one another unless the laggards run faster than the leaders. Moreover, if it is true that richer countries are better customers for American products, as they surely are, it follows incontestably that

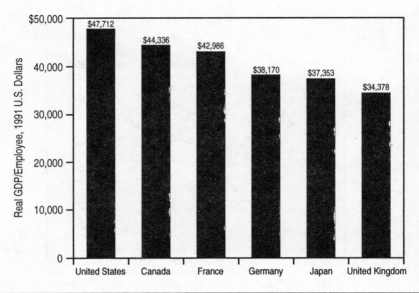

FIGURE 7.5 Overall Labor Productivity, 1991 *Source:* U.S. BLS (1993a).

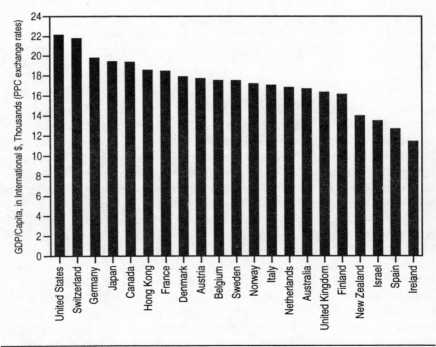

FIGURE 7.6 Per Capita GDP, OECD Countries, 1991 (U.N./OECD/World Bank data, 1993) *Source:* World Bank (1993). Uses purchasing power of currency exchange rates.

the more rapid growth of the other (laggard) countries has been a benefit to this country rather than a threat.

Figures 7.5 and 7.6 show the bottom line—they indicate where the U.S. economy stands in relation to the others. Figure 7.5 shows by how much we still lead in overall productivity, whereas Figure 7.6, based on a recent and much-publicized World Bank study, shows the universality of our lead in real per capita income. Slow relative growth in productivity (and, incidentally, in per capita income) turns out, properly interpreted, not to be as serious a problem as it seems.

Services, Manufacturing, and Deindustrialization— Everyone Is Doing This Too

We come, finally, to the last of the three pieces of evidence that is cited to show that the U.S. economy is in serious trouble: the rising share of the service sector, both as a percentage of our labor force employment and as a proportion of GDP. It is implied that this entails a double failure. First, it is suggested, the explanation must be that the United States is losing its competitive advantage as an industrial producer, so that we are forced into services because other countries are stealing our manufacturing markets away. In addition, it is suggested that service jobs are low-wage jobs that offer workers little hope for the future. The facts do not support the second contention, with the bulk of the new service jobs falling in the expanding information sector of the economy. But this will not be my focus here. Rather, I will devote my discussion to the first contention, that the United States is losing its edge in manufacturing and therefore is left with little option but to shift to services.

Figure 7.7, by itself, is enough to dispel this view of the matter. The black bars, for each of the nine countries reported upon, show the rise in the percentage of the national labor force that is employed in that country's service sector over the period 1967 to 1992. The dates are those for which I have been able to obtain statistics. What the graph shows, in brief, is that *if the United States is becoming a service economy, every other country in the group is doing so also, and is going in that direction faster (most of them substantially faster) than we*. The point is that this fact undermines the view that our country's service sector growth is attributable to loss of manufacturing jobs to others. Who are those others? Apparently, on this interpretation, all of the countries shown must be losing their manufacturing jobs to a country or countries unknown. Of course, that is nonsense. The explanation lies elsewhere. After providing that explanation, I will show that in fact the United States is not falling behind in manufacturing—far from it.

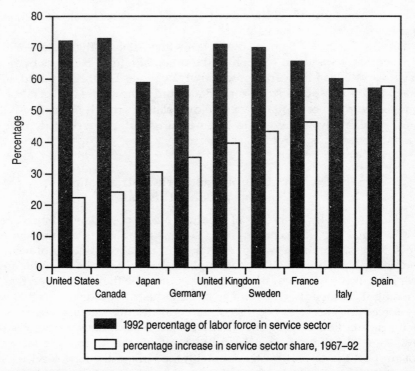

FIGURE 7.7 Growth in Service Sector of Nine Countries, 1967–92 *Source:* OECD, *Labour Force Statistics,* various years.

The reason for the common growth in share of service sector jobs is not hard to find. At one time, all of these countries experienced growth in manufacturing jobs at the expense of agriculture. The reason for that was the explosive growth in agricultural productivity. Soon after the Revolutionary War, some 90 percent of the U.S. labor force was employed in agriculture, and yet managed to produce far less than an abundance of foodstuffs. Today, less than 3 percent of our workforce is on the farm, but overabundant agricultural production is a continuing problem. Thus, as the demand for farm labor fell, although overall unemployment rates did not rise (except during relatively brief recessions), workers had to move elsewhere, and they moved to manufacturing and services, as the data clearly show. In recent decades the story has been repeated, only this time with manufacturing rather than agriculture experiencing the rapid growth in productivity that leads to a reduction in demand for labor.

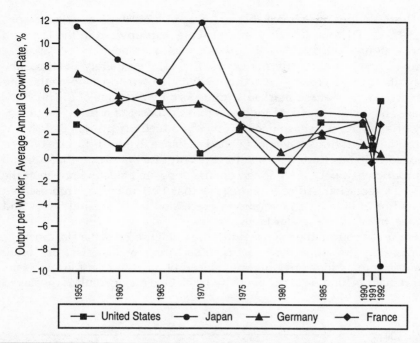

FIGURE 7.8 Manufacturing Productivity Growth, 1950–92 *Note:* The extreme swings in growth rates from 1990 to 1992 are probably attributable to different stages of recession. *Source:* U.S. BLS (1993b).

Further evidence that the shift to the services cannot be attributed to poor manufacturing productivity performance in the United States is provided by the last two figures. Figure 7.8 provides data on manufacturing productivity *growth rates* for the United States, France, Germany, and Japan, over the period 1950–92. This graph has a number of remarkable implications. First, it shows that, although there has been a marked decline in *overall* U.S. productivity growth, as we have seen, in *manufacturing* the trend in the growth rate has been (very slightly) upward. Certainly there has been no decline.

Second, Figure 7.8 shows that although, as might have been expected, soon after the war the other three countries started off with manufacturing productivity growing far faster than that in the United States, since then their pace of growth has had a declining tendency and has brought all three either close to or below the U.S. growth rate. And this failure to continue outpacing the United States has occurred while the United States still remains well ahead of the others in terms of manufacturing productivity levels (data not reported here).[1]

Third, there is the remarkable anomaly in the behavior of the graphs in 1991–92. There is, in that year, a striking leap upward in the U.S. and French figures on productivity growth, and a collapse in the Japanese figure. These are probably not errors. Rather, they merely illustrate the insignificance of year-by-year productivity growth developments, and the fact that they are so markedly influenced by the stage of the business cycle. The historical record indicates that the onset of a recession generally brings with it a sharp decline in the productivity growth statistic, as output falls but firms have not yet had a chance to adjust the size of their labor forces, thus leading to a fall in the output-labor ratio—that is, a fall in productivity. For the same reason, the opposite tends to happen at the end of a recession. All of this suggests that 1991 may have represented an end or at least an amelioration of recession in the United States and France, but a downturn for Japan.

For us, of course, the main significance of Figure 7.8 is the steadiness of productivity growth in American manufacturing, and the fact that other countries are no longer significantly ahead of us in terms of growth rate, and remain behind us in productivity level. One major result is displayed

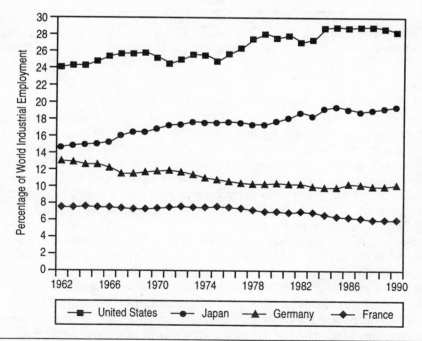

FIGURE 7.9 Shares of World Industrial Employment, 1962–90 *Source:* OECD, various publications, various years.

in Figure 7.9, which shows the performance of four countries, France, Germany, Japan, and the United States, in terms of their share of world industrial employment. We see that Japan's share has grown steadily over the period of available statistics, 1962–90. However, the U.S. share has also grown over most of this period, at the expense of the other two countries, and we and Japan together now account for about half of the world's industrial employment. That is not exactly in line with the deindustrialization story.

Concluding Comment

Most of the observations I have offered in this chapter are quite well documented. The evidence is extensive and offers relatively little ambiguity and inconsistency. It is clear that the United States has, indeed, undergone a number of developments that, on first examination, are disquieting. It is equally clear that in most of these areas a closer look at the facts reveals that they are far less menacing than they appear and that some of them are really surface manifestations of essentially beneficent developments.

None of this is meant to say that the United States is assured of a future with absolutely nothing to fear. The future is sure to bring surprises, and some of them are bound to be unpleasant. But apart from this vague generality, we do face threats whose shapes can already be discerned. These include low savings and investment rates and, along with them, deteriorating infrastructure. Perhaps most disturbing of all is the continuing poor educational performance of ethnic groups that provide a significant and growing share of the labor force. Such matters are not safely ignored; they are in urgent need of attention. They do not imply, however, that the U.S. economy is already well on its way to mediocrity.

Notes

1. A recent study run by a number of leading economists, and carried out through McKinsey and Company, confirms the very felicitous U.S. productivity performance in manufacturing. See, for example, *New York Times*, October 22, 1993, pp. D1 and D6.

References

Maddison, A. (1991). *Dynamic Forces in Capitalist Development: A Long-Run Comparative View*. New York: Oxford University Press.

Maddison, A. (1992). "Explaining the Economic Performance of Nations, 1820–1989." Unpublished manuscript.

Organization for Economic Cooperation and Development (OECD). (various years). *Indicators of Industrial Activity*. Paris: Author.

Organization for Economic Cooperation and Development (OECD). (various years). *Labour Force Statistics*. Paris: Author.

Organization for Economic Cooperation and Development (OECD). (various years). *Quarterly Labour Force Statistics*. Paris: Author.

U.S. Department of Labor. (various years). Unpublished data.

U.S. Bureau of Labor Statistics. (1993a). *Comparative Real Gross Domestic Product per Capita and per Employed Person, Fourteen Countries, 1960–1991*. Washington, DC: Government Printing Office.

U.S. Bureau of Labor Statistics. (1993b). *International Comparisons of Manufacturing Productivity and Unit Labor Cost Trends, 1992*. Washington, DC: Government Printing Office.

U.S. Bureau of Labor Statistics. (1993c). (Unpublished background data for comparative real GDP per capita and per employed person, 14 countries, 1950–91).

World Bank. (1993). *World Development Report 1993*. New York: Oxford University Press.

Comment

John Haltiwanger

In their chapters, William Baumol and Walter Oi both do an excellent job of putting the current concerns about productivity growth and job creation into perspective. The themes that they emphasize are somewhat different and deserve separate consideration.

William Baumol emphasizes a historical and international perspective in evaluating current productivity statistics. His main points may be summarized briefly as follows:

- Over the past 170 years, the United States has been phenomenally successful in the growth of living standards in both absolute and relative terms.
- The relative post-World War II experience in the United States in terms of productivity growth has been influenced by a number of factors, including the following:

    the inevitable catch-up of other industrialized economies in their postwar recovery;

    the pent-up demand for durables coupled with the pent-up supply of new inventions that led to a golden age for productivity in the first couple of decades following the war;

    the post-1973 slowdown in productivity that has been widespread across the globe; and

    the downsizing and increasing productivity growth in the manufacturing sector that is similar to what occurred early in this century in agriculture.

Walter Oi emphasizes the difficulties in measuring and interpreting output, employment, and thus productivity. He stresses many factors related to these measurement issues:

- On the output side, there are difficult conceptual and measurement issues for merit and public goods—for employment, the increasing role of temporary and contingent workers as well as outsourcing, makes interpretation of the typical statistics difficult.

- Downsizing is an important phenomenon connected with rising productivity. That is, downsizing is the result of technological progress.
- Workers displaced by downsizing may face prolonged unemployment because workers who are technologically obsolete may have difficulty relocating. Current government policies to assist such workers are not very effective.

The main points made by both Baumol and Oi are well taken and help us in evaluating current productivity and job growth behavior. In the comments that follow, I do not quarrel directly with either of these authors. Rather, I elaborate on some of the themes they raise in order to add to (and change somewhat) the perspective they have provided. The two themes on which I focus here are (a) the process of downsizing and its association with productivity growth, and (b) the displacement of workers associated with such downsizing.

At an aggregate level, there clearly has been downsizing in the manufacturing sector from the 1980s to early 1990s in the sense that employment (and particularly the share of employment) has fallen. Further, over this period there has been an increase in productivity growth (both labor and total factor productivity) in the manufacturing sector. It is, however, quite misleading to draw inferences from these aggregate data to characterize what has been happening at the micro level to individual workers and firms. In fact, one of my main messages here is that the process of downsizing and productivity growth at the aggregate level is at the micro level a very noisy and complex process. During this period of declining employment and rising productivity at the aggregate total manufacturing level, some firms were upsizing, some downsizing, some entering and some exiting—further, among all of these, some were increasing productivity and others were experiencing productivity decreases.

To begin this characterization of the noisy process of downsizing and productivity growth, it is useful to examine the evolution of the size distribution of employers and employees. The key fact to start with is that most firms are small, but most workers work for large firms. This skewness in the size distribution of firms makes the drawing of inferences about the process of downsizing quite difficult from typical aggregate data. That is, the average establishment or firm size is not a particularly useful indicator of the size of the establishment for the typical worker—the establishment mean is driven too much by the millions of very small establishments that make up most of the establishments but employ only a small fraction of the workers.[1] In previous work with Steven Davis, we found it useful to define a summary measure of the size of the establishment for the typical worker (Davis and Haltiwanger, 1990). We call this measure the coworker mean.[2] To understand the relationship between the establishment and the coworker mean, consider the following two experiments. Suppose one called up all establishments in the Yellow Pages, asked how many employees worked at each establishment, and then took the average of the responses. This would yield the mean establishment size. Alternatively, suppose one called up each worker in the white pages, asked how many employees work at the establishment where the worker is employed, and then took the average of these responses. This latter calculation yields what we call the coworker mean—again, it is the size of the establishment for the typical worker.

Figure 1 depicts the coworker mean for the total private sector, for manufacturing, and for services. There are three main points to be learned from this figure. First, the coworker mean is large relative to the establishment mean—the typical worker in 1985 worked for an establishment

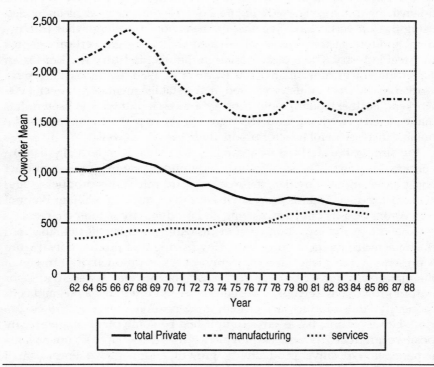

FIGURE 1 Coworker Means for Different Sectors   Note: The coworker mean is the size of the establishment for the typical worker. *Source*: Davis and Haltiwanger (1990).

with more than 600 workers. In contrast, the establishment mean in 1985 was 17 workers. The fact that the typical establishment has fewer than 20 workers is sometimes used misleadingly to characterize the importance of small businesses in the economy. In fact, the typical worker is employed at an establishment with more than 600 workers. The second main point to see from the figure is that there has been downsizing in the private sector and in the manufacturing sector, but this has been occurring since 1967. In fact, the sharpest decline in the coworker mean for the manufacturing sector occurred between 1967 and 1972. Since that time, the coworker mean in manufacturing has fluctuated, but has exhibited no strong trend. The third main point is that some sectors (e.g., services) have experienced a steady increase in the coworker mean.

In terms of the decline in employment in the manufacturing sector observed over the 1980s, we see that there has not been a decline in the size of the establishment for the typical worker. This finding is striking in light of the conventional wisdom on downsizing. Is there no truth to the conventional wisdom? The conventional wisdom is correct for some important sectors. For example, the steel industry experienced dramatic downsizing in the early 1980s. Figure 2 depicts the coworker mean (scaled using the left vertical axis) against the behavior of average labor productivity and total factor productivity (scaled using the right vertical axis) for the steel industry. The typical worker in the steel industry worked for an establishment of more than 7,000 workers in 1980. By 1986, the typical worker in the steel industry worked at an establishment of just over 4,000 workers. Further, coming out of the 1982 recession, there has been a dramatic increase in labor productivity growth above prerecession rates and a notable increase in total factor productivity growth as well.

Put simply, the steel industry exhibits the patterns underlying the conventional wisdom. The steel industry has undergone the type of product and process innovation (i.e., the move toward mini-mills producing specialized products) that is associated with the story that William Baumol and Walter Oi tell about downsizing and productivity in their chapters.

Analysis at the four-digit level of disaggregation is still not sufficient to characterize the noisy process of downsizing and productivity. Figure 3 presents a plant-level decomposition of labor productivity growth in the manufacturing sector over the 1980s.[3] For the total, we see that labor output growth has been positive, employment growth negative, and consequently labor productivity growth quite positive over the 1979–88 period. However, this has been accomplished by some plants experiencing positive productivity and employment growth (Group 1), some plants experiencing positive productivity growth and negative employment growth (Group 2), some experiencing negative productivity growth and

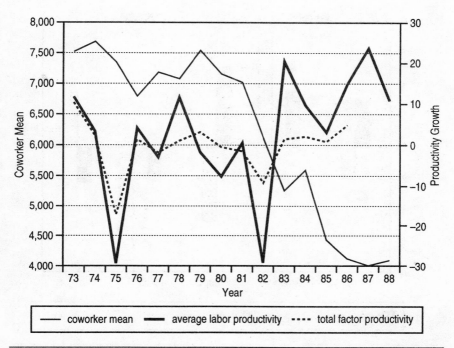

FIGURE 2 Downsizing in the Steel Industry *Source*: Tabulations from the LRD and Gray (ASM) data set.

negative employment growth (Group 3), and some experiencing negative productivity growth and positive employment growth (Group 4). In terms of employment shares in 1988, Group 1 (which I call the upsizing winners) accounted for 35 percent of employment, Group 2 (which in the figure I call downsizing winners) accounted for 43 percent of employment, Group 3 (downsizing losers) accounted for 11 percent of employment, and Group 4 (upsizing losers) also accounted for 11 percent of employment. Put simply, this implies that a substantial fraction of the productivity growth in manufacturing over this period was accounted for by plants that upsized rather than downsized.

To restate the point, at the aggregate level we know the manufacturing sector has increased productivity and shed workers. This has led to conventional wisdom that rising productivity in the manufacturing sector is caused by firms' downsizing—becoming lean and mean. The micro evidence indicates that this is misleading—an important fraction of the increase in productivity over this period is associated with those plants that were upsizing.

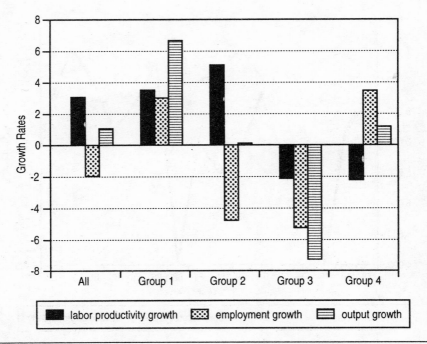

FIGURE 3 Decomposition of Manufacturing Productivity Growth, (1979–88) Note: Group
1 = upsizing winners; Group 2 = downsizing winners; Group 3 = downsizing losers; Group
4 = upsizing losers. *Source*: Baily et al. (1994).

Recognizing that the process of productivity and job growth is noisy
(some firms going one way, others another) helps put the displacement of
workers caused by some firms' downsizing in perspective. Figure 4 aids
in this perspective by depicting the rates of establishment-level job creation and destruction in the manufacturing sector. Remember that the job
creation rate is measured as the total employment increases by expanding plants (including start-ups) as a fraction of employment. The job destruction rate is measured similarly as the total employment decreases by
declining plants (including shutdowns) as a fraction of employment.

Three key points emerge from Figure 4. First, the annual rates of job
creation and destruction are large. Roughly 1 out of every 10 jobs each
year is created and 1 out of 10 jobs is destroyed in the manufacturing
sector. These gross job flow rates are large in absolute terms and very
large relative to the net rates of growth that are commonly examined
from aggregate data. Examination of evidence for other sectors reveals
that, if anything, job creation and destruction rates are even larger in
nonmanufacturing. In addition, examination of international evidence

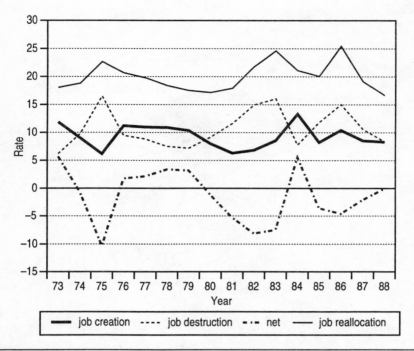

FIGURE 4 Manufacturing Gross Flows 1973–88 *Source*: Davis et al. (1994).

indicates that the United States is not an outlier in its gross flow rates (for a review of the evidence, see Davis, Haltiwanger, and Schuh, 1994). Second, although the rates of both creation and destruction are cyclical, it is particularly the rate of job destruction that is cyclically sensitive. What happens in a typical recession is that job destruction rises sharply but, surprisingly, job creation falls only mildly. For the present context, there is evidence (as in the steel industry) that this rise in job destruction in recessions is associated with plants that are concentrating on permanent restructuring. Third, there is no clear trend in the rates of creation and destruction (and hence no clear trend in the total rate of reallocation—the sum of creation and destruction).

Figure 5 shows that not only are the rates of creation and destruction large, but they are driven by establishments experiencing dramatically large employment adjustments. More than two-thirds of job creation and destruction is accounted for by establishments experiencing employment adjustments that are greater than 25 percent in absolute value.

Taken together, these points suggest the following characterization of employment dynamics. The U.S. economy is continuously undergoing

Job Creation

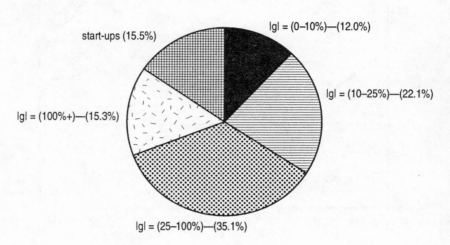

start-ups (15.5%)

|g| = (0–10%)—(12.0%)

|g| = (10–25%)—(22.1%)

|g| = (100%+)—(15.3%)

|g| = (25–100%)—(35.1%)

Job Destruction

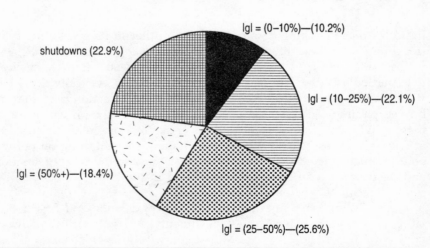

shutdowns (22.9%)

|g| = (0–10%)—(10.2%)

|g| = (10–25%)—(22.1%)

|g| = (50%+)—(18.4%)

|g| = (25–50%)—(25.6%)

FIGURE 5 Concentrations of Annual Job Creation and Destruction Note: g = growth rate. *Source*: Davis et al. (1994).

dramatic patterns of job gain and job loss. Even during economic booms (and even in the fastest-growing industries), there is substantial job destruction. Even during the worst recession and in shrinking industries, there is still substantial job creation. This is not a new phenomenon—it has been occurring at roughly the same rate for the past two decades. Further, these rates of creation and destruction are accounted for by plants experiencing large changes in employment.

Hence, in examining the impact of downsizing on displaced workers, one needs to recognize that large-scale employment reductions among individual employers are not rare; rather, they are part of the ongoing process of reallocation. For the most part, large-scale employment reductions by some plants in a sector are offset by large-scale employment increases by others. To the extent that this is not the case, some workers will obviously need to relocate to other sectors. This need for between-sector reallocation is clearly relevant in the manufacturing sector, but it is useful to note that within-sector reallocation dwarfs between-sector reallocation.

Conclusion

In thinking about the process of productivity growth and downsizing, examination of the microdata forces one to recognize that this is a very complex and noisy process. What is at work are a host of idiosyncratic factors that make some firms successful and grow (at least for some time) and others fail and shrink. These factors arguably include noisy technological innovations (e.g., in some years R&D at an individual firm yields better product or process innovations than in others), heterogeneity in entrepreneurial and managerial ability, and idiosyncratic cost and demand shocks (e.g., weather conditions and energy prices affect the relative costs and demand for alternative technologies and products).[4] This perspective suggests downsizing will be right for some, but not for others. Further, even if it is right, some will do it successfully and others will not.

In this noisy environment, picking winning industries is difficult, and picking winning firms within industries is impossible. Neutral policies that allow this complex, noisy process to unfold make the most sense. The basic idea is to establish a level playing field that permits those with the best products, the best technology, and the best managers to succeed. This perspective clearly implies that industrial policy or other targeted policies that attempts to pick winning industries or winning types of firms are doomed to failure.

A reasonable question is, What type of government policies are appropriate? This is a tough question of course. William Baumol and Walter Oi have touched on these matters, and they provide some useful guidance. First, the government's role in education in terms of providing basic skills is very relevant here. In the complex, noisy environment that firms and workers operate, a well-educated, adaptable labor force is essential. Second, as Walter Oi discusses in his chapter, some type of transition assistance for workers caught up in the inevitable turbulence may be advisable. One can interpret many U.S. labor market policies as attempting to do just this. However, as Oi ably notes, the existing set of assistance programs (e.g., publicly provided worker training for dislocated workers, UI benefits) can hardly be deemed an overwhelming success. Nevertheless, there are legitimate concerns about the ability of workers to insure appropriately against such risk. Further, there may be spillover effects from the reduced consumption of dislocated workers in transition. Given the importance of allowing the dynamic selection process of firms to unfold, it may be better to provide this safety net through various worker assistance programs than to interfere in the success and failure of firms.

Notes

1. The establishment mean is easily calculated from aggregate data simply by dividing total employment for a sector by the number of establishments.

2. The following discussion from Davis and Haltiwanger (1990) is based on tabulations from the Longitudinal Research Database (LRD) and U.S. Bureau of the Census (1963–88). As such, it represents a characterization of the size distribution of establishments, not firms.

3. The decomposition reported in Figure 3 is based on analysis by Baily, Bartelsman, and Haltiwanger (1994).

4. These are the factors that determine whether firms are operating in what Oi calls the production possibility frontier. Having examined the microdata, I believe that the precise characterization of such a frontier is difficult. Presumably, it might be the frontier of those using best practices (at least best practices for this year, given that next year cost shocks may make current best practices inferior). Put differently, I prefer to think of the production function at the micro level as including a number of idiosyncratic factors that might include managerial/entrepreneurial ability but also idiosyncratic technology shocks.

References

Baily, M., Bartelsman, E., and Haltiwanger, J. (1994). "Downsizing and Productivity Growth: Myth or Reality." University of Maryland Working Paper No. 94-07.

Davis, S., and Haltiwanger, J. (1990). "The Distribution of Employees by Establishment Size: Patterns of Change in the United States, 1962-85." Mimeo.

Davis, S., Haltiwanger, J., and Schuh, S. (1994). *Job Creation and Destruction in U.S. Manufacturing*. Washington, DC: U.S. Bureau of the Census.

U.S. Bureau of the Census. (1963–1988). *County Business Patterns*. Washington, DC: Government Printing Office.

Comment

Patrick Savin

Convergence: The Private Sector View

Professors Oi and Baumol have presented cogent rebuttal to the declinest argument propounded by certain elements of the economic and journalistic community over the past several years.

As countries appear to converge on us, the United States has seemed to lose its self-confidence. Americans have the sense that since 1950 foreign competitors have been "catching up" to us. This is certainly true, and this convergence will continue. The current economic developments in China and India illustrate this reality. Their position is broadly similar to some of the EEC countries and Japan in 1950. China and India have recently experienced productivity growth between 8 percent to 12 percent annually. Both countries are experiencing very high levels of investments as a backdrop to this surge in productivity. If present trends continue, they will become as competitive in manufacturing as the Europeans and Japanese have been in the past 20 years. This growth in productivity will tend to decelerate slowly. Government policies across Southeast Asia encourage investment, and it appears to me that what will happen is something similar to what occurred in the United States from the end of the Civil War through 1960, a period of enormous investment and rise of the United States as an economic power.

It is important to consider what the government can do to help American businesses in these circumstances. In my opinion, there is not much the government can do. Government will try to act on some fronts, but most of the things it does will probably be counterproductive. Moreover, government does not know what to do. As social scientists, we are not well trained to tell people that we lack solutions. In any event, smart American companies and individuals will make direct investment and engage in joint ventures in these areas as a means of maintaining their competitiveness.

Dr. Oi's example of government efforts in summer job training programs clearly illustrates that these efforts amount to a redistribution of income with little solid long term effects. The evidence suggests that these training programs do not work for people in distress, but for middle-class people who have other skills or options. These programs are ineffective. In his chapter, Baumol reminds us that the process of growth and shrinkage is constant. What should we do with the numbers of people who "fall through the cracks," who need to be retrained? The private sector would do well to become more involved in such efforts. Rather than wait for government mandates, the private sector should respond actively in this area. Government, in my opinion, is far less able to come up with an effective solution to this problem than are individual corporations who would obviously have a clearer sense of their own demand.

I think we ought not to expect a rapid return to high sustained economic growth or what has been called the "golden age." This period was a result of an explosion of new technology, the end of the Great Depression, the onset of World War II, and an era of relatively high investment. I agree with Dr. Baumol's recommendation that we have to be extremely cautious in determining how to deal with issues of convergence. Demographic problems, access to skills, and issues of immigration all would play disparate roles. In my view, recent attempts to curtail immigration to this country are poorly founded. The skill levels of the immigrants coming to this country might continue to decrease, and we must therefore focus on educating people and encouraging the acquisition of skills. To meet the changed immigration patterns, we have to allocate more of our educational resources to primary and secondary education and less to higher education. To meet job demands, we need to make it attractive for people to prepare themselves to join the workforce. We have to take some steps to encourage people to relocate by tax measures, if need be. We have to make it fiscally attractive as well for private companies to become involved in retraining. A coalition of forces is needed—private and public—to deal with the continuing problem of job growth that we are likely to experience over the next 10 years.

PART FOUR

Government Mandates, Labor Costs, and Employment

Introduction

The debate over the use of government mandates to achieve desired public policy objectives is typically political and always contentious. Liberals frequently argue that the cost of social programs should be borne by employers; while conservatives fight against employer mandates because they interfere with the normal functioning of the labor market. The session, "Government Mandates, Labor Costs, and Employment," brought together two points of view on this issue that, when taken at face value, would appear to be opposing.

In his chapter, "How Government Reduces Employment," Murray Weidenbaum makes the argument that the proponents of government mandates often seek to use them to promote particular social objectives, such as eliminating discrimination, protecting unskilled workers, or helping the disabled. He argues, however, "It is another matter and far less acceptable for them to say that all of these burdens [the costs of the mandates] can be justified on economic grounds." Given the cumulative disemployment effects of all the government mandates currently in place —the disemployment effects of wrongful termination lawsuits alone are estimated to be 2–5 percent of the entire workforce—he concludes that it must be possible to find alternatives to government mandates.

On the other hand, Alan Krueger, in his chapter, "Observations on Employment-Based Government Mandates, with Particular Reference to Health Insurance," takes an apparently much more conciliatory approach to the use of government mandates. In particular, his chapter notes that mandates may be useful to solve market imperfections or inefficiencies. For example, workers may not know the true risks involved in a particular production process. Mandatory workers' compensation insurance guarantees that workers will be covered in case of accidental injury, thereby forcing the firm to internalize the cost of potential injuries. Further, mandates may be the best available option if the political climate makes other alternatives untenable.

Though these papers may appear to be diametrically opposed, they actually represent two different elements of a broad political-economic approach to the analysis of government mandates. There are roughly three parts to this approach: (a) identify the set of available policies, including mandates; (b) conduct a cost-benefit analysis of each of the policies; and (c) determine which of the policies, if any, have benefits that outweigh costs and are politically viable.

Assume that the goal is to make the income distribution more equitable. Three available policies are (a) increase the minimum wage, (b) give direct income transfers through the welfare system or earned income tax credit, financing them by an increase in income taxes, (c) provide tax breaks to employers who hire low-wage workers, also financed by an increase in income taxes.

Each policy has its merits and drawbacks. An increase in the minimum wage is very cheap to implement; but most people would agree that there are disemployment effects of raising the minimum, so that some workers gain at the expense of others. Direct income transfers do not have such disemployment effects (aside from the distortions created by raising income taxes), but they may create a disincentive to work and the bureaucracy needed to implement them is more costly than raising the minimum wage. Tax breaks to employers who hire low-wage workers should expand the number of available jobs; but a large bulk of the costs would involve subsidies to employers for workers already on the payroll, not just new hires.

Unfortunately, conducting a cost-benefit analysis of a policy is a highly subjective undertaking: The estimates are sensitive to the underlying assumptions. For example, Weidenbaum's chapter cites a projection by June and David O'Neill that the proposed Clinton health reform will cost 3.1 million jobs. Krueger's chapter, by contrast, has an upper-limit prediction of about 500,000 lost jobs. While these two estimates are strikingly different, it is noteworthy that Krueger's estimates alone range from 200,000 to 500,000. This should make it clear that cost-benefit analysis is not an exact science; so one should carefully weigh the assumptions and analysis used to derive estimates of the effects of instituting a particular policy.

Identifying what policy, if any, is politically viable is the final step. Continuing with our previous example, an increase in the minimum wage may be easy to implement because the law is already on the books, so the precedent has already been set. Further, mandating an increase in wages allows politicians to look like they are being "tough" with employers who are "exploiting" low-wage workers. Direct income transfers also have a precedent in the form of both welfare benefits (e.g., Aid to Families with Dependent Children) and the earned income tax credit. However, the form in which the benefits are delivered may be crucial to political viability. During his first year in office, Bill Clinton has railed against the existing welfare system—including the structure of direct income transfers through programs such as AFDC—at the same time that he gave his full support to the recent increase in the earned income tax credit. Finally, employer subsidies may not be politically viable because they would constitute a new program (lack of precedent); and because the large sum of money transferred to employers who already have low-wage workers on their payrolls could subject politicians to charges of using the program as a way to help "rich" firms, not "poor" workers.

As Krueger argues in his essay, the costs of mandates are hidden, whereas explicit taxes to fund a government spending program are not. At the same time, the benefits of mandates are highly visible, whereas market incentives such as price subsidies or vouchers are harder for a politicians to point out as yielding tangible benefits to their constituencies. In some cases, then, mandates may be the best—or only—viable option given political constraints.

Weidenbaum emphasizes in his essay that the supporters of particular policies frequently discount or assume away any disemployment effects or other costs when lobbying on Capitol Hill. While this may be politically expedient, if there are potential disemployment effects of a proposed policy, they should be acknowledged. In such a case it is incumbent on economists to point out that jobs will be lost. This has indeed been the case (as Weidenbaum notes) for the proposed health care reforms. Political viability should not require misrepresenting the truth.

We can see that rather than representing diametrically opposite positions, Weidenbaum and Krueger each give voice to particular concerns that are relevant to the analysis of mandates. In their comments following the two chapters, each discussant provides further insights into the effects of mandates. Ronald Ehrenberg details and critiques the issues involved in determining the costs and benefits of mandates. Stanley Zax in turn offers some key insights from his position on the the firing line of the workers' compensation system in California.

As a final note, neoclassical economics allows for the possibility of nonmarket solutions if there is a market imperfection or inefficiency. In such a case, government intervention in the form of taxes and transfers is usually preferred over mandates, which are frequently more distortionary (as in our minimum wage example). Critics of "big government" note, however, that once a government spending program has been started, it can take on a life of its own. In such cases a program can survive long after the wrong is was meant to address has been righted.

Neoclassical economics encourages using the income tax over many other forms of taxation because it is one of the least-distortionary ways for the government to raise revenue. However, its effects are dispersed over the entire electorate. This means that each voter incurs a minuscule cost from a program financed by income taxes. If each person would save only a penny in taxes from the elimination of a transfer program, there is little personal incentive to lobby against that program when the time has come for it to go. This may indeed be one of the reasons why income tax financing of government spending programs is so prevalent. The costs of an employer mandate, on the other hand, are incurred by a relatively small group—the affected employers—guaranteeing a vocal opposition ready to argue for the program's demise at the appropriate time, if not earlier.

Finally, mandates are carried out by the individuals directly affected by the law: employers. They have the greatest incentive to meet the requirements of a mandate in the lowest-cost way, or risk going out of business. All three of these issues mean that the neoclassical concern over mandates may need to be tempered. Assuming the mandate allows employers to achieve the desired objective with a good deal of latitude— rather than specifying every detail—long-term economic efficiency may actually prescribe the use of mandates over government spending.

8

How Government Reduces Employment

Murray Weidenbaum

At a time of widespread concern that government is not doing enough to promote employment, we can no longer overlook the other side of the coin: the many ways in which government is doing too much, by reducing the ability of the private sector to create jobs. Through a variety of legislative mandates on and regulation of employers, government laws and rules weaken the demand for labor and, often, the supply of labor as well. Although that is not the intent of such legislation, the rising presence of government in the employment process slows down the growth of employment in the United States. The sad, hard fact is that more people would be at work if government were a less conspicuous force in the American economy.

As this chapter will show in detail, government, especially the federal government, conducts many activities that greatly influence the ability of the private sector to create jobs. The term *private sector* is not a misnomer, because it covers nonprofit as well as business enterprises. Colleges, hospitals, and museums are affected as much as business firms. And the direction of impact is the same and thus cumulative. Each of the government programs discussed below raises the cost of hiring people and thus discourages the creation of new jobs.

The central point of this chapter should not be misinterpreted. The aim is not to oppose efforts to eliminate discrimination, protect unskilled workers, or help the disabled. Rather, this report is designed to show that, quite unwittingly, much of the government's social legislation has been written in a way that is oblivious to its negative impact on employment.

Authors Note: I am greatly indebted to Sam Hughes, Frederick Deming Fellow at the Center for the Study of American Business, for extremely helpful research assistance.

If that undesirable side effect accompanied only one or two of these programs, perhaps it could be soft-pedaled. However, because the harm to employment is so pervasive and cumulative, it cannot be ignored. Surely, ways can be developed of meeting these important social objectives with less economic damage to the intended beneficiaries. However, the design of specific reforms is beyond the scope of this study.

Civil Rights Act

Of the numerous laws and regulations that discourage or slow down job creation, the most conspicuous example is the Civil Rights Act, including the affirmative action program. Although most of us do not like to think about it, this popular law does have some negatives. For example, it lengthens the amount of time that many jobs stay vacant. Any employer subject to affirmative action requirements who simply goes out and hires people does so at his or her peril. In order to reduce but not eliminate the likelihood of being sued, prospective employers must go through a lengthy and expensive process that includes advertising in specified types of media. The advertised position must stay open long enough to provide those interested with adequate opportunity to respond.

I once had the occasion to study a fascinating unintended phenomenon caused by this legislation. It turns out that an admonition in the affirmative action guidebook issued by the U.S. Equal Employment Opportunity Commission—namely, that covered employers should advertise in media specifically directed toward minorities—has helped to generate a new market. An example was the *National Black Register*, which charged $85 per column inch at a time that the Sunday edition of the *New York Times* charged $64 an inch to reach its circulation of 1.4 million. The *Register* was distributed to 42,500 organizations and individuals, a circulation equal to 3 percent that of the *Times* (Weidenbaum and Rockwood, 1978).

A study of affirmative action-induced advertising by colleges and universities in the mid-1970s concluded that the cost was "at least $6 million a year, though few professional placements ever result from such national advertisements" (Bonham, 1975–76, p. 11). Even though the outlay is likely much larger now, this advertising expense seems relatively insignificant when compared with the total cost imposed by the civil rights laws, including law enforcement, compliance, and resources directed from other activities. However, to most citizens, $6 million still is a great fortune.

Precise measures of the total costs imposed by civil rights laws and regulations are illusive. Nevertheless, Peter Brimelow and Leslie Spencer (1993) recently came up with an aggregate estimate of $236 billion a year, or approximately 4 percent of the gross domestic product. Because these authors' estimate is so dramatically large, it is useful to examine its individual elements. For example, Brimelow and Spencer estimate the direct-compliance expenses of private business necessary to respond to civil rights rules at a smaller but still substantial amount—$5–8 billion a year. Educational institutions spend $11 billion annually for the purpose. These direct costs are clearly very substantial. However, the truly huge costs imposed by these regulations—the remaining $220 billion plus— are indirect, such as the opportunities forgone because of the diversion of management time, energy, and resources.

Wrongful Termination Liability

If civil rights laws are an extremely conspicuous aspect of government's impact on the employment process, judicial narrowing of employers' right to fire is among the least publicized. Yet the repercussion of the resultant rise in wrongful-termination liability is very substantial. The RAND Institute for Civil Justice has revealed the high costs that have resulted from the tendency of state courts around the country to change traditional employment law.

As recently as a decade ago, courts in all but 13 states continued to recognize the long-standing common-law doctrine that allowed private employers to fire "at will" workers not protected by collective bargaining agreements or specific statutes. In recent years, a virtual landslide of cases has brought the law closer to the requirement that an employee can be fired only for cause. Courts have also been allowing plaintiffs to collect punitive damages as well as lost wages when they can prove wrongful conduct on the part of the employer. RAND researcher James N. Dertouzos (1993) sums up the findings: "In a nutshell, the efforts of the state judiciaries to protect workers' job securities are altering employers' hiring and firing practices. And one of the results is less hiring" (p. 6).

Dertouzos and Lynn Karoly (1992) note that, because of the substantial costs associated with wrongful-termination lawsuits, firms have responded by treating labor as a more expensive input to production. They estimate that, in the adjustment process, aggregate employment drops by 2–5 percent.

Family Leave Act

The Family and Medical Leave Act of 1993 is the most recent example of government-imposed costs on the employment process. It is fascinating to recall the debates on the bill as it wended its way through the Congress. Proponents kept asking, "How could anyone object to this obviously desirable measure that doesn't cost anything?" Just as soon as the bill became law, we were "reminded" that employers are required to maintain health insurance coverage for employees on leave. The U.S. General Accounting Office estimates this cost alone at $674 million a year (cited in Koltz, 1993, p. 14). One area of uncertainty is the ability of employers to recover the cost of the premiums they pay to employees who do not return from the leaves of absence mandated by the new law. Nor does this estimate cover the money involved in hiring and training temporary workers, who may be both more expensive and less productive than the employees on leave.

Research supports the thesis that the costs of mandated benefits such as employee leave are ultimately borne by the employees themselves. In a recent working paper published by the National Bureau of Economic Research, MIT economist Jonathan Gruber (1992) reports on a study of three states that passed laws, effective in 1976, requiring basic health insurance to include comprehensive coverage for maternity expenses. Gruber estimates that the mandate increased the cost of insuring women of child-bearing age by 1 to 5 percent of their wages. He arrived at this conclusion by analyzing data from the U.S. Census Bureau's *Current Population Survey*. Gruber found that real wages of married women of child-bearing age fell by 3.4 percent between 1974–75 and 1977–78 in the three states that required maternity coverage. In striking contrast, real wages for the same segment of the population rose 2.8 percent in five control states that did not require such coverage. At the same time that the "benefited" group of employees suffered a loss of real wages, employment among married women of child-bearing age declined. Not surprisingly, hours per worker in that population category rose. That is a logical response by employers, given that the fixed costs of employing these women had risen, regardless of the length of the workweek.

Gruber concluded that the increased cost of this employee leave mandate was shifted to the women's wages, or to their husbands' if they had insurance. He found similar effects from the passage of the 1978 Federal Pregnancy Discrimination Act, which extended comprehensive maternity coverage to insured women throughout the United States. In sum, the enactment of this government mandate seems to result in lower employment, lower wages, and higher hours worked.

Mandated Health Care

The largest prospective government mandate on employment is health care. At this point, nobody knows what specific type of health care "reform" will be enacted by the Congress, or even if such a bill will become law in the near future. In late August 1993, the *New York Times* did a roundup of views of various labor economists of the Clinton style of health care reform (Nasar, 1993). Their reactions are not comforting:

- Barbara Wolfe of the University of Wisconsin: "You'd expect to see fewer low-wage jobs because it would be more expensive to hire less-skilled workers. There's reason to be very concerned and very cautious."
- Daniel Hamermesh of the University of Texas at Austin: "Either there are going to be job cuts or wage cuts or, more likely, a combination of both."
- June O'Neill at Baruch College: "Many workers will be totally unaffected, but it will have a serious effect on low-wage workers."
- Robert Topel of the University of Chicago: "Somebody who keeps their job and has health insurance may be better off. But you have to think about the millions who no longer have jobs."

This near unanimity on the part of labor economists concerning the negative effects of employment mandates contrasts sharply with the view of former consultant Ira C. Magaziner, the top Clinton health care adviser, who was recently quoted as calling worries about job losses "crazy" (Nasar, 1993, p. A9). Perhaps the Clinton administration should reexamine its position on limiting the portion of mental health care to be covered by its health plan. After all, should it be enacted, the number of people meeting Magaziner's definition of crazy is likely to skyrocket.

Some analysts have tried to estimate the employment effects of imposing a health care mandate on American business. Professors June O'Neill and David O'Neill of Baruch College estimate that the increased cost of providing workers with health insurance will lead to the loss of 3.1 million jobs. Not surprisingly, the O'Neills show that low-wage industries (such as restaurants) would be hit very hard. The cost of the administration's health insurance package is likely to be the same for a highly paid worker as for an employee with a more modest wage scale. Thus, the researchers estimate that a health care mandate will result in an increase of 5 percent in labor costs in construction and a 19 percent rise in eating and drinking establishments (see Table 8.1; cited in Bonilla, 1993, p. A10).

As would be expected, other analysts have come up with different figures on the employment impact of the Clinton health program. Professor Alan Krueger of Princeton estimates that the plan would mean 200,000–400,000 fewer jobs in 10 years than would otherwise be the case. In contrast, presidential adviser Ira Magaziner believes that "some gain" in employment is likely in the short run as well as the long run (quoted in Wartzman, 1993, p. A26).

TABLE 8.1
Impacts of Clinton Health Care Mandate

	Increase in Labor Costs (%)	*Job Loss*
Eating and drinking establishments	19.1	828,000
Other retailing	7.9	726,000
Construction	5.1	241,000
Personal services	11.3	217,000
Agriculture	15.6	194,000
Private household services	32.9	190,000
Repair services	8.2	77,000
All other	2.8	627,000
TOTAL	3.8	3,100,000

Source: Bonilla (1993).

The short-term effects of imposing a health care mandate on employers differ from the long-run effects in important respects. In the short run, the great bulk of the costs (80 percent in the basic Clinton plan) is paid by employers, which should reduce their demand for labor. In the longer run, those costs are largely shifted back to workers in the form of lower real wages and reduced nonmedical benefits (McKenzie, 1991). As a result, the effect on the supply of labor is likely also to be negative. In any event, Barbara Presley Noble (1993) may have identified most succinctly a fundamental shortcoming of mandating health care benefits—the lack of adequate financing: "The tooth fairy, who has emerged as a major policy player, doesn't pay for health care" (p. F23).

Minimum Wage Legislation

Without doubt, of all the government regulations affecting employment, the statutory minimum wage has been the focus of the greatest amount of professional attention. With a few, albeit conspicuous, exceptions, the great mass of the research has concluded that increases in the compulsory minimum wage cause a rise in unemployment. The segment of the workforce most affected consists of those at or near the minimum wage. This is a group made up primarily of teenagers and others with low skills who thereby lose the opportunity to gain their initial work experience (McKenzie, 1991; Zycher, 1993).

After analyzing a great number of studies, the Minimum Wage Study Commission concluded in 1981 that a 10 percent increase in the minimum wage generates a 1–3 percent increase in unemployment among those holding minimum wage jobs, mainly teenagers. A smaller adverse effect was noted for 20–24-year-olds, mostly because a smaller percentage of that age group earns the minimum wage. Confidence in the commission's estimates is enhanced by the fact that David Neumark (1992) recently replicated the 1981 findings using panel data from all 50 states over a period of 15 years.

What about the workers who manage to retain jobs at the new minimum wage? Here, the data provide an interesting twist. According to Edward Gramlich of the University of Michigan, many minimum wage workers are the dependent children of the middle class. In the quotable words of Peter Passell (1993) in the *New York Times*, much of the gain from a higher minimum would go into surfboards and stereos, not into rent and baby formula.

More seriously, several economists have demonstrated that the benefits of the minimum wage to those receiving it are offset by reductions in other benefits. For example, a study of the 1967 rise in the statutory minimum wage showed that workers gained 32 cents an hour in money income, but lost 41 cents an hour in training benefits, for a net loss of 9 cents an hour in total compensation (Hashimoto, 1982; see also Leighton and Mincer, 1981). This empirical finding reinforces Martin Feldstein's (1973) more general conclusion on the point:

> The minimum wage law has an unambiguously harmful effect on some young workers. Even if an individual were willing to "buy" on-the-job training by taking a very low wage for six months or a year, the minimum wage law would not permit him to do so…. For the disadvantaged, the minimum wage law may have the ironic effect of lowering lifetime incomes by a very large amount. (p. 15)

It is instructive to estimate the effects of the recent proposal by Secretary of Labor Robert Reich to raise the compulsory minimum wage from $4.25 an hour to $4.50. We can obtain a rough idea of the disemployment effect by assuming that the past relationship continues to hold a 1–3 percent increase in the unemployment of the affected portion of the labor force for each 10 percent rise in the wage. Let us apply that ratio to the approximately 5 million affected employees, those now earning between $4.25 and $4.50 an hour. This procedure yields an increase in unemployment in the range of 29,500 to 88,500 workers. To those who dismiss the importance of such "small" numbers, it is pertinent to ask, When was the last time they generated 80,000 new jobs, or 20,000, or even 20?

Studies of retail establishments in New York found that many stores responded to increases in the minimum wage by reducing commission payments, eliminating bonuses, and cutting paid vacations and sick leave (Fleisher, 1981). One researcher estimated that, for every 1 percent increase in the minimum wage, restaurants reduced shift premiums by 3.6 percent, severance pay by 6.9 percent, and sick pay by 3.4 percent (Alpert, 1983).

It must be noted, however, that three distinguished economists have recently come up with a contrary conclusion. David Card of Princeton (1992a, 1992b) and Lawrence Katz of Harvard (currently at the U.S. Department of Labor) and Alan B. Krueger of Princeton estimate that the 27 percent rise in the statutory minimum wage in April 1990 had virtually no negative effect on employment (Katz and Krueger, 1992). These researchers reached this conclusion after studying the question from several viewpoints, using data on individual states and on fast-food restaurants in Texas, as well as examining the impact of the 1988 rise in the California minimum wage.

As would be expected in the case of research that departs from the conventional wisdom, many criticisms have been leveled at these contrary studies. Ronald Ehrenberg (1992) of Cornell notes that the studies do not take into account the possibility that some firms may go out of business because of the cost increase to them from raising the compulsory minimum wage. Finis Welch (1993, p. 12) of Texas A&M notes that the three researchers ignore changes in product demand among the establishments analyzed. Perhaps employment would have increased had the minimum wage not been raised. Also, the effects of a rise in the minimum wage may not show up quickly. Employers need time to make personnel decisions and to substitute machinery for workers; the studies cover only a year or two (Kramer, 1993).

The bulk of the evidence continues to support the traditionally negative view of minimum wage laws. Interestingly, Gallaway and Vedder (1993) also recently examined the effects of minimum wage increases on the American restaurant industry. Using U.S. Bureau of Labor Statistics data from 1980 through mid-1991, they estimated the effects of two minimum wage hikes that occurred in 1990 and 1991 (bringing the minimum wage to $4.25 an hour). They conclude that a 1 percent increase in money wage rates reduced employment in eating and drinking places by 0.83 percent.

The first of these two minimum wage hikes was less significant. At that time, the minimum wage had not been increased in almost a decade, and most establishments were already paying in excess of the federal minimum. Nevertheless, allowing for this as well as the fact that some portion of wage increases is passed on to consumers in the form of higher prices, Gallaway and Vedder's estimated range of possible job losses associated with the rise to a $4.25 minimum wage is 111,000 to 130,000.

In a study of the federal minimum wage increases in an earlier period (1979 and 1980), Janet Currie and Bruce Fallick (1993) also found negative effects on employment. Specifically, these two analysts at the National Bureau of Economic Research estimated that the employed individuals who were affected by the increases in the minimum wage were 3–4 percent less likely to be employed a year later. They describe their methodology as "similar in spirit" to Card's recent work on the minimum wage. However, they use individual data from the National Longitudinal Survey of Youth, rather than state-level data, and also cover an earlier period of time. In any event, in a vigorous response to the critics of the work that he and his colleagues have done, Professor Krueger (1993) states, "I want to emphasize that my comments should *not* be interpreted as support for the position that increasing the minimum wage is sound public policy" (p. 11).

Other Regulation of Employment

By no means have we exhausted the list of costs that government imposes on the job creation process in the United States. Some of the remaining employment-affecting programs are discussed briefly below.

Disability Insurance

Some public sector actions operate to reduce the demand for labor, whereas others decrease the supply of labor. Let us examine the disability portion of the social security program (technically, this is the D of OASDI, or old-age, survivors, and disability insurance, the formal way of describing social security). The disability program is a cogent example of a government mandate reducing the labor supply.

Jonathan S. Leonard (1991) reports that social security disability insurance beneficiaries rarely return to work. Once initial eligibility is established, the program resembles an early retirement system. In 1987, fewer than 8,000 disabled beneficiaries—less than one-half of 1 percent of the total—successfully completed a trial work period and thus stopped receiving their monthly social security checks. Leonard states his conclusions in good scholarly terms: "The statistical evidence supports the proposition that the target population of severely disabled persons who are unable to undertake any gainful activity is an elastic one" (pp. 46–47). In plain English, he is saying that the more generous the benefits, the less willing the recipients are to return to work.

Economist Walter Oi (1991) of the University of Rochester concludes from the evidence that the disability program creates an employment disincentive, encouraging working people with disabilities to drop out of the labor force and nonworking beneficiaries to remain out of the workforce. As benefit levels rise, the number of disabled beneficiaries expands and the male labor force participation rate declines. Between 1955 and 1985, for example, the portion of 45- to 55-year-old men not in the labor force rose from 2.5 percent to 8.2 percent; among 55- to 65-year-old males, the ratio climbed from 12.1 percent to 32.1 percent.

OSHA

Whereas disability benefits reduce the supply of labor, the rules and activities of the Occupational Safety and Health Administration (or OSHA, the small business executive's favorite four-letter word) operate to reduce the demand for labor. That feat is accomplished by increasing the indirect costs of maintaining a company workforce. Virtually every serious study of OSHA concludes that, although the costs are substantial, the benefits, if any, are modest. In his most recent work on the subject, W. Kip Viscusi (1992) of Duke University states, "Most available studies fail to show examples where the benefits of OSHA standards exceed the costs, although the recent OSHA hazard communication standard is a prominent exception" (p. 220).

Studies of OSHA performance in the 1970s concluded that the agency had no statistically significant impact on worker safety (Ruser and Smith, 1991). However, Viscusi believes that some modest improvement occurred in the 1980s. In his calculations, OSHA now prevents from 1 to 2 injuries involving at least one lost day of work per 1,000 workers annually.

At the present time, Congress is considering an ambitious extension of OSHA. In July 1993, the Senate and House Committees on Education and Labor each held hearings on the proposed Comprehensive Occupational Safety and Health Reform Act (H.R.1280/S.575). This bill would amend the existing OSHA statute to require each employer of 11 or more (an estimated 1.6 million firms) to undertake two new initiatives. The first is to create a joint labor-management safety and health committee that is granted broad authority to influence workplace safety and health programs. The second is to establish and implement a detailed written safety and health program.

In addition, OSHA inspectors would no longer have to go to court to get the authority to order an immediate shutdown if they considered a business operation unsafe. Each inspector would have discretion to do so. Also, the pending bill would preclude any consideration of economic impact in setting job safety or health standards.

Researchers at the Employment Policy Foundation have estimated that this package of changes in employment regulation will cost the American economy nearly $62 billion a year, a figure representing 11.8 percent of 1990 net business income. The major components of this very large cost estimate are the required new safety and health programs, training, and committees (for a total of $38.7 billion). Also significant are the costs of record keeping and reporting ($3.6 billion) and litigation ($8.6 billion). The cost of monetary penalties is estimated at "only" $90 million annually (Holt, Bruening, and Simon, 1993).

Workers' Compensation

Another expensive burden on the employment process, and one whose cost is rising very rapidly, is workers' compensation. As shown in Table 8.2, the cost of this mandate to U.S. companies is escalating. In real terms, the cost of workers' compensation more than doubled from 1977 to 1991. In nominal terms, this required outlay rose from $14 billion in 1977 to $55 billion in 1991. During the same period, lost work time owing to injuries and illnesses rose far more modestly, from about 60 days per 100 workers per year to approximately 70 days per 100 workers. Even taking into account the rise in unit medical costs, the workers' compensation program is an increasingly generous one and extremely costly to employers (Nelson, 1991).

TABLE 8.2
Employer Cost for Workers' Compensation

Year	Cost (in billions of current dollars)
1977	$14.1
1982	22.8
1986	34.0
1987	38.1
1988	43.3
1989	47.9
1990	53.1
1991	55.2

Note: Employer cost includes payments to worker compensation funds, private insurance systems, and payments from self-insurance funds. *Source:* Nelson (1991).

Some legislation affecting jobs is so recent that it is premature to attempt to estimate the specific impacts on labor costs and on labor supply or demand. An example is the Americans with Disabilities Act (ADA), which took effect on July 26, 1992, in the case of employers with 25 or more workers (and on July 26, 1994, in the case of employers with 15 or more employees). The officials charged with carrying out the statute explain that it will take extended litigation to determine the full scope of the vague and often sweeping provisions of the law, which covers an estimated 43 million Americans. However, early experience indicates that the costs will be substantial. The Equal Employment Opportunity Commission is now receiving about 1,000 ADA claims each month on top of its already heavy caseload dealing with other discrimination claims ("Lawyers Disable Disability," 1993).

Conclusion

Amid all the scary headlines about massive layoffs, some important but undramatic perspective is necessary. It is true that, in recent months, IBM, Procter & Gamble, et al. have announced unprecedented large reductions

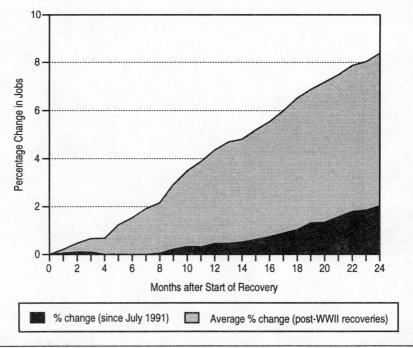

FIGURE 8.1 Job Growth since 1991 Compared with Earlier Economic Recoveries *Source:* U.S. Department of Labor data.

in their workforces. But one of the best-kept secrets in the U.S. economy continues to be that the total number of jobs is growing. Net job expansion from late 1991 to late 1993 has averaged a little over 1 percent a year. However, that is far below the rate of employment growth during typical recoveries (see Figure 8.1). We should be able to improve on that record.

The upbeat point that needs to be made is that the concern with removing government obstacles to job creation is reasonable and manageable. There is no need to throw up our hands in despair. There are many reasons for the slowdown in job formation in the American economy, and some of them are amenable to sensible policy changes.

Surely, an important and often overlooked factor is the rising load of regulation and mandates that government is imposing on business and other employers. The direct cost of meeting employment mandates imposed by the federal government has risen far faster than wages and salaries. As shown in Figure 8.2, federal mandates were equal to almost 3 percent of total wages and salaries in 1960. By 1990, the ratio of mandated benefits to wages and salaries had more than doubled, to over 7 percent.

It is one thing for the proponents of these mandates and regulations to justify them on social grounds. It is another matter and, far less acceptable, for them to say that all of these burdens can be justified on economic grounds. The case comes to mind of blind people who require "readers"

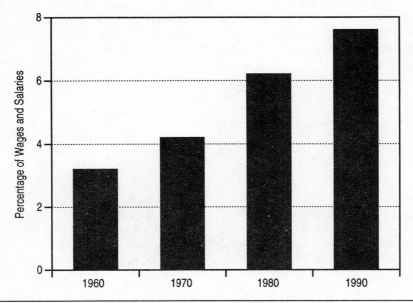

FIGURE 8.2 The Cost of Government Mandates as a Percentage of Worker Compensation
Source: McKenzie (1991).

to be employed to help them. Surely, the feeling of increased self-worth on the part of the newly employed blind person is a socially desirable accomplishment. But forcing the employer to pay two persons to do one job is often difficult to justify on economic grounds.

The indirect costs of employment regulations, many of which are both substantial and hidden, all share a common characteristic: They make adding workers to the payroll more expensive. At least initially, they also create a substantial gap between the cost to the employer and the benefit to the employee. These facts are often lost amid political debates on these issues. Many times, more regulation seems a costless way to achieve policy goals.

A review of the estimates presented in this chapter alone is staggering (see Table 8.3). Compliance with the civil rights laws may cost the U.S. economy as much as $236 billion a year, or 4 percent of the gross domestic product. Wrongful termination lawsuits may result in lowering employment by 2–5 percent. Mandating health care may involve the loss of 3.1 million jobs. In addition, employer costs are rising rapidly for workers' compensation. Moreover, the Clinton administration appears to be developing further impositions on the job creation process, such as another increase in the statutory minimum wage.

In the words of University of Chicago law professor Richard A. Epstein (1992), "Public discourse proceeds as if employment laws are unrelated to wage levels, job creation, or labor output" (p. A11). His colleague, economist Sam Peltzman, states the matter more pungently: "People who say there is no trade-off between regulation and employment are smoking something" (quoted in Farrell, 1993, p. 70).

TABLE 8.3
Estimates of Economic Cost for Major Employment Regulations and Mandates

Program	*Estimated Cost*
Civil rights programs	$236 billion a year (or 4% of GDP)
Wrongful termination lawsuits	2–5% lower employment
Mandating health care	3.1 million fewer jobs
Compulsory minimum wage	1–3% increase in teenage unemployment for each 10% increase in minimum
Workers' compensation	More than $43 billion a year
Comprehensive OSHA reform	$62 billion a year
Parental leave insurance costs	$674 million a year

Note: Sources of figures in this table are cited in text.

On occasion, we can find specific evidence to support the close and inverse relationship between onerous government regulation and the willingness to hire. Here are two recent examples: WorldClass Process Inc., a new and growing Pittsburgh processor of flat-rolled steel coils, has increased its workforce to 49. According to Jack Teitz, the company's chief financial officer, "We're going to keep at 49 as long as we can," in order to avoid being subject to the 50-or-more threshold for coverage under the Family Leave Act (quoted in Bowers, 1993, p. R16).

Similarly, the Schonstedt Instrument Company of Reston, Virginia, a profitable, high-tech firm, deliberately keeps its workforce below 50 employees. It does so in order to avoid having to file Form EEO-1 every year. An excerpt from a letter to the editor of the *Washington Times* from the company's president makes the point effectively, although not in scholarly fashion: "A friend went over 50 employees on a government contract. He gave me his EEO file...it weighs more than 8 pounds...I have kept my employment under 50" (Schonstedt, 1992). Perhaps fate will arrange a meeting between Mr. Schonstedt and Ira Magaziner. The tooth fairy could serve as the referee.

References

Alpert, W. T. (1983). *The Effects of the Minimum Wage on the Fringe Benefits of Restaurant Workers*. Bethlehem, PA: Lehigh University.

Bonham, G. W. (1975–76, Winter). "Will Government Patronage Kill the Universities?" *Change*, vol. 7, no. 10, 10–13, 60–61.

Bonilla, C. (1993, August 20). "The Price of a Health Care Mandate." *Wall Street Journal*, p. A10.

Bowers, B. (1993, October 15). "Regulation Play." *Wall Street Journal*, p. R16.

Brimelow, P., and Spencer, L. (1993, February 15). "When Quotas Replace Merit, Everybody Suffers." *Forbes*, pp. 80–82, 86, 90, 94, 96, 99, 102.

Card, D. (1992a, October). "Do Minimum Wages Reduce Employment?" *Industrial and Labor Relations Review*, vol. 46, no. 1, pp. 38–54.

Card, D. (1992b, October). "Using Regional Variation in Wages to Measure the Effects of the Federal Minimum Wage." *Industrial and Labor Relations Review*, vol. 46, no. 1, pp. 22–37.

Currie, J., and Fallick, B. (1993). "A Note on the New Minimum Wage Research." Working Paper 4348, National Bureau of Economic Research.

Dertouzos, J. N. (1993, Spring). "The Hidden Costs of 'Worker Protection'" *RAND Research Review*, pp. 6, 9.

Dertouzos, J. N., and Karoly, L. A. (1992). *Labor-Market Responses to Employer Liability*. Santa Monica, CA: RAND Corporation.

Ehrenberg, R. B. (1992, October). "New Minimum Wage Research." *Industrial and Labor Relations Review*, vol. 46, no. 1, pp. 1–4.

Epstein, R. A. (1992, September 2). "As Unions Decline, Labor Laws Constrain the Job Market." *Wall Street Journal*, p. A11.

Farrell, C. (1993, February 22). "The Scary Math of New Hires." *Business Week*, p. 70.
Feldstein, M. (1973, Fall). "The Economics of the New Unemployment." *Public Interest*, p. 15.
Fleisher, B. M. (1981). *Minimum Wage Regulation in Retail Trade*. Washington, DC: American Enterprise Institute Press.
Gallaway, L., and Vedder, R. (1993). "The Employment Effects of Social Security Tax Changes and Minimum Wage Regulations: A Case Study of the American Restaurant Industry." *Journal of Labor Research, 14*, 367–374.
Gruber, J. (1992). "The Efficiency of a Group-Specific Mandated Benefit: Evidence from Health Insurance Benefits for Maternity." Working Paper 4157, National Bureau of Economic Research.
Hashimoto, M. (1982, December). "Minimum Wage Effects on Training on the Job." *American Economic Review*, vol. 72, no. 5, pp. 1070–1085.
Holt, J. S., Bruening, T. M., and Simon, A. E. (1993). *COSHRA Legislation in the 103rd Congress: An Update of Estimated Private and Public Sector Employer Costs*. Washington, DC: Employment Policy Foundation.
Katz, L.F., and Krueger, A. B. (1992, October). "The Effect of the Minimum Wage on the Fast-Food Industry." *Industrial and Labor Relations Review*, vol. 46, no. 1, pp. 6–21.
Koltz, G. (1993, August 3). "The High Cost of Employees' Rights." *Wall Street Journal*, p. 14.
Kramer, J. (1993, October). "Taking a Hike." *Reason*, vol. 25, no. 3, p. 19.
Krueger, A. B. (1993, Summer). "Have Increases in the Minimum Wage Reduced Employment?" *Jobs & Capital*, vol. 2, no. 2, pp. 10–11.
"Lawyers Disable Disability." (1993, January 11). *Wall Street Journal*, p. A14.
Leighton, L., and Mincer, J. (1981). "Effects of Minimum Wages on Human Capital Formation." In S. Rothenberg (Ed.), *The Economics of Legal Minimum Wages*. Washington, DC: American Enterprise Institute.
Leonard, J. S. (1991). "Disability Policy and the Return to Work." In Carolyn Weaver (Ed.), *Disability and Work*. Washington DC: American Enterprise Institute Press.
McKenzie, R. B. (1991). *The Mandated-Benefit Mirage*. St. Louis, MO: Washington University, Center for the Study of American Business.
Nasar, S. (1993, August 30). "Health Care Quandary: Will Coverage Cost Jobs?" *New York Times*, p. A9.
Nelson, W. J. (1991, March). "Workers' Compensation." *Social Security Bulletin*, pp. 12–20.
Neumark, D., and Wascher, W. (1992, October). "Employment Effects of Minimum and Subminimum Wages." *Industrial and Labor Relations Review*, vol. 46, no. 1, pp. 55–81.
Noble, B. P. (1993, August 29). "The Employee Side of Health Care." *New York Times*, p. F23.
Oi, W. Y. (1991). "Disability and a Workfare-Welfare Dilemma." In C. Weaver (Ed.), *Disability and Work*. Washington, DC: American Enterprise Institute Press.
Passell, P. (1993, February 18). "Does Raising the Minimum Wage Still Mean Fewer Jobs?" *New York Times*, p. C2.

Ruser, J., and Smith, R. (1991, Spring). "Reestimating OSHA's Effects." *Journal of Human Resources*, vol. 26, no. 2, pp. 212–235.

Schonstedt, E. O. (1992, February 16). "'Robber Reg' has Backfired" (Letter to the editor). *Washington Times*, p. B5.

Viscusi, W. K. (1992). *Fatal Tradeoffs*. New York: Oxford University Press.

Wartzman, R. (1993, September 27). "Clinton Aides Predict Health-Care Plan Will Result in Net Job Gain in Long Term." *Wall Street Journal*, p. A26.

Weidenbaum, M. L., and Rockwood, L. L. (1978). "Government as a Promoter and Subsidizer of Advertising." In D. G. Tuerck (Ed.), *The Political Economy of Advertising*. Washington, DC: American Enterprise Institute.

Welch, F. (1993, Summer). "The Cruelty of the Minimum Wage." *Jobs & Capital*, vol. 2, no. 2, pp. 1, 12.

Zycher, B. (1993, Summer). "Replace the Minimum Wage." *Jobs & Capital*, vol. 2, no. 2, pp. 1, 13–14.

9

Observations on Employment-Based Government Mandates, with Particular Reference to Health Insurance

Alan B. Krueger

A government typically has three options in securing universal access to a good or service: It can provide the good or service directly, as in the case of public education, defense, and national parks; it can mandate that employers arrange for provision of the good or service for their workers and dependents, as in the case of workers' compensation insurance and certain pension safeguards; or it can mandate that individuals purchase the good or service themselves, as in the case of automobile insurance.[1] In addition, the government can alter market incentives to encourage individuals to purchase a good or service themselves, although there is no guarantee that every citizen will purchase the good or service. These approaches may have different implications for the efficiency and equity of a public program.

Employment-based mandates are widely used to accomplish social goals in the United States. Examples of such mandates include the recently passed Family Leave Act, which requires firms to give leave to workers; WARN legislation, which requires employers to give workers advance notice of plant closings; workers' compensation insurance, which requires employers to provide insurance against work-related injuries and diseases; unemployment insurance, which requires employers to pay a tax for unemployment benefits; the Fair Labor Standards Act, which mandates a minimum wage and overtime payments; and ERISA, which, among other things, requires firms to provide pension benefits to all workers if they provide them to some. In addition, in several states

Author's Note: I am grateful to Norman K. Thurston for excellent research assistance, and to Tim Besley, David Card, and Victor Fuchs for useful conversations.

the common law has imposed a quasi-mandate on firms that restricts their ability to fire workers at will, and Montana has passed a law requiring just cause to fire a worker. And, perhaps most significant, several recent proposals for universal health care, including the Clinton proposal, involve some form of an employment-based mandate.

In a textbook neoclassical economic model of the labor market, employment-based mandates can only reduce efficiency. If workers are fully informed, sufficiently mobile, and rational decision makers, then they will be willing to trade off wages for fringe benefits. In this model, as long as there are no other distortions in the economy, the optimal level of fringe benefits will result without government mandates. The necessary assumptions for this fortuitous result may not hold perfectly in the actual economy. For example, there are preexisting distortions, such as progressive income taxation. In addition, workers and firms often lack perfect information about things like work hazards and job opportunities. In a more complete model of the labor market, there conceivably may be an efficiency role for mandates.[2]

Opponents of employment-based mandated benefits tend to ignore market failures that may be improved by government intervention. Supporters of employment-based mandates tend to ignore the distortions that mandates create, and overlook implementation problems. In this chapter, I present several observations on the economic impact of employment-based mandates. I begin by reviewing possible rationales under which employment-based mandates may be an efficient mechanism. Next, I consider the efficiency costs of mandates. In short, mandates reduce efficiency because they restrict employers' and employees' freedom of contract. Mandates may also adversely affect employment and wage levels. I provide a detailed analysis of the possible employment and wage effects of the Clinton health care proposal to illustrate these points. I then consider some practical issues of mandates, such as lack of compliance and implementation issues. Finally, I present a discussion of the political economy of mandates.

The benefits of mandates must be weighed against their costs. My main conclusion in this chapter is that, in most cases, employment-based mandates are probably not the best way to structure a program. Nevertheless, mandates have proved an attractive alternative to policy makers in the United States and elsewhere because alternative financing mechanisms have been politically infeasible, largely because they would involve new taxes. The costs of mandates are hidden, which makes them politically feasible. Although mandates are probably not the best way to structure many policies, evidence suggests that the employment loss resulting from to most mandates is modest because labor supply is relatively insensitive to the wage rate. As a consequence, the burden of employer mandates is typically shifted to workers in the long run.

Possible Efficiency Rationales for Employment-Based Mandates

Adverse Selection

Some economists have tried to justify employment-based mandates on the basis of "adverse selection" (see, e.g., Levine, 1991). Adverse selection is a problem that has been of concern in the insurance industry for a long time. In the context of insurance, adverse selection means that if a firm offers a certain policy that is pitched for the average person, a disproportionate share of the "bad risks" will come forward to take up the policy.

To see how adverse selection might be relevant in the labor market, consider the case of a firm deciding whether to announce a policy that it will never fire workers, thus giving them lifetime jobs. In some industries, such a personnel policy may be desirable to firms because workers will then not fear losing their jobs if they develop new, labor-saving technologies. A no-firing rule may encourage workers to develop new technologies, which would help their firm and its shareholders. But workers who have a high propensity to be fired—bad workers—will find this personnel policy particularly attractive. Thus, a company that voluntarily chooses to provide lifetime jobs as a condition of employment will attract a disproportionate number of bad workers. If the firm cannot detect the bad workers in advance of hiring them, the firm will have a workforce composed largely of bad workers, which is likely to defeat the firm's original goal of encouraging workers to develop new technologies. Although a no-firing rule may be beneficial to the firm (and to other firms like it), the firm will not find it beneficial to provide a no-firing clause if it is the only firm in the industry to do so. But if all firms in the industry offer no-firing clauses, then the bad workers will not all flock to one firm, and productivity may rise, because job security encourages innovation and loyalty. Several observers have commented that Japanese companies have been successful in part because of their commitment to lifetime jobs, which is encouraged by government policy.

The no-firing rule is a stylized example, but there are other situations where, because of adverse selection, certain benefits that all firms would like to provide to workers are not provided because it is not profitable for any firm to offer the benefit individually. In this situation, total welfare may be higher if all firms are required to provide the benefit.

Adverse selection is likely to be a problem for employers' provision of health care benefits. For example, as part of their health packages firms can offer generous drug rehabilitation programs that reduce drug abuse, increase worker productivity, and improve the morale of workers. Workers may even be willing to take somewhat lower pay in exchange for such a benefit. But if other firms do not offer this policy, any firm that voluntarily offers such a policy is likely to find a high number of drug users among its job applicants. If those applicants are not screened out in advance, they may lower the firms' productivity and poison morale. As a consequence, individual firms have little incentive to provide these benefits. Indeed, individual firms have an incentive to test workers for drug use to avoid hiring them. There is a strong element of a prisoner's dilemma here: Firms must use up resources to test for drug use, but the drug users just end up working for other firms, so aggregate labor market efficiency is not improved.[3]

In principle, a government mandate is capable of solving the adverse selection problem by compelling every firm in the industry to provide a benefit. This may be grounds for a government mandate, and solving adverse selection may be one of the functions that government does best. But the gains of alleviating adverse selection must be weighed against the costs of the policy. In particular, some firms may not profit from having drug rehabilitation policies. For example, in some industries drug use probably does not reduce work productivity.

It should also be pointed out that in some industries private coalitions of firms or workers have managed to overcome adverse selection on their own, without government involvement. For example, the American Association of University Professors has established rules and procedures regarding tenure; these rules essentially govern lifetime jobs for tenured professors.

Finally, there are other alternatives to employment-based government mandates for solving adverse selection. For example, broad individual mandates or public provision (e.g., drug rehabilitation centers) may also solve adverse selection. Although individual mandates are not plausible for certain employment benefits, such as firing rules, they are feasible for others, such as drug rehabilitation. The costs and benefits of individual mandates versus employment-based mandates versus public provision must also be weighed. The case for employment-based mandates seems to me to be strongest in situations where programs cannot be structured without involving working conditions, such as firing rules or workplace safety. Moreover, the case for employment-based mandates over individual mandates would be stronger if employers have some unique advantage in implementing a program. For example, employers may be especially adept at detecting false injury claims (e.g., claims made by individuals who were not really injured at work) or at identifying and correcting hazardous working conditions.

Imperfect Information and Irrationality

The most obvious case to be made for mandating a certain benefit is that workers do not bargain for a particular benefit that they would desire because they have imperfect information. For example, in some industries workers are likely to underestimate the risks they face at work because employers have an incentive to understate the true level of risks. In other situations, it is not possible to know the health consequences of certain risks, given the current state of medical knowledge and long latency periods for some illnesses. If they receive systematic misinformation, workers will fail to request compensating payments for the risk of work-related disabilities. As a consequence, firms in dangerous industries will overproduce compared with the first-best level because they fail to account for the total social costs of their production. Mandates such as workers' compensation insurance and OSHA may be justified in this situation.

Workers' compensation insurance is especially appealing because workers can be compensated after injuries or illnesses have occurred. Moreover, workers' compensation is highly experience rated in the United States, which causes firms to internalize the costs of accidents that occur as by-products of production. On the other hand, workers' compensation insurance introduces a set of distortions of its own (see Butler and Worrall, 1983; Krueger, 1990). For example, workers have an incentive to claim benefits for injuries that might not be work related, or to take fewer precautions on the job.

In principle, OSHA regulation works by restricting the use of hazardous technologies. These restrictions may also create several distortions that must be weighed against the benefit of fewer industrial accidents. For example, by regulating the technology that firms can use, OSHA may not achieve the goal of reducing accidents at the least possible cost. (For a critical evaluation of OSHA, see Smith, 1976.)

Another issue is whether workers use rationally the information they do have. Psychologists have consistently found that individuals underweight outcomes that are merely probable in comparison with equally preferred outcomes that are obtained with certainty (see Kahneman and Tversky, 1979). This phenomenon may be relevant for the purchase of insurance coverage for catastrophic events. Fuchs (1976) and others note that individuals often prefer health insurance programs that offer limited coverage with a low or zero deductible and copayment over comparable policies that offer higher maximum coverage and higher deductibles and copayments. If employers have efficiencies in providing insurance because they can reduce adverse selection and lower transaction costs by purchasing coverage for a large unit, then trades that would take place under rational decision making may not take place if individuals are irrational. In addition to the preferred tax treatment of employer-provided health insurance, a tendency toward irrational evaluation of probabilities may explain why individuals tend to overinsure against predictable, small losses and underinsure against unpredictable, catastrophic losses.

Finally, it should be stressed that the knowledge and decision-making processes of the "marginal worker" are most relevant for labor market outcomes such as wages. Firms in an industry will set wages equal to the amount necessary to hire the profit-maximizing number of workers. If the industry cannot attract enough workers at a certain wage, wages will be bid up to attract a sufficient quantity of workers. The workers who are most mobile therefore determine the equilibrium wage, provided firms cannot pay workers doing the same job differently. As a consequence, if the workers who are on the margin of working or not working in an industry are well-informed and rational decision makers, then the "right" wage premiums for working conditions and fringe benefits will surface even if the average worker is misinformed or irrational.

Externalities

Some employment conditions involve externalities, meaning that the costs and benefits of particular actions may accrue to more than just the parties involved. For example, suppose a hazardous chemical is used improperly in the workplace. Any individual worker can take the time to investigate whether the use of the chemical is hazardous, and then use that information to improve working conditions (or demand a compensating wage premium). The information gathered will benefit not only the worker who invested the time and resources to learn about the chemical, but his or her coworkers who also use the chemical as well. Unfortunately, an individual worker does not have an incentive to take the benefits that accrue to the coworkers into account in making a decision to investigate working conditions. When externalities are involved, the independent actions of individuals will lead to a suboptimal allocation of resources. It is possible that, by mandating employers to disclose fully information about work hazards, the government can improve the operation of the labor market. More generally, mandates could improve distortions created by externalities.[4]

It is also worth noting that, in some situations, society inadvertently creates externalities through charitable programs. For example, the fact that society is often unwilling to deny some health care benefits to uninsured individuals when they become seriously ill creates an altruistic externali\ (see Pauly, 1971). The uncompensated cost of treating the uninsured is shifted to insured consumers, health care providers, or taxpayers. Thus, an uninsured individual who obtains a job that provides health insurance reduces costs for others. But the benefit to society will not be reflected in the individual's personal calculation of costs and benefits of obtaining health insurance. As a result, the fraction of the workforce that receives health insurance would tend to be less than optimal, and mandated health insurance could improve this distortion.

Finally, some activities and circumstances inherently produce externalities. For example, an individual who has an untreated contagious disease imposes a negative externality on the rest of society. Mandating that individuals have health insurance, which increases the probability that contagious diseases will be treated, reduces the spread of disease to others and limits the negative externality.

Lack of Fully Compensating Wage Differentials

If the labor market operates smoothly, then one would expect wages to adjust in response to the level of fringe benefits firms offer. Firms that offer more desirable benefits will be able to offer lower wages, other things (e.g., worker skills) being equal. If imperfect information or barriers to mobility are important features of labor markets, then compensating wage payments may not surface. The case for government mandates is stronger if the actions of individuals and firms fail to produce compensating wage payments for workers who take jobs that offer less generous benefits. Notably, the empirical literature on compensating wage payments has provided little systematic support for the view that wages adjust to compensate workers fully for fringe benefits and working conditions (for a dissenting view, see Rosen, 1986).

Smith and Ehrenberg (1983), Leibowitz (1983), and Monheit, Hagan, Berk, and Farley (1985) all failed to find that workers who receive more generous health insurance benefits also receive lower wage payments as a result. Economists have also had great difficulty establishing a tradeoff between other benefits and pay. In fact, with the major exception of work-related fatalities, the labor economics literature has not found consistent evidence of compensating wage differentials for work amenities (see Brown, 1980; Smith, 1979).

One of the difficulties in interpreting this literature, however, is that because of data shortcomings studies of compensating wage differentials have been able to hold constant only a limited number of worker characteristics. There is nothing in the theory of compensating differentials to suggest, for example, that lawyers should receive less-generous fringe benefits than manual laborers because of their higher wage. Indeed, if fringe benefits are a "normal good," one would expect higher-paid workers to take some of their compensation in the form of better working conditions and fringe benefits. Nevertheless, the past literature on compensating differentials should challenge researchers to search for additional evidence before assuming that employee valuation of fringe benefits will be reflected in the incidence of those benefits.

Preexisting Distortions

The labor market should not be considered in isolation; it is affected by a wide network of government policies. Similarly, other markets may fail (e.g., because of adverse selection, the market for private health insurance may be less than perfect), causing distortions that could be rectified by labor market policy. Government intervention in the labor market may help to improve distortions created elsewhere, and sometimes these interventions may involve steps in counterintuitive directions.

For example, consider the effect of welfare benefits. Employees who receive low-enough wages may qualify for a range of support, including food stamps, Aid to Families with Dependent Children, subsidized housing, and the earned income tax credit. Paying for this support imposes a burden on the rest of society, which could be expected to distort work effort and other behaviors. A mandate that transfers income to low-wage workers (e.g., a minimum wage if the elasticity of labor demand is less than 1) may be worth more to society than the cost of meeting that mandate to employers, because by meeting the mandate the firm reduces transfer payments that its low-wage workers would otherwise receive, and thus eases the burden of poor support imposed on the rest of society (this example is from Freeman, 1993).

To take another example, progressive income taxation reduces the incentive for individuals to invest in education because part of the return to that investment is taxed away. In this situation, it is possible that government-mandated on-the-job training will lead society to be closer to the production possibility frontier. One way to think about this issue is to take the view that there is a third party to any training arrangement between the worker and the firm; that third party is the government. The government receives some of the return to investments in human capital, so firms and individuals have an incentive to invest less than the optimal amount. By mandating training, the government can rectify this distortion caused by progressive taxation. However, mandated training may create other distortions, and there may be more efficient ways of increasing training (e.g., scholarships and public schools).

Many government policies create preexisting distortions. Although one could argue that eliminating these policies will rid the economy of the preexisting distortions, for many policies it is not realistic to imagine that the government program will be done away with. Instead, additional government programs could conceivably lead to a better outcome given these constraints. Likewise, failures in markets outside the labor market may be improved as a result of government intervention in the labor market. For example, owing to adverse selection, the private market for insurance may fail, causing a "second-best" solution. As a general rule, if we start from a "second-best" position because of preexisting distortions, then government mandates could possibly improve the operation of the economy.

Efficiency Cost of Mandates

The case typically made against mandated benefits is that they cause employers and employees to lose their freedom to contract. The argument is that presumably employees and employers know what is best for them, and they will strike bargains that lead to the greatest mutual gain. For example, a working mother may benefit from child-care services and choose to take a job with lower pay because of this fringe benefit, whereas a childless worker does not directly benefit from child-care benefits and would not be willing to take a job that pays a lower wage but offers child-care services. If the labor market works smoothly, workers can sort into the jobs that offer the bundles of wage and nonwage characteristics that best meets their desires. Similarly, firms can choose to offer the bundles of benefits and wages that give them a competitive advantage. A mandate that requires all firms to offer child-care services would prevent workers and firms from attaining a gain from sorting into jobs that offer the best match for their circumstances.[5]

The sorting of workers into jobs that are good matches for them is a powerful and simple argument against mandates. However, as discussed previously, adverse selection, imperfect information, externalities, and other distortions may not lead the market to provide the optimal mix of employment and wage benefits. In my view, unless a compelling case can be made that the market fails, there is good reason to allow freedom of contract for employment benefits because of the flexibility and independence that it affords.

The efficiency loss caused by mandates will depend on how much workers value the benefit that is mandated.[6] For example, if employers are mandated to provide health insurance to their employees, and the dollar value employees implicitly place on health insurance is exactly equal to the employers' cost of providing the health insurance, then in equilibrium workers' wages will decline by the full amount of the benefit, and there will be no efficiency loss. In this situation, employment will be unaffected by a mandate. Summers (1989) argues for the efficiency of employment-based mandates on the grounds that labor supply will shift out in response to mandates, cushioning their negative effect on employment.[7]

At the opposite extreme, if employees place no weight on health insurance benefits (e.g., perhaps because they expect to be in good health), then wages will not adjust in direct response to the mandate. In this case, the mandate is like an employment tax on the firm, which will tend to reduce employment and wages. The incidence of this tax, and the size of the efficiency loss, will depend on the elasticities of demand for and supply of labor. If labor supply is insensitive to the generosity of compensation, as is widely believed, then wages will fall and employment losses will be blunted.

A final case to consider is whether the health insurance mandate is structured in such a way as to provide coverage to nonworkers at no out-of-pocket cost. In this situation, regardless of how much workers prize health insurance, they will place no value on the insurance that employers are mandated to provide because they would receive the same benefit whether or not they worked. The analysis of a mandated benefit here is just like the analysis of an employment tax.

Estimated Employment and Wage Effects
of the Clinton Health Care Proposal

An important theme of this chapter is that the distortions caused by an employment-based mandate must be weighed against any possible gains associated with labor market imperfections and preexisting distortions. And the efficiency costs of an employment-based mandate must be compared with the costs and benefits of other means of assuring universal access, such as individual mandates. Such a comparison will require a tremendous amount of data and will rely on several untested assumptions. Most observers agree that health insurance reform in the United States is a priority, and that universal coverage is desirable. A key question is, Should universal coverage be achieved through a firm-based mandate or through other means? To illustrate the efficiency costs of an employment mandate, I present several calculations below to gauge the possible employment loss associated with the Clinton proposal for an employment-based health insurance mandate.

Key features of the Clinton health care mandate reportedly include the following: Employers will be required to pay a large portion of the health insurance premiums for their employees. Premiums will be based on four family situations (single with no children, single with children, married with no children, married with children), and there will be community rating within these classifications. For each employee, employer contributions will be 80 percent of the average cost of premiums for workers in that family status in the region.[8] Employees will be able to choose among health plans that provide at least a minimum package of benefits. Employees will be responsible for covering the rest of their premium costs. Total employer contributions will be capped at 7.9 percent of each firm's payroll. Small firms (with fewer than 50 employees) with low average wages will have lower caps, ranging between 3.5 percent and 7.9 percent. Workers in families earning less than 150 percent of the poverty level will also receive subsidies for their contributions. Revenues from other sources will be used to finance the subsidies to small employers and low-income employees.

Conceptually, one could think of the Clinton health care reform bill as a payroll tax on firms that do not currently offer health insurance, or that offer health insurance that is below the minimum standard. In the long run it should not matter whether the nominal burden is paid by firms or by workers, so for purposes of this analysis let us assume it is all paid by firms. From the outset, it should be stressed that there is considerable uncertainty in the economics profession as to how a health care mandate would affect employment. This uncertainty arises because there is uncertainty regarding the proper theoretical framework for modeling the labor market, and because there is considerable uncertainty over the magnitude of the relevant behavioral parameters in any model. The theoretical approach to modeling employment that I take in this chapter adheres to a standard neoclassical economic model. The analysis is strictly partial equilibrium, but the results give a flavor for the magnitude of employment losses that would result from the Clinton proposal.

To simplify the analysis, one can separately consider the effect of the mandate on two sectors: one sector composed of firms that do not offer insurance initially and the other sector composed of firms that do offer insurance. Figure 9.1A illustrates the employment effects for the sector where health insurance is not currently provided. In the figure, the wage is shown on the vertical axis and employment is on the horizontal axis. Because the cost of hiring a worker at any given wage is higher because of the health insurance requirement, the demand curve shifts in, from D to D'. The wage falls for these workers, and employment falls as well. Notice that the more inelastic (i.e., steeper) the supply curve, the larger the wage decrease and the smaller the employment decline.[9] Some of the workers who are no longer demanded in this sector may find employment in the other sector, but I consider a worst-case scenario, where these workers remain in the same sector.

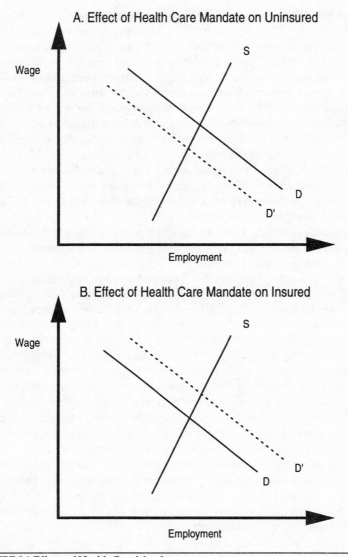

FIGURE 9.1 Effects of Health Care Mandate

For firms that already offer insurance that is more generous than the minimum benefit, the mandate causes the demand curve to shift out, from D to D' (see Figure 9.1B). This occurs because many of these firms will have lower health care costs after the reform than before because they currently subsidize family benefits of their workers, and because some of their premiums go to cover uninsured individuals. As a result, employment and wages will rise in this sector. In this case, if the demand curve is relatively more inelastic, wages will rise more and employment will grow less.

How big are the two sectors? How much of an employment change should one expect? Table 9.1 gives estimates of the number of employed workers in each sector. The estimates are derived from the March 1992 *Current Population Survey* (CPS) (U.S. Bureau of the Census, 1992) and pertain strictly to non-self-employed workers.[10] In 1992, there were 111.4 million wage and salary workers.[11] Some 101 million of these workers would be legally covered by the employment mandate in the Clinton proposal.[12] An estimated 40 million covered workers currently do not receive health insurance coverage from their own employer. This sector will have its employment demand curve shift in.

Table 9.1 also presents estimates of the average premium for insured and uninsured workers (combined employer and employee payments), based on the draft of the Clinton proposal released in October 1993. Of

TABLE 9.1
Two-Sector Model of Employment Effects of Clinton Health Care Mandate

	Uninsured	*Insured*	*All*
Number of wage and salary workers (in millions)	50.1	61.3	111.4
Percentage covered by employment mandate	80.6	99.1	90.8
Number of workers covered by mandate (in millions)	40.3	60.8	101.1
Average annual earnings of covered workers ($)	14,692	30,993	23,986
Current health insurance premium ($)	0	2,989	1,798
Forecast premium ($)	1,426	2,575	2,117
Premium change as percentage of average earnings predicted	9.71	–1.34	1.33
Employment change	279,595	67,679	–211,916
Predicted earnings change ($)	–1,019	345	–199

Note: Average annual earnings were converted from 1991 dollars to 1993 dollars, assuming 3 percent wage growth per year. See text for a discussion of the predicted employment and earnings changes. *Source:* Author's calculations from U.S. Bureau of the Census (1992). Employment is based on figures in Council of Economic Advisers (1993) and author's estimates of the number of private household and agricultural workers.

course, any forecast of what average premiums will be if the Clinton proposal is passed will necessarily involve considerable uncertainty. The estimates used here take account of workers' family status in each sector, payroll caps, firm subsidies based on firm size and average earnings, and worker subsidies based on family income. The results indicate that, after accounting for these factors, the average premium in the currently uninsured sector will be $1,426. The subsidies keep the premium relatively low in this sector. In the currently insured sector, premiums will change because (a) the portion of premiums that pertain to uncompensated care will decline, (b) there will be a decline in costs for workers whose spouses work but do not receive health insurance coverage from their own employers, and (c) some current plans will not meet the minimum standard, and benefits there will rise. The net effect of these changes is that the average premium will fall by 13.9 percent in this sector. With these assumptions, total premiums would be $31 billion more than currently paid.

Table 9.2 summarizes characteristics of workers who are covered by the health care employment mandate, broken down by whether they currently receive health insurance from their own employers. As the table shows, 54 percent of workers in the uninsured sector are women, compared with 42 percent in the insured sector. Uninsured workers are also more likely to be minorities, to be employed in the retail and construction industries, and to be employed in service jobs. The average workweek of uninsured workers is 36.8 hours, compared with 42.1 hours for insured workers. It is also noteworthy that 57 percent of those who are not insured by their own employers receive health insurance from other sources, mostly commonly from their spouses' employers.

The employment effects of a mandate depend critically on the magnitude of the labor supply and demand elasticities in each sector. There is a consensus among labor economists that labor supply is relatively inelastic, especially for male workers. For example, in his survey of male labor supply studies, Pencavel (1986, p. 94) concludes, "The vast proportion of that work—both that based on the static model and that based on the life-cycle model—indicates that the elasticities of hours of work with respect to wages are very small." Even for low-income and female workers, estimated labor supply elasticities tend to be small. For example, the median estimated uncompensated-own wage elasticity from studies based on the negative income tax experiments is less than .12 for wives, for husbands, and for single female household heads (see Killingsworth, 1983, Table 6.2). In the future, I would expect that women's labor supply behavior will resemble men's even more closely. One reason the labor supply elasticity may truly be low is that economic theory predicts that

TABLE 9.2
Selected Characteristics of Workers Covered by
Health Care Mandate, by Employer-Provided Insurance Status

Characteristic	Uninsured	Insured
Average age	34.4	40.0
Average weekly hours	36.8	42.1
Insured (%)	57.0	100.0
Female (%)	54.4	41.9
White (%)	82.9	86.7
Black (%)	13.2	9.9
Selected industries (%)		
retail	23.3	10.6
wholesale	3.5	4.6
manufacturing	11.5	23.6
construction	7.5	4.9
Selected occupations (%)		
managers	8.4	15.3
professionals	8.9	16.2
administrative support	15.9	17.9
sales	12.7	9.5
service	17.6	5.9
private household	1.4	0.02

Note: Figures are the percentages of workers in each column who fall into the reported group. Insurance must be in own name for a person to be considered insured. *Source:* Author's calculations from U.S. Bureau of the Census (1992).

income and substitution effects have opposing impacts on the labor supply elasticity. I initially assume a value of .1 for the labor supply elasticity in each sector.[13]

In his recent book, Hamermesh (1993) concludes that the aggregate employment demand elasticity is probably "bracketed" by −.15 and −.75. Past estimates tend to be sensitive to the data set, industry, and estimation technique. There are no separate estimates of the elasticity of demand for labor in the insured and uninsured sectors that I am aware of. One could plausibly argue that the elasticity of demand for labor is higher in the sector that offers insurance than in the one that does not, because the insured sector is overrepresented by firms in traded goods industries, which also face competition from abroad. Demand for workers in the uninsured sector would be more like the low-wage sector more generally. Moreover, studies of the impact of the minimum wage on employment find elasticities around 0 to –.3 for teenagers, whereas studies of employment demand in manufacturing find a wide range of estimates, but they are centered near –.5. I initially assume the elasticity of demand for labor is –.5 in the insured sector and –.25 in the uninsured sector.

Under these assumptions, the net employment loss associated with the Clinton mandate would be 212,000 jobs. Employment in the uninsured sector will decline by 280,000, whereas employment in the currently insured sector will rise by 68,000. Under the assumed elasticities, most of the cost of meeting the mandate will be shifted to workers in the form of lower wages. Studies of other mandates (e.g., workers' compensation insurance) tend to bear out this forecast (see Gruber and Krueger, 1991)[14], with about 80% of employers' costs shifted to workers in the form of lower wages. Annual wages in the uninsured sector will fall by some $1,019 per year under these assumptions, whereas annual wages will rise by $345 in the insured sector.

Table 9.3 reports results in which the assumed values of the elasticity of demand and supply in each sector are varied. Specifically, I vary the employment demand elasticity between .25 and .75 and the labor supply elasticity between .1 and .2. Although the results do not change much if the elasticity of demand is varied, the predicted employment decline is very sensitive to the elasticity of supply in the insured sector. If that elasticity is set to .2 instead of .1, then the predicted net employment decline is 491,000 jobs.[15] Overall, the forecasts tend to fall in the 200,000–500,000 range for the parameters reported in the table. Under the elasticities that strike me as most plausible, the employment loss from the Clinton health care mandate would be near the bottom of the range—but one has to admit a wide range of uncertainty here.

Is this a large or a small change in employment? Although the loss of some 200,000 jobs is surely something to be lamented, this represents less than 0.2 percent of the workforce. The predicted job loss in this model is on the same order of magnitude as monthly blips in the employment series. Moreover, since turnover tends to be very high in the uninsured sector, the burden of the job loss will be spread out over many workers. A decline of 200,000 full-time jobs averages out to just 3.4 hours less work per worker per year. Why is the estimated employment change this small? The main reason is that, given a low elasticity of supply, most of the cost of meeting a mandate will be shifted to workers. If the elasticities of supply and demand are .1 and .25, respectively, then the conventional economic model predicts that 71 percent of the health care costs will be shifted to employees in the form of lower wages. In addition, the sector that currently offers health insurance will have lower employment costs after reform, and should thus expand. Finally, firms whose employment

TABLE 9.3
Alternative Estimates of Employment and Wage Effects of Health Care Mandate

Uninsured		Insured		Employment Change			Annual Wage Change		
e_s	e_d	e_s	e_d	Uninsured	Insured	All	Uninsured	Insured	All
0.10	−0.50	0.10	−0.50	−326194	67679	−258515	−1188	345	−267
0.10	−0.25	0.10	−0.50	−279595	67679	−211916	−1019	345	−199
0.20	−0.50	0.10	−0.50	−559190	67679	−491511	−1019	345	−199
0.20	−0.25	0.10	−0.50	−434926	67679	−367247	−792	345	−109
0.10	−0.50	0.10	−0.75	−326194	71660	−254534	−1188	365	−254
0.10	−0.25	0.10	−0.75	−279595	71660	−207935	−1019	365	−187
0.20	−0.50	0.20	−0.50	−559190	116021	−443169	−1019	296	−187
0.20	−0.25	0.20	−0.50	−434926	116021	−318905	−792	296	−138

Note: e_s and e_d represent the assumed values of the elasticity of supply of labor and demand for labor in each sector respectively.

costs rise because of the mandate will not totally be at a competitive disadvantage because many of their competitors who did not offer insurance will also see their employment costs rise.

Finally, it should be stressed that the estimated employment changes are relative to the current level of health care costs. If, as expected, the Clinton proposal reduces the rate of growth of health care costs relative to what it otherwise would be, then the baseline level of employment change would be even lower if wages do not perfectly adjust to reflect health care benefits.

Additional Employment Effects

Supply Effects

Because under the Clinton plan health insurance will be provided to nonworkers as well, there may be supply effects as well as demand effects, depending on how generously benefits are provided to nonworkers. Revenue from sin taxes and possibly other taxes will be used to provide health insurance for nonworkers. If benefits are provided to nonworkers, the supply curve of labor will shift in, because leisure will become more attractive.[16] This is illustrated in Figure 9.2 for the aggregate labor market. For example, older workers will be encouraged to retire early because of subsidized benefits for nonworkers, and because of community rating. Some observers have also argued that this shift in of

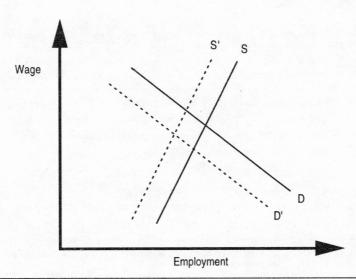

FIGURE 9.2 Effect of Health Care Mandate on Labor Market: Demand and Supply Shifts

the labor supply curve may be important for woman. However, a comparison of female labor force participation between Canada and the United States, before and after Canada adopted universal health insurance, suggests that female labor force participation rose in Canada relative to the United States (see Card and Riddell, 1993).

The current availability of Medicaid for poor nonworkers and the low elasticity of labor supply make it unlikely that the supply shift will be significant for workers other than early retirees. Gruber and Madrian (1993) recently found that continuing health insurance coverage induces early retirement.

Minimum Wage Constraint

Workers who are paid the minimum wage, or near the minimum wage, obviously cannot have their wages adjusted to offset fully the compensation increase caused by a health care mandate. Because wage offsets are a major reason large employment losses from a mandate are not predicted, this is a potentially important issue. How much should we expect the minimum wage constraint to affect employment? The following calculations suggest that the minimum wage constraint could be expected to reduce employment owing to a health care mandate, but not by an overwhelming amount.

As mentioned earlier, a reasonable expectation is that about 80 percent of the cost of financing the health care mandate will be shifted to workers. Employers' health care costs for minimum wage workers are difficult to predict because of the payroll cap and firm subsidies. Minimum wage workers are overrepresented in low-wage, small firms, so they are especially likely to be affected by the payroll caps. If we suppose that the typical low-wage employer's health care contribution equals 7.9 percent of earnings, then workers who earn between $4.25 and $4.52 per hour will be constrained by the minimum wage. From the CPS, I estimate that 4.93 million workers who will be covered by the employment mandate earn between the minimum wage and $4.52, and 803,000 of these workers already receive health insurance. This leaves 4.13 million workers who are likely to be constrained by the minimum wage.[17]

If we make the extreme assumption that there are no wage offsets at all for these workers, and assume an elasticity of demand of −.3, then there will be a loss of 98,000 more jobs as a result of the minimum wage constraint. This estimate should probably be regarded as an upper bound, because workers earning $4.50 per hour, say, could have slower wage growth—or other fringe benefit reductions—as a result of the health care mandate, which would cushion employment losses.

Another reason for tempering forecasts of job loss caused by an employment-based mandate is that several studies indicate that recent minimum wage increases have not had adverse effects on employment (see Card, 1992; Card and Krueger, 1993; Katz and Krueger, 1992). This evidence has been cited by the Clinton administration as support for the view that the health care mandate will not reduce employment. Even though I am a contributor to this literature, I am not sure it applies to a health care mandate. The reason for my skepticism is that the leading models that explain the findings of no or positive employment effects of a minimum wage rise involve monopsony and search models. A minimum wage increase makes work more rewarding, and may thus enable firms to fill vacancies and reduce turnover, whereas a health care mandate that extends to nonworkers as well does not have the advantageous supply-side effects of a minimum wage. Thus, in my calculations I have used a conventional model to predict the effects of a health care mandate with a minimum wage constraint.

Distortions Created by Payroll Caps and Subsidies

Certain provisions of the Clinton plan are likely to create distortions that are of greater significance than the employment losses forecast above. First, the fact that employer contributions are capped as a percentage of *total salary* in the firm gives firms an incentive to split up into smaller units, placing high-wage workers in one firm and low-wage workers in another. To take a hypothetical example, consider a firm with

50 workers earning $10,000 per year and 50 workers earning $100,000 per year (see Table 9.4). Suppose the premium cost of meeting the mandate is $2,000 per worker for the firm. The firm's payments are capped at 7.9 percent of payroll. If the firm remains intact, its health care costs will be $200,000, but if it splits into two firms—one with high-wage workers and the other with low-wage workers—its costs will be $139,500, producing a savings of 30 percent on its health care bill. The reason for this gain is that if the firm remains intact the high-wage workers prevent the firm from benefiting from the payroll cap. Firms that have high variability in the salaries of their workers will have a strong incentive to break into smaller units as a result of the firm-level payroll cap.[18] One can also envision a rise in staff-leasing arrangements to remove either low-wage or high-wage workers from a firm's payroll so the firm can benefit from the payroll cap.[19]

TABLE 9.4
Effect of Firm Payroll Cap on Incentive to Subdivide Hypothetical Firm

One Firm			
50 employees @ $10,000			
50 employees @ $100,000			
1) Total payroll	$5.5 million		
2) 7.9% of payroll	$434,500		
3) $2,000 x 100 employees	$200,000		
4) Health care costs (lesser of 3 and 2)	$200,000		

Two Firms			
Firm A		*Firm B*	
50 employees @ $10,000		50 employees @ $100,000	
1) Total payroll	$500,000	1) Total payroll	$5,000,000
2) 7.9% of payroll	$39,500	2) 7.9% of payroll	$395,000
3) $2,000 x 50	$100,000	3) $2,000 x 50	$100,000
4) Health care costs (lesser of 3 and 2)	$39,500	4) Health care costs (lesser of 3 and 2)	$100,000

Bottom line

Combined health care costs of Firm A and Firm B	$139,500
Savings from splitting up	$60,500

Second, the current draft of the Clinton proposal dictates a lower payroll cap for small firms, as low as 3.5 percent depending on the average salary. The current draft of the legislation has a discrete jump in the cap once a firm exceeds 50 employees. Obviously, firms with 49 employees will resist hiring more workers because they will lose their subsidy. And firms with more than 50 employees will have an incentive to shrink to 49 employees or split up into units of 49 or smaller to benefit from the lower cap. It should be noted that these incentives will remain even if the cap is smoothly increased to 7.9 percent as a firm reaches 50 employees. Essentially, a subsidy to small firms turns firms into monopsonists, because the marginal cost of hiring a worker is greater than the worker's compensation. Similarly, the fact that subsidies are more generous for lower-wage, small employers will give employers an even stronger incentive to resist wage increases.

Third, the small-firm subsidy provides perverse organizational incentives. For example, company-owned McDonald's stores would be considered big firms and not eligible for the small-firm subsidy, whereas franchised McDonald's stores would be considered small firms and thus eligible for the subsidy. As there may be good economic reasons for the current division of stores among company-owned and franchised outlets, this provision will upset that equilibrium. In a dynamic economy, these distortions could have a further negative effect on employment.

Fourth, because health care costs are a fixed cost, a mandate will give firms incentives to employ full-time workers over part-time workers. This incentive effect will be somewhat muted because the Clinton proposal prorates premiums for employees who work between 10 and 32 hours per week and exempts employees who work fewer than 10 hours per week. But employers will still have an incentive to use more overtime hours for full-time workers (because the marginal health insurance costs are zero). In addition, employers will have an incentive to employ workers to work very short hours, because those working fewer than 10 hours per week are excluded. It should also be noted that hours of work are notoriously poorly reported, by individuals and by firms, so prorating of contributions for work hours will be difficult to implement.

As a result of these incentive effects, the Clinton mandate will raise less premium revenue than expected. In this situation, either the payroll cap will have to rise or other sources of revenues will be required. Moreover, the contortions that firms go through to minimize their health care payments may reduce economic efficiency. Phasing out the small-firm subsidy over time would help to alleviate some of these distortions.

All the perverse disincentive effects of the Clinton proposal discussed in this subsection would come about because the financing of the plan is based on the firm level, rather than the individual level. This differs from social security, unemployment insurance, workers' compensation insurance, and most other social insurance programs. If employer contributions were capped at 7.9 percent of each worker's earnings, up to some limit, then the perverse incentives for firms to shrink, resist wage increases, and so on would not arise. It should also be noted that a pure payroll tax mechanism with a constant individual cap would still confer a subsidy to small employers because small employers tend to pay lower wages than large employers.

Practical Observations on Mandates

There are several practical implications of mandates that should be considered. For one thing, mandates are not always followed. Past experience suggests that, unless there is a strong enforcement mechanism or stiff penalties for noncompliance, many employers will not follow mandates. For example, Ashenfelter and Smith (1979) and subsequent researchers have found that many covered employees are paid less than the minimum wage. The estimates of noncompliance range from 25 percent to 40 percent of covered employees who are paid the minimum or less. Similarly, Addison and Blackburn (1994, pp. 181–190) recently found extremely low compliance with the WARN law. Remarkably, they found no change in the percentage of displaced workers who reported receiving advance notice of firm closures after the law was passed.[20] De La Rica and Lemieux (1993) report that 12 percent of workers in Spain are employed by firms that do not contribute to their health insurance, even though it is mandated by law. Noncompliance in Spain tends to be higher in industries that have low health care insurance rates in the United States. Although there is a tradition of high voluntary compliance with laws in the United States, one should not overlook the possibility of noncompliance. Noncompliance should be of special concern as it relates to such legislation as the Family Leave Act, because workers may fear retaliation if they take advantage of the newly enacted law.

Because of noncompliance, mandated benefits may be far less successful at achieving their aims than anticipated by lawmakers. Certainly, the possibility of noncompliance suggests the importance of monitoring the parties involved. Such monitoring will require substantial resources. It should also be noted that, if compliance with mandates is low, the employment distortions that they create will also be smaller than anticipated.

Another feature of mandates is that "escape clauses" are rarely utilized in some programs. To take an example, the 1990 amendments to the Fair Labor Standards Act allowed firms to pay a subminimum wage to teenagers. There were hardly any administrative requirements on firms that used the subminimum wage. Several studies have found that less than 2 percent of minimum wage employers have taken advantage of the subminimum wage clause (see Katz and Krueger, 1992; Spriggs, Swinton, and Simmons, 1992). One reason for this behavior is that firms are concerned about internal equity; they do not want to pay workers performing the same work differently. But this finding suggests that minimum wage mandates are less distressing to firms than is commonly claimed.

Perhaps an even more remarkable example of a rarely used "escape clause" is found in Hawaii, where the health insurance employer mandate created a fund for "distressed employers." Employers who are in financial distress because of the mandate are able to apply for relief from this government fund but only a tiny minority of employers have requested such assistance (Office of Technology Assessment, 1993). One has the sense that employer behavior would be different on the mainland, but Hawaii's experience suggests that the health insurance mandate did not create an overwhelming burden on employers.

From a practical standpoint, there are two important reasons to phase in new mandates slowly, over time. First, wages will have a chance to adjust to the mandate if it is known that the mandate will be imposed well in advance. Given that wage adjustments are important for blunting employment losses, this will be an advantage. Second, employers will have time to adjust personnel policies in response to the mandate.

Another practical issue is how much of the nominal financing burden of a mandate should be borne by employees and how much by employers. The answer to this question typically given by economists is that in the long run it doesn't matter, because wages will adjust to offset whatever division there is between employer and employee costs. However, there are three practical considerations that make the division of the nominal burden of interest. First, because of the minimum wage constraint, wages cannot always adjust in the long run. Making employees bear a larger share of the nominal burden will then cushion any employment losses caused by this constraint.[21]

Second, for a fixed tax rate, the amount of revenue collected will vary depending on the nominal burden. For example, suppose that a tax rate of 10 percent is set to finance a mandate, and workers earn $300 per week. If the nominal burden of the tax is placed on employers, then wages would be expected to fall, and a reasonable expectation is that 80 percent of the burden will be shifted to workers in the form of lower wages. Thus, wages could be expected to fall by around $(.80)(\$30) = \$24$ per week. As a result, in the long run the tax will be applied to a salary of $276 per week. However, if the 10 percent tax is split evenly between workers and employers, then before-tax wages will fall by just $9 per week. Because revenues are determined by the multiplication of the before-tax wage by the tax rate, at a fixed tax rate the amount of money collected will be higher if workers pay a larger share of the nominal burden. In this example, 5 percent less revenue will be collected if employers pay the full tax and the tax rate is constant at 10 percent.

A third reason it is possibly preferable for workers to shoulder a larger share of the nominal tax burden is that, in the long run, one would expect that workers will bear most of the cost of the tax, so the long run will arrive sooner if workers' share of the nominal burden is larger. If wages are downwardly rigid in the short run, then shifting a larger share of the nominal burden to workers will reduce job loss.

Finally, it should be stressed that, if possible, there are often advantages to making mandated benefits "tradable." For example, suppose firms are mandated to provide a benefit that workers do not value, and that the benefit serves no other purpose. If provision of this benefit is costly to firms, then everyone could be made better off if firms were allowed to "buy off" workers instead of providing the mandate. This is just a special case of the Coase principle, which asserts that as long as property rights are tradable and well established, then the initial allocation of property rights will not affect the efficiency of the market. A clear example of this principle has to do with employment at will (see Krueger, 1991). Until recently, the tradition in the United States has been that employers could fire workers at will. Firms owned the property right to the job. Workers and firms, of course, could write contracts to restrict this right, and unions typically negotiate just-cause firing standards. Legislation in Montana restricts employers' ability to fire at will, but allow the parties the authority to write limited contracts that allows the firm to fire the worker for any reason after a specified period. This legislation essentially shifts (part of) the property right to jobs to workers, but allows the parties to trade that right subsequently.

Political Economy of Mandates

Several factors explain the current political popularity of employment-based mandates in general, and of employment-based health insurance mandates in particular. First, the costs of mandates are hidden. Rather than directly raise revenue, the government can conceal the costs of mandates by having workers and firms bear them. The revenue needed to finance the mandate does not go through the government, so the government can avoid the appearance of raising new taxes. Mandates have gained increased popularity in the United States because of concern over the high budget deficit and rising resistance to direct taxation. These factors may explain the already high use of payroll taxation to finance social programs in the United States.

Second, unlike the costs, the benefits of mandates are highly visible. It is clear to all that workers receive the benefits because they are mandated. But if the government uses market incentives (e.g., price subsidies or vouchers) to encourage consumption of some benefit, increased consumption may result, but it is unlikely that politicians will receive credit for the greater access. Furthermore, many politicians are skeptical that altering market incentives will result in changed behavior, even though, as noted above, there is substantial noncompliance with mandates.

Third, mandated health insurance builds on an existing structure, and that existing structure creates lobbies that want to preserve features of the current system. More than two-thirds of the uninsured are full-time, full-year workers or are in families that are headed by full-time, full-year workers. Moreover, nearly 80 percent of those with medical insurance already obtain their insurance from an employer-sponsored plan (Chollet, 1987). Consequently, an employer mandate has the potential to extend health insurance coverage to a large number of uninsured individuals without radically restructuring the insurance industry.

Finally, it is often underappreciated that a strong social insurance system (perhaps funded by mandates) may make other desirable policies more politically feasible. For example, a key political issue in the debates preceding the passage of the North American Free Trade Agreement (NAFTA) was that freer trade with Mexico would create some winners and some losers among U.S. workers. The winners would probably be made better off by more than the losers would be made worse off. But unless the losers were to be compensated, they had a legitimate reason to oppose NAFTA. A strong safety network would cushion the losses of those who lose under such policies, and would make their passage more likely and less contentious.

Conclusion

If one starts from the position that the labor market works according to the assumptions of the conventional neoclassical model, there are no good economic reasons to use employment-based mandates. In this chapter I have reviewed some reasons the classical assumptions may fail, in which case employment-based mandates may be useful. The decision about whether to have an employment-based mandate must be made on a case-by-case basis, weighing the efficiency losses of mandates against the gains, as well as comparing employment-based mandates to other financing mechanisms. The strongest case for employment-based mandates seems to me to be in situations where the employer has some direct control over a behavior and requiring the employer to bear some of the cost of the mandate can improve economic efficiency. An example of this situation is experience rating in workers' compensation and unemployment insurance. In many other situations, employment-based mandates are unlikely to dominate alternative financing mechanisms.

George Stigler (1992, p. 459) argues that "all durable social institutions, including common and statute laws, must be efficient." He even goes on to say that, "lacking a cheaper way of achieving domestic subsidy, our sugar program is efficient" (p. 459).[22] There may be a grain of truth to Stigler's view—at least it is a useful antidote for those who assume that everything the government does is evil. Employment-based mandates are widely used in the United States and elsewhere, and they have clearly been durable. Employment-based mandates thus pass the Stigler test. But the reason for the popularity of employment-based mandates probably lies more in their political feasibility than in their inherent efficiency. Other financing schemes are difficult to achieve because politicians resist raising new taxes. The better route for policy may be to remove the barriers that prevent alternative, more efficient mechanisms from being used, rather than to use a "second-best" solution.

There is no obvious efficiency reason mandated health insurance should be tied to work. The historical reasons for work-related health insurance stem from responses to price and wage controls in the 1940s, union bargaining, and adverse selection problems (see Munts, 1967). Price and wage controls are no longer an issue, and there are other ways the government can solve adverse selection that do not involve employer mandates. Other solutions to failures in the health care market may be more efficient than an employment-based mandate. Nevertheless, my calculations of the employment and wage effects of an employment-based health care mandate indicate that the employment loss caused by the mandate would not be great, mainly because workers' labor supply decisions are relatively insensitive to wages. If this is correct, then an employment-based health insurance mandate may not be much more inefficient than other, probably less politically feasible, policies.

Notes

1. Some programs may be hybrids. For example, in the case of social security and unemployment insurance, the government requires employers and workers to pay a tax to cover workers' benefits, but the government provides the benefits directly.

2. This point has been made several times before; for examples, see Ehrenberg (1986) and Mitchell (1990).

3. Of course, if there is a match component, and drug use has different effects on productivity in different jobs, efficiency can be improved by testing.

4. On the other hand, in some situations firms have an incentive to solve informational externality problems themselves. Firms have incentives to provide clear information, use their bargaining power to obtain quantity discounts, and help educate workers with regard to their benefit choices, because by doing so firms make working conditions more desirable, at a lower cost than the value workers place on the benefit.

5. Notice that individual mandates also restrict freedom of contract.

6. See Summers (1989), Danzon (1989), and Sheiner (1993) for theoretical discussions of employment effects of employment-based mandates.

7. Tim Besley has pointed out to me that this feature is not unique to employment-based mandates. Specifically, the government could finance a program through some other means, but restrict benefits to those who work. In this way, the positive labor supply effects could be accomplished without an employment-based mandate.

8. More precisely, the employer's payments will be 80 percent of the average premium for the family status divided by the average number of workers per families of that type.

9. Mathematically, the wage and employment changes from a health care mandate are given by $dW/dC = -e^d/(e^d - e^s)$ and $dL/L = [(dC + dW)/W] \, e^d$, where dW is the change in the wage, dC is health insurance costs, L is employment, dL is the change in employment, e^d is the elasticity of demand for labor, and e^s is the elasticity of labor supply.

10. The reason for deleting the self-employed from consideration is that there is a strong presumption that the self-employed will offset the health care mandate by taking lower cash income. The only issue for the self-employed is whether some will leave the labor force because they are unhappy with the mix of benefits.

11. According to the Council of Economic Advisers, in 1992 there were 108.4 million wage and salary workers, excluding agricultural and private household workers. From the CPS I have estimated that 2.76 percent of wage and salary workers are in agricultural or private household jobs.

12. Coverage is determined from the provisions of the Clinton draft proposal. Specifically, workers who usually work 10 or fewer hours per week, are age 18 or younger, or are unmarried, full-time students, age 23 or younger, are deemed ineligible for the employment mandate.

13. Although one may expect that labor supply is less responsive to the wage in the insured sector, if wages rise in the insured sector I suspect workers will be willing to move to that sector from the uncovered sector or from nonemployment, even if this mobility requires some additional training. Furthermore, one could argue that to some extent the two sectors are already noncompeting, and that there are some workers in the uncovered sector who are as equally skilled as workers in the covered sector, even though their compensation differs.

14. Also, in an analysis of a sharp natural social experiment, Holmlund (1983) used time-series data on payroll taxes in Sweden to examine wage growth in a period when the payroll tax increased from 14 percent to 40 percent. He estimates that roughly 50 percent of the employer payroll tax was shifted to wages in the short run.

15. If we set the elasticity of demand at −1 and the elasticity of supply to .2 in both sectors, then the forecast job loss is 517,000.

16. On the other hand, some workers who are "locked" out of the labor force because they would lose Medicaid by working may join the workforce under the Clinton plan, thereby causing the labor supply curve to shift out.

17. The 4.13 million low-wage workers who lack health insurance were already counted among the 40.3 million workers in the uninsured sector. This results in some double counting of the job loss, on the order of 20,000–40,000 jobs.

18. More generally, this result occurs because of Jensen's inequality, and the payroll cap creates a concave budget set.

19. Another effect is that firms considering hiring new workers will behave differently depending on whether the new workers are high- or low-wage workers. A firm that is constrained by the payroll cap will not want to hire high-wage workers because it will relax the cap.

20. One reason for the low compliance with WARN is that firms have many possible exemptions. In addition, enforcement involves taking action through the courts, which may not be worth workers' expense for the small rewards available.

21. An alternative approach is to allow employers who provide health insurance to pay a subminimum wage, as is done in Washington, D.C., for laundry workers. With universal coverage, a credit toward the minimum wage could be allowed.

22. This point has also been made by Victor Fuchs (1972) in regard to national health insurance.

References

Addison, J., and Blackburn, M. (1994, Winter). "Policy Watch: Mandatory Notice." *Journal of Economic Perspectives, 8*, pp. 181–190.

Ashenfelter, O., and Smith, R. S. (1979). "Compliance with the Minimum Wage Law." *Journal of Political Economy, 87*, 333–350.

Brown, C. (1980). "Equalizing Differences in the Labor Market." *Quarterly Journal of Economics, 94*, 113–134.

Butler, R., and Worrall, J. (1983). "Workers' Compensation: Benefit and Injury Claims Rates in the Seventies." *Review of Economics and Statistics, 60*, 580–589.

Card, D. (1992). "Using Regional Variation in Wages to Measure the Effects of the Federal Minimum Wage: 1992." *Industrial and Labor Relations Review, 46*, 22–37.

Card, D., and Krueger, A. (1993). "Minimum Wages and Employment: A Case Study of the Fast Food Industry in New Jersey and Pennsylvania." Working paper, Princeton University, Industrial Relations Section.

Card, D., and Riddell, W. C. (1993). "A Comparative Analysis of Unemployment in Canada and the United States." In D. Card and R. Freeman (Eds.), *Small Differences That Matter* (pp. 149–189). Chicago: University of Chicago Press.

Chollet, D. (1987). "Public Policy Options to Expand Health Insurance Coverage among the Nonelderly Population." In *Government Mandating of Employee Benefits*. Washington, DC: Employee Benefits Research Institute.

Council of Economic Advisers. (1993). *Economic Report of the President.* Washington, DC: Government Printing Office.

Danzon, P. (1989). "Mandated Employment-Based Health Insurance: Incidence and Efficiency Effects." Mimeo, University of Pennsylvania.

De La Rica, S., and Lemieux, T. (1993). "Does Public Health Insurance Reduce Labor Market Flexibility or Encourage the Underground Economy? Evidence from Spain and the United States." NBER Working Paper 4402.

Ehrenberg, R. (1986). "Workers' Rights: Rethinking Protective Labor Legislation." In R. Ehrenberg (Ed.), *Research in Labor Economics* (Vol. 8, pp. 285–318). Greenwich, CT: JAI

Freeman, R. (1993). "Minimum Wages—Again!" Mimeo, Harvard University.

Fuchs, V. (1976). "From Bismarck to Woodcock: The 'Irrational' Pursuit of National Health Insurance." *Journal of Law and Economics, 19,* 347–359.

Gruber, J., and Krueger, A. B. (1991). "The Incidence of Mandated Employer-Provided Insurance: Lessons from Workers' Compensation Insurance." In D. Bradford (Ed.), *Tax Policy and the Economy* (Vol. 5, pp. 111–144). Cambridge: MIT Press.

Gruber, J., and Madrian, B. (1993). "Health Insurance and Early Retirement: Evidence from the Availability of Continuation Coverage." Mimeo, Massachusetts Institute of Technology.

Hamermesh, D. S. (1993). *Labor Demand.* Princeton, NJ: Princeton University Press.

Holmlund, B. (1983). "Payroll Taxes and Wage Inflation: The Swedish Experience." *Scandinavian Journal of Economics, 85,* 1–15.

Kahneman, D., and Tversky, A. (1979). "Prospect Theory: An Analysis of Decisions under Risk." *Econometrica, 47,* 313–327.

Katz, L., and Krueger, A. B. (1992). "The Effect of the Minimum Wage on the Fast Food Industry." *Industrial and Labor Relations Review, 46,* 6–21.

Killingsworth, M. (1983). *Labor Supply.* Cambridge, England: Cambridge University Press.

Krueger, A. B. (1990). "Incentive Effects of Workers' Compensation Insurance." *Journal of Public Economics, 41,* 73–99.

Krueger, A. B. (1991). "The Evolution of Unjust Dismissal Legislation in the United States." *Industrial and Labor Relations Review, 44,* 644–660.

Leibowitz, A. (1983). "Fringe Benefits in Employee Compensation." In J. E. Triplett (Ed.), *The Measurement of Labor Cost.* Chicago: University of Chicago Press.

Levine, D. (1991). "Just-Cause Employment Policies in the Presence of Workers' Adverse Selection." *Journal of Labor Economics, 9,* 294–305.

Mitchell, O. (1990). "The Effects of Mandating Benefits Packages." In R. Ehrenberg, (Ed.), *Research in Labor Economics,* (Vol. 11, pp. 297–320). Greenwich, CT: JAI.

Monheit, A., Hagan, M., Berk, M., and Farley, P. (1985). "The Employed Uninsured and the Role of Public Policy." *Inquiry, 22,* 348–364.

Munts, R. (1967). *Bargaining and Health: Labor Unions, Health Insurance and Medical Care.* Madison: University of Wisconsin Press.

Office of Technology Assessment. (1993). *Health Insurance: The Hawaii Experience.* Washington, DC: Government Printing Office.

Pauly, M. (1971). *Medical Care at Public Expense.* New York: Praeger.

Pencavel, J. (1986). "Labor Supply of Men: A Survey." In O. Ashenfelter and R. Layard (Eds.), *Handbook of Labor Economics*, (Vol. 1, pp. 3–102). Amsterdam: North Holland.

Rosen, S. (1986). "The Theory of Equalizing Differences." In O. Ashenfelter and R. Layard (Eds.), *Handbook of Labor Economics*, (Vol. 1, pp. 641–692). Amsterdam: North Holland.

Sheiner, L. (1993). "The Efficiency Costs of Health Care Financing Reforms." Mimeo, Board of Governors of the Federal Reserve.

Smith, R. (1976). *The Occupational Safety and Health Act: Its Goals and Its Achievements*. Washington, DC: American Enterprise Institute for Public Policy Research.

Smith, R. (1979). "Compensating Wage Differentials and Public Policy." *Industrial and Labor Relations Review, 32*, 339–352.

Smith, R. S., and Ehrenberg, R. G. (1983). "Estimating Wage-Fringe Trade-Offs: Some Data Problems." In J. E. Triplett (Ed.), *The Measurement of Labor Cost*. Chicago: University of Chicago Press.

Spriggs, W., Swinton, D., and Simmons, M. (1992). "The Effects of Changes in the Federal Minimum Wage: Restaurant Workers in Mississippi and North Carolina." Mimeo, Economic Policy Institute.

Stigler, G. (1992). "Law or Economics." *Journal of Law and Economics, 39*, 455–468.

Summers, L. H. (1989). "Some Simple Economics of Mandated Benefits." *American Economic Association, Papers and Proceedings, 79*, 177–183.

U.S. Bureau of the Census. (1992). *Current Population Survey*. Washington, DC: Government Printing Office.

Comment

Ronald G. Ehrenberg

A friend and economist, Marvin Kosters from the American Enterprise Institute, once told me that I have a serious problem in that liberals think I'm conservative and conservatives think I'm liberal. So, whatever group I am addressing can usually find something objectionable or "politically incorrect" in what I say. I suspect I will prove Marv correct with my commentary here.

How can one distinguish a liberal from a conservative? One way is by the language he or she uses. A liberal refers to government employment standards and social programs as "protective labor legislation" and "social insurance." The liberal's notion is that these interventions do something positive for workers. A conservative refers to the same interventions as "government mandates." The conservative's focus, as is Murray Weidenbaum's, is on the costs of such mandates.

Another, perhaps better, distinction comes from another friend and economist, Walter Oi, who is also a contributor to this volume. Walter once told me that the definition of a liberal is someone who wants to demonstrate his or her good intentions, whereas the definition of a conservative is someone who wants to know if a proposed, or actual, policy change makes sense. Viewed from this perspective, Alan Krueger's chapter and my comments suggest that we can both be viewed as Oi-type conservatives. However, as my remarks below will indicate, Krueger and I are conservatives in a very different sense than is Weidenbaum.

In fact, my commentary here will focus almost exclusively on Weidenbaum's chapter. In part, this is because Krueger was an undergraduate student of mine at Cornell, and to criticize one's former students is to indirectly criticize oneself. More substantively, it is because I agree with virtually everything Krueger says and thus find little to criticize in his chapter.

In his chapter, Weidenbaum presents in great detail estimates of the costs to business, along with estimates of job loss, from various forms of

Author's Note: The views expressed here are my own and should not be attributed to Cornell University or the National Bureau of Economic Research.

labor market legislation and regulation. These interventions include the Civil Rights Act, wrongful-termination liability and the abandonment by the courts of the employment-at-will doctrine, the Family Leave Act, possible Clinton administration-mandated health insurance reform, minimum wage legislation, disability insurance, OSHA, workers' compensation, and the Americans with Disabilities Act. In contrast to his extensive discussion of costs, however, he never provides any estimates of the benefits to society of these government interventions.

In some cases, these benefits are or will be primarily distributional. In the words of Arthur Okun (1975), there is a "big trade-off" between equality and efficiency, and society should not necessarily choose to maximize the latter at the expense of the former. In other cases, the benefits may be primarily productivity enhancing, even though Weidenbaum also does not allow for this possibility. For example, in the original debate over the Civil Rights Act, then Senator Hubert Humphrey and others argued that by breaking down discriminatory barriers that prevent workers from flowing to their most productive uses, the act would actually enhance efficiency, not reduce it.[1] Krueger similarly points out in his chapter that mandates may improve efficiency in situations in which adverse selection, imperfect information, irrational behavior, or externalities are present. Krueger stresses, however, and, as I indicate below, I concur, that the costs of any such mandates must be weighed against their potential benefits in deciding their desirability.

Are situations in which government mandates might enhance productivity in labor markets rare? Although a pure "Chicago" economist would argue that they are, and thus that competitive markets eliminate the efficiency rationale for mandates, other economists would disagree. Indeed, one former Chicago labor economist (who later presided over two major universities, one of which is in a northern suburb of Chicago) is reputed to have said, "The invisible hand is all thumbs in the labor market." That is, situations in which externalities exist and the decisions of private actors (firms and workers) diverge from what is socially optimal may not be that rare.

As Krueger notes in his chapter, I have previously articulated a simple framework that can be used to evaluate the merits of labor market interventions and, in a series of publications, have used this framework to analyze overtime pay and plant closing legislation, as well as proposals to implement comparable worth and to move away from employment at will (Ehrenberg, 1989; Ehrenberg and Jakubson, 1989; Ehrenberg and Schumann, 1982; Ehrenberg and Smith, 1987). I sketch the framework below and then ask how Weidenbaum's chapter relates to it.

My framework has three components. First, I ask if there is any evidence that an externality exists that justifies contemplating government action. That is, is there evidence of a divergence either between the marginal social and private costs or between the marginal social and private benefits of the actions taken by employers or employees in the labor market? Second, I ask whether economic theory tells us anything about unintended side effects of proposed policies, including the possible reductions in employment that Weidenbaum stresses. Finally, I ask whether there is empirical evidence, or whether one can obtain new empirical evidence, on the magnitudes of both the expected benefits and the expected costs of policy changes to help one ultimately conclude whether or not the policy changes are desirable.

Weidenbaum focuses *only* on the unintended side effects of a set of labor market interventions: the additional costs to employers that surely must lead to compensating reductions in wages and/or to employment losses. There is virtually no discussion in his chapter of whether a rationale for government intervention exists in each case and no discussion of the magnitude of the actual or potential benefits from the intervention.[2] Thus, we have no way of evaluating whether the negative effects on employment that he claims exist mean that on balance having these mandates leaves us worse off.

To be fair, Weidenbaum does assert early in his chapter:

> The central point of this chapter should not be misinterpreted. The aim is not to oppose efforts to eliminate discrimination, protect unskilled workers, or help the disabled. Rather, this report is designed to show that, quite unwittingly, much of the government's social legislation has been written in a way that is oblivious to its negative impact on employment. If that undesirable side effect accompanied only one or two programs, perhaps it could be soft-pedaled. However, because the harm to employment is so pervasive and cumulative, it cannot be ignored. Surely ways can be developed of meeting these important social objectives with less economic damage to the intended beneficiaries. However, the design of specific reforms is beyond the scope of this study.

In this statement, he seems to be acknowledging implicitly a rationale for government intervention and arguing that more efficient ways of achieving desired social goals exist. However, by not enumerating these alternatives, the overall impression he leaves with the reader is that government intervention in the labor market is always bad. This is simply incorrect.

Although Weidenbaum is unprepared to go out on a limb to suggest policies that might achieve desired social objectives and simultaneously stimulate employment growth, I feel no such constraint, so here are three. First, expansion of the earned income tax credit, as was done in 1993, surely is a better way of reducing poverty *and* expanding employment growth than is raising the minimum wage. (Burkhauser and Finegan, 1992). Second, increasing an individual's human capital through provisions of more education and training is more likely to pull him or her out of poverty than is mandating an increase in the minimum wage. Finally, requiring employers, as is done under the Americans with Disabilities Act, to bear the costs of "reasonable accommodation" for disabled employees is less likely to lead to an expansion of employment opportunities for the disabled than would providing tax credits for employers who undertake such accommodations.

Note that none of the three policies I suggest increases employers' costs for a given quality of labor. Hence, none should have adverse effects on employment. Yet, save perhaps for the earned income tax credit, we have not actively pursued these policies. Why we have not is instructive: Each would, at least in the short run, increase the size of the federal budget deficit. Despite the advantage of running social interventions through government budgets (namely, that taxpayers eventually become aware of their costs), we tend not to be willing to do so any longer. Moreover, the very conservative economists who typically oppose increased mandates also tend to oppose increases in government budget deficits. Do these economists, as Weidenbaum asserts that he does, actually care about the groups that government mandates would protect?

Ultimately, I suspect that Weidenbaum and many of these economists really believe that the invisible hand works in the labor market and that, save for distributional considerations (which could be handled through the tax and transfer system), the case for government intervention in the labor market is quite weak. As Krueger notes, however, one can test whether labor markets are competitive by seeing if they produce compensating wage differentials for unfavorable job characteristics. By now, a rather long literature that has addressed job characteristics such as pace of work, risk of injury, and restrictions on hours of work, has concluded that compensating wage differentials tend to be larger in unionized than in nonunionized work environments (Dickens, 1984; Duncan and Stafford, 1980; Ehrenberg and Schumann, 1984). That is, unions appear to win compensating wage differentials for undesirable job characteristics for their members that the labor market does not always produce for nonunion workers on its own. The decline in unionization in the United States that has occurred thus seems to enhance the case for government intervention in the labor market.

I cannot resist noting that in some cases Weidenbaum's specific cost estimates appear to be very large primarily because he implicitly assumes that labor markets are *not* competitive. For example, his estimates of the rapidly rising costs of workers' compensation insurance seem to ignore a number of studies that suggest that higher workers' compensation benefits (higher ex post compensation for work injuries) lead to compensatingly lower wage rates (less ex ante insurance for work injuries) (see the studies surveyed in Ehrenberg, 1988). That is, as workers' compensation benefits rise, workers apparently at least partially pay for the increase in the form of lower wage levels or wage increases. Hence, the true cost to employers of the workers' compensation program is considerably less than the estimates Weidenbaum offers in his chapter.

I probably should also note, as Krueger (1991) has reminded us in a recent article dealing with unjust dismissal legislation, that the workers' compensation system was developed at the start of the twentieth century *with* the support of the National Association of Manufacturers in response to ad hoc changes in the common law that led to employers' bearing a risk of extremely high judicial awards for work-related injuries. So, in the absence of the workers' compensation system, employers' labor costs might be higher, or at least more uncertain, than they actually are today.

Rather than quibbling over Weidenbaum's estimates of the magnitudes of the impact of various mandates on employment (e.g., do we really believe that the cost to society of civil rights laws and regulations is 4 percent of GNP), I will conclude by reiterating my main points. Distributional considerations matter along with efficiency. Rationales for government intervention may be present. Dispassionate evaluators of labor market policies and proposed policy changes (as contrasted to liberal or conservative lobbyists and policy advocates) should evaluate the benefits of actual policies and proposed policy changes as well as the costs. If they judge a policy or proposed policy change to have employment effects that are too adverse, it would be nice if they would suggest some alternatives. Viewed in the context of these points, Weidenbaum's chapter is only partially successful.

Notes

1. Statements by Humphrey and other legislators to this effect are cited in Gold (1985). Gold notes that such views were expressed in Congress at least as far back as 1948 by Senator Irving M. Ives from New York, the legislator for whom the chair I occupy at Cornell is named.

2. I am overstating things a bit here in the case of proposed minimum wage increases; he does talk about their likely limited effect on reducing poverty.

References

Burkhauser, R., and Finegan, T. A. (1992). "The Economics of Minimum Wage Legislation." Mimeo, Syracuse University.

Dickens, W. (1984). "Differences between Risk Premiums in Union and Nonunion Wages and the Case for Occupational Safety Regulation. " *American Economic Review Papers and Proceedings, 96,* 320–323

Duncan, G., and Stafford, F. (1980). "Do Union Members Receive Compensating Wage Differentials?" *American Economic Review, 70,* 355–371

Ehrenberg, R. G. (1988). "Workers' Compensation, Wages, and the Risk of Injury." In J. Burton (Ed.), *New Perspectives in Workers' Compensation.* Ithaca, NY: ILR Press

Ehrenberg, R. G. (1989). "Workers' Rights: Rethinking Protective Labor Legislation." In D. L. Bawden and F. Skidmore (Eds.), *Rethinking Employment Policy.* Washington, DC: Urban Institute Press.

Ehrenberg, R. G., and Jakubson, G. H. (1989). *Advance Notice Provisions in Plant Closing Legislation.* Kalamazoo, MI: Upjohn Institute for Employment Research.

Ehrenberg, R. G., and Schumann, P. L. (1982). *Longer Hours or More Jobs.* Ithaca, NY: ILR.

Ehrenberg, R. G., and Schumann, P. L. (1984). "Compensating Wage Differentials for Mandatory Overtime." *Economic Inquiry, 22,* 460–478.

Ehrenberg, R. G., and Smith, R. S. (1987). "Comparable Worth in the Public Sector." In D. Wise (Ed.), *Public Sector Payrolls.* Chicago: University of Chicago Press.

Gold, M. E. (1985). "Griggs' Folly: An Essay on the Theory, Problems and Origin of the Adverse Impact Definition of Employment Discrimination and a Recommendation for Reform." *Industrial Relations Law Journal, 7.*

Krueger, A. B. (1991). "The Evolution of Unjust Dismissal Legislation in the United States. " *Industrial and Labor Relations Review , 44,* 644–660.

Okun, A. (1975). *Equality and Efficiency: The Big Trade-Off.* Washington, DC: Brookings Institution.

Comment

Stanley Zax

My focus in these comments is workers' compensation insurance, which is my business, and its effects on business. Our company, Zenith Insurance, insures 21,000 businesses in California. I appreciate the comments that Professor Erhenberg makes in his preceding commentary about the history of workers' compensation because I want to discuss whether workers' compensation insurance—which today pays most claims for insubstantial injuries—is really intelligent public policy. Workers' compensation programs exist in 47 states. Texas is the largest state where participation is voluntary. In Texas, my estimate is that 30–40 percent of the businesses have opted out of the system and subjected themselves to tort liability. Professor Ehrenberg suggests that it is costlier for businesses to be in the tort liability system. I would like to suggest to you just the opposite.

The injuries that are primarily covered by workers' compensation consist of back injuries, strains, sprains, and carpel tunnel syndrome. A very real issue is how to reduce the frequency of insubstantial and fraudulent claims, particularly for injuries that are hard to prove. What we can learn from the experience in Texas is that when you leave the injured worker to the tort system, workers' compensation insurance goes back to what it was really intended to cover: serious work-related injuries. I believe a fertile area for study is whether or not businesses would be better off utilizing the tort system rather than the government-regulated workers' compensation system.

Several years ago, Zenith Insurance was receiving multiple bills from different medical clinics treating the same allegedly injured workers for 18 hours each on the same day for psychiatric testing. We even received five bills for the same person at the same clinic on the same date. The problem with the current system is that claims processors identify with injured workers, and so do not act objectively. They look the other way too often.

Once we realized that fraudulent multiple billing was taking place, we asked ourselves, What could we do differently? The solution we suggested was the use of federal RICO statutes. Zenith Insurance filed four suits against workers' compensation claimants, lawyers, and medical clinics. The legal process was widely publicized and the concern we exhibited gained support within the system. The result has been that over the past two years, the frequency of claims in California is down as much as 20 percent from a few years ago.

This has alerted businesses and insurers that they can accomplish a great deal without legislative remedy. In the past, the routine has been that every few years there would be a request for increased benefits; business would counter, saying increased benefits were feasible only if the system were to be reformed as well. In California in 1989, when this dialogue again took place, what started out as reform ended up as increased cash benefits and increased mandates on workers' compensation companies with no reform. The effect of this legislation was to increase the cost of doing business in California by 15 percent. As a result, the business community has learned that the best route to reform is to avoid the legislature and find solutions on our own.

When Proposition 103 passed in 1989 it rolled back insurance prices 20 percent retroactively. This initiative passed by only 1 percent of the vote. The California Supreme Court interpreted the law as rolling back rates 20 percent, but only if the insurance industry was still able to earn a "fair profit." In the five years since this decision, the insurance industry has not known what a "fair profit" is, because legal action is pending. In addition, the 1989 workers' compensation legislation imposed restrictions in terms of the handling of claims. The effect has been to increase our cost of settling claims by almost 100 percent. The mandates have forced us to seek higher profit margins, which means higher costs to our customers, who today are primarily small businesses. In California, large businesses have adopted self-insurance policies and small businesses turn to the insurance industry.

In closing, I suggest that the chief executive officers of American business must join with politicians and intellectuals in some type of joint venture. For good public policies to be made, we need to lay out options and fact-based research to inform our politicians of the implications of the decisions they make.

The single most discouraging thing about doing business in the workers' compensation system is the so-called reform process. When recent legislation was enacted in California, I would venture that there was not a handful of state representatives and the governor's staff who knew a sufficient amount about the subject to legislate public policy intelligently. That was true when the process was started, and it was true when it ended. Now, businesses, workers, lawyers, and insurance companies must live with the aftermath. I spend about half my time working in the political process in California, trying to discuss basic and critical ideas with the principal actors in this drama. I attempted to have the creation of a think tank or research institute included in the latest legislation. This think tank would not be operated by the insurance industry. It would bring together representatives of the many constituencies involved in the workers' compensation field to work on policy proposals and the research process. We have in California a legislature subject to term limitations. The question I pose is, Where will the institutional memory come from in this system? Given that the legislature will no longer have the institutional memory necessary to deal with these issues, we will need something like a think tank to tackle the hard job of reasonable reform proposals and options in the future.

PART FIVE

Labor Force Demographics/ Income Inequalities/ Returns to Human Capital

Introduction

The debate over income inequality in America has raged for years. Wage differentials between blacks and whites in the first half of this century have been attributed primarily to unequal access to educational opportunities. Now that society has dismantled many of the overt barriers to decent schooling that African-Americans once faced, there is a growing sentiment that the socioeconomic status of one's family while growing up is a much more important determinant of racial differences in income.

In a similar vein, conventional wisdom holds that the key to moving up the income distribution ladder is to work hard. The implicit assumption in this image of American society is that equality of economic opportunity reduces any differences in income to simple differences in ability or desire, at least when comparing people of the same race. There is much debate over this claim, however. On the one hand, there is significant mobility within the income distribution in the United States. At the same time, the notions of a permanent underclass and inescapable cycles of poverty for the urban poor permeate our thinking about problems in the inner city. These two different images have vastly different implications when assessing a potential role for government in addressing inequality.

One thing is clear in the debate on inequality: College-educated workers have always commanded higher wages than those with a high school diploma or less. Until recent decades, lack of a college degree was not a barrier to membership in the middle class. Relatively high-paying blue collar jobs were widely available, providing a decent standard of living to those who shunned college. In recent years such opportunities seem to have evaporated, however. The chapters by Gary Burtless and Ray Marshall in Part 1 described the trends toward more education-intensive and skill-intensive employment in manufacturing. At the same time, college graduates have enjoyed an increase in their relative wages. Simply put, a college education today commands more of a premium than at any time in recent history.

The session on "Labor Force Demographics/Income Inequalities/Returns to Human Capital" was convened to try and find explanations for the rise in inequality in recent years. In their chapter, "Relative Wages and Skill Demand 1940–90," Chinhui Juhn and Kevin Murphy trace the increase in the demand for skilled workers (those at the upper end of the income distribution) over the past half century. There are two competing explanations for this rise: sectoral shifts and technical change. Sectoral shifts (between-industry shifts in labor demand) are a factor if the industries that expand are those that disproportionately employ highly skilled workers. Technical change (within-industry shifts in labor demand), in turn, leads to an increase in demand for highly skilled workers within the same industry. Comparing the differences in the evolution of inequality and labor demand during the 1940s and 1980s, they conclude that in recent years the rise in inequality is more consistent with the within-industry technological change story.

Juhn and Murphy make a compelling argument that technological change has led to a rise in inequality. But what does that mean in terms of specific skills used by workers? An answer can be found in the chapter by Frank Levy and Richard Murnane, "Skills, Demography, and the Economy: Is There a Mismatch?" They find that those with better math skills were paid more of a premium in 1986 than in 1978. They also find less evidence of a rise in the wage premiums for good reading and vocabulary skills. This is consistent with the popular perception that in order to survive in today's work place, people need more technical skills than ever before.

Based on their findings, Levy and Murnane argue for increased emphasis on bolstering basic math skills. They also note, however, that changing demographics today may make it more difficult to raise public money for additional spending on children. As average family size has fallen, and more people delay having children (or decide not to have any at all), a larger and larger fraction of households have become childless. This means that the constituency ready to argue directly for the needs of children has shrunk. Though this paints an apparently bleak picture of the future for those who are not getting the right basic skills training, Levy and Murnane's assessment is not shared by all. Barbara Wolfe's comments point out that there seems to be no lack of voter support for truly needy people. And both Wolfe and June O'Neill note that advocating a general increase in spending alone is no guarantee of success. What really matters is whether educational resources are targeted toward the most needy students, and whether they are used to improve directly the classroom situation of such students (as opposed to being siphoned off for administrator salaries and the like).

The discussion concludes with some observations by Richard Sandor on the difficulties that business leaders face when trying to deal with the skills gap. His comments highlight the fact that there are many in the business community who want to take an active role in improving the quality of the workforce. There are significant institutional impediments to doing so, however. Though none of the participants in this session was able to come up with a simple solution to the problems facing low-skilled workers today, this dialogue should help further our understanding of exactly what needs to be done and how we can get started.

10

Relative Wages and Skill Demand, 1940–1990

Chinhui Juhn and Kevin M. Murphy

Wage inequality across and within schooling levels for males in the United States increased dramatically during the 1980s. Between 1979 and 1990, the weekly earnings of college graduates increased by 2 percent, whereas the real weekly earnings of high school graduates decreased by more than 16 percent. As a result, the wage premium for college graduates increased from 42 percentage points in 1979 to 71 percentage points in 1990. The increase was even more dramatic for workers in their first five years out of school, where the wage differential increased from 38 percentage points in 1979 to 79 percentage points in 1990.

These increases in inequality have been widely discussed and described (see, e.g., Blackburn, Bloom, and Freeman, 1990; Levy and Murnane, 1992; Murphy and Welch, 1991, 1992). Although there is general agreement on the facts, the precise causes of these changes in inequality are the subject of growing debate. Most researchers associate the rise in inequality with a rise in the relative demand for skilled workers (see, e.g., Murphy and Welch, 1992; Juhn, Murphy, and Pierce, 1993). The basic logic is simple. Although there has been a slowdown in the rate of growth of the college population since the baby boom, the share of total aggregate hours worked by college graduates has still increased significantly as wage inequality has expanded. The observation that both skill quantities and skill prices increased over the 1980s implies that demand for skill must have increased over this period.

Although demand shifts in favor of more skilled workers stand as the leading explanation, there is little direct evidence of this, owing at least in part to the difficulties in measuring demand changes. The most widely used method attempts to measure changes in the demand for

skill by measuring employment shifts across different sectors (i.e., industries and occupations) in the economy. To the extent that employment
grows in those sectors that intensively use highly skilled factors, one
would conclude that there has been a general increase in demand for
skill in the economy. Indeed, Katz and Murphy (1992), Juhn et al. (1993),
and others have found that these measured demand shifts go in the right
direction and take them as indicators of even larger unmeasured shifts
in demand. The existence of further unmeasured shifts seems like a necessity, because the size of the measured demand changes is much too
small to account for the observed rise in skill prices. The measures of the
growth in skill demand capture the two major demand-side forces suggested in the literature: industrial change and biased technological
change (see, e.g., Bound and Johnson, 1989). One major question has
concerned the relative importance of technological changes (such as skill
upgrading) and industrial change (e.g., the growth of the service economy). In this chapter, we attempt to provide evidence on this front by
analyzing the recent experience from a longer-term perspective.

We begin our analysis with a summary of the recent evidence on relative wages and wage inequality over the 1967–91 period using data from
the March *Current Population Survey*. In addition to summarizing past
findings, we also add somewhat to the existing literature by extending
the analysis into the early 1990s. We find that inequality has continued
to increase during the "white-collar recession" of the early 1990s and that
real wages have declined sharply for all skill groups. In spite of the
"white-collar" nature of the recent recession (which is evident in some of
our employment calculations), wage inequality across and within schooling levels has continued to increase, suggesting a continuation of the underlying marketwide changes that dominated the 1980s.

After summarizing the wage trends, we link changes in wage inequality to changes in employment rates of individuals and their spouses.
Here we find that relative employment responses to growing wage inequality and shifts in labor supply have served to magnify the effects of
growing wage inequality on individual and family earnings. For example, employment and participation rates among males (traditionally
thought to be invariable for prime-aged men) have displayed diverging
patterns by both wage and education levels. We find that the employment rate for men in the lowest quintile of the wage distribution declined by more than 20 percentage points from the late 1960s to 1990,
whereas the employment rate for men in the highest wage quintile remained essentially unchanged. The increasing disparity of labor market
outcomes can be seen at the family level as well, in that the covariance
between husbands' and wives' wages and weeks worked have all increased over time. Although the labor supply of all women has been on

the rise over the past two decades, we find that by far the largest increases in labor supply have been among women married to relatively high-wage men.

Following our summary of recent trends, we look at wage data for a much longer period, using the 1940–80 decennial census files together with the 1989–92 CPS to look at wage and employment changes over five decades. Our findings on wages are similar to those reported in Goldin and Margo (1992) and Juhn (1993), who examined some of these same data. We find that wage inequality fell sharply during the 1940s, with the wage differential between men in the top and bottom quintiles declining by about 20 percentage points. Inequality was relatively constant over the 1950s, began to increase during the 1960s, and then increased sharply over the 1970s and 1980s. Our goal, then, is to exploit these time-series differences in inequality growth to identify the most promising explanation for the recent trends. Demand- or supply-side factors that seem to track the history of wage inequality best over this period we interpret to be those that are most likely to explain the recent trends.

What does account for the dramatic contrast in wage inequality growth between the 1940s and the 1980s? Again, a reasonable starting point is to examine shifts in employment demand across sectors of the economy. One might expect from the wage evidence that employment in the skill-intensive sectors grew much faster during the 1980s compared with the 1940s. Contrary to expectations, however, we find that overall, the relative demand for skill (as measured by our demand index) grew no faster during the 1980s than during the 1940s. At least as measured by employment shifts across different industries and occupations, the evidence suggests that the U.S. economy has been moving toward more skill-intensive sectors relatively steadily since 1940. What does distinguish the 1940s and the 1980s is the *composition* of the change in relative demand for skill. In particular, the shift in demand toward more skilled workers within industry has accelerated over time, along with the rise in wage inequality. In contrast, industrial shifts increasing the demand for skill have decreased in importance over time. Based on this analysis, we conclude that changes in the rate of measured technological change within industries fit best with the historical patterns of change in wage inequality. Both changes in industrial structure and changes in the supply of skilled workers (two competing explanations) line up much less well with the long-term changes in inequality. These results add support for those who argue for technological change as the primary driving force behind the growing inequality in men's wages.

We also find that demand shifted from the bottom to the middle skill categories during the 1940s and from the middle to the top during the 1980s. Given that skill prices fell during the 1940s and rose dramatically during the 1980s, one hypothesis consistent with the data is that workers find it easier to make the transition from the bottom to the middle skill categories than from the middle to the top skill categories. In other words, what distinguished the 1980s from previous decades may have been the increase in demand for the types of skills that are inelastically supplied in the economy.

In the next section, we describe the recent history of male wage inequality and relative wages and show how changes in labor supply have served to magnify these effects. We then present the historical evidence on wage growth as well as changes in some key supply and demand factors for the 1940–90 period.

The Recent History of Wage Inequality

The rise in wage inequality during the 1980s is best illustrated by the ratio of wages for college graduates to those of high school graduates. Figure 10.1 plots this ratio for men in two experience categories: new entrants (those with 1–10 years of experience) and more experienced workers

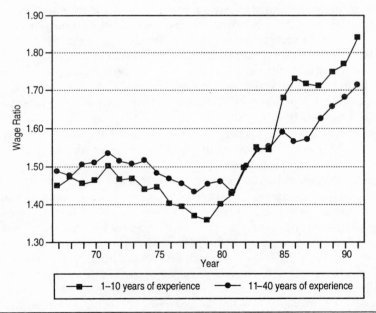

FIGURE 10.1 College High School Wage Ratios, 1967–91 *Note:* The data are for white males with 1–40 years of potential labor market experience who worked full-time and worked at least 13 weeks or more during the previous year. The sample is further limited to wage and salary workers and excludes farm workers, students and military personnel. *Source:* Based on authors' calculations from 1968–92 March *Current Population Survey.*

(those with 11–40 years of experience). The data are from the 1968–92 March *Current Population Survey* and are for white males with 1–40 years of potential labor market experience who worked full-time during the survey year.[1] The change is most dramatic for new entrants. Among new entrants, college graduates earned about 37 percent more than high school graduates in 1979. By 1991 this wage differential had more than doubled, to more than 80 percent. The fact that relative wages for college graduates have resumed their rise after a brief decline in the late 1980s is important. It illustrates that the forces leading to rising inequality are still at work and did not abate during the recent white-collar recession. In fact, as the figure illustrates, between 1987 and 1991 the college wage premium rose almost 20 percentage points for both older and younger workers (a rate of increase equal to that of the rapid rise in wage differentials during the early 1980s). Figure 10.2 shows that relative wages for more experienced workers follow a similar pattern, particularly among the less educated. Among high school graduates, the experience differential rises from about 49 percent in 1979 to about 66 percent in 1991.

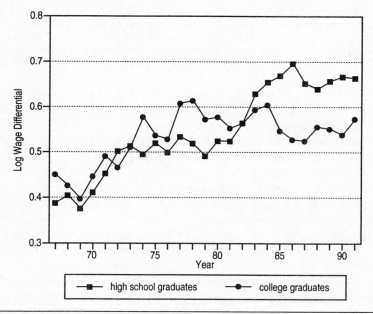

FIGURE 10.2 Experience Differentials by Education Level, 1967–91 *Note:* The data are for white males with 1–40 years of potential labor market experience who worked full-time and worked at least 13 weeks or more during the previous year. The sample is further limited to wage and salary workers and excludes farm workers, students, and military personnel. *Source:* Based on authors' calculations from 1968–92 March *Current Population Survey.*

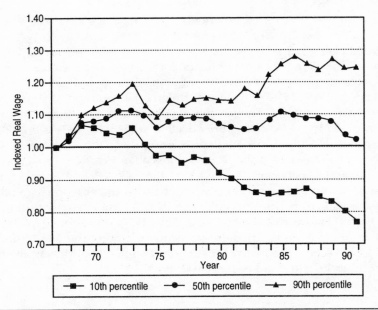

FIGURE 10.3 Indexed Real Wages by Percentile, 1967–91 *Note:* The data are for white males with 1–40 years of potential labor market experience who worked full-time and worked at least 13 weeks or more during the previous year. The sample is further limited to wage and salary workers and excludes farm workers, students, and military personnel. *Source:* Based on authors' calculations from 1968–92 March *Current Population Survey.*

Figure 10.3 provides another perspective on the rise in wage inequality by giving indexed real wages for three points in the male wage distribution: the 10th percentile, the median (or 50th) percentile, and the 90th percentile. For all three groups, we index wages to 100 in 1967 and examine how real weekly wages progress from there. Once again, data are from the 1968–92 March *Current Population Survey* and are for white males with 1–40 years of potential labor market experience who worked full-time during the survey year. As the figure illustrates, real weekly wages for the median worker peak in 1973 and again in 1985, and end up in 1991 only slightly ahead (by about 2 percent) of where they were in 1967. Real wages for workers at the 90th percentile do significantly better and end up in 1991 about 26 percent above where they started in 1967. In sharp contrast, wages for workers at the 10th percentile of the wage distribution did significantly worse than the median. For these workers, wages began to decline after 1969 and ended up in 1991 more than 20 percent below where they started in 1967. The divergence among the three wage indices in Figure 10.3 illustrates the enormous rise in inequality over the past two decades.

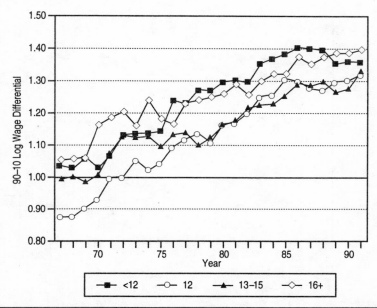

FIGURE 10.4 Weekly Wage Inequality by Education Level, 1967–91 *Note:* The data are for white males with 1–40 years of potential labor market experience who worked full-time and worked at least 13 weeks or more during the previous year. The sample is further limited to wage and salary workers and excludes farm workers, students, and military personnel. *Source:* Based on authors' calculations from 1968–92 March *Current Population Survey.*

Finally, Figure 10.4 shows that wage inequality also increased dramatically even within observed characteristics such as education levels. For both college graduates and high school graduates, the wage differential between workers at the 90th percentile of the wage distribution and workers at the 10th percentile of the wage distribution increased dramatically, increasing by 14 points for college graduates and 19 points for high school graduates.

Although these wage inequality changes have been widely discussed, what is less well known is that relative employment responses to growing wage inequality and shifts in labor supply have magnified the effects of growing wage inequality on individual and family earnings. For example, Figure 10.5 illustrates the changes in male employment levels by wage percentile category. Whereas the employment rate of the bottom quintile declined as much as 20 percentage points, employment rates in the higher wage categories remained essentially unchanged. This divergence in employment has further contributed to rising inequality of individual earnings.

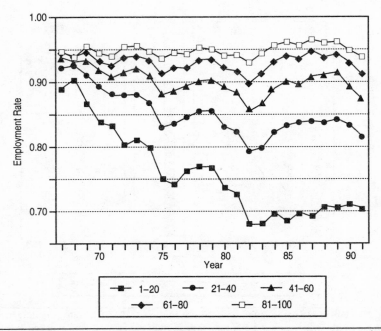

FIGURE 10.5 Employment by Wage Quintile for Men, 1967–91 *Note:* The data are for males with 1–30 years of potential labor market experience. Students and military personnel are excluded from the sample. *Source:* Based on authors' calculations from 1968–92 March *Current Population Survey.*

Finally, Figure 10.6 contrasts the wife's employment rate by husband's wage decile in the late 1960s and the late 1980s. This figure illustrates the point that although labor supply of all women has increased, the largest increases have occurred among women married to relatively high-wage men. Although the increase in wife's earnings as a share of total family income has had a somewhat mitigating effect, the increases in the covariance of husband's and wife's time worked have contributed to rising inequality of family incomes (see Cancian, Danziger, and Gottschalk, 1993; Juhn and Murphy, 1992).

Changes in Relative Wages and Skill Demand, 1940–1990

Changes in Relative Wages

In the preceding section we described the major changes in relative wages and employment during the period, 1970–90. In this section we take a more long-term approach and investigate the changes in relative wages and demand for skill over the period 1940–90. The data are from

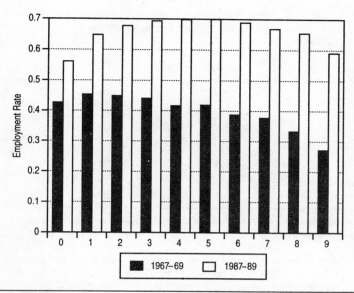

Figure 10.6 Wife's Employment Rate by Husband's Wage Decile *Note:* The data are for a sample of matched husbands and wives where the husband has 1–30 years of potential labor market experience and where neither the husband nor the wife worked part year due to school or military service. *Source:* Based on authors' calculations from 1968–92 March *Current Population Survey.*

the 1940–80 Public Use Microdata Samples (PUMS) and from the 1988–92 March *Current Population Surveys.* For the purposes of looking at wage changes, we selected a sample of white males with 1–40 years of potential labor market experience who worked full-time in the nonagricultural sector, were not self-employed, worked a minimum of 40 weeks, and earned at least one-half of the legal minimum weekly wage.

Table 10.1 presents the decade changes in log weekly wages of men in different quintiles of the wage distribution. Changes in the average wage and in the relative wage (here defined as the differential between the top and the bottom quintile wages) are presented in the bottom rows of the table. As Table 10.1 illustrates, there was a dramatic decline in wage inequality during the 1940s, with the wage differential between the top and the bottom quintiles of the distribution falling more than 20 percent over the decade. Since the 1940s, there have been progressively larger increases in wage inequality, with the differential between the top and bottom quintiles growing 9.5 and 11.5 percent, respectively, during the 1960s and the 1970s. The most significant increase in male wage inequality, however, occurred during the 1980s, with the top quintile gaining more than 23 percent relative to the bottom quintile. To summarize,

TABLE 10.1
Changes in Log Weekly Wages of Men

Percentile	1939–49	1949–59	Years 1959–69	1969–79	1979–89
1–20	.289	.289	.209	−.024	−.196
21–40	.277	.292	.207	.015	−.115
41–60	.197	.301	.232	.073	−.071
61–80	.127	.302	.252	.096	−.021
81–100	.081	.302	.304	.091	.037
Average wage	.194	.297	.241	.050	−.074
Relative wage	−.209	.013	.095	.115	.233

Note: The sample includes white males with 1–40 years of experience who worked in the nonagricultural sector, worked full-time, were not self-employed, worked a minimum of 40 weeks, and earned at least one-half the legal minimum weekly wage. "Relative wage" refers to the differential in wages between workers in the top and the bottom quintiles. *Source:* Numbers for 1939–79 are based on the 1940–80 Public Use Microdata Samples. Numbers for 1989 are based on a five-year average of the 1988–92 surveys from the March 1992 *Current Population Survey.*

between the 1940s and the 1980s there is a differential of more than 40 percentage points in inequality growth. Alternative measures of skill, such as educational and occupational differentials, indicate similar contrasts in wage inequality growth. For example, the college/high school wage ratio fell by 8.6 percent during the 1940s and increased 13.4 percent during the 1980s. Similarly, the wage ratio of professionals to laborers fell by up to 23 percent during the 1940s and increased almost 22 percent during the 1980s (see Juhn, 1993).

Changes in Industrial and Occupational Distribution of Employment

What accounts for the tremendous contrast in wage inequality growth between the 1940s and the 1980s? If demand for skill is an important part of the explanation, then one would expect that demand for skill grew much faster during the 1980s than in the 1940s. A starting point in answering this question is to measure demand changes via employment shifts across different sectors of the economy. To the extent that overall aggregate employment shifted toward more skill-intensive sectors, this would indicate that there has been a general increase in demand for skilled workers in the economy. Tables 10.2 and 10.3 begin this analysis by examining employment distributions across different industries and occupations over the period 1940–90. Table 10.2 presents industry employment shares (measured in efficiency units). For the purposes of measuring demand

TABLE 10.2
Distribution of Employment across Industries

Industry	Year					
	1940	1950	1960	1970	1980	1990
Mining	2.9	2.2	1.5	1.2	1.5	0.9
Constructlon	6.2	7.2	7.2	6.7	6.7	6.8
Manufacturing						
low tech	12.5	10.0	9.7	7.5	6.2	4.8
basic	13.0	16.1	17.9	17.1	15.3	12.5
high tech	2.8	3.3	4.7	4.7	4.1	3.8
Transportation and utilities	10.0	9.9	8.4	7.9	7.9	7.3
Wholesale	3.9	4.7	4.4	5.0	5.1	4.8
Retail	18.1	16.6	14.1	13.0	12.1	12.5
Professional services, finance, insurance, and real estate	9.4	9.8	2.4	15.4	19.1	23.6
Education and welfare	5.3	5.1	7.0	9.4	10.4	11.1
Public administration	5.0	6.1	6.7	7.2	7.2	6.5
Other services	10.9	7.8	6.1	4.9	4.4	5.4

Note: The sample includes men and women with 1–40 years of experience who were in the nonagricultural sector, and who were not enrolled in school or the military during the survey week. Employment shares are calculated as the fraction of total wage-weighted count of workers in the nonagricultural sector. Source: Numbers for 1940–80 are based on the Public Use Microdata Samples. Numbers for 1990 are based on a five-year average of the 1988–92 March Current Population Survey.

changes, both men and women with 1–40 years of labor market experience who have reported industry and occupation categories are included in the sample. For the sake of consistency, we concentrate on only the nonagricultural sector in our analysis. Table 10.2 indicates that the least skill-intensive industries, such as "low-tech" manufacturing, have been declining since at least 1940, with the share of employment falling from 12.5 percent in 1940 to 4.8 percent in 1990. Moreover, the declines in employment share are actually larger during the earlier decades (2.5 percentage points over the 1940s) than during the more recent decades (1.4 percentage points over the 1980s). In contrast, the skill-intensive industries such as professional services have been rising rapidly every period, ending with an employment share of more than 23 percent by 1990.

Table 10.3 presents employment shares across occupation categories. Again, the employment share of highly skilled occupations such as professionals increased every period, rising from 11.1 percent in 1940 to 23.5 percent in 1990. Low-skilled occupations such as laborers lost in employment share from 7.8 percent in 1940 to 3.1 percent in 1990. Again, the

TABLE 10.3
Distribution of Employment across Occupations

Occupation	Year					
	1940	1950	1960	1970	1980	1990
Professionals	11.1	13.1	16.7	19.9	21.1	23.5
Managers	13.1	13.0	12.6	12.8	15.5	19.5
Sales workers	7.5	8.2	7.8	7.4	6.7	6.8
Clerical workers	13.5	12.8	13.6	14.6	14.9	13.6
Crafts workers	15.6	18.3	17.8	16.7	15.8	13.3
Operatives	15.2	15.7	14.2	12.5	10.1	7.4
Transport operatives	5.8	5.1	5.1	4.4	4.2	3.9
Laborers	7.8	6.0	4.4	3.5	3.1	3.1
Domestic workers	3.3	1.3	1.1	0.5	0.2	0.3
Service workers	7.3	6.6	6.7	7.6	8.3	8.9

Note: The sample includes men and women with 1–40 years of experience who were in the nonagricultural sector, and who were not enrolled in school or the military during the survey week. Employment shares are calculated as the fraction of total wage-weighted count of workers in the nonagricultural sector. Source: Numbers for 1940–80 are based on the Public Use Microdata Samples. Numbers for 1990 are based on a five-year average of the 1988–92 March Current Population Survey.

largest declines in employment share among these low-skilled occupations appear to have occurred during the 1940s and the 1950s. In summary, the employment shares of the least- and most-skilled industries and occupations appear to have followed a long-run trend; based on these tables, it would be difficult to conclude that there is an observable difference in the pace of demand growth in favor of more skilled workers between the 1940s and the 1980s.

Changes in Demand for Skill 1940–1990

Tables 10.2 and 10.3 gave preliminary indications that demand for skill has been increasing since at least 1940. In this section, we quantify the impact of the employment changes presented in Tables 10.2 and 10.3 by constructing demand indexes for various skill groups. The indexes we calculate measure the percentage change in the demand for a particular skill group as the weighted average of percentage changes in employment shares of different industries and occupations, where the weights are the group's initial employment distribution across these industry and occupation categories (see Katz and Murphy, 1992, for a more detailed discussion of these demand indexes). Intuitively, those groups predominantly located in sectors with overall employment growth will experience a rise in demand for their services, and those groups located in the shrinking sectors will experience a decline in demand.

These demand indexes are "biased" measures to the extent that they understate the demand shift favoring groups with rising relative wages. For example, as the college-high school wage premium rose during the 1980s, this would have a dampening effect on the growth of sectors that intensively utilize college graduates. Without taking this effect into account, the measured demand shifts will understate the true demand shift in favor of college graduates under constant relative wages. To account for this bias, we make a simplifying assumption that the factor demand curves in each sector have unit own-price elasticities and zero cross-price elasticities. Computationally, this amounts to adjusting the demand indexes calculated as described above by adding the group's percentage price change to its percentage change in share. These demand indexes adjusted for relative wage changes are presented in Table 10.4. The first panel of the table reports demand indexes based on employment shifts across both industries and occupations, whereas the second and third panels report the between-industry and within-industry components, respectively.

As suggested earlier in Tables 10.2 and 10.3, Table 10.4 indicates that the relative demand for skill observed and documented during the 1980s is not a new phenomenon, but a continuation of a trend dating back to the 1940s. For example, as shown in the first panel, the relative demand for workers in the top skill category (the top quintile of the wage distribution) grew approximately 15 percent faster than the demand for those in the bottom category (the bottom quintile) during the 1940s and the 1950s. The pace of demand growth in favor of skilled workers actually slowed during the more recent period, the 1970s and the 1980s, in that demand for the top group grew approximately 9 percent and 11 percent faster during the 1970s and the 1980s, respectively. The first panel of Table 10.4 suggests that a simple relative demand for skill hypothesis that compares the demand growth for the top versus the bottom skill groups would not be able to account fully for the dramatic contrast in wage inequality growth between the 1940s and the 1980s.

Although the relative demand for the most- versus the least-skilled workers does not exhibit a pattern of acceleration over the decades, Table 10.4 does indicate that there have nevertheless been significant differences in the *nature* of demand changes over the decades. The second and third panels of Table 10.4 show that there have been important differences in the between- and within-industry components of relative demand shifts over the decades. More specifically, the between-industry

TABLE 10.4
Changes in Relative Demand for Men by Wage Percentile

Percentile	Years				
	1939–49	1949–59	1959–69	1969–79	1979–89
Based on employment shifts across industries and occupations					
1–20	−.07	−.09	−.08	−.05	−.08
21–40	−.00	−.05	−.05	−.04	−.08
41–60	.04	−.02	−.04	−.04	.09
61–80	.07	.01	−.03	−.02	−.07
81–100	.08	.06	.03	.04	.03
all men	.02	−.02	−.03	−.02	−.06
Based on employment shifts across industries only					
1–20	−.03	−.06	−.06	−.03	−.03
21–40	.01	−.02	−.03	−.03	−.04
41–60	.03	−.01	−.03	−.03	−.06
61–80	.05	.01	−.02	−.02	−.07
81–100	.06	.01	−.00	.00	−.04
Based on employment shifts across occupations within industries					
1–20	−.04	−.04	−.02	−.02	−.05
21–40	−.02	−.03	−.02	−.02	−.04
41–60	.00	−.02	−.02	−.01	−.02
61–80	.02	.00	−.00	.00	.00
81–100	.02	.05	.03	.04	.07

Note: The change in relative demand for a particular group is calculated as the change in the national composition of employment across industries and occupations multiplied by the group's initial employment distribution across industries and occupations. Both men and women are included in the calculation of the national employment shares. The agricultural sector is excluded from all calculations.

component appears to have been much more important during the 1940s and the 1950s than during the later decades. During the 1940s, for example, the between-industry component accounted for well over half (9 out of 15 percentage points) of the differential in demand growth between the top and bottom skill groups. However, during the 1980s, the within-industry component (as measured by shifts across occupations within industries) alone more than accounted for the entire 11-percentage-point differential in demand growth between the top- and bottom-quintile workers. These results offer some evidence supporting those who argue that skill-biased technological change has been the primary driving force behind the recent increases in wage inequality.

Another notable difference between the 1940s and the 1980s is the change in demand for the medium skill categories. As the first panel of Table 10.4 illustrates, the demand for the middle (the 41–60 percentile category) grew 4 percent over the 1940s, whereas the demand for this same group fell as much 9 percent during the 1980s. In fact, one may characterize the decade of the 1940s as a period when the middle and the top skill groups gained on the very bottom skill groups. In contrast, the 1980s were a period when both the least and the medium skilled lost and only very highly skilled workers gained.

How could the declining demand for the medium skilled account for the dramatic increase in wage inequality during the 1980s? A rapidly declining demand for the middle may lead to wage inequality if the medium-skilled workers are relatively good substitutes for workers in the bottom skill categories but poor substitutes for workers in the very top skill categories. For example, as medium-skilled sectors such as basic manufacturing grew over the 1940s, workers may have found it relatively easy to make the transition from the lower-tech manufacturing or agricultural sectors to the growing medium-skilled manufacturing sectors. The transition from these middle manufacturing sectors to the professional services sector may have proved to be more difficult, however, as the manufacturing sector contracted severely and the skilled services sectors grew rapidly during the 1980s. Although we can draw only tentative conclusions at this point, we believe that the results reported in Table 10.4 suggest that one of the key distinguishing features of the 1980s in comparison with the earlier decades is the increase in demand for the types of skills that are more inelastically supplied in the economy. Whether or not it is indeed true that workers are more mobile across certainly categories of skill than others, as well as the precise reasons such may be the case, we leave to be investigated further in the future.

Changes in the Relative Supply of Skill

So far, we have focused on differences in the rate of demand growth for skill in the economy. An equally likely explanation for the large contrast in wage inequality growth between the 1940s and the 1980s, however, may be differences in the rate of growth of skill in the economy. We address this question in Table 10.5, where we present changes in the relative supply of skill in the economy. The supply of workers of a particular skill category (again measured in wage quintiles) is predicted by multiplying the group's initial distribution over five educational categories (<8, 8–11, 12, 13–15, 16+ years of schooling) with the aggregate changes in the educational distribution. As the population attains more schooling over time, we observe a decline in the relative supply of the lower percentile groups (who are predominantly in the less-educated groups) and an increase in the relative supply of the higher percentile groups.

The main finding to report from Table 10.5 is that explanations based on relative supplies will fall short of accounting for the differences in wage inequality growth between the 1940s and the 1980s. In fact, compared

TABLE 10.5
Changes in Relative Supply of Skill

Percentile	Years				
	1939–49	*1949–59*	*1959–69*	*1969–79*	*1979–89*
1–20	−.05	−.08	−.13	−.15	−.09
21–40	−.01	−.03	−.05	−.08	−.03
41–60	−.00	−.01	−.00	−.03	.00
61–80	.01	.02	.04	.05	.03
81–100	.06	.09	.13	.20	.09

Note: The change in supply reported above is predicted by multiplying the change in ed-ucational distribution across the decennial censuses with the percentile group's initial distribution across five educational categories, <8, 8–11, 12, 13–15, and 16+.

with the later decades, the 1940s appear to be the decade of the slowest growth in the relative supply of skill, with the relative supply of the top quintile group growing 11 percent faster than the bottom quintile group. During the 1970s, the relative supply of the top quintile grew as much as 35 percent faster than the bottom quintile. Even though the relative sup-ply of skill did not grow as dramatically during the 1980s, the supply of the top group grew approximately 18 percent faster than the bottom group, a rate of growth that is nevertheless significantly greater than the rate observed over the 1940s.

Conclusion

In this chapter we have examined changes in wage inequality and skill demand over a substantial period, 1940 to 1990, to identify the most promising explanation for the recent trends in inequality growth. We find that skill demand has grown relatively steadily since 1940, whereas skill prices fell sharply during the 1940s and increased dramatically dur-ing the 1980s. Although the overall demand for skill grew at a steady pace, we find significant differences in the *nature* of these increases be-tween the 1940s and the 1980s. First, we find evidence that within-indus-try shifts in demand for skill accelerated over time, as between-industry shifts have diminished in importance. Based on these results, we con-clude that factors such as changes in product demand and international trade had only minor influence during the 1980s. What appears to be more important during the 1980s is pervasive skill upgrading, which occurred within all industries. We also find that relative demand shifts from the bottom to the middle skill categories were much more important during the 1940s (when wage inequality fell), whereas while demand shifts from the middle to the top were more important during the 1980s (when wage inequality increased). This suggests that there may be important differences in supply responses across different skill categories, and that what distinguished the 1980s from the earlier decades may be increases in demand for the types of skill that are less elastically supplied in the economy.

Note

1. The sample is further limited to include only wage and salary workers, excluding farmers as well as those who were in school or in the military, and is limited to those who worked 13 or more weeks during the year.

References

Blackburn, M., Bloom, D., and Freeman, R. B. (1990). "The Declining Economic Position of Less-Skilled American Men." In G. Burtless (Ed.), *A Future of Lousy Jobs? The Changing Structure of U.S. Wages*. Washington DC: Brookings Institution.

Bound, J., and Johnson, G. (1989). "Changes in the Structure of Wages during the 1980's: An Evaluation of Alternative Explanations." NBER Working Paper 2983.

Cancian, M., Danziger, S., and Gottschalk, P. (1993). "Working Wives and Family Income Inequality among Married Couples." In S. Danziger and P. Gottschalk (eds.), *Uneven Tides: Rising Inequality in America*. New York: Russell Sage Foundation.

Goldin, C., and Margo, R. A. (1992). "The Great Compression: The Wage Structure in the United States at Mid-Century." *Quarterly Journal of Economics, 107*, 1–34.

Juhn, C. (1993). "Wage Inequality and Industrial Change: Evidence from Five Decades." Working paper, University of Houston.

Juhn, C., and Murphy, K. M. (1992). "Wage Inequality and Family Labor Supply." Working paper, University of Chicago.

Juhn, C., Murphy, K. M., and Pierce, B. (1993). "Wage Inequality and the Rise in Returns to Skill." *Journal of Political Economy, 101*, 410–442.

Katz, L., and Murphy, K. M. (1992). "Changes in the Wage Structure 1963–1987: Supply and Demand Factors." *Quarterly Journal of Economics, 107*, 35–78.

Levy, F., and Murnane, R. J. (1992). "U.S. Earnings Levels and Earnings Inequality: A Review of Recent Trends and Proposed Explanations." *Journal of Economic Literature, 30*, 1333–1381.

Murphy, K. M., and Welch, F. (1991). "Wage Differentials in the 1980's: The Role of International Trade." In Marvin Kosters, (Ed.), *Workers and Their Wages: Changing Patterns in the United States*. Washington, DC: American Enterprise Institute.

Murphy, K. M., and Welch, F. (1992). "The Structure of Wages." *Quarterly Journal of Economics, 107*, 285–326.

U.S. Bureau of the Census. (1967–1992). *Current Population Survey.* Washington, DC: Government Printing Office.
U.S. Bureau of the Census. (1940–1980). [Public Use Microdata Samples].

11

Skills, Demography, and the Economy: Is There a Mismatch?

Frank Levy and Richard J. Murnane

One of the most widely publicized aspects of earnings trends during the 1980s was the increasing differential between the earnings of college-educated and high school-educated workers. For 25–34-year-old males, this differential stood at 18 percent in 1979; in 1989, it was 43 percent. First reported in 1987, the widening gap between the earnings of college-educated and high school-educated workers has been the subject of countless media reports (see Levy and Michel, 1987). It is no longer news.

Attempts to understand earnings trends and their causes continue, however. Recent work has clarified the nature of education-related earnings trends and their causes in the following ways:

1. The increase in education-related earnings differentials stems from a large decline in the real earnings of high school graduates and high school dropouts, not from an increase in the real earnings of college graduates. This is illustrated in Figure 11.1, which displays trends in the annual earnings (in 1991 dollars) of 25–34-year-old males with different educational attainments.

2. As illustrated in Figure 11.1, young college-educated males experienced a 5 percent decline in earnings between 1989 and 1991. However, high school-educated males of the same age experienced a 9 percent decline over this same "white-collar recession." As a result, the earnings premium college-educated workers received over the earnings of high school-educated workers increased from 43 percent in 1989 to 50 percent in 1991.

3. The increase in the earnings of college-educated workers relative to those of high school-educated workers primarily reflects changes taking place within industries rather than shifts in the distribution of workers among industries (Murphy and Welch, 1993).

4. The increasing relative earnings of college-educated workers does not reflect a recent decline in the skills of high school-educated workers. The earnings of older high school-educated workers, who completed school before the test score decline, have also fallen during the 1980s (see, e.g., Levy and Murnane, 1992).
5. Earnings inequality also increased among workers with the same educational attainments.

The accumulated evidence about the nature of recent earnings trends has led most economists to conclude that a major explanation for these trends is an increased demand for skills. In this argument, employers are willing to pay an increasing earnings premium for college graduates in order to obtain critical skills that these graduates possess. Similarly, the widening earnings variation *among* high school graduates and *among*

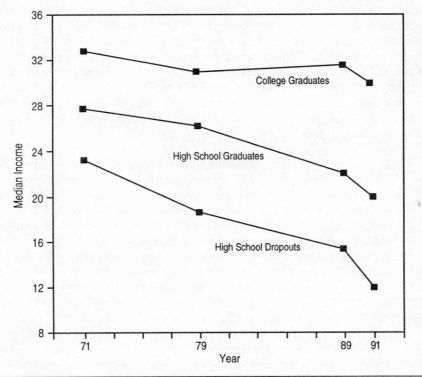

FIGURE 11.1 Median Income of 25–34-Year-Old Males (in 1991 $), by Education Level
Source: Author's tabulations of U.S. Bureau of the Census, *Current Population Survey Annual Demographics Files,* March 1971 and March 1991.

college graduates reflects increasing demand for skills that some individuals have and other individuals (with similar levels of schooling) do not.

It is important to recognize that support for the increasing demand for skills hypothesis comes primarily from evidence that alternative hypotheses do not explain the earnings trends very well. To date, there is little direct evidence that particular well-defined skills are more important in determining wage levels today than in the past.[1] This lack of direct evidence is particularly problematic for the assessment of whether strategies to enhance the skills of high school students will markedly improve their earnings prospects.

In this chapter we present evidence directly bearing on the increasing demand for skills hypothesis. First, we show that one type of skill, the ability to understand and use basic mathematics, has become more important in determining wages. Second, we describe the distribution of this skill in the population of high school students and evaluate the importance of skill differences in predicting subsequent wages. Third, we describe changes over the past decade in high school students' basic math skills and evaluate the relative importance of changes in schooling and changes in home environments in contributing to these changes. Finally, we present an explanation for why the United States has made so little progress in either raising average cognitive skills or closing the gap between the cognitive skills of poor children and those from more affluent families.

The Increasing Importance of Basic Mathematical Skills

As part of a study sponsored by the U.S. Department of Education, called the National Longitudinal Study of the High School Class of 1972 (NLS72), several thousand high school seniors in the graduating class of 1972 completed a battery of tests assessing reading and mathematics skills. The math test focused on the extent to which each student read well enough to follow directions, knew how to manipulate and use fractions and decimals, and could interpret graphs. In other words, the mathematics test assessed the extent to which students had mastered quite basic skills. The test did not assess students' mastery of more advanced mathematics, such as algebraic problem solving or probability theory (see Figure 11.2).

Eight years later, the U.S. Department of Education repeated the survey, asking several thousand high school seniors in the graduating class of 1980 to take essentially the same tests. Students in both surveys were followed as they went to college or entered the labor market. Periodic interviews provided information about subsequent schooling and labor market experiences of the subjects.

Directions: Each problem in this section consists of two quantities, one placed in Column A and one in Column B. You are to compare the two quantities and circle the letter

A if the quantity in Column A is greater;
B if the quantity in Column B is greater;
C if the two quantities are equal;
D if the size relationship cannot be determined from the information given.

	Column A	**Column B**	
1.	Length represented by 3 inches on a scale of 4 feet to an inch	A length of 12 feet	A B C D
2.	$\dfrac{1}{P} = \dfrac{4}{3}$	$\dfrac{1}{Q} = \dfrac{3}{4}$	
	P	Q	A B C D
3.	Cost per apple at a rate of $2.00 per dozen apples	Cost per apple at a rate of 3 apples for $0.50	A B C D
4.	245	$2(10)^3 \div 4(10)^2 + 5(10)$	A B C D

FIGURE 11.2 Questions from Mathematics Exam Administered to Samples of American High School Seniors in 1972 and 1980 *Source:* U.S. Department of Education (1972).

These two longitudinal surveys of large samples of American high school seniors, begun eight years apart, provide a rare opportunity for us to learn whether mastery of basic skills was more important in the 1980s in determining high school graduates' ability to earn middle-class wages than had been true in the late 1970s. We explored this question by comparing, for the two cohorts of high school seniors, the importance of math scores in predicting hourly wages six years after high school graduation (when the graduates were age 24). Essentially, our analysis addressed the question: Among men and women with the same family backgrounds and same post-high school educational attainments, how important is the score on the math test taken as a high school senior in predicting wages at age 24? We focus our discussion on the math score results, because they were the most compelling.

For both young men and young women, the ability to follow directions and manipulate fractions and decimals was a more important determinant of wages in 1986 than it was in 1978. This pattern is illustrated in Figure 11.3. Among 24-year-old males in 1978 who graduated from high school six years earlier but did not go to college, those who left high school with a strong grasp of the basic skills measured on the math test earned an average of 5 percent more (54 cents per hour in 1991 dollars) than their peers who had the same amount of formal education but lacked facility with fractions and decimals. Thus, in 1978, the ability to follow directions and manipulate fractions and decimals did affect wages six years after high school for males, but the effect was modest.

Eight years later these same skills had much greater influence on the wages of young male high school graduates. Instead of a 5 percent wage difference (54 cents per hour), the difference between mastery of basic math skills and very poor facility with these skills was associated with a 16 percent difference in wages ($1.34 per hour).

The abilities to follow directions and to work with fractions and decimals did not affect only the earnings of men. In fact, these skills were

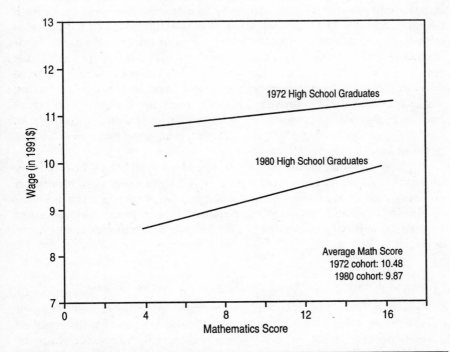

FIGURE 11.3 Relationship between Math Score of Male High School Seniors and Predicted Wage Six Years Later *Source:* Author's tabulations from U.S. Bureau of the Census (1972, 1992), *Current Population Survey Annual Demographic Files,* March 1971 and March 1991.

more important in predicting the earnings of women in any given year. Among 24-year-old females in 1978 whose highest educational attainment was high school graduation, those with mastery of basic math skills earned 11 percent (86 cents per hour) more than those who had very weak math skills. As with males, mastery of basic math skills was more important in determining wages in 1986 than was the case in 1978. Among 24-year-old female high school graduates in 1986, those with mastery of basic math skills earned 24 percent ($1.66 per hour) more than those with very weak math skills.

Just how important are basic math skills in predicting wages six years after high school? The question is important politically because it bears on the debate about the relative importance of changes in schools and changes in firms in restoring real wages to their earlier levels. As illustrated in Figure 11.3, males who graduated from high school in 1980 with *strong* basic math skills (one standard deviation above the mean) earned less in 1986 than 1972 high school graduates with *weak* math skills (one standard deviation below the mean) earned in 1978. Thus, success in helping all students to achieve mastery of basic mathematics skills would contribute only modestly to restoring the earnings of high school graduates to their 1971 level. It is possible that other skills students learn in school or at home have grown in importance in the labor market even more than have basic mathematics skills, but such skills have not yet been identified. In fact, the other skills for which we have measures, reading and vocabulary, grew less in importance in predicting wages than did basic mathematical skills. Thus, improving schooling, at least as measured by performance on standardized tests, is unlikely, *by itself*, to be a powerful strategy for restoring real earnings to their level of 20 years ago.[2]

At the same time, Figure 11.3 also shows that 1980 high school seniors who lack mastery of basic mathematical skills end up at a much greater disadvantage in the labor market relative to their peers than was the case for 1972 seniors weak in basic math. Thus, helping all children to acquire the ability to understand and use basic mathematics is an important goal.

Which Students Lack Basic Mathematics Skills?

Evidence from the National Assessment of Educational Progress (NAEP) shows that lack of mastery of basic mathematical skills is not an isolated problem affecting only a relatively small number of students. The 1982 NAEP mathematics assessment showed that only half of the nation's 17-year-olds had achieved the "300 level of mastery," meaning that they could compute with decimals and fractions, interpret simple inequalities, evaluate formulas, and use logical reasoning to solve problems (for a full description, see National Center for Education Statistics, 1991, pp. 76–77). The NAEP data also showed that 17-year-olds from minority groups and those whose parents had relatively little formal education were the least likely to have mastered basic mathematics. Whereas 57 percent of white students had a 300 level of proficiency, only 17 percent of black students and 22 percent of Hispanic seniors had. Whereas 64 percent of 17-year-olds whose parents had four-year college degrees had achieved the 300 level of mastery, only 42 percent of students whose parents were only high school graduates had achieved the 300 level.

The NAEP does not report mathematics scores by socioeconomic status (SES), but reports based on the High School and Beyond data, collected by the U.S. Department of Education, do. The average mathematics scores of 1980 high school seniors whose families were in the lower quartile of the SES distribution were one standard deviation lower than the average scores of students whose families were in the top SES quartile.

Of course, it is not news that race, ethnicity, parents' educational attainments, and socioeconomic status are strong predictors of students' cognitive achievement levels. This was a major finding of James Coleman's report, *Equality of Educational Opportunity*, published more than a quarter century ago. What is relatively new is the increase in the size of the handicap that deficiencies in basic cognitive skills create for recent labor market entrants. For example, the one standard deviation difference between the average mathematics score of high-SES high school seniors and low-SES seniors corresponds to a predicted wage difference (at age 24) of 32 cents per hour for 1972 male high school graduates and a corresponding difference of 85 cents per hour (or $1,700 per year) for 1980 male graduates (both expressed in 1991 dollars).

Achievement, Schools, and Demography

If mathematical skills are becoming increasingly important in the labor market, how well are schools doing at teaching these skills? Trends in mathematics achievement test scores provide clues, but the scores typically reflect an interaction of the quality of schooling with student family backgrounds—characteristics such as parental education, income, and family size. If student backgrounds are improving in these dimensions, we would expect rising achievement test scores even if schools are unchanged. If student backgrounds are deteriorating, even modest increases in test scores could represent a substantial achievement as schools "swim upstream." It follows that assessing schools' performance requires looking at both trends in achievement and trends in student background.

Trends in mathematics achievement are available from the recent publication of the National Center for Education Statistics (NCES), *America's High School Sophomores: A Ten Year Comparison* (1993), and by using data from High School and Beyond (one of the sources for our wage estimates) and the National Education Longitudinal Study of 1988 (NELS88), a U.S. Department of Education survey that compares mathematics achievement test scores of high school sophomores in 1980 and 1990. The results show modest gains on the order of one-fifth of a standard deviation between the two years.

Equally important, the gains are spread throughout the student population. When NCES divided students by an index of socioeconomic status, they found students in the bottom quartile, in the middle one-half, and in the top quartile of SES all saw test score gains of about 8 percent (Figure 11.4). Similarly, black students had significantly lower scores than white students in both 1980 and 1990, but the black-white gap closed moderately as black students' scores increased at a significantly faster rate.

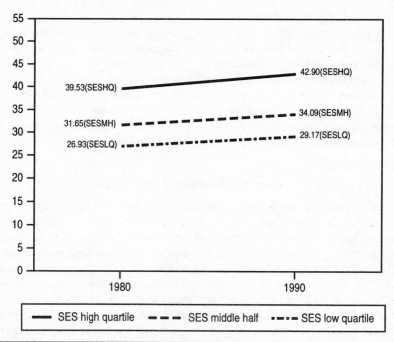

FIGURE 11.4 Gains in Mathematics by SES Quartiles, 1980–90 *Source*: National Center for Education Statistics (1993, p. 25).

The mathematics achievement gains during the 1980s are heartening, especially following a decade in which the mathematics proficiency of the nation's 17-year-olds declined slightly (see NCES, 1991, p. 62). However, the gains are extremely modest. The average achievement gain of one-fifth of a standard deviation translates into a predicted wage gain at age 24 of 13 cents per hour, or approximately $250 per year. This was for a decade in which the median earned income of 25–34-year-old males who entered the labor market right after high school fell by $4,300.

There remains the question of whether changes in demographics facilitated achievement gains, thereby making the contribution of improved schooling very modest, or whether the schools were forced to swim upstream against unfavorable demographic trends. Since the publication of *Workforce 2000* (Johnston and Packer, 1987), there has been a public perception that children's backgrounds are changing for the worse because a growing proportion of children are being raised in low-income families and minority families, groups both historically associated with low academic achievement.

Although this perception has some truth, it is seriously incomplete. To begin with, other dimensions of children's backgrounds have been changing in ways associated with higher achievement. Today's "average" child grows up with fewer siblings than the child of 10 or 20 years ago, a statistical plus in virtually all achievement studies.[3] Similarly, the mother of today's average child has significantly more education than the mother of a child one or two decades ago—a second plus in achievement studies.

Beyond this, any attempt to characterize changes in the "average" child (including the statements just made) are potentially misleading. To see why, consider the case of the income of the "average" child's family. During the 1980s, family income inequality increased substantially and, as we show below, the proportion of low-income children and the number of upper-income children both increased significantly. In this case, changes in the "average" child's income (e.g., changes in the mean of the distribution) tell very little.

To deal with these problems, we return to the NCES evidence on achievement test gains by SES quartile. Because the NCES does not explain precisely how it defined socioeconomic status, we use family income as a proxy to ask the following questions: Consider the quartile of children with the lowest incomes in 1980 and the quartile of children with the lowest incomes in 1990. How do these two groups compare in terms of absolute income levels? Family structure? Number of siblings? Mother's education? As with the NCES data, we repeat these questions for children in the middle 50 percent and top quartile of the 1980 and 1990 distributions. The data are presented in Table 11.1.

TABLE 11.1
Changes over the 1980s in the Characteristics of Children's Families
(children ranked by income quartiles)

| | Bottom Quartile | | Middle Half | | Top Quartile | |
	1980	1990	1980	1990	1980	1990
Math test score	26.93	29.17	31.65	34.09	39.53	42.90
Mean household income (1991 $)	10,226	8,911	33,385	33,587	70,648	81,509
% in female-headed households	.51	.57	.12	.16	.04	.04
Average no. of siblings	1.77	1.62	1.72	1.52	1.42	1.26
% of mothers who did not finish high school	.49	.42	.26	.20	.12	.06
% reporting welfare receipt	.29	.31	.04	.04	.01	.01
% white	.58	.54	.81	.77	.89	.88
% black	.28	.28	.12	.12	.07	.07
% Hispanic	.14	.18	.08	.11	.04	.05

Source: Test scores from NCES (1991); all other statistics from authors' tabulations of data in U.S. Bureau of the Census, Current Population Survey Annual Demographic Files (March 1981, March 1991).

In the case of income, data for these children mirrored the pattern in the larger society: absolute drops in the bottom quartile and absolute gains at the top. By contrast, changes in other characteristics were more constant across groups. The proportion of mothers who failed to finish high school fell by about .06 in all three income classes. Similarly, a child's average number of siblings fell by .20 in all three income classes. In terms of achievement, both of these developments were positive. By contrast, the proportion of children in female-headed families rose by about .05 in each of the two lower income classes, a negative factor for achievement.

What do these demographic changes imply about schools? Rough estimates based on similar data sets suggest that schools are showing modest improvement, particularly in the education of the lowest income group.[4] For this group, demographic changes are largely offsetting in their effects in achievement scores. Given the net effect of more female-headed families, better-educated mothers, lower incomes, and fewer siblings, one would predict essentially no change in achievement scores. In fact, however, these scores rose by 10 percent, suggesting a modest improvement in schools. Similar calculations for the middle and upper income groups suggest that changing demographic characteristics per se should have produced small gains in achievement. Again, however, the actual gains were somewhat larger than one would have predicted based on demographic characteristics.

In sum, it appears that observed gains in mathematics test scores over the 1980s reflect modestly better school performance—the gains cannot be explained by the students' changing demographic characteristics. But to date, observed test score gains imply far smaller wage gains than the wage losses that occurred for male high school graduates during the 1980s.

The Politics of Improvement

In the preceding sections, we argued that deficiencies in basic cognitive skills are a substantial handicap in today's labor market. We also showed that improvements in mathematics skills during the 1980s were modest, especially when compared with either the percentage of students who lack basic mathematical skills or the income losses experienced by non-college-bound youth, especially males, over the decade. In this last section, we consider one set of obstacles to more substantial improvement—the evolving politics of children's issues.

For much of this century, the United States has seen itself as a child-centered nation in which support for the next generation is an important priority. Slowly and without much fanfare, however, the privileged position of children has declined. The decline stems from the interaction of two factors: the changing demographics of children and the way we provide children's services.

Begin with the provision of services. In the United States, the principal public provider of services for children is the local government, often backed by the state. Education is provided by local school districts. Local governments also shape and finance large parts of the welfare, health, protection, and social services that touch many children's lives. In this respect, the provision of children's services differs sharply from the provision of services for the elderly. Among the elderly, the two most important programs—social security and Medicare—are provided by the federal government. This centralization of benefits magnifies the elderly's political power vis-à-vis other groups. Because these important benefits are national, elderly persons from San Diego, California, to Augusta, Maine, focus on the same decisions. The fact that those decisions are made in a single place makes the job of lobbying—for example, the job of the American Association of Retired Persons—that much easier.

Local government's provision of children's services has the opposite effect. Decisions affecting children's education are divided among 15,000 school districts and, to a lesser extent, 50 state capitols. In this fragmented context, two conditions are required for children's issues to attract national attention:

- Children have to reside in a significant fraction of the nation's households, leading to a large constituency.
- Families with children must be fairly "similar" in terms of income and other characteristics so that families with children in different jurisdictions perceive similar interests.

At the height of the baby boom, both of these conditions held to a reasonable degree. Today, that is no longer true.

Begin with simple demographics. In 1970, there were, by census count, 67.6 million U.S. children under age 18, a number not much different from the number of children today. But whereas the number of children has stayed the same, the rest of the population has grown substantially. Since 1970, people have married at later ages, have had smaller families, and have lived longer. As a result of these trends, the number of households *without* children, at some point in time, has grown dramatically. In 1970, 55 percent of families and 45 percent of all households had at least one child. Today, less than half of all families (45 percent) and only about *one-third* of households have one or more children. These numbers suggest that, in any election, a declining number of voters will have children as a primary concern.[5]

Over the same period, differences among families with children have grown, particularly with respect to income. The children of 1970 were products of the baby boom, a time when marriage, sex, and children occurred together, and occurred for most women (Cherlin, 1988, pp. 3–4). By 1990, marriage had become separated from both sex and children. At younger ages, women were increasingly likely to have children outside of marriage. At older ages, married women with children were increasingly likely to divorce their husbands. Two facts resulted:

- In 1990, slightly more than 25 percent of all children were born to unwed mothers compared with 5 percent in the 1960s. The number reflects a growing proportion of unmarried women, rising birthrates among unmarried women, and declining birthrates among married women.
- In 1990, 22 percent of all children lived in mother-only families, compared with about 12 percent in 1970. (In addition, in 1990, 3 percent of all children lived in father-only families.)

At the same time, those children who were in two-parent families were increasingly likely to have both parents working. The result was a moderately growing split in the income distribution of children's families. Between 1970 and 1990, the proportion of children in families with income less than $10,000 rose from 9.6 percent to 12.7 percent (see Figure 11.5). At the same time, the proportion of children in families with income greater than $50,000 also increased from 27.8 percent to 40.7 percent. The remaining piece of the picture—the proportion of children in families with incomes between $10,000 and $50,000—declined from 63 percent to 50 percent.

Moreover, different income levels were increasingly associated with different jurisdictions, a stratification most obvious in the case of central cities. In 1970, slightly fewer than one in five central-city children were poor, a number that reflected two facts. First, despite the urban riots of the 1960s, large numbers of middle-class and working-class children still lived in cities. Second, significant numbers of poor persons were in rural areas, particularly the South, with its very low incomes. This meant that urban poor children attended city schools in which significant numbers of nonpoor parents had a stake. By 1990, the situation was reversed in two respects. In the intervening decades, large numbers of middle-class families had left central cities for the suburbs. At the same time, poor families had left rural areas and migrated to cities. As a result, the incidence of poverty for central-city children rose from fewer than one in five to almost one in three, and central cities now contain 44 percent of all poor children.

The growing coincidence of poor children and cities further weakens the constituency for children's issues. Among middle-class parents, worrying about education now means worrying about education in their own suburban communities, a battle that leaves poor central-city children untouched. It also means that poor children are concentrated in jurisdictions that face increasing needs of all kinds—expenditures for health, drug treatment, police, courts, and welfare—at a time when the out-migration of the middle class has reduced resources.[6]

Together, these trends point to the need for an increased federal and state presence if problems of education—in particular, the education of poor children—are to improve substantially. Some of this increased presence is already in the making. The development of national standards in subjects such as mathematics and science will, if properly implemented, give clear signals about which schools are in trouble. Once these schools are identified, the issue becomes, What happens next? If our argument is correct, many of these schools—particularly schools serving the poorest children—will require resources that their local communities either cannot or will not provide. As unfashionable as it sounds, if these resources do not come from higher levels of government, they will not come at all.

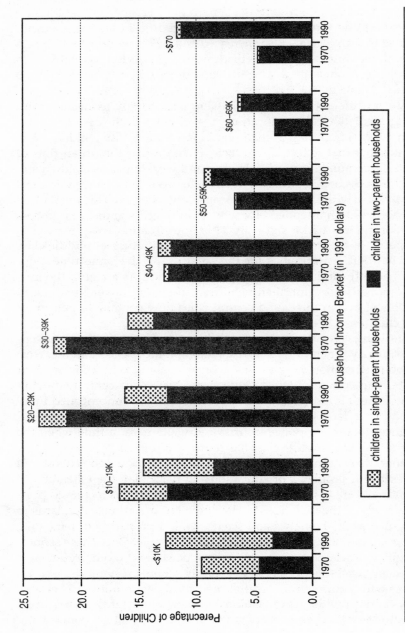

FIGURE 11.5 Distribution of Children by Family Income: 1970 and 1990 *Source:* Author's tabulations from U.S. Bureau of the Census (1972, 1992), *Current Population Survey Annual Demographic Files*, March 1971 and March 1991.

Notes

1. One exception is the work of Grogger and Eide (1992), who argue that the 1980s demand for college graduates was centered on business administration and science majors, whereas demand for other graduates slackened. Alan Krueger (1993) has shown that the spread of computer use contributed to the increase in the education-related wage gap.

2. If there is a case to be made for educational improvements to play a critical role in improving productivity, it is that better-prepared labor force entrants will catalyze firms to invest in training and reorganizations that increase productivity. To date, this is only an unsupported hypothesis. It is also important to keep in mind that the modest size of the relationship between skills learned in school and subsequent earnings does not refute the view that an increasing demand for skills is the major source of the increase in earnings inequality. It does require a realization that skills include not only the abilities that job applicants take to interviews, but also skills that workers acquire on the job as a result of training.

3. This is presumably because fewer siblings allow a child to receive more parental attention.

4. These calculations are based on models relating achievement test scores to demographic characteristics in Murnane, Willett, and Levy, (1990).

5. During this time, the number of households has grown much faster than the number of families, as a rising number of young, unmarried persons as well as older divorced persons have opted to live alone.

6. Between 1987 and 1991, the number of murdered black men and women, ages 15–19, rose from 658 to 1,600/100,000. If we assume that men and women each constitute half of the population, and that men are the victims in 80 percent of the murders, then the 1991 murder rate for men is .0128. If that rate applies to each of the five years, ages 15–19, then these young men have 1-in-200 chance of being murdered (i.e., $[1 - (.9872)^5]$ as they pass through that age range. These numbers are taken from the FBI's *Uniform Crime Reports* (1988, 1992).

References

Cherlin, A., ed. (1988). "The Changing American Family and Public Policy." in *The Changing American Family and Public Policy*. Washington, DC: Urban Institute.

Coleman, J. et al. (1966). *Equality of Educational Opportunity*. Washington, DC: Government Printing Office.

Federal Bureau of Investigation. (1988, 1992). *Uniform Crime Reports*. Washington, DC: Government Printing Office.

Grogger, J., and Eide, E. (1992). "Changes in College Skills and the Rise in the College Wage Premium." Unpublished manuscript, University of California, Santa Barbara, Department of Economics.

Johnston, W. B., and Packer, A. E. (1987). *Workforce 2000: Work and Workers for the 21st Century*. Washington, DC: Hudson Institute.

Krueger, A. B. (1993). "How Computers Have Changed the Wage Structure Evidence from Microdata, 1984–89." *Quarterly Journal of Economics, 108*, 33–60.

Levy, F., and Michel, R. (1987). "Understanding the Low Wage Jobs Debate." Mimeo, Urban Institute.

Levy, F., and Murnane, R. J. (1992). "U.S. Earnings Levels and Earnings Inequality: A Review of Recent Trends and Proposed Explanations." *Journal of Economic Literature, 20,* 1333–1381.

Murnane, R. J., Willett, J. B., and Levy, F. (1990, July). "Skills, Skill Payments and the Mismatch Hypothesis." Paper presented at the NBER Summer Labor Workshop.

Murphy, K. M., and Welch, F. (1993). "Industrial Change and the Rising Importance of Skill." In S. Danziger and P. Gottschalk (Eds.), *Uneven Tides: Rising Inequality in America.* New York: Russell Sage Foundation.

National Center for Education Statistics (NCES). (1991). *Trends in Academic Progress.* Washington, DC: Government Printing Office.

National Center for Education Statistics (NCES). (1993). *America's High School Sophomores: A Ten Year Comparison.* Washington, DC: Government Printing Office.

U.S. Bureau of the Census. (1972, 1980, 1990, 1992). *Current Population Reports. Series P-60,* Washington, DC: Government Printing Office.

U.S. Department of Education. (1972). *National Longitudinal Study of the High School Class of 1972* (NLS 72). Princeton, NJ: Educational Testing Service.

U.S. Department of Education. (1988). *National Education Longitudinal Study of 1988.* Washington, DC: Government Printing Office.

Comment

Barbara L. Wolfe

Both of the preceding chapters raise a number of interesting suppositions. They are both significant contributions to an important topic, and both bring together a number of areas in the human resources literature, and from education production functions, labor market research, and inequality of earnings and income to demography. These chapters lead the reader to contemplate a number of subissues, and I compliment the authors on their insightful work.

In both chapters, the analysis and assertions made seem reasonable and appeal to the reader's (or at least my) intuition. The story they tell seems to fit together, and seems to offer an explanation for the growing earnings disparity. Further, Levy and Murnane seem to suggest both a reason for concern with investment in today's schools and motives to invest further in schooling, especially for youths in inner cities.

My task is not, however, to suggest that the intuition appealed to by the preceding chapters is reasonable; it is to ask whether the authors have established reasonable scientific grounds to support their thesis. In the comments that follow, I will explore several dimensions. I begin with Chapter 11, by Levy and Murnane.

In their presentation of statistical evidence on returns to math skills, Levy and Murnane suggest that the payoff to math skills has increased over the period studied. Perhaps it has, but I would raise the following issues.

First, are those who do not work included in the estimates? That is, do the wages reported include only full-time, full-year workers, or do they include everyone who completed high school and did not go on to college? Either is likely to create a possible problem. If only full-time, full-year workers are included, there is selection going on; to the extent this proportion has changed, and those who work are not a random sample of those who took the test, this proportion will influence the calculated returns to math skills. If the averages are based on everyone, then the zeros or nonworkers will influence the results. If more low-skilled persons did not have jobs and the proportion increased (decreased) over time, the resulting wage rates would reflect not only returns to productivity but also returns in terms of the probability of getting a job—but the discussion should then reflect labor market conditions or the impact of skills on getting a job rather than only differential wages. Finally, if the reported wages are based on those who work at all, a similar bias could be present in which those who work part-time may be paid less and also may have lower scores. (Yes, this is still differential returns, but the implications for productivity would be viewed differently.)

Second, are the tests identical over time? (And is the extent of teaching toward the test approximately equal over time?) If not, the results are not meaningful, for the test would not capture the same skills. And if, for example, the test became less racially biased, the results could reflect only the test rather than true differences in knowledge.

Third, the proportion of youths who took the test may have changed: The proportion who graduate from high school is higher in 1980 than in 1972 or earlier. To the extent a higher proportion of students now take the standardized tests, one would expect the reported means to change simply as the composition of those taking the exam changes. (There is a parallel to the analysis of the decline in SAT scores: That more now take the test is one explanation for the decline in SAT scores.)

Fourth, in the 1992 Green Book (p. 1141), there is related evidence; comparing 1978 with 1990 mathematics scores for 17-year-olds for categories by area and socioeconomic class, the scores changed as follows:

Mathematics	1978	1990
advantaged urban	321	317
disadvantaged urban	273	285
extreme rural	295	304
suburban/other	301	306

These results suggest that disadvantaged urban youth have improved somewhat and do nearly as well as suburban and rural youth. These data then do not seem consistent with some of Levy and Murnane's discussion and interpretation and raise questions about some of their claims.

Continuing with questions related to data, Levy and Murnane suggest that the problems of poor children have become more concentrated in inner cities. Again turning to the 1992 Green Book, we find that fewer children lived in rural areas (consistent with Levy and Murnane's claims) but fewer children lived in poverty areas in 1988 compared with 1976 (18.9 compared with 20.9 percent; pp. 1171–1172.)

Turning to more general issues, Levy and Murnane lay out the primary caveat of their chapter as follows:

Success in helping all students to achieve mastery of basic mathematics skills would contribute only modestly to restoring the earnings of high school graduates to their 1971 level. It is possible that other skills students learn in school or at home have grown in importance in the labor market even more than have basic mathematics skills; but such skills have not yet been identified.

Yet the authors go on to call for increased investments in school to increase such skills. Is this reasonable public policy?

Even if we accept the premise that increasing mathematics skills would increase earnings, do we know how to do so? We have but limited know-ledge and mixed evidence on the topic. I do think there is evidence that school resources matter, but these are particular resources for particular students. Simply spending more dollars is not likely to be successful. (Spending on better teachers and smaller classes for disadvantaged children may, however, pay off and certainly would be worth an experiment or two, or more.)

What is the basis of Levy and Murnane's claims regarding educational production functions? On what basis do they claim that growing up in a female-headed family negatively affects achievement? This may "seem reasonable," but are there studies that establish this and give some quantitative dimension to the claim? The same type of question can be raised for income, average number of siblings, and the proportion of mothers who completed high school.

To go further, simple positive relationships will not be convincing here. "Selection" could lie behind simple relationships. If mothers with higher IQs are more likely to complete high school, the children of mothers who completed high school will be more likely to score well on standardized tests—but it may be mother's and hence child's IQ that is the explanation, rather than mother's education. If this is the case, then having more mothers graduate from high school could have no independent influence on the scores of their children.

Levy and Murnane go far in their claims. They state, "Given the net effect of more female-headed families, better-educated mothers, lower incomes, and fewer siblings, one would predict essentially no change in achievement scores." Really? What is the basis of this claim? It requires not just causal relationships but also quantitative magnitudes to have been estimated.

Another statement Levy and Murnane make cannot be justified: "Scores over the 1980s reflect modestly better school performance—the gains cannot be explained by the students' changing demographic characteristics." We just do not have estimates to warrant this claim, reasonable though it may seem.

Tables 1–3 present some results from a study I am conducting with Robert Haveman that looks at the determinants of level of education—a measure of the quantity of education rather than the quality or achievement in qualitative terms. The results are based on data collected over 21 years for the Michigan Panel Study of Income Dynamics from more than 1,700 children ages 0–6 in 1968 who were studied through 1988. These results suggest the following:

- Having parents with at least a high school education is significantly related to the child's level of schooling.
- Growing up with more siblings is a significant (negative) factor in predicting years of schooling, but not high school completion (competition for resources may be more important for college, which involves greater direct expenditures by parents).
- Income (poverty) is also significant in determining level of schooling, but not high school completion (see the point above with regard to siblings).
- Having a mother who works while the child is growing up seems to be positively associated with the probability of graduating from high school (possibly a role model effect).
- Living in a household whose head is disabled is negatively associated with amount of schooling.
- Stress—such as that caused by moving—appears to be negatively related to level of schooling.
- Consistent with Levy and Murnane's views, more years lived with a single parent appears to be negatively associated with amount of schooling (divorce per se does not seem to be).

Concerning Levy and Murnane's final section, "The Politics of Improvement," again questions can be raised by reasonable persons about the extent of evidence or basis for the authors' assertions. Let me make an

TABLE 1
Determinants of High School Graduation, Full Sample, Probit Estimation $(N = 1,705)$

	Coefficient	t Statistic	Coefficient	t Statistic
Constant	.54	2.56**	1.29	4.38**
Background				
African-American	.40	3.94**	.25	1.68*
female	.19	2.43**	−.03	.24
African-American x female	—	—	.40	2.40**

(continues)

TABLE 1 *(continued)*

	Coefficient	t Statistic	Coefficient	t Statistic
Parental choice/opportunities				
religion	.12	.84	—	—
Catholic	—	—	.22	1.25
Jewish	—	—	4.12	.01
Protestant	—	—	.12	.27
number of siblings	−.07	2.56**	−.04	1.37
number of years lived with one parent	−.03	3.12**	−.03	1.62
father high school graduate +	.49	4.33*	—	—
father high school graduate	—	—	.34	2.76**
father some college	—	—	.62	2.80**
father college graduate	—	—	.29	1.24
mother high school graduate +	.34	3.60**	—	—
mother high school graduate	—	—	.28	2.85**
mother some college	—	—	.63	2.71**
mother college graduate	—	—	4.87	.01
average family income ÷ poverty line	.07	1.59	—	—
years in poverty	—	—	−.01	.35
years in poverty x AFDC	—	—	−.01	.38
years mother worked	.02	2.00**	.03	2.17**
years lived in SMSA	−.01	.86	−.01	1.05
number of location moves	—	—	−.13	5.35**
number of parental separations	—	—	.07	.66
number of parental remarriages	—	—	−.06	.43
Family circumstances				
years family head disabled	−.07	4.91**	−.06	3.89**
firstborn	—	—	.28	2.35**
grandparents poor	—	—	−.03	.30
Neighborhood attributes (%)				
families headed by a female	—	—	−.16	.34
youths who are dropouts	—	—	−.02	3.46**
households headed by a person with a high-status occupation	—	—	−.42^{-2}	.64
Goodness of fit				
log likelihood	−644		−608	
proportion predicted correctly	.845		.853	

* Significant at 10% level
** Significant at 5% level

Note: The model specifications also include controls for whether both parents are in the sample in 1968, and whether child's father was foreign-born. *Source:* Haveman and Wolfe (1994), pp. 152–153.

TABLE 2
Determinants of High School Graduation, Full Sample, Tobit Estimation ($N = 1,705$)

	Coefficient	t Statistic	Coefficient	t Statistic
Constant	11.40	52.63**	12.36	44.91**
Background				
African-American	.41	4.03**	.27	1.83*
female	.35	4.35**	.03	.28
African-American x female	—	—	.66	4.22**
Parental Choice/Opportunities				
religion	.24	1.48*	—	—
Catholic	—	—	.37	2.20**
Jewish	—	—	−.14	.36
Protestant	—	—	.15	1.03
number of siblings	−.07	2.30**	−.09	3.23**
number of years lived with one parent	−.04	3.03**	−.04	2.62**
father high school graduate +	.66	6.22**	—	—
father high school graduate	—	—	.49	4.37**
father some college	—	—	.83	5.20**
father college graduate	—	—	1.13	5.86**
mother high school graduate +	.46	4.96**	—	—
mother high school graduate	—	—	.40	4.27**
mother some college	—	—	.66	3.90**
mother college graduate	—	—	1.27	4.93**
average family income ÷ poverty line	.21	5.75	—	—
years in poverty	—	—	−.06	2.53**
years in poverty x AFDC	—	—	.04	1.69*
years mother worked	.01	.79	.01	.98
years lived in SMSA	−.00	.31	−.00	.10
number of location moves	—	—	−.10	3.91**
number of parental separations	—	—	.14	1.19
number of parental remarriages	—	—	−.24	1.79*
Family circumstances				
years family head disabled	−.05	2.87**	−.04	2.61**
firstborn	—	—	.11	1.08
grandparents poor	—	—	−.02	.21
Neighborhood attributes (%)				
families headed by a female	—	—	−.75^{-2}	1.59
youths who are dropouts	—	—	−.83^{-2}	1.52
households headed by a person with a high status occupation	—	—	.42^{-2}	.69
Goodness of fit				
log likelihood	−2686		−2645	

*$p < .05$
**$p < .01$

Note: The model specifications also include controls for whether both parents are in the sample in 1968, and whether child's father was foreign-born. *Source*: Haveman and Wolfe (1994), pp. 152–153.

TABLE 3
Simulated Effects of Changes in Explanatory Variables:
Predicted Value of Attainment Variable and Percentage Change from Population
(Base) Value of Attainment Variable

	Probability of Graduation	Percentage Change from Base	Years of Completed Schooling	Percentage Change from Base
Base	.88	—	13.0	—
Mother/father are high school graduates	.93*	6.4	13.6*	4.3
Family zero years in poverty [a]	.88	0.5	13.0*	.3
not on welfare, if poor [b]	.88	.2	13.0	−.2
on welfare, if poor [c]	.88	−.1	13.0	.1
Family zero years lived with one parent	.89	1.1	13.1*	.6
Four family location moves	.83*	−5.9	12.8*	−1.8
Zero family location moves	.91*	4.2	13.1*	1.1
Grew up in "bad" neighborhood [d]	.80*	−9.0	12.5	−4.0
Grew up in "good" neighborhood [e]	.91*	3.9	13.26	2.1
Mom worked 10 years	.90*	2.1	13.0	.4
Mom worked 0 years	.85*	−3.0	12.9	−.5
Parent disabled 10 years	.77*	−11.8	12.6*	−3.0
Parent disabled 0 years	.89*	1.7	13.0*	0.3
One more sibling	.87	−.8	12.9*	−.7

[a] If family is poor, in any year, income equal to the poverty line is assigned.

[b] If family is poor, in any year, welfare = 0 is assigned.

[c] If family is poor, in any year, welfare = 1 is assigned.

[d] Proportion in neighborhood of households headed by a female and proportion of youths who are dropouts set = 40; proportion of those who work in neighborhood who are in high-prestige occupations set = 0.

[e] Proportion in neighborhood of households headed by a female and proportion of youths who are dropouts set 0; proportion of those who work in neighborhood who are in high-prestige occupations set = 40.

* Based on a coefficient that is statistically significant at 5 percent level.

Source: Haveman and Wolfe (1994), p.165.

alternative argument. It is easier to influence politicians in smaller areas, where there are limited legislators with more narrowly defined interests. Parents can move to areas with good schools, and this demand can positively influence property values. Alice Rivlin (1992 talk, Columbia University, N.Y.) has made a similar argument—that more independence should be given to local areas (including states), for they will have more interest in increasing investment in schools.

Second, there is evidence that the elderly care about children and will vote to provide services to them. Americans of all ages seem to be willing to provide assistance for those viewed as "innocent victims." Today there seems to be increased awareness that children are facing a relatively un-attractive future and that private resources will not be sufficient to com-pensate for this.

For these reasons, Levy and Murnane's argument that federalizing education decisions would lead to improvements in schooling seems to be highly questionable.

Are there alternative views on this? First, not all children are not doing well—the issue is increasing inequality. Children at the bottom of the dis-tribution are confronting multiple risks, such as poor education, poverty, single-parent families, unstable families, and dysfunctional neighbor-hoods. I see the problem primarily as one in which the bottom tail has drifted away from the median. We need to target measures on specific children, rather than concern ourselves with increasing resources for all children.

Children themselves do not complain much and are not politically or-ganized, and, as Levy and Murnane point out, the number of voting units with children in them is now smaller than in the past. However, the future well-being of today's middle-aged and older population, from their wage rates to the security of their pensions and health care benefits, rests at least in part on future productivity and economic growth—in other words, on the quality of the nation's workforce. This, of course, ar-gues for intergenerational redistribution.

Finally, I would like to make some minor points concerning Levy and Murnane's Table 11.1. It would be useful to know the ages of the chil-dren included in the data, and a column showing all children would make possible some interesting comparisons. It would also be helpful to know if the percentage reporting welfare receipt include those who have *ever* received welfare or only those who were receiving it at a certain point in time.

Turning to Juhn and Murphy's chapter, I have only a few points to raise. First, changing patterns of labor market earnings reflect three com-ponents: the proportion who work, the hours worked, and the wage rate. If the proportion who work changes, or the average hours changes, this too can influence overall inequality. The answer one gets may reflect whether one is looking at all three components or only a subset.

Second, in the analysis concerning the contribution of wives to eco-nomic inequality, I think we might be a bit skeptical of what Juhn and Murphy's figures seem to tell us, for several reasons. The proportion in the population who are married has changed over time. Hence, the pattern with regard to contribution of earnings will in part reflect who is married. But the problem may be more compelling. There is some evi-dence that poverty influences marital status, including the stability of marriage. Hence, part of the inequality will be masked if only married couples are included in an analysis. And this is a problem for comparisons over time if the pattern of marriage changes (which it has over this time period).

Further, it is worth noting that the Gini coefficient—or other measures of inequality of income or earnings—will be lower generally (show greater equality) when two earnings or income distributions are combined, compared with a single one. Hence, the contribution of a wife's earnings to that of the household decreases inequality when calculated as Juhn and Murphy have done. Why begin with husbands rather than wives? One could certainly ask a similar question beginning with wives' earnings that would also shed some light on growing inequality.

The issue of the response to higher returns for college graduates should be studied with all groups (see Table 4). The big shifts have taken place among women rather than among men. The shifts are large and substantial. This pattern suggests that it is important to study inequality including all adults, not just men, white men, or married men.

Table 4 shows the proportion of those aged 21–25 who were economically inactive in 1973 and 1988. This table highlights the importance of adjusting for the proportion in school when looking at the picture for young adults. The results, based on CPS data, suggest that the only group that has become less economically active over this time period is nonwhite men. Table 4 also highlights the pattern of increasing schooling among women in the population, although all groups had larger proportions in school in 1988 than they did in 1973.

TABLE 4
Inactivity Rates, Persons Aged 21–25
1973 and 1988 (percentages)

	Males		Females	
	1973	1988	1973	1988
White				
inactive	10.2	9.7	11	8.1
in school	19.3	20.2	13.3	17.2
Nonwhite				
inactive	15.8	19.7	12.2	11.7
in school	12.8	14.8	9.5	12.0

Source: 1973 and 1988 CPS tapes as reported in Haveman and Wolfe (1994).

References

Haveman, R., and Wolfe, B. L. (1994). *Succeeding Generations: On the Effects of Investments in Children.* New York: Russell Sage Foundation.

U.S. House of Representatives, Committee on Ways and Means. *1992 Green Book: Background Material and Data on Programs within the Jurisdiction of the Committee on Ways and Means.* Washington, DC: U.S. Government Printing Office.

Comment

June E. O'Neill

One of the more intensive "whodunits" or, more appropriately, "what-done-its" of the past few years has been the search for the causes of the growing inequality in the income distribution that became apparent in the 1980s. One important finding, clearly demonstrated in the preceding chapters by Juhn and Murphy and Levy and Murnane, is the recognition that the widening gap between rich and poor stems at least in part from a widening gap in earnings between college graduates and high school graduates as well as between high school graduates and those with still less schooling. Put less ominously, the payoff to additional schooling has increased. Rephrasing the question in this case has helped point to some plausible answers. The authors of the two chapters I will comment on here have contributed to this emerging literature.

As discussed in a recent paper by Jacob Mincer (1993) and as is evident in the historical data presented in Chapter 10 by Juhn and Murphy, the rising return to education in the 1980s was, in part, a rebound from the 1970s—the era of the "overeducated American," when the payoff to a college education fell to record lows.[1] There is a supply-and-demand story here. The 1970s decline in college graduates' pay is widely believed to have been the result of a surge in the number of college graduates entering the labor market—a consequence of an increase in college attendance on the part of those in the huge baby-boom cohort. (The increase in college attendance rates was a response to the high payoff to a college education in the 1960s as well as to liberalized government subsidies, rising parental incomes, and the Vietnam War, given that college attendance was a way to avoid or at least to postpone the draft.) During the 1970s, college enrollment rates ebbed, this time in response to a relative decline in college graduates' wages. By the 1980s, the slack supply of new college graduates could not counter what appeared to be a strongly rising demand for skilled workers, thereby resulting in the large increases we have observed in the relative earnings of college graduates.

It has proven difficult to identify and measure the contribution of the factors underlying the rise in demand for highly skilled workers. There is some evidence to suggest that technological change has enhanced the productivity of college-trained people and increased the value of college-learned skills; and increased levels of foreign trade also may have favored the skilled (see the review by Levy and Murnane, 1992). At the same time, a supply factor—the substantial increase over the past two decades of immigrants from Central America with extremely low levels of schooling—may have added to downward pressure on the wages of the unskilled generally.[2]

One important question is whether the wage gap between the more and less educated will continue to widen. As Mincer (1993) shows, a self-correcting mechanism is already at work; college enrollment rates increased sharply in the 1980s. But there is a long lag between the initial enrollment response and the point at which the new college graduates actually have an impact on relative supply in the market—Mincer estimates an 8 year lag. In consequence, the increased enrollments of the 1980s are projected to eliminate half of the skill shortage resulting in a significant reduction in the college wage premium shortly after the turn of the century, other things the same. But as Mincer warns, the demand for skills could continue to grow and other negative factors (rising tuition, stagnating family income) may curtail a continuing enrollment response.

The widening pay gap between college and high school graduates is not the only source of widening inequality, as wages have become more unequal among high school graduates and among college graduates. As Juhn, Murphy, and Pierce (1991) have suggested, there are considerable skill differences among people with the same nominal schooling level, and it is reasonable to inquire whether these skill differences have also led to wider wage differentials. But lack of data has made it difficult to measure these skill differences directly. In their chapter, Levy and Murnane provide a particularly interesting analysis that bears on this issue. Their findings are important. First, they show that there is a sizable pay gap related to differences in math skills among people who have completed only high school. Second, the payoff to these math skills rose from the 1970s to the 1980s. (Although Levy and Murnane do not report here on changes in the return to math skill differences among college graduates, they tell me that the pattern is similar.)

I believe that these findings help explain why some groups fared worse than others during the 1980s (and continuing into the 1990s). For example, after several decades of significant progress, the earnings of young black men slipped relative to the earnings of young white men even when schooling is controlled for. However, achievement levels, as measured by test scores, are lower for black workers than for white workers with the same years of school completed. For example, among the large sample of youth in the National Longitudinal Survey of Youth

(NLSY) administered the Armed Forces Qualifying Test (AFQT), black men scored almost a standard deviation below white men when those with a high school education are compared, and the differential widens above a standard deviation at the college graduate level. Among both blacks and whites, AFQT scores are highly correlated with earnings. In my own research I have found that an increase of one standard deviation in the AFQT score of black men increases their wages by 10.6 percent (all other things being the same), whereas a comparable increase in scores increases white men's earnings by 7 percent (O'Neill, 1990).

As shown in Table 1, differences in human capital as measured by AFQT scores, as well as by such factors as schooling and work experience, could account for nearly all of the earnings gap between 22–29-year-old black and white men in 1987. In the study from which this table is drawn, I speculated that an increasing payoff to the types of skills measured by the AFQT might account for the widening black-white gap in wages during the 1980s but I had no second cohort to compare with the NLSY men

TABLE 1

Effect of Adjusting for Differences in AFQT Scores
and Other Characteristics on the
Black/White Hourly Wage Ratio, Men Age 22–29, 1987

	Actual Black/White Ratio	*Predicted Black/White Wage Ratios*		
		1	*2*	*3*
Predicted black wage (given white characteristics) as percentage of actual white wage				
all schooling levels	82.9	87.7	95.5	99.1
0–12 years	84.5	85.0	90.4	93.8
13 years and over	85.9	95.6	108.0	110.4
Factors held constant				
region		yes	yes	yes
schooling		yes	yes	yes
potential work experience		yes	yes	yes
AFQT score			yes	yes
actual work experience				yes

Note: Predicted wages were estimated as follows: Separate hourly wage regressions were estimated for black and white men. A predicted wage for blacks was estimated by substituting white mean characteristics into the regression results for black men. The predicted wage varies depending on the explanatory variables in the model. Three model specifications are shown. The analysis is restricted to full-time workers who are not self-employed. For details see O'Neill (1990). *Source*: Author's estimates using the National Longitudinal Survey of Youth, microdata files.

as did Levy and Murnane. Levy and Murnane have constructed parallel analyses using comparable data for two cohorts separated by about a decade. Their results support the presumption that rising returns to cognitive skills can help explain why earnings differentials would have widened between groups whose academic achievement levels differ although they have completed the same number of years of schooling.

Not all groups who typically have lower earnings and less human capital fared badly in the 1980s, women being a notable exception. This seeming exception, however, helps explain the rule. Women's earnings at all levels of schooling increased sharply relative to men's as the ratio of women's wages to men's rose above 70 percent after having been stuck at around the 60 percent level for several decades. Given that the Reagan administration has never been accused of enforcing affirmative action with more zeal than its predecessors, it is unlikely that the shrinking gender gap can be attributed to government action. Sol Polachek and I attribute the narrowing in the gender gap primarily to a narrowing in human capital differences, particularly in the skills acquired through work experience (O'Neill and Polachek, 1993). Although women's schooling and academic achievement have usually been comparable with that of men, women on average have always worked less than men over their lifetimes, and consequently they have invested less in acquiring work-related skills. It is this gender differential in skills acquired through market experience that has been the primary source of the gender gap in pay. But things have changed. Women now work longer and more continuously; their schooling is more vocationally directed; and employers, recognizing that women will remain at work even after bearing children are more likely to give women chances to train for more responsible and higher-paying jobs. Sol Polachek and I found that increases in women's actual years of work experience relative to men's can account for one-fourth of the narrowing in the gender gap since the late 1970s. In addition, a relative rise in the payoff women receive from a year of experience explains an additional 30–40 percent of the convergence. Women have also gained relative to men in terms of schooling at the college level, and this helped narrow the gap. And the fact that women never much went into blue-collar work helped them avoid the earnings losses suffered by many blue-collar male workers in recent years.

Levy and Murnane conclude their chapter with a discussion of what the future may hold for labor force entrants from disadvantaged families—a matter of concern widely shared. They point to small gains in achievement among children from low-income groups, but show that these gains are not large enough to produce a significant improvement in earnings. It should, however, be recognized that the achievement gains observed among schoolchildren today will not have an impact on the labor force for quite a few years. Moreover, it is difficult to determine the extent to which these gains will result in higher levels of school completion or in enhanced skills among those with a given level of schooling.

I support the view that improvements in the schools are essential. However, I do not think that much will be gained from an infusion of federal funds alone. Extreme deprivation of money resources clearly can affect performance, but few children today, even in our older central cities, attend schools with such low levels of funding. In fact, expenditures per pupil in cities such as New York and the District of Columbia are considerably above the national average. Nor do studies show any measurable impact on achievement of the tangible inputs most school systems purchase (see a review of these studies in Hanushek, 1986). Expenditures per pupil in public elementary and secondary schools in the United States have steadily increased. After adjusting for inflation, they were 80 percent higher in 1990 than in 1970 (and 200 percent higher in 1990 than in 1960) (National Center for Education Statistics, 1991, Table 157). Moreover, in international comparisons U.S. children rank poorly in standardized tests of mathematics achievement, although the United States is second, just behind Switzerland, in expenditures per student (National Center for Education Statistics, 1991, Tables 388, 395).

What is needed is a reorganization of the way in which schooling is delivered. For example, vouchers for low-income children would provide incentives for educators to develop schooling suited to the needs of a disadvantaged population. Children who are raised in unstable families with weak educational backgrounds start school with significant handicaps. The failure of our schools to offset these handicaps suggests that radical new approaches are needed.

Notes

1. For a discussion of the 1970s drop in the earnings of college graduates see Freeman (1976).

2. The 1980 census of population (U.S. Bureau of the Census) shows that immigrants from Mexico on average had completed only seven years of school, five years less than the average U.S. worker. Immigrants from Central and South America made up about half of the total legal immigration to the United States during the 1980s and are likely to have made up a significant share of the illegally admitted immigrants as well.

References

Freeman, R. B. (1976). *The Overeducated American*. New York: Academic Press.
Hanushek, E. A. (1986). "The Economics of Schooling." *Journal of Economic Literature*, 24, 1141–1177.

Juhn, C., Murphy, K. M., and Pierce, B. (1991). "Accounting for the Slowdown in Black-White Wage Convergence." In M. H. Kosters (Ed.), *Workers and Their Wages: Changing Patterns in the United States.* Washington, DC: American Enterprise Institute Press.

Levy, F., and Murnane, R. J. (1992). "U.S. Earnings Levels and Earnings Inequality: A Review of Recent Trends and Proposed Explanations." *Journal of Economic Literature, 20,* 1333–1381.

Mincer, J. (1993). "Investment in U.S. Education and Training." Discussion Paper 671, Columbia University. Revised version: February 16, 1994.

National Center for Education Statistics. (1991). *Digest of Education Statistics.* Washington, DC: Government Printing Office.

O'Neill, J. (1990). "The Role of Human Capital in Earnings Differences between Black and White Men." *Journal of Economics Perspectives,* 4(4), 25–45.

O'Neill, J., and Polachek, S. (1993). "Why the Gender Gap in Wages Narrowed in the 1980s." *Journal of Labor Economics, 2,* 205–228.

Comment

Richard L. Sandor

I very much enjoyed the preceding chapters. Based on my experience as a businessman who has spent the last three decades developing new businesses and helping to establish new financial markets, it seems apparent to me that the twenty-first century is going to require the next generation of students to develop a set of skills that will help them to adapt to our country's rapidly changing business environment. I believe that the task of preparing our country's future employees is both complex and challenging, difficult but certainly not impossible.

The financial futures revolution began on October 20, 1975, when the Chicago Board of Trade launched the first interest rate futures contract. As chief economist and later as a member of the Board of Directors, I was fortunate to be involved in creating numerous new markets. In the years that followed I had the challenge of developing new businesses associated with these new markets. It was my responsibility and that of my colleagues not only to hire the workforce that would fuel these businesses but to train them as well. Our experiences should help give some insight into the frustrations faced by businesspeople trying to change the system in a positive way.

When our work first began the exchange was dominated by traditional commodities, such as soybeans, corn, and wheat. New skills would soon be required in almost every segment of the industry from the salesroom to the back office. Some of us developed programs to recruit in the inner cities, to train people to be runners and clerks, and to serve in a variety of other entry-level positions within the exchange community. We immediately recognized a tremendous inadequacy in human capital.

At the time of our involvement, of the thousands of students graduating annually from Chicago's high schools, about one-third graduated and did not find employment. In order to help solve problems in the schools, the mayor appointed a businessperson advisory committee to the Chicago Board of Education. The committee members represented exchanges, industrial corporations, service industries, and universities. I enthusiastically accepted the appointment as a representative of the exchange community. Our principal purpose was to provide information to educators on how to improve the education process so that high school graduates would have high probabilities of being employed. After considerable debate, the committee of businesspeople unanimously agreed that the most tangible contribution we could make would be to create jobs. We proposed the following to the Board of Education: A six-year program with a guarantee of 1,000 jobs in the first year, 2,000 jobs in the second year, 3,000 jobs in the third year, etc. In effect, by the sixth year every high school graduate in the city of Chicago would be guaranteed an entry-level job by the business community. The quid pro quo was that the verbal and mathematical skills of the typical graduate would equal national averages. We had close to 30 parent groups supporting our proposal including every major ethnic community, such as Latino, African-American, and Asian American.

Unfortunately, the Chicago School Board and its bureaucracy refused our request to use test scores as a determinant for jobs, even though Chicago high school students had tested at less than 75 percent of the national average. Their opposition was based on claims of racial bias in all of the exams. We responded that Chicago underperformed New York, which had an even higher percentage of minority students. We pleaded with them. "We only want to use the scores to get a sense of relative performance and minimal skills. We understand that scores don't mean everything. We have 6,000 jobs for 16- and 17-year-old kids that would be guaranteed." Their response was final. "No way, we're not interested in any performanced-based system."

The first thing the business community learned was that in spite of our belief that we could use standardized test scores as a basis for providing jobs and particular wage levels, the administration and its bureaucracy refused to initiate any program based on performance. Individual educators, parent groups, and students agreed with the business community but their opinion did not have any impact. Bureaucracies need to be convinced both that there is a relationship between skills and jobs and that businesses will provide opportunities when skills are quantitatively demonstrated.

Over the years our work with new markets also taught us that basic skills could be adapted for use in new markets. In addition, we learned that it was not necessary to offer higher wages in new businesses. Whether they were traders, salespeople, or operations personnel, all new entrants recognized that whereas there were high risks in retraining for a new industry, upward mobility was easier and higher rewards could be significant.

The educational challenge fostered by financial futures innovation was enormous. The first contract was GNMA futures. These are securitized mortgages guaranteed by the Government National Mortgage Association. Financial instruments with changing coupons and uncertain duration provided new challenges to existing industry participants as well as new individuals attracted to the business. Options on futures, with new terminology such as strike price, puts, calls, buy rights, etc., would provide the same challenge.

Fortunately, Chicago's futures markets had made the city the center of speculative capital. Thus, existing market makers would provide some liquidity for the new market. However, a new class of traders would have to be attracted. Special purpose memberships were sold at low prices and the exchange instituted training programs. The program attracted individuals ranging from members of the Chicago police force to former bond salespeople. Women were attracted to the business because it offered opportunities not available in the more established and male-dominated trading pit. Salespeople were equally diverse. Individuals that had sold hedging strategies in traditional commodities as diverse as cocoa and corn were attracted to the industry. Back office personnel came from both traditional commodity futures as well as the fixed income world. In virtually all instances, the adaptability of existing skill sets was the driver in providing the human capital that was necessary to revolutionize the futures industry.

I believe that the lessons learned from financial futures can be applied to other businesses, for example, insurance. From the mid-1960s to the mid-1980s, the average catastrophic loss to the U.S. insurance industry was about $4.5 billion/year. Starting in 1989 with Hurricane Andrew, Hurricane Iniki, numerous northeasters, and culminating with the March 1993 storm of the century, the insurance industry has been racking up about $12 billion/year in losses. The stated net worth of the industry is $175 billion in primary capital. That is $175 billion of primary capital to cover a $6 trillion economy with about $12 to $15 trillion of property. You do not have to be particularly analytic to see that this is not a viable situation. Markets respond: Capital flows into industries that are undercapitalized or have more perceived risks that are greater than actually exist. The result of the latter is the development of risk management techniques along with standardization and commodization.

The Chicago Board of Trade has started an insurance futures market. An "over-the-counter" (OTC) market has also become active. You can now buy puts and calls on hurricanes, tornadoes, and earthquakes. A significant portion (as much as 30 percent) of the insurance premiums are paid in sales commission to insurance brokers, reinsurance brokers, and retrocession brokers. The situation does not seem to be viable in the long run. What will be the market response? Perhaps catastrophe insurance will be sold on television. You will certainly see it on the financial news networks. Eventually, you will have commoditization. What does that mean? The uneducated high school graduate who wants to become an insurance salesman no longer has a career, because the product will be delivered in a standard form and even electronically. The people who will have the careers are those that structure these policies, hedge them, process them, and help deliver them.

Let me conclude by stating that based on my experience as a businessman and someone who has worked on new markets and new businesses, there are no franchises left. Speed and flexibility are the only true franchises. All of which suggests that the twenty-first century is going to require skill sets that are very strong and that can be adapted to changing business environments.

About the Editors and Contributors

Editors

Lewis C. Solmon is president of the Milken Institute for Job & Capital Formation in Los Angeles. Prior to assuming this position in July 1991, he served as dean of UCLA's Graduate School of Education for six years. He has served on the faculties of UCLA, CUNY, and Purdue, and currently is a professor emeritus at UCLA. He has published two dozen books and monographs and more than 60 articles in scholarly and professional journals. His books include *From the Campus: Perspectives on the School Reform Movement* (1989), *The Costs of Evaluation* (1983), *Underemployed Ph.D.'s* (1981), and three editions of *Economics*, a basic text. He has written on teacher testing programs, foreign students, demographics of higher education, education and economic growth, the effects of educational quality, and the links between education and work. He is currently an associate editor of the *Economics of Education Review*. He has served as an adviser to the World Bank, UNESCO, various government agencies, and many universities. He received his A.M. in 1967 and his Ph.D. in economics in 1968, both from the University of Chicago.

Alec R. Levenson is a research associate at the Milken Institute. He is a graduate of the University of Wisconsin-Madison (B.A., economics and Chinese language, 1988) and he received his M.A. (economics, 1990) and Ph.D. from Princeton University (economics, 1994). His principal areas of interest are labor economics, development economics, and applied econometrics. He is currently at work on the issues of whether bad job market opportunities upon entrance lead to permanently lower lifetime earnings, whether recent patterns of part-time employment in the United States are indicative of a structural shift away from full-time employment, the operation of informal financial market institutions within the ethnic communities in Los Angeles, and the evolution of self-employment for women and minorities.

Contributors

Laurie J. Bassi received a bachelor's degree in mathematics and economics from Illinois State University, a master's degree from the Industrial and Labor Relations School at Cornell University, and a Ph.D. in economics from Princeton University. She joined the economics faculty at Georgetown University in 1982, and in 1990 she received a joint appointment in both the economics and public policy programs at Georgetown. From 1988 to 1989, while on leave from Georgetown, she served as the deputy director for the Department of Labor's Commission on Workforce Quality and Labor Market Efficiency. Currently, she serves as the executive director of the Advisory Council on Unemployment Compensation. Her research efforts have focused on corporate decision making about training workers and the organization of work; the effects of training on the economy, from both microeconomic and macroeconomic perspectives; the impacts of job creation programs; the effects of income redistribution on behavior, in terms of both the dynamics of welfare spells and the impact of welfare on family structure and labor supply; the economics of children's well-being; and education production functions. She has published extensively in professional economics and policy journals, is coeditor of *Labor Economics and Public Policy*, and has recently completed a book-length manuscript titled "Getting America to Work."

William J. Baumol is professor of economics and director of the C. V. Starr Center for Applied Economics at New York University, and senior research economist and professor of economics (emeritus) at Princeton University. He is a graduate of the City College of New York (B.S.S., 1942) and the University of London (Ph.D., 1949). He is the author of some 20 books, which have been translated into nearly as many languages, as well as some 400 professional articles. His theoretical works include *Welfare Economics and the Theory of the State* (1952), *Economics: Principles and Policy* (1993, with Blinder), and *Superfairness: Applications and Theory* (1986). He has done extensive work in productivity, authoring *Inflation and the Performing Arts* (1984, ed. with H. Baumol), *Productivity and American Leadership: The Long View* (1989, with Batey, Blackman, and Wolfe), and *The Information Economy and the Implications of Unbalanced Growth* (1989, with Osberg and Wolff). His most recently published works are in the finance field. He is a fellow of the Econometric Society, honorary fellow of the London School of Economics, and distinguished fellow of the American Economic Association. He served as president of the American Economic Association in 1981, as president of the Association of Environmental and Resource Economists in 1979, and as an elected member of the American Academy of Arts and Sciences, the American Philosophical Society, and the National Academy of Arts and Sciences. His primary areas of research interest are application of micro-economic theory to welfare, productivity analysis, environmental policy, and financing of the arts.

Robert W. Bednarzik (Ph.D., economics, University of Missouri) is currently a senior economist in the Bureau of International Labor Affairs, U.S. Department of Labor (DOL). Prior to this, he was an economist at the Bureau of Labor Statistics. He is also vice chair to the Organization for Economic Cooperation and Development (OECD), Working Party on Employment, which makes labor policy recommendations to member countries. He has served as technical secretariat on an OECD panel to re-view individual country evaluations of reemployment programs. His an-alytic efforts are focused on how the employment conditions and wage levels of American workers are affected by international trade and invest-ment, the results of which are used to develop DOL policy positions. He was also instrumental in setting up DOL's technical assistance program in Poland and Hungary, and served on an OECD research team that re-cently reviewed labor market policy in Poland. His work has resulted in the publication of more than two dozen articles and reports. His expertise in labor market adjustment issues has been called upon to help develop federal assistance programs for serving displaced U.S. workers. His re-cent work has been on distinguishing trade-sensitive industries, espe-cially their geographic concentration and the likelihood of workers being displaced because of imports' receiving federal assistance.

David Birch is a leading authority in the areas of employment, busi-ness growth, and economic change. He has become well known for his landmark research in the late 1970s that identified the critical role of in-novation in job creation, particularly among smaller companies, and has published a book titled *Job Creation in America*. He has pioneered the de-velopment of microeconomic analysis techniques and has published a number of articles on how companies start and grow and how they choose places in which to do business. He has also studied the real estate implications of job change, and has recently published "America's Fu-ture Office Space Needs: Preparing for the Year 2000." He is currently president of Cognetics, Inc., in Cambridge, Massachusetts, and is direc-tor of the MIT Program on Jobs, Enterprises and Markets. He has served on the faculties of the Harvard Business School and MIT. He received his A.B. degree from Harvard University and his M.B.A. degree from Har-vard Business School.

Gary Burtless is a senior fellow in the economic studies program at the Brookings Institution in Washington, D.C. His research focuses on issues connected with public finance, aging, savings, labor markets, income distribution, social insurance, and the behavioral effects of government tax and transfer policy. He is coauthor of *Growth with Equity: Economic Policymaking for the Next Century* (1993) and of *Can America Afford to Grow Old? Paying for Social Security* (1989), and is editor and contributor to *A Future of Lousy Jobs? The Changing Structure of U.S. Wages* (1990) and *Work, Health, and Income among the Elderly* (1987). He has also published numerous articles on the effects of social security, welfare, unemployment insurance, and taxes. He graduated from Yale University in 1972 and earned a Ph.D. in economics from MIT in 1977. Before joining Brookings in 1981, he served as an economist in the Office of the Secretary of Labor and the U.S. Department of Health, Education and Welfare. In 1993 he taught as a visiting professor of public affairs at the University of Maryland.

Steven J. Davis received his Ph.D. in economics from Brown University in 1986. He is currently associate professor of business economics at the University of Chicago's Graduate School of Business and visiting associate professor of economics at the Massachusetts Institute of Technology for the 1993–94 academic year. His research on labor economics and macroeconomics has been published in leading academic and policy journals, including the *American Economic Review, Quarterly Journal of Economics, Journal of Monetary Economics, Brookings Papers on Economic Activity*, and the *NBER Macroeconomics Annual*. He has been cited as an economic authority in leading newspapers and magazines, including the *New York Times, Wall Street Journal, Business Week, The Economist, Financial Times*, and *Newsweek*.

Ronald G. Ehrenberg is Irving M. Ives Professor of Industrial and Labor Relations and Economics, director of research, and director of the Institute for Labor Market Policies at the School of Industrial and Labor Relations, Cornell University, and a research associate at the National Bureau of Economic Research. He received a Ph.D. in economics from Northwestern University in 1970 and has authored more than 100 papers and books in the areas of public sector labor markets, wages in regulated industries, the evaluation of labor market programs and legislation, resource allocation issues in education, and the incentive effects of compensation systems. He is the editor of *Research in Labor Economics* and has served or is serving on the editorial boards of the *American Economic Review, Industrial and Labor Relations Review*, and *Economic Letters*. He has been a staff economist at the Council of Economic Advisers and a member of the National Science Foundation Advisory Panel for Economics and the National Research Council Committee on Enlistment Standards. In recent years, much of his research has focused on educational issues. He is coauthor of *Economic Challenges in Higher Education* (University of Chicago Press, 1991). Currently, he is pursuing research on issues relating to the race, gender, and ethnicity of American teachers and students. His current research also addresses the relationship between labor markets and economic integration (e.g., NAFTA), and he is preparing a monograph for the Brookings Institution on the topic.

John Haltiwanger, professor of economics at the University of Maryland, received his Ph.D. in economics from the Johns Hopkins University in 1981. After serving on the faculty at UCLA and Johns Hopkins, he joined the faculty at Maryland in 1987. He has published more than 30 articles in the *American Economic Review, Quarterly Journal of Economics, NBER Macroeconomics Annual, Brookings Papers on Economic Activity*, and *Economic Journal*. He recently completed a two-year term on the Economic Advisory Panel for the National Science Foundation. He has been a research associate at the Center for Economic Studies at the U.S. Bureau of the Census since 1988. His current research exploits the recently created longitudinal establishment databases that are available at the Bureau of the Census. This research focuses on the process of reallocation, retooling, and restructuring in the U.S. economy. His forthcoming book based upon this research (coauthored with Steven Davis and Scott Schuh) presents a comprehensive analysis of job creation and destruction in the U.S. manufacturing sector over the past two decades.

James J. Heckman has a Ph.D. in economics from Princeton University (1971). He is Henry Schultz Professor of Economics at the University of Chicago, where he has been on the department of economics faculty since 1973. Since 1991, he has also served on the faculty of the Harris School of Public Policy at the University of Chicago, where he directs the Center for the Evaluation of Social Programs. He has written widely on the economics of job training and is currently finishing a book on the evaluation of the Job Training Partnership Act, the largest federal manpower training program. He has also written extensively on labor supply, unemployment, earnings, demographic wage differentials and affirmative action programs, fertility, and econometric methodology. He has edited or coedited, among others, the *Journal of Political Economy, Journal of Econometrics*, and *Journal of Labor Economics*. He is a member of the National Academy of Science and the American Academy of Arts and Sciences, and is a fellow of the Econometric Society.

Chinhui Juhn is currently an assistant professor of economics at the University of Houston. Dr. Juhn received her B.A. from Yale University and her Ph.D. in economics from the University of Chicago. Recently appointed an NBER faculty research fellow, her research interests are mainly in the field of empirical labor economics. She has published papers on such topics as rising wage inequality, declining male employment, and the black-white earnings gap. Her current work examines issues regarding changes in family labor supply, changes in marriage and sorting patterns, and the impact of industrial change on earnings inequality.

Alan B. Krueger holds the Bendheim Professorship in Economics and Public Affairs at Princeton University. He is also a research associate at the National Bureau of Economic Research and the Institute for Policy Reform. He recently served as a consultant to the Interagency Task Force on Health Care Reform. He has published numerous articles on the economics of education, wage determination, changes in the wage structure, employment demand, workers' compensation insurance, and social security. He serves as director of the Princeton Survey Research Center and is coeditor of the *Journal of Economic Perspectives* and of *Economics Letters*. He was named a Sloan Fellow in Economics in 1992 and was awarded an NBER Olin Fellowship in 1989. He received a B.S. degree in industrial and labor relations from Cornell University in 1983 and a Ph.D. in economics from Harvard University in 1987.

Frank Levy is Daniel Rose Professor of Urban Economics in MIT's Department of Urban Studies and Planning. Before joining MIT in 1992, he taught for 10 years each at the University of California at Berkeley and the University of Maryland at College Park, and worked for four years as a senior research associate at the Urban Institute. In addition to teaching at MIT, he is associated with the Brookings Institution and is a research adviser to Public/Private Ventures and Manpower Demonstration Research Corporation. He has written extensively in the areas of income inequality, living standards, and the economics of education. His 1987 book, *Dollars and Dreams*, is a standard reference on the development of U.S. income distribution, and he has discussed income trends with the media, including the *New York Times*, the *Washington Post*, *Science* magazine, and *Good Morning America*. He is currently working with Richard Murnane of Harvard on a book that applies the lessons of industrial restructuring to the problems of school reform. He has Ph.D. and master's degrees in economics from Yale University, and an undergraduate degree in economics from MIT.

Ray Marshall holds the Audre and Bernard Rapoport Centennial Chair in Economics and Public Affairs at the University of Texas, Austin. His previous UT positions include professor of economics, chairman of the Economics Department, and director and founder of the Center for the Study of Human Resources. From 1977 to 1981, he took leave from the university to serve as U.S. Secretary of Labor. His current positions also include director and founding economist of the Economic Policy Institute and cochair of the Commission on Skills of the American Workforce. His current research interests include the economics of education and learning systems; the organization of work for high performance;

comparisons of international worker-management relations; the competitiveness of the American economy; disadvantaged business development programs; the impact of the North American Free Trade Agreement and the integration of Europe on employment, wages, and income; school-to-work systems; workplace learning systems; and private pension reform. He has authored or coauthored more 30 books and monographs and approximately 175 articles and chapters. Some of his recent publications include *Thinking for a Living: Education and the Wealth of Nations* (1992, with Tucker), "Commons, Veblen and Other Economists" (*Journal of Economic Issues*, 1993), "What America Needs: A License to Skill" (*Washington Post*, 1993, with Brock and Tucker), and "Organizations and Learning Systems for a High-Wage Economy" (*Labor Economics and Industrial Relations*, edited by Kerr and Staudohar, 1994).

James Medoff graduated from Brown University in 1969. He received his master's and doctorate degrees in economics from Harvard University in 1973 and 1975, respectively. After receiving his Ph.D., he joined the economics faculty at Harvard, where today he is a tenured professor of economics. His research and teaching have focused on the operation of U.S. labor markets. He has published numerous articles as well as *Employers Large and Small* (with Brown and Hamilton, 1990) and *What Do Unions Do?* (with Freeman, 1984) concerning the treatment of workers in different work settings. His most recent studies have concerned the plight of the unemployed. He has concluded that we are witnessing a "new unemployment" that is far more threatening than the unemployment of recent decades.

Richard J. Murnane, an economist, is professor of education at the Harvard Graduate School of Education. He was chairperson of a National Academy of Sciences committee on improving indicators of the quality of K–12 mathematics and science education, and is a member of the National Academy of Education. Before studying economics, he was a high school mathematics teacher. He has written widely about the relationships between education and the economy, about public/private school comparisons and the effects of family choice in education, and about teacher labor markets. His most recent book is *Who Will Teach? Policies That Matter* (1991). He recently completed a chapter on federal education and training policies for a Brookings Institution volume titled *Setting Domestic Priorities*. His current research focuses on the effects that changes in the economy have had on the skills new labor force entrants need to get good jobs. This issue is the focus of a book he is currently completing with MIT professor Frank Levy.

Kevin M. Murphy received his A.B. in economics in 1981 from the University of California, Los Angeles, and his Ph.D. in 1986 from the University of Chicago. He is professor of business economics and industrial relations at the Graduate School of Business, University of Chicago. The recipient of a Sloan Foundation Fellowship, he has published widely in the field of labor economics, including "Wage Differentials in the 1980's: The Role of International Trade" (with Welch, in *Workers and Their Wages,* edited by Kosters, 1991), "The Allocation of Talent: Implications for Growth" (with Shleifer and Vishny, *Quarterly Journal of Economics,* 1991), and "Wage Inequality and Relative Wages" (with Welch, *American Economic Review Papers and Proceedings,* 1993).

Walter Y. Oi is Elmer B. Milliman Professor of Economics at the University of Rochester, where he has taught economics since 1967. He was chairman of the Economics Department from 1976 to 1982. He has also held teaching positions at Iowa State University, Northwestern University, and the University of Washington. He received the B.S. and M.A. degrees from UCLA in 1952 and 1954, and the Ph.D. in economics from the University of Chicago in 1961. He has been a visiting scholar at Princeton and Brigham Young universities, and at the Hoover Institution at Stanford University. He was recently the president of the Western Economics Association International, and he has been a frequent consultant on defense issues for the Department of Defense, the RAND Corporation, and the Institute for Defense Analyses. He coauthored two papers published in the Gates Commission volumes, *Studies Prepared for the President's Commission on an All-Volunteer Armed Force,* and a number of other papers on the volunteer force alternative to the draft. He has served on policy advisory panels on employment of the handicapped, civil rights, and poverty. He has published widely in microeconomic theory and policy. Much of his work has focused on issues in labor economics. He was recently elected as a fellow of the Econometric Society and to the American Academy of Arts and Sciences.

June E. O'Neill is director of the Center for the Study of Business and Government and professor of economics and finance at Baruch College and the Graduate Center, City University of New York. She has also served as director of the Office of Programs, Policy and Research at the U.S. Commission on Civil Rights; program director of the Urban Institute; chief of the Human Resources Cost Estimates Unit, Congressional Budget Office; senior staff economist for the Council of Economic Advisers; research associate at the Brookings Institution; and instructor at Temple University. She received her Ph.D. in economics in 1970 from Columbia University. Her numerous published works concentrate in the human resource and education areas and include *The Impact of a Health Insurance Mandate on Labor Costs and Employment* (with D.M. O'Neill, 1993) and *Affirmative Action Revisited* (ed. with Orlans, 1992).

Barry Rogstad is president of the American Business Conference (ABC), a coalition of 100 mid-size, fast-growing firms that seeks to promote public policies that encourage growth, job creation, and a higher stan-dard of living for Americans. Prior to joining the ABC, he was chief economist; managing partner, international management consulting; and partner, strategic management services, with Coopers & Lybrand. He received his A.B. in history at Clark University, master's in economics from Clark, and Ph.D. in economics in 1968 from Brown University.

Rebecca L. Roselius is an advanced graduate student in the Department of Economics at the University of Chicago and research associate at the Center for Social Program Evaluation. Her current research entails studying the impacts of government training programs on adults and developing econometric models to control for selection into social programs. She is also currently involved in evaluating the German apprenticeship program as it works in Germany.

Richard L. Sandor is chairman and CEO of Centre Financial Products Limited, a risk management firm that specializes in derivative market applications for the development of new products and new markets (the company is an affiliate of Centre Reinsurance Company, a subsidiary of the Zurich Insurance Group). He was previously an executive managing director at Kidder, Peabody, responsible for the derivative products and new ventures group. He has also held the positions of president and CEO of Indosuez International Capital Markets Corporation and various senior executive positions in the financial services industry. For more than three years, he was vice president and chief economist at the Chicago Board of Trade, where he earned a reputation as the "principal architect of interest rate futures markets." A faculty member of the School of Business Administration, University of California, Berkeley, he has held faculty positions at Stanford University and Northwestern University. He was recently appointed distinguished adjunct professor at Columbia University Graduate School of Business. He has served on numerous committees and boards, including the Chicago Board of Trade, the Chicago Mercantile Exchange, and the United Nations Commission on Trade and Development. He received his B.A. from City University of New York, Brooklyn College, and earned his Ph.D. in economics from the University of Minnesota in 1967.

Patrick Savin has been an economist and investment strategist on Wall Street for more than 20 years. For the past 10 years he has devoted himself to the propagation of high-yield bonds as an asset class and to the management of these securities in an alliance with a European firm. Savin Carlson Investment is a highly successful SEC-registered investment management company.

Scott Schuh is an economist at the Board of Governors of the Federal Reserve System. He has also held positions as a statistician at the Center for Economic Studies, U.S. Bureau of the Census, and junior staff economist at the President's Council of Economic Advisers. His research currently focuses on the macroeconomic implications of microeconomic heterogeneity, and his publications and research papers are in the fields of labor, inventories, and applied econometrics. He received his B.A. from California State University-Sacramento in 1985 and his M.A. and Ph.D. in economics from Johns Hopkins University in 1992.

Jeffrey A. Smith is an advanced graduate student in the Department of Economics at the University of Chicago and a research associate at the Center for Social Program Evaluation. His current research centers on the relative merits of experimental and nonexperimental evaluation methods, the process by which individuals select into employment and training programs, and new methods for using data from social experiments to learn about features of the distribution of impacts other than the mean.

Joel Stern has been managing partner of Stern Stewart & Co. since he cofounded the firm in 1982. He has degrees in physics and mathematics from Columbia University and CUNY and completed graduate studies in economics and finance at the University of Chicago. Stern Stewart is a financial policy advisory firm that applies modern financial economics to a variety of issues and problems faced by boards of directors and executive committees, with emphasis on the critical link between strategy and shareholder value. He has served on the faculties of graduate business schools both in the United States and abroad (among them Columbia, UCLA and UC Berkeley, the University of Wisconsin, and the University of Capetown in South Africa). Currently he is on the Executive Advisory Committee of the William E. Simon Graduate School of Business at the University of Rochester and serves as a member of the University of Chicago's Council on the Graduate School of Business and on the Fordham University Graduate School of Business Visiting Committee, and is adjunct professor at the Graduate School of Business at Columbia University and the University of the Witwatersrand in Johannesburg, South Africa. He spent four years as a financial policy columnist for the *Financial Times of London* in the 1970s, has been widely published in business newspapers and periodicals. He has presented his views on financial economics on national television on CNN's *Moneyline*, and for 17 years was a rotating panelist on *Wall Street Week*, where twice his stock picks won top performance for the year. His is author of two books in financial economics (*Analytical Methods in Financial Planning* and *Measuring Corporate Performance*) and coeditor of four others.

Murray Weidenbaum has been an economist in three worlds—business, government, and academia. He holds the Mallinckrodt Distinguished University Professorship at Washington University in St. Louis, where he also serves as director of the university's Center for the Study of American Business. From January 1981 to August 1982, Weidenbaum served as President Reagan's first Chairman of the Council of Economic Advisers. In that capacity, he helped to formulate the economic policy of the Reagan Administration and was a spokesman for the Administration on economic and financial issues. Weidenbaum was the first Assistant Secretary of the Treasury for Economic Policy. Earlier he served as fiscal economist in the U.S. Bureau of the Budget and as the corporate economist at the Boeing Company. He received his B.B.A. from City College of New York (1948), his M.A. from Columbia University (1949), and his Ph.D. from Princeton University (1958). He has been a faculty member at Washington University since 1964 and was the chairman of the economics department from 1966 to 1969. Weidenbaum is known for his research on economic policy issues, taxes, government spending, and regulation. He is the author of six books; his latest, *Small Wars, Big Defense: Paying for the Military After the Cold War*, was judged by the Association of American Publishers to be the outstanding economics book published in 1992. He has written several hundred articles in publications ranging from the *American Economic Review* to *The Wall Street Journal*. He also prepares regular columns for *The Christian Science Monitor* and the *Los Angeles Times*. Weidenbaum's international activities include serving as chairman of the Economic Policy Committee of the Organization for Economic Cooperation and Development in 1981–82, lecturing at universities and research institutes throughout Western Europe and Asia, and in 1984, receiving the National Order of Merit from France in recognition of his contributions to foreign policy.

Barbara L. Wolfe is professor in the departments of economics and preventive medicine at the University of Wisconsin, Madison. She is a co-editor of *Journal of Human Resources* and has published extensively in the field of health and economic well-being. A graduate of Cornell University (B.A., economics, 1965), she holds her M.A. from the University of Pennsylvania (economics, 1971) and Ph.D. from the same university (economics, 1973). Publications include "How Does Mother's Schooling Affect Family Health, Nutrition, Medical Care Usage and Household Sanitation?" (with Behrman, *Journal of Econometrics*, 1987), "Labor Market Behavior of Older Men: Estimates from a Trichotomous Choice Model" (*Journal of Public Economics*, 1988), and "Trends in the Prevalence of Disability, 1962–1984" (with Haveman, *The Milbank Quarterly*, 1990). Professor Wolfe is a member of the American Economic Association, Economics Screening Committee (Fullbright Fellowships), and the National Academy of Social Insurance.

Stanley Zax, chairman and president of Zenith Insurance Company, Woodland Hills, California, is an attorney who previously specialized in corporate and securities law. With a group of private investors, Zax negotiated the acquisition and financing of struggling Zenith Insurance in 1977. Over the last decade, he has dramatically expanded and diversified the company. He earned his B.A. and J.D. degrees from the University of Michigan. He began practicing law with Friedman, Mulligan, Dillon and Uris (presently Friedman and Koven) in Chicago. During this period he supervised the merger of Carte Blanche Corporation into a subsidiary of First National City Bank; the spin-off of Hilton International Company to the shareholders of Hilton Hotels Corporation; and the settlement of a 57-day grievance strike at the Pittsburgh Hilton. In 1966, he became a vice president, secretary, and general counsel of Hilton Hotels Corporation as well as an officer and director of subsidiaries and affiliates of Hilton Hotels Corporation. After leaving Hilton in 1972, Zax became a senior vice president, director and, general counsel of National General Corporation, a large conglomerate engaged in insurance, book publishing, real estate, motion picture, and other businesses. He later became president and chief executive officer of Great American Insurance Company and its subsidiaries.

Index

About the Book

This clear, accessible volume provides a comprehensive overview of the ongoing debate over the determining factors of and key influences on employment growth and labor market training, education, and related policies in the United States. Drawing on the work of distinguished labor economists, the chapters tackle questions posed by job and skill demands in the "new high-tech economy" and explore sources of employment growth; productivity growth and its implications for future employment; government mandates, labor costs, and employment; and labor force demographics, income inequality, and returns to human capital.

These topics are central concerns for government, which must judge every prospective policy proposal by its effects on employment growth. Washington keeps at least one eye firmly on the jobs picture, and public officials at every level are constantly aware of the issues surrounding American job security. The jobs issue reaches beyond this focus on the unemployment rate and on total employment, including the rate at which employment is seen as growing, the growth of real wages, the security of employment, returns to human capital, uncertainty about the education and training best suited for a world of rapidly changing economic conditions, and the distribution of the gains from growth across economic classes and population groups.